Recent Advances in Finite Element Methods with Applications

Recent Advances in Finite Element Methods with Applications

Guest Editor

Shuo Zhang

MDPI

Basel • Beijing • Wuhan • Barcelona • Belgrade • Novi Sad • Cluj • Manchester

Guest Editor
Shuo Zhang
Academy of Mathematics and
Systems Science
Chinese Academy of Sciences
Beijing
China

Editorial Office
MDPI AG
Grosspeteranlage 5
4052 Basel, Switzerland

This is a reprint of the Special Issue, published open access by the journal *Mathematics* (ISSN 2227-7390), freely accessible at: https://www.mdpi.com/journal/mathematics/special_issues/FEM.

For citation purposes, cite each article independently as indicated on the article page online and as indicated below:

Lastname, A.A.; Lastname, B.B. Article Title. *Journal Name* **Year**, *Volume Number*, Page Range.

ISBN 978-3-7258-6252-8 (Hbk)
ISBN 978-3-7258-6253-5 (PDF)
https://doi.org/10.3390/books978-3-7258-6253-5

Contents

About the Editor

Shuo Zhang

Shuo Zhang is currently an Associate Professor at the Academy of Mathematics and Systems Science, Chinese Academy of Sciences, China. He received his B.S. degree from the School of Mathematics, Shandong University, China, in 2003, and his Ph.D. degree from the School of Mathematical Sciences, Peking University, China, in 2008. Following his doctoral studies, he conducted postdoctoral research at The Pennsylvania State University, USA. As a first author or corresponding author, his published papers have been awarded the Second Prize and the First Prize of the Excellent Youth Paper Award by the China Society for Computational Mathematics. He is a Senior Member of the China Computer Federation (CCF), a member of the First Committee on FinTech and Algorithms and the Committee on Mathematics in Information and Communications Technology of the China Society for Industrial and Applied Mathematics (CSIAM). He has organized and co-organized more than 10 international special sessions, symposiums, and conferences. His main research focuses on numerical algorithms for partial differential equations, with interests including finite element methods, neural network methods, multilevel methods, structure-preserving algorithms, and computational problems in advanced manufacturing.

mathematics

MDPI

Article

Approximate Solution of Two Dimensional Disc-like Systems by One Dimensional Reduction: An Approach through the Green Function Formalism Using the Finite Elements Method

Alejandro Ferrero [1,*] and Juan Pablo Mallarino [2]

1 Departamento de Ciencias Básicas, Universidad Católica de Colombia, Bogotá 110231, Colombia
2 Facultad de Ciencias—Laboratorio Computacional HPC, Universidad de los Andes-Bogotá, Bogotá 111711, Colombia
* Correspondence: aferrero@ucatolica.edu.co

Abstract: We present a comprehensive study for common second order PDE's in two dimensional *disc-like* systems and show how their solution can be approximated by finding the Green function of an effective one dimensional system. After elaborating on the formalism, we propose to secure an exact solution via a Fourier expansion of the Green function, which entails solving an infinitely countable system of differential equations for the Green–Fourier modes that in the simplest case yields the source-free Green distribution. We present results on non separable systems—or such whose solution cannot be obtained by the usual variable separation technique—on both annulus and disc geometries, and show how the resulting one dimensional Fourier modes potentially generate a near-exact solution. Numerical solutions will be obtained via finite differentiation using Finite Difference Method (FDM) or Finite Element Method (FEM) with the three-point stencil approximation to derivatives. Comparing to known exact solutions, our results achieve an estimated numerical relative error below 10^{-6}. Solutions show the well-known presence of peaks when $\mathbf{r} = \mathbf{r}'$ and a smooth behavior otherwise, for differential equations involving well-behaved functions. We also verified how the Green functions are symmetric under the presence of a "weight function", which is guaranteed to exist in the presence of a curl-free vector field. Solutions of non-homogeneous differential equations are also shown using the Green formalism and showing consistent results.

Keywords: Coulomb interactions; finite elements method FEM; two-dimensional two-component plasma; two dimensions; Green function

MSC: 34B27; 35A25; 42B05; 74S05; 74S15

1. Introduction

In the present work, we elaborate on the FEM for solving complex two-dimensional partial differential equations (DE) using a Green *function* construction. Green's method has been employed extensively in physics for solving Laplace's equation and associates in a cornucopia of areas, such as Quantum and Statistical Mechanics. In quantum mechanics, for example, the method of non-equilibrium Green's functions (NEGF) has been used to study the Brownian motion of a quantum oscillator [1], quantum thermal transport [2,3], electron transport through single and two levels of interacting quantum dot [4], derive quantum kinetic equations [5,6], study hadronic physics [7], among others. In statistical mechanics, some of the applications of the Green functions include the predictions of some observables [8], help to describe 1D hydrodynamic models [9], finding electrical properties of some physical systems [10,11], study non-extensive statistical mechanics with new normalized q-expectation values [12], as well as time- and ensemble-average statistical mechanics of the Gaussian network model [13], and so much more. Even the Green functions are used in quantum field theory to describe the propagators of quantum fields in the perturbative regime.

Not only are Green functions useful to solve systems described by inhomogeneous differential equations, but they can also be used to describe thermodynamic properties. For instance, the density and correlations of particles immersed in two-dimensional two component plasmas at certain temperatures can be described by sets of Green functions [14–16]. The calculation of the energy gap in the one-dimensional Hubbard model can also be approached by means of the Green function formalism [17]. From a mathematical and more fundamental perspective, the Green functions and domains with uniformly rectifiable boundaries of all dimensions have been approximated [18]; an analysis of extra critical points of Green functions on Flat Tori has also been performed, in which their minimality has been emphasized [19].

In order to study how an inhomogenous partial DE can be solved by the method we propose, we start defining a differential operator

$$\hat{\mathcal{L}}_{\{\mathbf{r}\}}\square = (\vec{\nabla}_{\{\mathbf{r}\}} + \vec{f}(\mathbf{r})) \cdot (\vec{\nabla}_{\{\mathbf{r}\}}\square) + g(\mathbf{r})\square, \tag{1}$$

acting on a scalar field, denoted by $\square$, in $\mathbb{R}^d$, with d the dimension of the system—i.e., $\mathbf{r} \in \mathbb{R}^d$. This operator is known in other contexts as the Liouville operator; via this definition, we often describe the evolution of a relevant quantity ψ by means of the equation $\partial_t\psi(\mathbf{r},t) - \hat{\mathcal{L}}\psi(\mathbf{r},t) = 0$ as it is the case of the wave function in quantum mechanics. For example, in the diffusion phenomenon the functions take the form $\vec{f}(\mathbf{r},t) = \vec{\nabla}D(\mathbf{r},t)$ and $g(\mathbf{r}) = 0$, and for the Helmholtz equation $\vec{f}(\mathbf{r},t) = 0$ and $g(\mathbf{r}) = m^2$, with m a constant.

Finding solutions to the latter has motivated the development of numerical methods that grow in number and complexity. For instance, using Restricted Boltzmann Machines we can engineer an artificial neural network that is able to accurately sample the probability distribution for quantum statistical systems [20,21]. However, some effort can be made from a mathematical point of view prior to implementing a full scale numerical calculation.

Green's function—or more precisely, distribution—is perhaps the most interesting artifact of a huge bag of tricks that we have when facing differential equations. Its power relies on the possibility of inverting the differential operator $\hat{\mathcal{L}}$ to solve the inhomogeneous equation

$$\hat{\mathcal{L}}\psi(\mathbf{r}) = \phi(\mathbf{r}), \tag{2}$$

with $\psi(\mathbf{r})$ and $\phi(\mathbf{r})$ two scalar functions. Hinting that its existence, the Green Distribution, is conditioned by some properties of $\hat{\mathcal{L}}$.

A disadvantage of the Green methodology is the duplication of degrees of freedom, encouraging researchers to find $\psi(\mathbf{r})$ directly. Our aim is not to develop a generalized theory for an arbitrary problem and number of dimensions. Despite this, we can look into the consequences of breaking down one dimension by focusing on the simple two-dimensional case.

Two-dimensional systems are of great interest in statistical mechanics [14–16], material sciences [22–24], quantum computing [25,26], high-energy physics [27,28], ionic fluids [29], theoretical mathematics [30,31], and many others.

The outline of the paper is as follows. We first remind some relevant known results for the Green's function construction in Section 2 prior to presenting the strategy to move from 2D to 1D in Section 2.4. We lay out a clever geometric interpretation of the result in Section 2.1 followed by a connection to a relevant theory for Hilbert Space functions in Section 2.3. Consequently, we next discuss its implications towards finding the Green function using FDM in Section 3. We then present some mathematical results that include the solution of certain well known systems for testing purposes and the implementation of the method in a non-separable 2D system in Section 4; a discussion of such results and an explanation of how the algorithm can be adapted to solve the heat diffusion problem in thermal equilibrium is stated in Section 5. Finally, we wrap up the conclusions in Section 6. Intermediate calculations and numerical details are left for further inspection in appendices.

2. Framework and Methodology

We start studying the Green function formalism by postulating the convolution identity from the Dirac distribution,

$$\psi(\mathbf{r}) = \int_{\mathbf{r}'} \psi(\mathbf{r}')\,\delta(\mathbf{r}' - \mathbf{r})\,w(\mathbf{r}', \mathbf{r})\,\mathrm{d}\mathbf{r}' , \tag{3}$$

with $w(\mathbf{r}', \mathbf{r})$ a weight function properly defined by two conditions; the first of which $w(\mathbf{r}, \mathbf{r}) = 1$. Now by defining $G(\mathbf{r}', \mathbf{r})$ as,

$$\hat{\mathcal{L}}_{\{\mathbf{r}'\}} G(\mathbf{r}', \mathbf{r}) = \delta(\mathbf{r}' - \mathbf{r}) , \tag{4}$$

with $\delta(\mathbf{r}' - \mathbf{r}) = \delta(\mathbf{r} - \mathbf{r}')$ the $\mathbb{R}^d$ Dirac delta distribution, then,

$$\psi(\mathbf{r}) = \int_{\mathbf{r}'} \psi(\mathbf{r}') \left[\hat{\mathcal{L}}_{\{\mathbf{r}'\}} G(\mathbf{r}', \mathbf{r})\right] w(\mathbf{r}', \mathbf{r})\,\mathrm{d}\mathbf{r}'. \tag{5}$$

The second condition over $w(\mathbf{r}, \mathbf{r}')$ will be determined in such a way that $\hat{\mathcal{L}}$ is self-adjoint (Hermitian), or equivalently

$$\int_{\mathbf{r}'} \psi(\mathbf{r}') \left[\hat{\mathcal{L}}_{\{\mathbf{r}'\}} G(\mathbf{r}', \mathbf{r})\right] w(\mathbf{r}', \mathbf{r})\,\mathrm{d}\mathbf{r}' = \int_{\mathbf{r}'} \left[\hat{\mathcal{L}}_{\{\mathbf{r}'\}} \psi(\mathbf{r}')\right] G(\mathbf{r}', \mathbf{r})\,w(\mathbf{r}', \mathbf{r})\,\mathrm{d}\mathbf{r}' + \text{b.c.}, \tag{6}$$

with added Dirichlet or Neumann boundary conditions (b.c.). Direct substitution into Equation (5), using Equation (2), yields

$$\psi(\mathbf{r}) = \int_{\mathbf{r}'} G(\mathbf{r}', \mathbf{r})\phi(\mathbf{r}')\,w(\mathbf{r}', \mathbf{r})\,\mathrm{d}\mathbf{r}' + \text{b.c.}. \tag{7}$$

2.1. On the Nature of $w(\mathbf{r}, \mathbf{r}')$, and $\hat{\mathcal{L}}^{-1}$

This former known result deserves a more delicate look, particularly, on the existence of the weight function, and how previous solution relates with the usual convolution theorem $\psi(\mathbf{r}) = \int_{\mathbf{r}'} G(\mathbf{r}, \mathbf{r}')\phi(\mathbf{r}')\,\mathrm{d}\mathbf{r}' + \text{b.c.}$ As mentioned, an appropriate choice for the weight function ensures that Equation (5) reproduces Equation (7). This is performed by using the Green's and Divergence theorem in Equation (5) to perform an integration by parts. After simplifications, we realize that by choosing the weight function, such that $\vec{\nabla}_{\{\mathbf{r}'\}} w(\mathbf{r}', \mathbf{r}) - w(\mathbf{r}', \mathbf{r})\vec{f}(\mathbf{r}') = 0$ (See Appendix A for further details) we ensure that the operator is self-adjoint! This is essential to Green's method. Hence, if no weight function exists, we might be forced to use other analytical and/or numerical procedures in order to find ψ. For that matter, the range of problems that we aim to analyze is narrowed down to the few ones satisfying the aforementioned condition; despite this, a great many of this subset are of special interest for mathematics and physics.

Assuming $w(\mathbf{r}', \mathbf{r})$ exists we are able to incorporate the premise for Equation (7) yielding exactly,

$$\begin{aligned}\psi(\mathbf{r}) = &\int_{\mathbf{r}'} G(\mathbf{r}', \mathbf{r})\phi(\mathbf{r}')\,w(\mathbf{r}', \mathbf{r})\,\mathrm{d}\mathbf{r}' + \\ &\oint_{\partial\mathbf{r}'} w(\mathbf{r}', \mathbf{r}) \left[\psi(\mathbf{r}')\vec{\nabla}_{\{\mathbf{r}'\}} G(\mathbf{r}', \mathbf{r}) - G(\mathbf{r}', \mathbf{r})\vec{\nabla}_{\{\mathbf{r}'\}}\psi(\mathbf{r}')\right] \cdot \mathbf{n}\,\mathrm{d}S' .\end{aligned} \tag{8}$$

Notice how the second term depends on $\psi(\mathbf{r})$'s boundary conditions. By choosing identical conditions and trivial values for the Green distribution function at the boundaries ($G = 0$ for Dirichlet or $G' = 0$ for Neumann) we are capable of solving an infinite number of similar boundary value problems.

The discussion for the existence of the weight function can be answered mathematically. Given the relationship required, the weight is defined as $w(\mathbf{r}',\mathbf{r}) \equiv \exp[-\gamma(\mathbf{r}',\mathbf{r})]$, yielding $\vec{\nabla}_{\{\mathbf{r}'\}}\gamma(\mathbf{r}',\mathbf{r}) = -\vec{f}(\mathbf{r}')$. Considering that the curl of the gradient of any scalar function is trivial then $\gamma(\mathbf{r}',\mathbf{r})$ exists if, and only if, $\vec{\nabla} \times \vec{f} = 0$, which means that $\vec{f}$ must be a conservative vector field! Within this view, $\gamma(\mathbf{r}',\mathbf{r})$ represents the scalar potential associated with a force. Anticipating this last restriction, the solution for $\gamma(\mathbf{r}',\mathbf{r})$ is independent of a path that simply connects $\mathbf{r}$ to $\mathbf{r}'$ yielding,

$$w(\mathbf{r}',\mathbf{r}) \equiv \frac{e^{-\gamma(\mathbf{r}')}}{e^{-\gamma(\mathbf{r})}} = \frac{1}{w(\mathbf{r},\mathbf{r}')}, \tag{9}$$

reflecting on the symmetry of the distribution as it will be shown later. Finally, we are ready to define the inverse operator of $\hat{\mathcal{L}}$ as

$$\hat{\mathcal{L}}^{-1}_{\{\mathbf{r}\}}\Box = \int_{\mathbf{r}'} G(\mathbf{r}',\mathbf{r})\,\Box(\mathbf{r}')\,w(\mathbf{r}',\mathbf{r})\,\mathrm{d}\mathbf{r}', \tag{10}$$

conditioned by the boundary-value problem, which in turn defines $G(\mathbf{r}',\mathbf{r})$ from Equation (4).

There is one last piece of the puzzle to be resolved and it is related to the symmetry of the Green function distribution. Let us evaluate $\hat{\mathcal{L}}_{\{\mathbf{r}\}}G(\mathbf{r}',\mathbf{r})$—i.e., the operator acting on the second variable. Direct application of $\hat{\mathcal{L}}_{\{\mathbf{r}\}}$ on Equation (8), using Equation (2),

$$\phi(\mathbf{r}) = \int_{\mathbf{r}'} \hat{\mathcal{L}}_{\{\mathbf{r}\}}\{G(\mathbf{r}',\mathbf{r})\,w(\mathbf{r}',\mathbf{r})\}\phi(\mathbf{r}')\,\mathrm{d}\mathbf{r}' + \hat{\mathcal{L}}_{\{\mathbf{r}\}}\{\text{b.c.}\}, \tag{11}$$

hints how this operator appears to work and leads us to anticipate the convolution of a Dirac distribution. Indeed this is true. To clarify, here we exchanged integral and Liouville operators because they are acting on separate variables, and the weight and Green functions (except at $\mathbf{r}' = \mathbf{r}$) are differentiable.

This conjecture can be proved from the following statement: two separate problems with different boundary values and identical inhomogeneous differential equation—Equation (2)—share the same Green function distribution and satisfy Equation (11); therefore, by comparing equations for any two cases leads to $\hat{\mathcal{L}}_{\{\mathbf{r}\}}\{\text{b.c.}\} = 0$ because we can always choose convenient trivial boundary values (i.e., b.c. $= 0$) in one case. Consequently,

$$\hat{\mathcal{L}}_{\{\mathbf{r}\}}\{G(\mathbf{r}',\mathbf{r})\,w(\mathbf{r}',\mathbf{r})\} \equiv \delta(\mathbf{r}'-\mathbf{r}), \tag{12}$$

an equality that bears meaning in the sense of the distributions. These final result unravels the symmetry of the Green distribution function via the weight function, i.e.,

$$G(\mathbf{r}',\mathbf{r}) = G(\mathbf{r},\mathbf{r}')\,w(\mathbf{r},\mathbf{r}'). \tag{13}$$

An interesting question now arises, and it is related to the possibility of using Equation (13) to drop the weight function out of the equation. This operation, with the addition of the relation $\vec{\nabla}_{\{\mathbf{r}'\}}w(\mathbf{r},\mathbf{r}') = -w(\mathbf{r},\mathbf{r}')\vec{f}(\mathbf{r}')$, leads to,

$$\begin{aligned}\psi(\mathbf{r}) = &\int_{\mathbf{r}'} G(\mathbf{r},\mathbf{r}')\phi(\mathbf{r}')\,\mathrm{d}\mathbf{r}' + \\ &\oint_{\partial\mathbf{r}'}\Big[\psi(\mathbf{r}')\vec{\nabla}_{\{\mathbf{r}'\}}G(\mathbf{r},\mathbf{r}') - G(\mathbf{r},\mathbf{r}')\big[\psi(\mathbf{r}')\vec{f}(\mathbf{r}') + \vec{\nabla}_{\{\mathbf{r}'\}}\psi(\mathbf{r}')\big]\Big]\cdot\mathbf{n}\,dS'.\end{aligned} \tag{14}$$

Notice that for Neumann boundary conditions (NBC), unlike Dirichlet (DBC), both $\psi(\mathbf{r})$ and its derivative—at the boundaries—are necessary. Ergo, Equation (14) is inconvenient for NBC unless either ψ vanishes or $\vec{f}(\mathbf{r}) = 0$. In such a case, it deems necessary to use the version that incorporates weight function.

Actually, the vector field $\vec{f}$ does not appear in some of the Liouville operators used in physics. For instance, the Green function associated with the electrostatic field satisfies the relation $\vec{\nabla}^2 G(\mathbf{r},\mathbf{r}') = -4\pi\delta(\mathbf{r}-\mathbf{r}')$—the irrelevant factor of -4π appears by convenience. The static regime of the Klein Gordon equation—which also leads to the Yukawa potential—also follows a similar behavior, as its associated Green function in 2D is $K_0(\mu r)$, satisfying the DE $(\vec{\nabla}^2 - \mu^2)G(\mathbf{r}) = -2\pi\delta(\mathbf{r})$ [32]. Clearly, $\vec{f}$ is absent in both systems.

Yet, the DEs describing the behavior of other physical systems, such as the driven damped harmonic oscillator, (the one-dimensional driven damped harmonic oscillator is modeled by the DE $m\ddot{x} + b\dot{x} + kx = F(t)$. The damping constant b plays the role of $\vec{f}$ in this one dimensional system. Although the time t is the relevant variable describing this system (instead of the position x), the one dimensional formalism we describe is analog to this model.) the diffusion equation at thermal equilibrium with an anisotropic diffusion coefficient, and the electrostatic potential in the presence of anisotropic media, include the existence of a vector field $\vec{f}$—see Section 4 for more details about the first system.

Surprisingly, any dependence on the weight function in Equation (14) has vanished. As previously stated, the weight function can only be defined when $\vec{f}$ is a conservative field. Then, an important question now arises: is Equation (14) still valid for non-conservative vector fields? This in a fundamental question that can be addressed in a future work. Since the main purpose is to present a compact and rigorous algorithm to solve the Green function in 2D space, we will restrict our analysis to only the supported cases.

2.2. Boundary Conditions

As previously stated, the Green function conveniently inherits identical types of conditions as the target function ψ at the boundaries. These can be summarized as,

$$\text{DBC} : \rightarrow G(\mathbf{r},\mathbf{r}')|_{\mathbf{r}\text{ at }R_{\text{ext/int}}} = 0\,, \tag{15}$$

$$\text{NBC} : \rightarrow \partial_{\mathbf{r}} G(\mathbf{r},\mathbf{r}')|_{\mathbf{r}\text{ at }R_{\text{ext/int}}} = 0\,. \tag{16}$$

However, there are two hidden additional conditions that must be satisfied enforced by the presence of Dirac's distribution. The rationale behind this is that without them $G = 0$ will be a solution to the Green function for the simple boundary value problem. Although this is directly visible for Dirichlet, notice that it also applies for Neumann's case. The added restrictions appear at the artificial boundary $\mathbf{r} = \mathbf{r}'$ implying continuity of G and discontinuity of the local derivative. Both are essential to secure a non-zero solution. Continuity is often regarded considering that the Green distribution is still a function and its derivatives up to second order exist in the classical sense of the DE everywhere except at $\mathbf{r} = \mathbf{r}'$. Though there is a stronger argument that stems from the fact that the annulus and the disc are Lipschitz domains [33], in DE it always results convenient to decide what do we take as an acceptable solution to any problem, which is our particular case here.

Turning to the plane $\mathbf{r} = \mathbf{r}'$, conditions are derived directly from Equation (4) by integrating over $\mathbf{r}$ inside the volume delimited by the surface S_δ enclosing $\mathbf{r}'$ such that it is contained inside a vicinity—$\mathcal{V}_\delta$—of $\mathbf{r}'$ (see right of Figure 1 for an artistic view). Using the divergence theorem, the condition simplifies to,

$$\lim_{\delta\to 0} \oint_{S_\delta} \vec{\nabla}_{\{\mathbf{r}\}} G(\mathbf{r},\mathbf{r}') \cdot \hat{n}\, dS = 1\,, \tag{17}$$

where we have kept the leading contributing term while taking the limit. For the one dimensional case, it yields the relation $G'(r'_>, r') - G'(r'_<, r') = 1$.

2.3. Connection with the Sturm–Liouville Problem

The weight function, if existent, is able to transform the Liouville operator into a self-adjoint differential operator. Notice that action of $w(\mathbf{r}',\mathbf{r})$ on Equation (1),

$$w(\mathbf{r}',\mathbf{r})\hat{\mathcal{L}}_{\{\mathbf{r}'\}}\Box = \vec{\nabla}_{\{\mathbf{r}'\}} \cdot \left[w(\mathbf{r}',\mathbf{r})\vec{\nabla}_{\{\mathbf{r}'\}}\Box\right] + w(\mathbf{r}',\mathbf{r})g(\mathbf{r}')\Box\,, \tag{18}$$

yields the otherwise known Sturm–Liouville form for Partial Differential Equations (PDE)'s. Namely, the Sturm–Liouville differential operator reads then as,

$$\hat{\mathcal{L}}^{\mathrm{SL}}_{\{\mathbf{r}'\}}\square = w(\mathbf{r}',\mathbf{r})\hat{\mathcal{L}}_{\{\mathbf{r}'\}}\square\,. \tag{19}$$

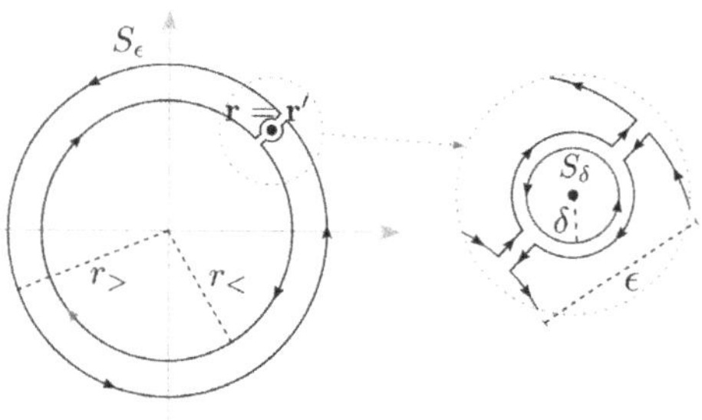

Figure 1. Contours used in the path integration: to the left S_ϵ and S_δ to the right. The radius and thickness are chosen purposely as $\delta < \epsilon/2$ to take the $\epsilon \to 0$ limit.

Consequently, operating onto the Green distribution function gives equal results for both operators, i.e., $\hat{\mathcal{L}}^{\mathrm{SL}}_{\{\mathbf{r}'\}}G(\mathbf{r}',\mathbf{r}) = \delta(\mathbf{r}-\mathbf{r}')$.

This last result connects the Sturm–Liouville problem with null eigenvalues and the Green function distribution problem where the former is the solution to the first strictly when $\mathbf{r} \neq \mathbf{r}'$ under either Dirithlet or Neumann boundary conditions. Resulting from this, $G(\mathbf{r}',\mathbf{r})$ is continuous everywhere and differentiable at $\mathbf{r} \neq \mathbf{r}'$; the behavior of its derivative at $\mathbf{r} = \mathbf{r}'$ is dictaminated by the Liouville operator in the domain of the problem and specified by the Dirac Delta distribution.

2.4. Moving from 2D to 1D: The Infinite Coupling

As noted before, let us elaborate on the simplest scenario where a reduction in the dimension of the problem significantly improves our chances of procuring a general solution. Assume we would like to find the two-dimensional Green function in accordance with Equation (4). Taking advantage of the completeness of the Fourier infinite expansion of any periodic function, we propose to solve the two-dimensional DE in polar coordinates; the dimensional reduction occurs due to the periodicity in θ that does not take place in Cartesian coordinates.

Although the Laplace operator in polar coordinates is known to be separable in the variables r and θ, the introduction of the additional terms in Equation (1), as already mentioned, may lead to a DE that cannot be split conveniently. Equation (4) is then given by,

$$\left[\frac{\partial^2}{\partial r^2} + \frac{1}{r}\frac{\partial}{\partial r} + \frac{1}{r^2}\frac{\partial^2}{\partial \theta^2} + f_r(r,\theta)\frac{\partial}{\partial r} + f_\theta(r,\theta)\frac{1}{r}\frac{\partial}{\partial \theta} + g(r,\theta)\right]G(\mathbf{r},\mathbf{r}') = \delta(\mathbf{r}-\mathbf{r}')\,, \tag{20}$$

where convenient periodic conditions that must be satisfied suggests we should expand the Green function distribution in Fourier modes. Tentatively, we can resort to a Fourier expansion of the form $\sum_\lambda e^{i\lambda(\theta-\theta')}G_\lambda$, where

$$f(r,\theta) = \sum_{\mu\in\mathbb{Z}} f_\mu(r)e^{i\mu\theta}\ ;\ f_\mu(r) = \frac{1}{2\pi}\int_0^{2\pi} f(r,\theta)e^{-i\mu\theta}d\theta\,,$$

to match the delta distribution expansion—i.e., $\delta(\mathbf{r}-\mathbf{r}') = \frac{1}{2\pi r}\delta(r-r')\sum_\lambda e^{i\lambda(\theta-\theta')}$—but since we cannot guarantee that the G_λ coefficients are θ'-independent (only under *proper* angular symmetry conditions) then we will assume $G(\mathbf{r},\mathbf{r}')$ expands as,

$$G(\mathbf{r},\mathbf{r}') = \frac{1}{2\pi}\sum_{\lambda\in\mathbb{Z}} e^{i\lambda\theta} G_\lambda(r,r',\theta')\,. \tag{21}$$

With that in mind and multiplying Equation (20) by r^2 to avoid divergences at $r = 0$,

$$\sum_{\lambda\in\mathbb{Z}} e^{i\lambda\theta}\left[r^2\frac{d^2}{dr^2} + r(1+rf_r)\frac{d}{dr} + (-\lambda^2 + i\lambda r f_\theta + r^2 g)\right]G_\lambda = \sum_{\lambda\in\mathbb{Z}} e^{i(\lambda-\lambda')\theta} r\delta(r-r')\,. \tag{22}$$

Notice how we cannot obtain a solution because there remains a residual dependence of θ in functions $\vec{f}$ and g. Despite this, a simplification can be manufactured when they are replaced by their Fourier series form before integrating on θ over a full period. This step yields our master equation where we deduce that the $G_\lambda(r,r',\theta')$ modes satisfy the DE (we have dropped out the dependencies of all functions on r, θ, r', and θ' facilitating a comprehensible reading),

$$\begin{aligned} &r^2 G_\lambda'' + r\,G_\lambda' - \lambda^2 G_\lambda + \sum_{\mu\in\mathbb{Z}} r^2 f_{r\,\mu} G_{\lambda-\mu}' + \sum_{\mu\in\mathbb{Z}} \left[ir(\lambda-\mu) f_{\theta\,\mu} + r^2 g_\mu\right] G_{\lambda-\mu} \\ &= r\delta(r-r') e^{-i\lambda\theta'}\,. \end{aligned} \tag{23}$$

This final result shows we have accomplished to reduce the rank of the effective Green function to solve at the expense of requiring a countable large number of these Green modes. It is remarkable how the dependence on θ' is delegated to a quasi-negligible term at the right hand side of the equation. We will develop this argument further in the following sections.

This formulation represents an infinitely coupled system of linear differential equations that unsurprisingly contains the solution to the Green function for the classical source-free wave function; the structure of functions $\vec{f}$ and g defines the strength of the entanglement of Green's free wave modes appearing in the rate at which the Fourier coefficients—functions—go to zero with increasing mode frequency. For simplicity, we opt to recall Green's Fourier modes as λ-modes, and $\vec{f}$ and g's modes as μ-modes suggested by the indexes employed in the equation above.

2.5. More on Boundary Conditions of the λ-Modes

One last effort must be made to explain how boundary conditions are inherited along the free-wave modes. The key to this understanding depends on the geometry of the problem and the originating expansion from Equation (21); we can identify two cases for disc-like systems: the annulus and the disc. Other geometries will be studied in a future work. For the annulus, either under Dirichlet or Neumann boundary conditions, the function or its derivative must vanish at the boundaries. This can be met if all modes preserve the vanishing values at both inner and outer boundaries—under uniform convergence. In doing so, we guarantee to meet all requisites for the Green function and a solution is obtained. Conversely, preserving boundary conditions for the disc is not trivial because we do not have one but two boundaries (the second at $r \to 0^+$). Due to the oscillating behavior of $e^{i\lambda\theta}$ with θ at $r \to 0^+$, all $\lambda \neq 0$ modes must vanish at the origin to ensure continuity of the Green distribution function. This can be enforced examining Equation (23) as $r \to 0^+$. Discontinuity due to the source at $r = r'$ may be neglected for now to realize that we can, while approaching the origin, consider the behavior of each r^0, r^1, and r^2 terms independently. We draw then conveniently,

$$r^0\left[-\lambda^2 G_\lambda\right] \underset{r\to 0}{=} 0\,, \tag{24}$$

$$r^1\left[G'_\lambda + i\sum_{\mu\in\mathbb{Z}}(\lambda-\mu) f_{\theta\mu} G_{\lambda-\mu}\right] \underset{r\to 0}{=} 0\,, \tag{25}$$

$$r^2\left[G''_\lambda + \sum_{\mu\in\mathbb{Z}} f_{r\mu} G'_{\lambda-\mu} + \sum_{\mu\in\mathbb{Z}} g_\mu G_{\lambda-\mu}\right] \underset{r\to 0}{=} 0\,, \tag{26}$$

where we can choose, via r^0 terms, that $G_\lambda = 0 \;\forall\, \lambda \neq 0$ and $G_0 \neq 0$. Plugging this sequentially into r^1 and r^2 terms hints $G'_\lambda = 0$ and $G''_\lambda = 0$ ($\forall \lambda \neq 0$) assuming that $\lim_{r\to 0} f_{\theta\mu} G_{\lambda-\mu} = 0$ and $\lim_{r\to 0} f_{r\mu} G'_{\lambda-\mu} = 0 \;\wedge\; \lim_{r\to 0} g_\mu G_{\lambda-\mu} = 0$ (with the exception of $\lambda = 0$ where the $\mu = 0$ term remains, thus we will choose $G''_0 = -g_0 G_0$), respectively.

This is supported from continuity of $g(\mathbf{r})$ everywhere in the disc and from the definition of $\vec{f}(\mathbf{r})$, where limited by the existence of $w(\mathbf{r}', \mathbf{r})$, as the gradient of a scalar function. If such functions, $\gamma(\mathbf{r})$, where to be free of pathologies and differentiable everywhere in the disc (including the origin) then $\lim_{r\to 0} f_{r\lambda} = 0$ and $\lim_{r\to 0} f_{\theta\lambda} = 0$ for $\lambda \neq 0$. It remains to say, that in order to fulfill all above conditions we will require that $f_{\theta 0}$ and f_{r0} are finite as $r \to 0^+$. Looking under the hood of these assumptions, note that consequently the 0-mode has a logarithmic divergence when $r' = 0$, i.e., $G_0 \underset{r\to 0}{\propto} -\log r$.

In summary, the conditions for the disc at the origin are the following two only for $r' > 0$ (see Section 3 for numerical details)

$$G_\lambda(0^+, r', \theta') = 0 \;\; \forall\, \lambda \neq 0\,, \tag{27}$$

$$G'_\lambda(0^+, r', \theta') = 0 \;\; \forall\, \lambda\,. \tag{28}$$

Exceptions and particularities emerging from the specific form of functions $\vec{f}$ and g must be taken into account when detailing the boundary conditions and may alter the relationships obtained above.

This relationship has to be completed with the resulting relationship at the artificial boundary $r = r'$ obtained when using a complementary surface S_ϵ corresponding to an open ring of $\epsilon > 0$ thickness—see left Figure 1 and Equation (17). This gives,

$$r' \lim_{\epsilon\to 0} \int_0^{2\pi} \left[\partial_r G(\mathbf{r}, \mathbf{r}')_> - \partial_r G(\mathbf{r}, \mathbf{r}')_<\right] d\theta = 1\,. \tag{29}$$

which entails the radial averaged contribution. We have eliminated angular contributions by selecting the convenient contour S_ϵ suggesting a pathway to extend it to the λ-modes. Direct substitution of Equation (21) along with a convenient choice of unity—inspired by Equation (23)—gives us ultimately,

$$r'\left[G'_\lambda(r'_>, r', \theta') - G'_\lambda(r'_<, r', \theta')\right] = e^{-i\lambda\theta'}\,, \tag{30}$$

where primes denote partial derivatives with respect to the first argument at both left ($<$) and right ($>$) hand sides of r'. Substituting this relationship in the differential equation, we obtain a similar relationship for the second derivatives, essential to the numerical method, as follows,

$$(r')^2\left[G''_\lambda(r'_>, r', \theta') - G''_\lambda(r'_<, r', \theta')\right] = -e^{-i\lambda\theta'}\left[1 + r' f_r(r', \theta')\right]. \tag{31}$$

For the disc, the $r' = 0$ case must be clarified. In polar coordinates, Dirac's distribution is best described as absent of angular dependence, which entails that for all λ-modes except $\lambda = 0$ it is exactly zero. Therefore, the boundary at the origin for each λ-mode is dictated by symmetry except for $\lambda = 0$. This last, carries the logarithmic divergence. This means that conditions for non-zero modes are unchanged. For the zero mode and due to symmetry

$G_0'|_{r\to 0^+} = -G_0'|_{r\to 0^-}$ and $G_0''|_{r\to 0^+} = G_0''|_{r\to 0^-}$; however, due to the divergence a cut-off must be set in place. Such a choice of cut-off will be discussed later.

3. Finite Differences Method, FDM, or FEM on a Regular Grid

The FDM, or uniform mesh FEM, has been used extensively in the literature to find approximate solutions for many physical systems and its stability makes it a suitable candidate to obtain a numerical Green distribution function. Some examples include the one-dimensional Schrödinger equation [34], the Poisson equation for Electrodynamics [35], the Euler equations of inviscid fluid flow [36], solutions to 1D and 2D Burgers' equation [37], and the time-fractional diffusion equation [38]. From the mathematical perspective, the same method has been implemented to solve elliptic, hyperbolic and parabolic partial DEs on irregular meshes [39], with interfaces [40], or in finding optimal algorithms on non-trivial meshes [41].

Orchestrating an exact solution to Equation (23) is virtually not possible. There are four cases where an analytical approach can be attempted: two cases where either $\vec{f}$ or g are zero, requiring to find a base of G_λ's that can decouple the system—hence, a diagonalization—the unique case where the same base applies to both coupling matrices accompanying G_λ' and G_λ, and the trivial free-wave ($\vec{f}$ and g zero). Excluding the latter, finding this diagonalizing operator for the first three cases will be addressed in a future study.

Therefore, we will compute a numerical solution where we approximate the operator with finite differentiation (the finite difference method—FDM or FEM for a regular grid) and bind expansions to include all relevant Green and function modes up to a calculated cut-off; maximum and minimum modes will be chosen, respectively, for λ- and μ-modes symmetrically as $|\lambda| \leq L$ and $|\mu| \leq M$ considering that $M \leq L$ for reasons that will be clarified afterwards.

Since the Green function is twice differentiable, when $\mathbf{r} \neq \mathbf{r}'$, its Fourier series converges uniformly and its coefficients decay at least as λ^{-2}, conditioned by equally well-behaved functions $\vec{f}$ and g. Then, a possible educated choice of L is the minimum integer such that the sum of $1/k^2$ up to L exceeds $\frac{\pi^2}{6}p$, with p a percentage of accuracy; for example, to achieve at most 1% of estimation error we require $L > 60$.

Numerical details and calculations performed henceforth are presented solely for the 3-point stencil. The strategy for the implementation of more accurate approximations will only be mentioned and briefly discussed; their details will be left for the reader to carry them out. Other minor and major details regarding the procedure will be addressed in future works.

3.1. A Large Matrix Equation

The Finite Differences Method (FDM) or Finite Elements Method (FEM) with uniform grid is a simple approach to computing derivatives of functions at a point by using Taylor expansions on a discretized mesh. (The choice of whether dissecting uniformly or non-uniformly is highly dependable on the problem. For example, if we were interested in fracture dynamics we would prefer a non-uniform grid to model complex material topologies.) In doing so, a derivative will rely on knowledge of the values of the function in neighboring sites. Such is the art of computing derivatives. The number of neighboring sites to be taken into consideration determines the degree of which the function approaches to the point value. For instance, in the so called three-point stencil (the site in question and its two adjacent neighbors), the first and second derivatives are accurate up to order square of the mesh size.

Going back to our problem in Equation (23), we turn to a simply redefined one dimensional DE for a sketch of the forthcoming operations. The left hand side reads rewritten as,

$$P(r)\frac{d^2}{dr^2}G_\lambda(r,r',\theta') + \sum_{\mu\in\mathbb{Z}} Q_\mu(r)\frac{d}{dr}G_{\lambda-\mu}(r,r',\theta') + \sum_{\mu\in\mathbb{Z}} R_{\lambda,\mu}(r)G_{\lambda-\mu}(r,r',\theta') .$$

In transforming the continuous variables r and r' into a discrete equally-spaced mesh of size h, we will adopt matrix notation for variables and functions; ergo, for N partitions defining $N+1$ points $h = (R_{\text{ext}} - R_{\text{int}})/N$ in a disc-like geometry. For clarity, we summarize notation changes in Table 1. This procedure applied over the aforementioned equation gives for $r \neq r'$,

$$P^j\left[\frac{1}{h^2}\sum_{\eta\in\mathcal{A}_{|j}} a^{(2)}_{\eta|j} G^{j+\eta,k}_{\lambda|\theta'}\right] + \sum_{\mu\in\mathbb{Z}} Q^j_\mu \left[\frac{1}{h}\sum_{\eta\in\mathcal{A}_{|j}} a^{(1)}_{\eta|j} G^{j+\eta,k}_{\lambda-\mu|\theta'}\right] + \sum_{\mu\in\mathbb{Z}} R^j_{\lambda,\mu} G^{j,k}_{\lambda-\mu|\theta'} + O(h^\xi),$$

with ξ the order of approximation, $\mathcal{A}_{|j}$ the set of neighbor site indices, and $a^{(n)}_{\eta|j}$ the respective coefficient (namely the finite difference coefficient included into a matrix representation $\mathbf{A}^{(n)}$—see Appendix B) of the η-th neighbor required to compute the n-th derivative up to a predetermined order of accuracy [42]; in the three-point stencil case, $\xi = 2$. Both sets of neighbor indices and coefficients depend on the information of the site j under inspection; if, for example, we are at or near an interface, boundary, or discontinuity, then the strategy for choosing neighbors may differ; we might be interested in computing derivatives using only points in regions where it makes sense.

Table 1. A summary on the change of notation from continuous to discrete form. We have $r^0 = R_{\text{int}}$ and $j \in \{0, 1, 2, \ldots, N\}$.

Variable or Function	Equivalent Array
r and r'	$r^j = r^0 + h\,j$,
$G_\lambda(r,r',\theta')$	$G^{j,k}_{\lambda\|\theta'} = G_\lambda(r^j, r'^k, \theta')$
$P(r) \equiv r^2$	$P^j = P\left(r^j\right)$
$Q_\mu(r) \equiv r^2 f_{r\,\mu}(r) + r\delta_{0,\mu}$	$Q^j_\mu = Q_\mu\left(r^j\right)$
$R_{\lambda,\mu}(r) \equiv r^2 g_\mu(r) - \lambda^2\delta_{0,\mu} + ir(\lambda-\mu) f_{\theta\,\mu}(r)$	$R^j_{\lambda,\mu} = R_{\lambda,\mu}\left(r^j\right)$

With some reorganization, the generated discrete DE can be regarded as a matrix multiplication. To see this, first we realize that by understanding $G^{j,k}_{\lambda|\theta'}$ as the (j,k)-th element of a constructed matrix $\mathbf{G}_{\lambda|\theta'}$—of size $N+1 \times N+1$—we can envision a column matrix vector $\mathbb{G}_{\theta'}$ that contains all λ-modes, or all of $\{\mathbf{G}_{\lambda|\theta'}\ \forall\,\lambda \in \mathbb{Z}\}$, where all operations from the previous complex array equation are condensed into an equally conceived matrix $\mathbb{U}$ multiplying $\mathbb{G}_{\theta'}$. The following is a view of $\mathbb{G}_{\theta'}$,

$$\mathbb{G}_{\theta'} = \begin{pmatrix} \vdots \\ \mathbf{G}_{-L|\theta'} \\ \vdots \\ \mathbf{G}_{-1|\theta'} \\ \mathbf{G}_{0|\theta'} \\ \mathbf{G}_{1|\theta'} \\ \vdots \\ \mathbf{G}_{L|\theta'} \\ \vdots \end{pmatrix}, \text{ with } \mathbf{G}_{\lambda|\theta'} = \begin{pmatrix} G^{0,0}_{\lambda|\theta'} & G^{0,1}_{\lambda|\theta'} & \cdots & G^{0,N-1}_{\lambda|\theta'} & G^{0,N}_{\lambda|\theta'} \\ G^{1,0}_{\lambda|\theta'} & G^{1,1}_{\lambda|\theta'} & \cdots & G^{1,N-1}_{\lambda|\theta'} & G^{1,N}_{\lambda|\theta'} \\ \vdots & \vdots & \ddots & \vdots & \vdots \\ G^{N-1,0}_{\lambda|\theta'} & G^{N-1,1}_{\lambda|\theta'} & \cdots & G^{N-1,N-1}_{\lambda|\theta'} & G^{N-1,N}_{\lambda|\theta'} \\ G^{N,0}_{\lambda|\theta'} & G^{N,1}_{\lambda|\theta'} & \cdots & G^{N,N-1}_{\lambda|\theta'} & G^{N,N}_{\lambda|\theta'} \end{pmatrix}. \tag{32}$$

In principle, both matrices are infinitely large but for practical terms they will be truncated on both λ- and μ-modes, as mentioned in the previous section. Despite this numerical simplification that will be carried out in the numerical analysis, the infinite matrix $\mathbb{U}$ has a well-defined structure, as will be detailed in Section 3.2.

Finally, the terms to the right of Equation (23) vanish for all $r \neq r'$ leading us to believe that if $\mathbb{U}$ is invertible then the solution to the discrete Green function $\mathbb{G}_{\theta'}$ is identically zero. However, attention should be paid at $r = r'$ for its effect discards the trivial solution. Along with the other geometrical boundary conditions the problem will now have a unique solution. These boundary conditions will be addressed in Section 3.3.

3.2. Infinite Matrix $\mathbb{U}$

To understand the structure of $\mathbb{U}$ we turn to the set of operations for a particular λ-mode. Seeing as $\mathbb{U}$ is infinite we may encode rows by the integer value of the mode being solved and columns by the value of the mode being correlated. Thus taking row λ from $\mathbb{U}$,

$$\mathbb{U}_\lambda \mathbb{G}_{\theta'} = \Big(\cdots, \overbrace{\tfrac{1}{h}\mathbf{Q}_\mu + \mathbf{R}_{\lambda,\mu}}^{\text{column } \lambda-\mu}, \cdots, \overbrace{\tfrac{1}{h^2}\mathbf{P} + \tfrac{1}{h}\mathbf{Q}_0 + \mathbf{R}_{\lambda,0}}^{\text{column } \lambda}, \cdots, \overbrace{\tfrac{1}{h}\mathbf{Q}_\mu + \mathbf{R}_{\lambda,\mu}}^{\text{column } \lambda-\mu}, \cdots \Big)_{\substack{\cdots,M,\cdots,3,2,1\leftarrow\mu \,|\, \mu=0 \,|\, \mu\rightarrow -1,-2,\cdots,-M,\cdots}} \begin{pmatrix} \vdots \\ \mathbf{G}_{\lambda-\mu|\theta'} \;\}\text{ row } \lambda-\mu \\ \vdots \\ \mathbf{G}_{\lambda|\theta'} \;\}\text{ row } \lambda \\ \vdots \\ \mathbf{G}_{\lambda-\mu|\theta'} \;\}\text{ row } \lambda-\mu \\ \vdots \end{pmatrix}, \tag{33}$$

with the following definitions for matrices $\mathbf{P}$, $\mathbf{Q}_\mu$, $\mathbf{R}_{\lambda,\mu}$,

$$\mathbf{P} = \begin{pmatrix} P^0 & 0 & \cdots & 0 \\ 0 & P^1 & \cdots & 0 \\ \vdots & \vdots & \ddots & \vdots \\ 0 & 0 & \cdots & P^N \end{pmatrix} \times \mathbf{A}^{(2)}, \tag{34}$$

$$\mathbf{Q}_\mu = \begin{pmatrix} Q^0_\mu & 0 & \cdots & 0 \\ 0 & Q^1_\mu & \cdots & 0 \\ \vdots & \vdots & \ddots & \vdots \\ 0 & 0 & \cdots & Q^N_\mu \end{pmatrix} \times \mathbf{A}^{(1)}, \tag{35}$$

$$\mathbf{R}_{\lambda,\mu} = \begin{pmatrix} R^0_{\lambda,\mu} & 0 & \cdots & 0 \\ 0 & R^1_{\lambda,\mu} & \cdots & 0 \\ \vdots & \vdots & \ddots & \vdots \\ 0 & 0 & \cdots & R^N_{\lambda,\mu} \end{pmatrix}. \tag{36}$$

One last remark on matrix $\mathbb{U}$ is that the density of non-zero entries is at most $3/N$ for the three-point stencil. For sufficiently large N, it will become essential to find a way to manage such sparsity for all speed-ups, data-compression, and efficiency in memory footprint.

3.3. Discrete Boundary Conditions

Using conditions detailed thoroughly in Section 2.2 and at end of Section 2.4 we are now in capacity of parameterizing the values of $G^{j,k}_{\lambda|\theta'}$. This parametrization should further reflect the behavior of the δ-function. The following are the conditions for the 3-point stencil: (*i.*) at $r = R_{\text{ext}}$,

$$G^{N,k}_{\lambda|\theta'} = 0 \quad \text{for DBC}; \tag{37}$$

$$G^{N+1,k}_{\lambda|\theta'} - G^{N-1,k}_{\lambda|\theta'} = 0 \quad \text{for NBC}, \tag{38}$$

(*ii.*) at R_{int} for the annulus,

$$G^{0,k}_{\lambda|\theta'} = 0 \quad \text{for DBC}; \tag{39}$$

$$G^{1,k}_{\lambda|\theta'} - G^{-1,k}_{\lambda|\theta'} = 0 \quad \text{for NBC}, \tag{40}$$

(*iii.*) for the disc at R_{int} (disregarding $G'_\lambda = 0$ for now),

$$G^{1,k}_{0|\theta'} - G^{-1,k}_{0|\theta'} = 0 \quad \lambda = 0, \tag{41}$$

$$G^{0,k}_{\lambda|\theta'} = 0 \quad \lambda \neq 0, \tag{42}$$

and, finally, (*iv.*) at the interface $r = r'$ the condition reads,

$$\left(G^{k_>+1,k}_{\lambda|\theta'} - G^{k_>-1,k}_{\lambda|\theta'}\right) - \left(G^{k_<+1,k}_{\lambda|\theta'} - G^{k_<-1,k}_{\lambda|\theta'}\right) = \frac{2h}{r^k} e^{-i\lambda\theta'}. \tag{43}$$

Here we have adopted the subscript convention of $<,>$ to refer to points to the left and right of the site of derivative evaluation. Note how all equations above reference and highlight a few fictitious points. The mesh points that lay outside or beyond the valid grid are $G^{N+1,k}_{\lambda|\theta'}$, $G^{-1,k}_{\lambda|\theta'}$, $G^{k_<+1,k}_{\lambda|\theta'}$, and $G^{k_>-1,k}_{\lambda|\theta'}$. These spurious terms must be dealt with and simplified in order to be able to incorporate readily all conditions.

3.4. A Non-Trivial Matrix Equation and a Solution

We will now show the explicit matrix equation associated with the conditions described above. As mentioned, they depend on the degree of accuracy that we choose, or equivalently, the stencil. We will describe the procedure for the three-point stencil and further discuss how to generalize for higher orders of approximation.

With the boundary relationships in mind, here in Equations (37), (39), (41) and (43), Equation (23) (multiplied by $-h^2$) equates partially to zero (when $r \neq r'$) as,

$$2P^j G^{j,k}_{\lambda|\theta'} - P^j(G^{j+1,k}_{\lambda|\theta'} + G^{j-1,k}_{\lambda|\theta'}) - h^2 \sum_\mu R^j_{\lambda,\mu} G^{j,k}_{\lambda-\mu|\theta'} - \frac{h}{2}\sum_\mu Q^j_\mu (G^{j+1,k}_{\lambda-\mu|\theta'} - G^{j-1,k}_{\lambda-\mu|\theta'}) = 0,$$

where via Equation (43) the latter can be used to simplify both spurious terms (appearing at $r = r'$) $G^{k_<+1,k}_{\lambda|\theta'}$ and $G^{k_>-1,k}_{\lambda|\theta'}$. After crossing out these terms by iterative substitution we obtain a generalized expression for the above valid for *almost* every point in the grid. The general discrete equation yields for $r' > 0$,

$$\begin{aligned} &2P^j G^{j,k}_{\lambda|\theta'} - P^j(G^{j+1,k}_{\lambda|\theta'} + G^{j-1,k}_{\lambda|\theta'}) - \frac{h}{2}\sum_\mu Q^j_\mu (G^{j+1,k}_{\lambda-\mu|\theta'} - G^{j-1,k}_{\lambda-\mu|\theta'}) - h^2 \sum_\mu R^j_{\lambda,\mu} G^{j,k}_{\lambda-\mu|\theta'} \\ &= -hr^j \delta^{j,k} e^{-i\lambda\theta'} \left\{ 1 - \frac{h^2}{4(r^k)^2}[1 + r^k f_r(r^k,\theta')]^2 [1 - \delta_{\lambda,0}] \right\}, \end{aligned} \quad (44)$$

where the new term that accounts for the boundary condition at $r = r'$ has appeared. Due to the absence of a left-hand limit as $r' = 0$, according to Equation (43), this term is exactly $-hr^j\delta^{j,k}e^{-i\lambda\theta'}$ at the origin. Actually, this condition holds for the mode $\lambda = 0$ in general due to translational invariance—this invariance is clearly absent for the other modes. The terms composing the right-hand side of last equation can be viewed as of order of mesh-size or order of radial distance from the origin as follows,

1. $-\frac{h^3}{4} f_r(r^k, \theta')$, a surprising third order correction due to the vector field appearing after substituting the interface difference in derivatives.
2. $h\, r^k = h\, R_{\text{int}} + h^2 k$, the leading order that substituted yields a first order constant term and a second order increasing term.
3. $-\frac{h^3}{4}\frac{1}{r^k} = -\frac{h^3}{4}\frac{1}{R_{\text{int}} + h\,k}$, a negative term significant closer to the origin. As expected, the behavior of the discrete version near zero validates our previous choice of boundary condition for the disc.
4. For $r' = 0$, we must implement a cut-off such that $r^0 = \epsilon > 0$ instead of zero to avoid numerical divergences. The choice for ϵ will be discussed below.

Because the error in the differential equation is of $O(h^4)$, we should incorporate all terms to the calculation. However, we will neglect the higher order term—first term—since this will simplify our calculations of $\psi(\mathbf{r})$.

This final expression is valid everywhere including the controversial $j = 0, N$ points, where either Dirichlet or Neumann conditions complete Equation (44) at the borders. In those two cases, substitutions must take place following Equations (37), (39) and (41). After replacements, and due to the nature of derivative calculation in the three-point stencil, rows from $\mathbb{U}$ corresponding to exterior and interior borders are modified. See the substitution rules in Tables 2 and 3.

Table 2. Non-vanishing matrix elements of $\mathbb{U}$ for $1 \leq j \leq N-1$ for an annulus and a disc.

Mode	$\mathbb{U}^{j,j}_{\lambda,\lambda}$	$\mathbb{U}^{j,j\pm1}_{\lambda,\lambda}$	$\mathbb{U}^{j,j}_{\lambda,\lambda-\mu}$	$\mathbb{U}^{j,j\pm1}_{\lambda,\lambda-\mu}$
$\forall\lambda$	$2P^j - h^2 R^j_{\lambda,0}$	$-P^j \mp \frac{h}{2}Q^j_0$	$-h^2 R^j_{\lambda,\mu}$	$\mp\frac{h}{2}Q^j_\mu$

Table 3. Non-vanishing matrix elements of matrix $\mathbb{U}$ that define DBC (D) and NBC (N) for an annulus. N/A specifies those elements that lay outside $\mathbb{U}$.

	Mode	j	$\mathbb{U}^{j,j}_{\lambda,\lambda}$	$\mathbb{U}^{j,j+1}_{\lambda,\lambda}$	$\mathbb{U}^{j,j-1}_{\lambda,\lambda}$	$\mathbb{U}^{j,j}_{\lambda,\lambda-\mu}$
(D)	$\forall\lambda$	$0, N$	1	0, N/A	N/A, 0	0
(N)	$\forall\lambda$	0	$2P^0 - h^2 R^0_{\lambda,0}$	$-2P^1$	N/A	$-h^2 R^0_{\lambda,\mu}$
(N)	$\forall\lambda$	N	$2P^N - h^2 R^N_{\lambda,0}$	N/A	$-2P^{N-1}$	$-h^2 R^N_{\lambda,\mu}$

We now define our complete matrix system as $\mathbb{U} \cdot \mathbb{G}_{\theta'} = -h\mathbb{V} \cdot \mathbb{E}_{\theta'}$. Among other things, the right-hand side accounts for the contribution of Dirac's distribution. The two additional definitions appearing correspond to first a distance parameter generalized into α^j_λ, a new object that incorporates the boundary conditions at both $j = 0$ and $j = N$. Notice, for instance, that keeping the term r^j at every point does not explain the vanishing of the Green function at the boundaries when DBC are considered, neither does it describe the correct behavior at $r = 0$ for a disk. Actually, when the last condition is considered, an ultraviolet cut-off ϵ—such that $\epsilon \to 0$—must be introduced to avoid divergences, as seen in previous works [14–16]. Such a cut-off is not surprising, as the 2D Green distribution has a natural divergence at $\mathbf{r} = \mathbf{r}'$ and a logarithmic behavior near the origin when $\mathbf{r}' = 0$. Although the appearance of this divergence can easily be visualized after studying the behavior of Equation (44) at $j = 0$ for the mode $\lambda = 0$ in a disk, its existence at any point—also for an annulus—is guaranteed by the infinite number of λ-modes that must be summed up to obtain an exact solution. Therefore, it is not surprising that ϵ and h are related—see Section 4 for more details.

Matrix terms are written as,

$$\mathbb{V}^{j,k}_{\lambda,\mu} = \alpha^j_\lambda \delta_{\lambda,\mu} \delta^{j,k}, \tag{45}$$

$$\mathbb{E}^{j,k}_{\lambda|\theta'} = e^{-i\lambda\theta'} \delta^{j,k}, \tag{46}$$

and the solution to the λ-modes matrix $\mathbb{G}_{\theta'}$ is,

$$\mathbb{G}_{\theta'} = -h\mathbb{A} \cdot \mathbb{E}_{\theta'}, \tag{47}$$

where we have defined $\mathbb{A} = \mathbb{U}^{-1} \cdot \mathbb{V}$ assuming that $\mathbb{U}$ is invertible.

Matrix $\mathbb{A}$ was declared because it has interesting symmetry properties that will be discussed in the next section. Tables 2–5 outline how to fill the matrix elements of the objects we have described.

Table 4. Non-vanishing matrix elements of matrix $\mathbb{U}$ that define DBC (shown above) and NBC (shown below) for a disc. N/A specifies those elements that lay outside $\mathbb{U}$.

Mode	j	$\mathbb{U}^{j,j}_{\lambda,\lambda}$	$\mathbb{U}^{j,j+1}_{\lambda,\lambda}$	$\mathbb{U}^{j,j-1}_{\lambda,\lambda}$	$\mathbb{U}^{j,j}_{\lambda,\lambda-\mu}$
$\lambda = 0$	0	$2 - h^2 g^0_0$	-2	N/A	0
$\lambda = 0$	N	1	N/A	0	0
$\lambda \neq 0$	$0, N$	1	0, N/A	N/A, 0	0
$\lambda = 0$	0	$2 - h^2 g^0_0$	-2	N/A	0
$\forall\lambda$	N	$2P^N - h^2 R^N_{\lambda,0}$	N/A	$-2P^{N-1}$	$-h^2 R^N_{\lambda,\mu}$
$\lambda \neq 0$	0	1	0	N/A	0

Table 5. Elements α^j_λ that define DBC and NBC for an annulus (A) and a disc (D).

Mode	j	α^j_λ (DBC)	α^j_λ (NBC)	Geom.
$\lambda = 0$	0	ϵ^{-1}	ϵ^{-1}	(D)
$\lambda = 0$	0	0	r^0	(A)
$\lambda = 0$	$1 \leq j \leq N-1$	r^j	r^j	(A, D)
$\lambda = 0$	N	0	r^N	(A, D)
$\lambda \neq 0$	0	0	0	(D)
$\lambda \neq 0$	0	0	$r^0 - \frac{h^2}{4r^0}$	(A)
$\lambda \neq 0$	$1 \leq j \leq N-1$	$r^j - \frac{h^2}{4r^j}$	$r^j - \frac{h^2}{4r^j}$	(A, D)
$\lambda \neq 0$	N	0	$r^N - \frac{h^2}{4r^N}$	(A, D)

3.5. The Parameter α and the Symmetry of $\mathbb{A}$

A closed relation can be found for the matrix describing the entire Green function. Using the results from previous section, it is

$$G^{j,k}_{\theta,\theta'} = -\frac{h}{2\pi} \sum_{\lambda,\mu} e^{i\lambda\theta} e^{-i\mu\theta'} \mathbb{A}^{j,k}_{\lambda,\mu}, \tag{48}$$

where $\mathbb{A}^{j,k}_{\lambda,\mu} = [\mathbb{U}^{-1}]^{j,k}_{\lambda,\mu}\alpha^k_\mu$. As previously mentioned, the parameter α^k_λ generalizes the radial parameter r^k, including the boundary conditions. On the other hand, it is worthwhile to state the symmetry conditions that $\mathbb{A}$ satisfies (a more detailed derivation can be found in Appendix D; $\bar{z}$ denotes the complex conjugate of z.)

$$\mathrm{Im}\left(\mathbb{A}^{j,k}_{0,0}\right) = 0, \tag{49}$$

$$\mathbb{A}^{j,k}_{-\lambda,0} = \overline{\mathbb{A}^{j,k}_{\lambda,0}}, \quad \mathbb{A}^{j,k}_{0,-\mu} = \overline{\mathbb{A}^{j,k}_{0,\mu}}, \tag{50}$$

$$\mathbb{A}^{j,k}_{-\lambda,\mu} = \overline{\mathbb{A}^{j,k}_{\lambda,-\mu}}, \quad \mathbb{A}^{j,k}_{-\lambda,-\mu} = \overline{\mathbb{A}^{j,k}_{\lambda,\mu}}. \tag{51}$$

Using Table 5, it is easy to see that the matrix elements $[\mathbb{U}^{-1}]^{j,k}_{\lambda,\mu}$ satisfy the same symmetry properties.

3.6. The Algorithm

The algorithm for a numerical solution can be summarized as follows:

1. The values of L and M are determined according to the required level of approximation.
2. We fill all elements described in Table 1; the matrix elements $\mathbb{U}^{j,k}_{\lambda,\mu}$ are filled by blocks using the rules shown in Tables 2–4. Matrix elements α^j_λ are also filled according to Table 5.
3. Matrix $\mathbb{U}$ is inverted and so matrix $\mathbb{A}$ is computed.
4. The Green function is computed according to Equation (48).

Using previous results, we can deduce a closed form for $\psi(\mathbf{r})$ for both DBC and NBC using the conventions stated in Equations (8) and (14). Although there are many ways to perform the integrals stated in previous equations, and the reader can choose the method that he or she prefers, a sketch of these solutions, using the trapezoid rule, is shown in Appendices F and G.

3.7. Particular Cases and Properties

We will analyze some particular cases that can be deduced from the procedure explained above. We will start focusing on the one-dimensional case.

One-Dimensional Case

The analysis of a Green function in one dimension requires an appropriate definition of a general DE obeyed by the Green function $G(x, x')$. Unfortunately, a direct analysis of the results by studying Equation (23) is not straightforward due to the clear differences between the Laplacians in Cartesian and polar coordinates. Let us imagine a general second order DE of the form $\mathcal{L}_x\psi(x) = \phi(x)$, where the Green function satisfies the relation

$$\mathcal{L}_x G(x, x') = P(x)\frac{d^2G}{dx^2} + Q(x)\frac{dG}{dx} + R(x)G = \beta\delta(x - x')\,. \tag{52}$$

The function $P(x)$ might not be necessary, as it can be eliminated by division, but its inclusion allows us to have a more general analysis. The constant therm β seems clumsily placed, as its value is usually 1. Nonetheless, some formalisms define the Green function by means of the operator $\mathcal{L}_x G(x, x') = -\delta(x - x')$, thus introducing a change of sign that can be contemplated in our study.

By following a similar analysis as that shown above, we can deduce an appropriate recurrence relation for Equation (52), which is

$$(2P^j - h^2R^j)G^{j,k} - (P^j + \frac{h}{2}Q^j)G^{j+1,k} - (P^j - \frac{h}{2}Q^j)G^{j-1,k} = -h\beta\,\delta^{j,k}\,. \tag{53}$$

Having confined the system within the domain $x \in [x^0, x^N]$, our step size is now $h = (x^N - x^0)/N$.

From this point on, we can apply the results obtained for the two-dimensional problem in this study. Notice that, in the absence of modes that account for the angular dependence, we can always say that $\mathbb{A}^{j,k}_{\lambda,\mu} = \mathbb{A}^{j,k}_{\lambda,\mu}\delta_{\lambda,0}\delta_{\mu,0}$. Therefore, Equation (48) becomes

$$G^{jk} = -h\mathbb{A}^{j,k}\,, \text{ where } \mathbb{A}^{j,k} = [\mathbb{U}^{-1}]^{j,k}\alpha^k \tag{54}$$

and α^k accounts for the boundary conditions. By making the association $x^j = x^0 + hj$, the elements described in Equation (54), for $1 \leq j \leq N-1$, are now filled using the following rules:

1. $\mathbb{U}^{j,j} = 2P^j - h^2R^j$.
2. $\mathbb{U}^{j,j\pm1} = -P^j \mp \frac{h}{2}Q^j$.
3. $\mathbb{U}^{0,0} = \mathbb{U}^{N,N} = 1$ for DBC. For NBC: $\mathbb{U}^{0,0} = 2q^0 - h^2b^0$, $\mathbb{U}^{N,N} = 2P^N - h^2R^N$, $\mathbb{U}^{0,1} = -2P^1$ and $\mathbb{U}^{N,N-1} = -2P^{N-1}$.
4. $\alpha^j = \beta$.
5. $\alpha^0 = \alpha^N = 0$ for DBC. For NBC: $\alpha^0 = \beta$ and $\alpha^N = \beta$.

The weight function, which guarantees the symmetry condition $G^{kj} = w^{jk}G^{jk}$ takes the form

$$w(x', x) = \frac{e^{U(x')}}{e^{U(x)}}\,, \quad U(z) = \frac{1}{P(z)}\exp\left[\int_{z_0}^{z}\frac{Q(y)}{P(y)}dy\right], \tag{55}$$

where z_0 is an irrelevant constant. Solutions for $\psi(x)$ with both DBC and NBC using the trapezoid rule as method of integration are shown in Appendix G.

Monopole-like Case

This takes place when both $\vec{f}(\mathbf{r})$ and $g(\mathbf{r})$ have no significant angular dependence, so the mode $\mu = 0$ is their only relevant contribution; this implies that $Q^j_\mu = R^j_{\lambda,\mu} = 0$ for $\mu \neq 0$. The off-diagonal matrices $\mathbb{U}^{j,k}_{\lambda,\lambda-\mu}$ thus vanish—this leads to a block diagonal $\mathbb{U}$ matrix—and so the system becomes separable in the radial and angular variables. Having now the relation $\mathbb{A}^{j,k}_{\lambda,\mu} = \mathbb{A}^{j,k}_{\lambda,\mu}\delta_{\lambda,\mu}$, Equation (48) reduces to

$$G^{jk}_{\theta\theta'} = -\frac{h}{2\pi}\sum_{\lambda} e^{i\lambda(\theta-\theta')}\mathbb{A}^{j,k}_{\lambda,\lambda}\,. \tag{56}$$

Notice that each mode can now be solved independently.

3.8. Beyond the Three-Point Stencil

As mentioned, we only showed an explicit analysis for a three-point stencil approximation. This method can be generalized to include the contribution of more neighbors in the derivative terms, i.e., higher order stencils that provide more accurate degrees of approximation in h. In spite of its simplicity, the three-point stencil has the great advantage that the spurious terms that arise from the boundary conditions can be eliminated in a simple fashion.

The description of the system with a five-point stencil, for instance, will increase the amount of terms different from zero in $\mathbb{U}$—for example, terms of form $\mathbb{U}^{j,j\pm 2}_{\lambda,\lambda-\mu}$ will provide non-zero contributions. Having a higher degree of approximation, that demands the inclusion of more non-trivial matrix terms, the grid size can be reduced. Although there is no guarantee that the inversion process is optimized in time when the contributions of more neighbors are included, as the matrices are highly sparse, there is a clear optimization of memory storage.

Yet a great disadvantage that higher stencils inherit is the elimination of the spurious terms that come from the boundary conditions. For instance, when we deal with the condition at $j = k$ $(r = r')$, Equation (43) will include more coefficients outside the grid, so the recurrence relation that is obtained will not be able to eliminate all of them—at least, using the same procedure we implemented. Therefore, a different approach must be performed. A possible solution could be expanding the derivatives around a point different from the center, so avoiding the spurious terms; this process is studied in detail in [42]. Nonetheless, this could be discussed in a future study.

4. Numerical Results

We will use the formalism described above to solve some particular examples. This section is particularly focused on presenting our results; such results will be discussed in the following section. Three examples will be presented.

Example 1: a one-dimensional case

As a first example, let us study a one-dimensional system with a known analytical solution, useful to test the formalism we have described. Let us suppose we want to solve the DE in the domain $[0,4]$

$$x^2\psi''(x) + x\psi'(x) + (x^2 - 4)\psi(x) = J_4(x)\,, \tag{57}$$

where $J_n(x)$ and $Y_n(x)$ are the Bessel functions of first and second kind of order n. Using Equation (55), we can easily deduce that $w(x', x) = x/x'$.

The conditions $\psi^0 = 0$ and $\psi^N = 2$ (Dirichlet), lead to the analytical solution,

$$\psi(x)^{\text{DBC}} = \frac{1}{24J_2(4)}\Big[J_2(x)(48 - 2J_4(4) + +\pi x J_2(4)J_4(x)Y_1(x)) - \pi x J_2(4)J_1(x)J_4(x)Y_2(x)\Big]. \tag{58}$$

Conversely, with conditions $f'^0 = 0$ and $f'^N = 2$ (Neumann), the analytical solution yields,

$$\psi(x)^{\text{NBC}} = \frac{1}{C(x)}\Big[(2J_0(4) + 3J_1(4))\left(x(x^2 - 24)J_0(x) - 8(x^2 - 6)J_1(x)\right) + x^3 J_2(x)(96 + 2J_0(4) - 3J_1(4))\Big], \tag{59}$$

with $C(x) = 24x^3(J_1(4) - J_3(4))$.

Analytical and numerical results are compared for both cases in Figure 2 and Table 6—see Equations (A25a) and (A25b) for explicit expressions using a numerical approach.

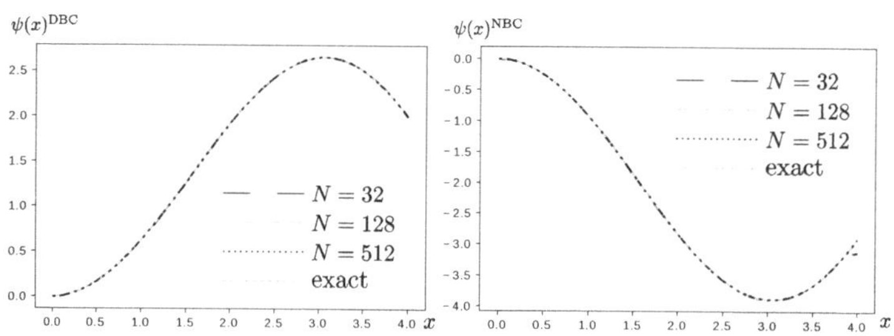

Figure 2. Left: solution to the DE given by Equation (57) with the initial conditions $\psi(0) = 0$ and $\psi(4) = 2$. **Right**: solution to the DE given by Equation (57) with the initial conditions $\psi'(0) = 0$ and $\psi'(4) = 2$. Table 6 analyzes the accuracy of the numerical solutions. Note: we made $x_0 = 10^{-6}$ to avoid numerical divergences at $x = 0$.

Table 6. Analysis of the accuracy of the two numerical solutions to Equation (57). The first two blocks use the conditions $\psi(0) = 0$ and $\psi(4) = 2$ and show the value of the maximum—exact value $\psi^{\text{DBC}}_{max} = 2.6524822\ldots$, its percentage error (PE) (from 0 t 100%), and mean square error (MSE) of the function along the domain $[0, 4]$; the first block uses the weight function, the second one does not. The block below shows something similar for the conditions $\psi'(0) = 0$ and $\psi'(4) = 4$ and focus on the global minimum—exact value $\psi^{\text{NBC}}_{min} = -3.88574186\ldots$ using the weight function—remember that for NBC the formalism with the weight function is required.

Func.	$\psi_{N=32}$	$\psi_{N=128}$	$\psi_{N=512}$
ψ^{DBC}_{max}	2.6510	2.6526	2.6525
PE	5.6550×10^{-2}	3.7700×10^{-3}	1.9221×10^{-4}
MSE	3.2824	2.6156×10^{-9}	1.0287×10^{-11}
ψ^{DBC}_{max}	2.7372	2.6736	2.6577
PE	3.1939	7.9615×10^{-1}	1.9671×10^{-1}
MSE	3.4935	2.1177×10^{-4}	1.3148×10^{-5}
ψ^{NBC}_{min}	−3.8852	−3.8853	−3.8856
PE	1.4438×10^{-2}	1.2060×10^{-2}	3.1806×10^{-3}
MSE	1.6316×10^{-3}	2.3096×10^{-5}	3.5993×10^{-7}

Example 2: the two-dimensional Helmholtz equation with imaginary wave number

We now shift our attention to solve a two-dimensional system. Let us consider the DE

$$(\vec{\nabla}^2 - m^2)G(\mathbf{r}, \mathbf{r}') = \delta(\mathbf{r} - \mathbf{r}') \,. \tag{60}$$

In the absence of the vector field $\vec{f}(\mathbf{r})$, we conclude that $w(\mathbf{r}, \mathbf{r}') = 1$; besides, the system is separable in the radial and angular coordinates. The solution to last equation confined in a large disc of radius $r^N = R_{\text{ext}}$ with Dirichlet boundary conditions can be found analytically. For $\theta = \theta'$ and different values of r', solutions are presented in Figure 3.

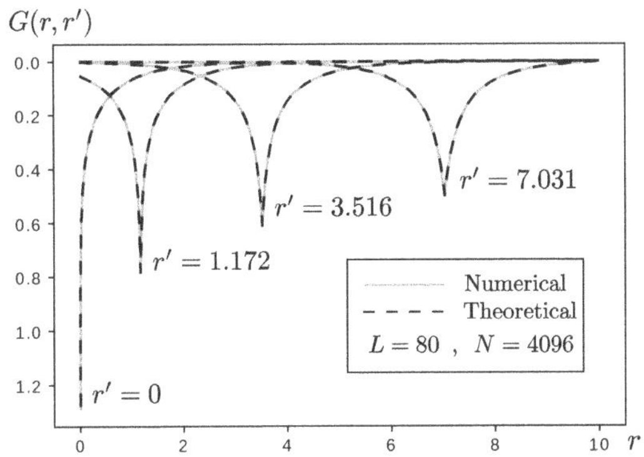

Figure 3. Solution to Equation (60) using the numerical solution explained in Section 3 (continuous gray lines) and using Equation (62) (black dashed lines) for $\theta = \theta'$ and different values of r'. We have chosen in all cases units such that $m = 1$. We also used $L = 80$ for both cases. In the numerical solutions $N = 4096$ and $\epsilon = 0.25h$, in the analytical solution $s = 0.15h$. The values of the minima and the mean square error (MSE) are shown in Table 7.

Last numerical result will now be used to solve a non-homogeneous equation of the form $(\vec{\nabla}^2 - m^2)\psi(\mathbf{r}) = \phi(\mathbf{r})$, whose general solution is provided in Appendix G with $r^0 = R_{\text{int}} = 0$.

Now, let us consider $\phi(\mathbf{r})$ to be a function defined over a disc of radius $R = 10$ and study the two following cases:

(a) $\psi^{(a)}(r, \theta)$, with $\phi(\mathbf{r}) = -\frac{1}{10} r \sin\theta$, and $\psi(R, \theta) = 2$.

(b) $\psi^{(b)}(r, \theta)$, with $\phi(\mathbf{r}) = \begin{cases} r^{-1/2} & , \quad 0 \leq \theta < \pi \\ -r^{-1/2} & , \quad \pi \leq \theta < 2\pi \end{cases}$, and

$$\psi(R, \theta) = \begin{cases} 1 & , \quad 0 \leq \theta < \pi \\ -1 & , \quad \pi \leq \theta < 2\pi \end{cases} .$$

Solutions to $\psi^{(a)}(r, \theta)$ and $\psi^{(b)}(r, \theta)$ for some angles are shown in Figures 4 and 5, respectively.

It is important to mention that Equation (60) is a particular case of a DE that describes the behavior of a two-dimensional two-component plasma in thermal equilibrium at a fixed temperature in the absence of an external electric field. Here the function $\psi(\mathbf{r})$ is naturally identified with $G(\mathbf{r}, \mathbf{r}')$ (actually, a Green function), which generates the n-body correlation functions of the system. When the plasma is confined in a disc (or annulus) and it is subjected to an external field, $\vec{E}(\mathbf{r})$, the system can be solved numerically with the presented method, once the identifications $g(\mathbf{r}) = -m^2 - E^2(\mathbf{r})$, $f_x(\mathbf{r}) = -2iE_y(\mathbf{r})$, and $f_y(\mathbf{r}) = 2iE_x(\mathbf{r})$ are performed; more details can be found in [14–16].

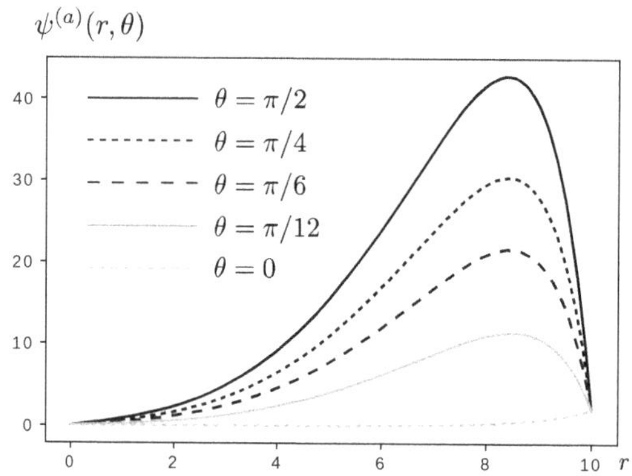

Figure 4. Solution to $\psi^{(a)}(r,\theta)$ for different values of θ in units in which $m = 1$. We used $N = 256$.

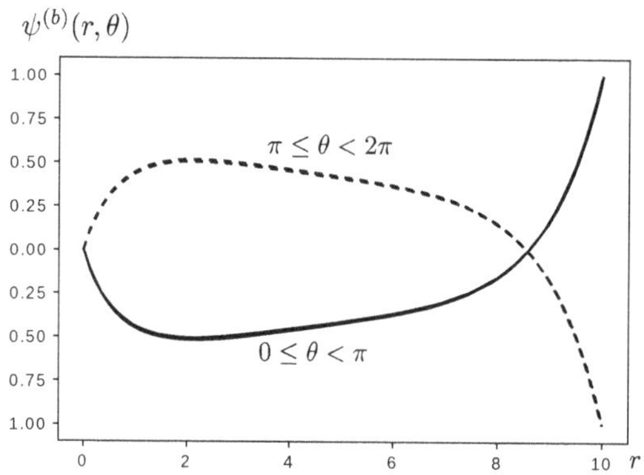

Figure 5. Solution to $\psi^{(b)}(r,\theta)$ for different values of θ in units in which $m = 1$. The continuous line shows the solution for $\theta = \{\frac{\pi}{12}, \frac{\pi}{6}, \frac{\pi}{4}, \frac{\pi}{2}\}$, the dotted line for $\theta = \{-\frac{\pi}{12}, -\frac{\pi}{6}, -\frac{\pi}{4}, -\frac{\pi}{2}\}$. We used $N = 256$ and $L = 80$.

Example 3: a pedagogical example

Now let us apply the same formalism to solve another two-dimensional problem. Let us suppose that we want to find the Green function associated with the two-dimensional DE $[\vec{\nabla} + \vec{\nabla}Z(\mathbf{r})] \cdot \vec{\nabla}\psi(\mathbf{r}) = \phi(\mathbf{r})$, where $Z(x,y) = 2x^2y^2$. After transforming the system to polar coordinates, we can see that $f_r = r^3(1 - \cos 4\theta)$ and $f_\theta = r^3 \sin 4\theta$. The elements defined in Table 1 now become

$$Q^j_\mu = r^j\delta_{0,\mu} + (r^j)^5\left[\delta_{0,\mu} - \frac{1}{2}(\delta_{4,\mu} + \delta_{-4,\mu})\right], \tag{61a}$$

$$R^j_{\lambda,\mu} = -\lambda^2\delta_{0,\mu} + \frac{1}{2}(r^j)^4(\lambda - \mu)(\delta_{4,\mu} - \delta_{-4,\mu}). \tag{61b}$$

The system will be confined in an annulus or internal radius $R_{\text{int}} = 1$ and external radius $R_{\text{ext}} = 2$. Figure 6 shows the Green function for DBC and some particular parameters but different values of L. Figure 7 shows the results for different parameters under NBC.

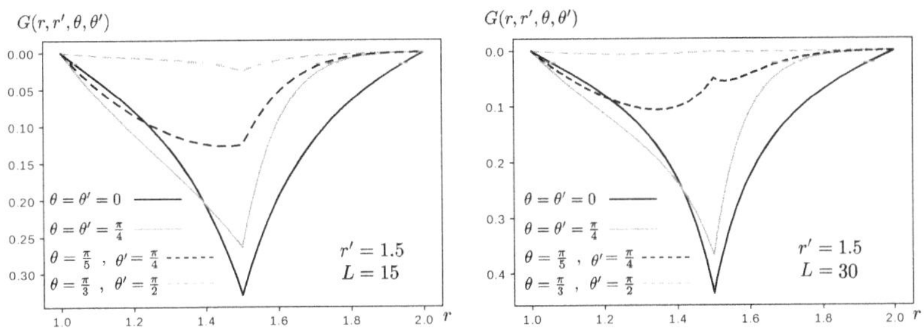

Figure 6. Solution to $G(\mathbf{r}, \mathbf{r}')$ with DBC, as given in example 3 for different values. We set $h = \frac{1}{256}$. We made $L = 15$ in the left plot and $L = 30$ in the right one.

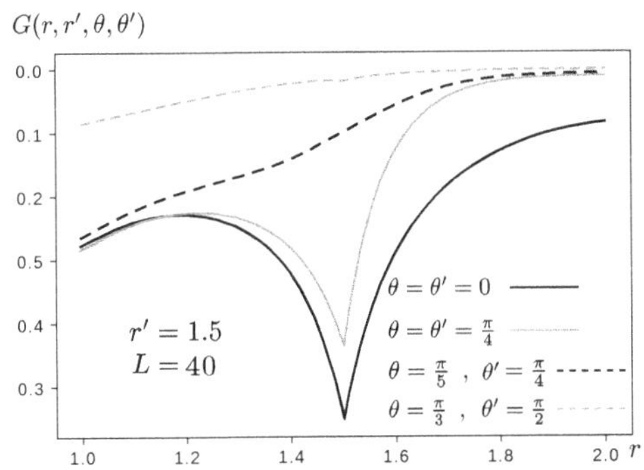

Figure 7. Solution to $G(\mathbf{r}, \mathbf{r}')$ with NBC, as given in example 3 for different values. We set $h = \frac{1}{256}$ and made $L = 40$.

5. Discussion

It is worthwhile to discuss the results found in the previous section. We will analyze the three examples presented above in respective order followed by an explanation on how the method can be adapted to solve the diffusion equation.

Example 1. *In the one-dimensional case it is interesting to contrast the numerical solutions shown in Figure 2 using the weight function and the one that arises without the weight function formalism—performing the replacement $w^{jk}G^{jk} \to G^{kj}$ (graphs that illustrate the results using the weight function were not shown, but comparisons will be given. Interestingly, from Table 6, we conclude that the introduction of the weight function leads to a more accurate result in this case. Notice that the use of a modest grid sizes ($32 \leq N \leq 512$) leads to very accurate results.*

Example 2. *This two-dimensional example has an analytical solution. Adapting the result found in [16], we deduce that the Green function associated with Equation (60) is*

$$G(\mathbf{r}, \mathbf{r}') = -\frac{m^2}{2\pi} \sum_{\lambda} e^{i\lambda(\theta-\theta')} \left[I_\lambda(mr_<)K_\lambda(mr_>) - t_\lambda(R) I_\lambda(mr) I_\lambda(mr') \right], \tag{62}$$

where $r_>$ and $r_<$ are the maximum and minimum between r and r', $I_\lambda(x)$ and $K_\lambda(x)$ are the well-known modified Bessel function of the second kind and $t_\lambda(R) = \frac{K_\lambda(mR)}{I_\lambda(mR)}$. Taking a look at Equation (62), we deduce that the Green function diverges—many distributions are formally infinite. Actually, the first term of previous sum can be reduced to $-\frac{m^2}{2\pi} K_0(m|\mathbf{r} - \mathbf{r}'|)$.

Notice that the Green function diverges logarithmically, in the limit $\mathbf{r} \to \mathbf{r}'$, as $K_0(x)_{x \to 0} \sim \ln(2/x) - \gamma$, with γ the Euler Mascheroni constant. A cut-off s, which represents a minimum separation distance between $\mathbf{r}$ and $\mathbf{r}'$ [14], is usually introduced to address this divergence. In turn, s might be related to L and ϵ.

We now implement the numerical analysis to verify last solution noticing that $P^j = (r^j)^2$, $Q^j_\mu(r) = \alpha^j = r^j\delta_{\mu,0}$, and $R^j_{\lambda,\mu} = -(\lambda^2 + m^2P^j)\delta_{\mu,0}$.

The following step is determining an appropriate value for ϵ. From Figure 3, we see that the solution for a fixed value of r' shows a peak at $\mathbf{r} = \mathbf{r}'$. As we sum up all modes the magnitude of the height of the peaks must be infinite. However, the introduction of L guarantees the peaks to be finite. The height of the peak at $r = r' = 0$ is associated with ϵ, as the functions $K_\lambda(r)$ diverge at $r = 0$. The cut-off ϵ is chosen in such way that the height of the peaks in the neighborhood of $r = r' = 0$—i.e., $|r - r'| = O(h)$—are close enough. We found that for $N \geq 2^7$, $\epsilon \simeq 0.25h$. Surprisingly, we found that ϵ does not depend on L for large enough L.

We recall that this is an approximation; the exact solution for the distribution is found in the limits $\epsilon \to 0$ and $L \to \infty$. In addition to the graphical comparison between the numerical and analytical results already shown in Figure 3, Table 7 also presents numerical details that ratify the accuracy of our results.

Table 7. Values of the minima shown in Figure 3 for the numerical solution (NS) and analytical solution (AS). PE means percentage error (from 0 to 100%) and MSE is the mean square error.

	Values of the Minima			
$G(r,r')$	$r' = 0$	$r' = 1.172$	$r' = 3.516$	$r' = 7.031$
NS	-1.288	-0.783	-0.609	-0.498
AS	-1.2778	-0.7835	-0.6087	-0.4984
PE	0.8263	$3.566 \times 10{-}2$	5.148×10^{-3}	1.603×10^{-3}
MSE	3.629×10^{-8}	1.343×10^{-10}	5.053×10^{-12}	6.379×10^{-13}

Regarding the inhomogeneous solutions shown in Figures 4 and 5, we do not have an analytical solution to test the algorithm; however, results show to be consistent. Particularly, the function $\psi^{(a)}(r,\theta)$ shows maxima for similar values of r—the value of such maxima gradually decreases with the angular direction; interestingly, the location of the critical points seems to occur for approximately the same value of r. Since $\phi(\mathbf{r})$ obeys a diffusion equation, this suggests that the concentration of the analyzed quantity shows maximum (or minimum) values at a certain radial location; this critical concentration, nonetheless, is favored for larger angles—this is consistent because of the non-homogeneous function $\phi(\mathbf{r}) = -\frac{1}{10}r\sin\theta$ that has been chosen. As expected, $\psi^{(a)}(r,\theta)$ takes the required values at the borders for every angle. On the other hand, $\psi^{(b)}(r,\theta)$ presents the same solution for two sets of angles: $0 \leq \theta < \pi$ and $\pi \leq \theta < 2\pi$, which is expected due to the form chosen for $\phi(\mathbf{r})$—notice that the only difference between such two sets of conditions is a global sign; this difference is clearly reflected in Figure 5. Interestingly, $\phi(\mathbf{r})$ is finite at $r = 0$, in spite of the clear divergence of $\phi(\mathbf{r})$ at this value. However, such difference is weak enough as it goes like $r^{-1/2}$. Like in previous example, the presence of a critical point is evident.

Example 3. *Notice from Figure 6 how the Green functions become zero at the borders and their derivatives present a discontinuity at $r = r'$. As expected, the larger L, the larger the magnitude of the value at that point; however, this value decreases as $|\theta - \theta'|$ increases; under this condition, the behavior of the Green function is smoother, but it seems to be too much more sensitive respect to the value of L. Interestingly, for the parameters that have been analyzed, the Green function only shows a "mirror symmetry" respect to r' as $\theta = \theta' = 0$. For NBC, as illustrated in Figure 7, something similar happens. However, the derivatives at the borders are now the ones which tend no be zero. Although this is clear as $r \to 2$, the asymptotic behavior toward zero close to the inner border can be appreciated. The values of the Green function at the border, however, clearly differ for different parameters. Similarly to the case where DBC where analyzed, the "mirror symmetry" around r'*

is also absent (also when $\theta = \theta' = 0$); the variation of the Green function is also larger as $\theta \simeq \theta'$, showing sharper peaks.

When using the Green function to solve a particular inhomogeneous equation, it is clear that $\vec{\nabla} \times f = 0$, so the weight function exists. It is

$$w(\mathbf{r}', \mathbf{r}) = \frac{e^{\frac{1}{4}r'^4(1-\cos 4\theta')}}{e^{\frac{1}{4}r^4(1-\cos 4\theta)}} = \frac{\sum_\lambda w_\lambda(r')e^{i\lambda\theta'}}{w(\mathbf{r})}, \tag{63}$$

whose only non-vanishing modes in discrete coordinates are given by the relation $w^j_{4\lambda} = (-1)^\lambda e^{\frac{1}{4}(r^j)^4} I_\lambda(\frac{1}{4}(r^j)^4)$. Although we are not interested in finding $\psi(\mathbf{r})$ for a particular boundary problem, all the steps are carried out to accomplish this goal.

The Stationary Diffusion Equation

It is worthwhile to describe how our formalism can be adapted to solve the diffusion equation at "thermal" equilibrium. Let $\psi(\mathbf{r})$ and $D(\mathbf{r})$ represent the density of the diffusion material and the anisotropic diffusion coefficient, respectively. In the stationary regime, $\psi(\mathbf{r})$ satisfies the DE

$$D(\mathbf{r})\vec{\nabla}^2\psi(\mathbf{r}) + \vec{\nabla}D(\mathbf{r}) \cdot \vec{\nabla}\psi(\mathbf{r}) = 0. \tag{64}$$

Although Equation (64) does not have the standard form shown in Equation (2), after dividing Equation (64) by $D(\mathbf{r})$ and defining $\vec{f}(\mathbf{r})$ as $\vec{f}(\mathbf{r}) = \frac{1}{D(\mathbf{r})}\vec{\nabla}D(\mathbf{r})$, the standard form can be obtained. (The diffusion coefficient is assumed to be well-behaved within the annulus or disc. However, $\vec{f}$ can have poles within the same domain.) The weight function is now guaranteed to exist, as $\vec{\nabla} \times \vec{f} = -\frac{1}{D^2}\vec{\nabla}D \times \vec{\nabla}D + \frac{1}{D}\vec{\nabla} \times \vec{\nabla}D = 0$. Actually, $w(\mathbf{r}, \mathbf{r}') = \frac{D(\mathbf{r})}{D(\mathbf{r}')}$.

The viability of our method to solve Equation (64) depends on the particular form of the diffusion coefficient. The following possibilities may arise: (a) $\vec{f}$ has no poles in the two dimensional domain; (b) $\vec{f}$ has a divergence in $r = 0$ that can be eliminated once $\vec{f}$ is multiplied by r; (c) the divergence at $r = 0$—or any other radial divergence—previously discussed still persists after multiplication by r; and (d) D^{-1} has poles for some $\theta \in [0, 2\pi)$.

The cases (a) and (b) can be solved with the regular procedure we have described; the modes $f_{r\,\mu}$ and $f_{\theta\,\mu}$ are well-behaved and so the elements Q^j_μ and $R^j_{\lambda,\mu}$ defined in Table 1 exist. The possibility stated in (c) demands a redefinition of $\vec{f}$ to eliminate any possible radial divergence; however, this redefinition does not guarantee the existence of the weight function. The situation described in (d) is problematic, as some of the modes $f_{r\,\mu}$ and $f_{\theta\,\mu}$ are divergent. The last situation is alleviated by working with the original DE, Equation (64); nonetheless, the process that we must follow to solve a system whose mathematical form differs from Equation (2) has not been described in this work.

Similar analysis can be performed as we deal with the Poisson's equation associated with electrostatic potential in an anisotropic media, among others.

6. Conclusions

In this paper we have analyzed the Green function formalism and studied under which conditions such mechanisms can be used to obtain the solution of an inhomogeneous DE. We consider that the main contribution of this research has been the proposition of a numeric algorithm to solve a family of partial differential equations for two-dimensional systems in polar coordinates, the Green function formalism was used for this purpose.

After decomposing the Green function as a sum of Fourier modes, an infinite set of coupled second order DE for the radial variable is found. Although such set decouples when the initial DE is separable in the radial and angular variables, the coupling in the modes arises as the vector field $\vec{f}(\mathbf{r})$ and the scalar function $g(\mathbf{r})$ are expressed as a sum of

Fourier modes. The presented analysis allows us to state the following highlights: (a) we found that there exists a function, which we called the weight function, that makes the Liouville operator self-adjoint. This function also defines the symmetry properties of the Green function (how it is transformed under the exchange of $\mathbf{r}$ and $\mathbf{r}'$) and is guaranteed to exist as $\vec{\nabla} \times \vec{f} = 0$; (b) a non-separable DE in r and θ leads to a large matrix system that is non-diagonal by blocks; (c) there exist a natural diverge due to the usual properties of the Dirac Delta distribution; however, this divergence can by absorbed only in the $\lambda = 0$-mode; and (d) the λ-modes satisfy DBC at $r = 0$ for a disk geometry.

An algorithm to solve the Green function associated with a general class of Liouville operator was solved using a FEM. We used a simple three-point stencil approach to approximate the solution and focused on both Dirichlet and Neumann boundary conditions. A set of approximations was made, which included a truncation of the infinite number of modes, a minimum distance when the system is confined in a disc, and the discard of the term $-\frac{h^3}{4} f_r(r^k, \theta')$. Although the first two approximations are well-justified because the Green function has a natural divergence, the last one was performed by convenience (anyway, it provides a very small contribution).

The algorithm was verified by comparing with known results and obtaining very small percentage errors. An additional example whose solution cannot be found by means of the regular algorithms was shown.

We consider that the presented method is a useful attempt to solve Green functions of operators whose radial and angular variables cannot be separated. However, we expect this algorithm can be improved by other authors in the future to obtain more accuracy without the need of creating huge matrix systems, which demand large storage memory and computational time. Some of the improvements may include the implementation of the method for higher order stencils, an optimized calculation either mathematically or numerically of ϵ, simplified formulas for the calculation of $\psi(\mathbf{r})$ or "on the go" algorithms that do not require the inversion of the matrix or the storage of temporal information.

Author Contributions: A.F. was in charge of writing the article, developing the introduction and the main steps of the methodology, working on the numerical codes, and obtaining the results. Additionally, he proposed the project that did lead to the realization of this work. J.P.M. made relevant corrections and suggestions to the main document, proved some of the equations that are stated, help to consolidate the numerical codes, and gave some ideas to extend this work to future research projects. All authors have read and agreed to the published version of the manuscript.

Funding: This work was funded by Universidad Católica de Colombia and Universidad de los Andes. The authors would like to thank both institutions for their support.

Data Availability Statement: Not applicable.

Conflicts of Interest: The authors declare no conflict of interest.

Abbreviations

The following abbreviations are used in this manuscript: Finite Elements Metyhod (FEM), Finite Difference Method (FDM), Diichlet Boundary Conditions (DBC), Neumann Boundary Conditions (NBC), Differential Equation (DE), Boundary Conditions (b.c.), Partial Differential Equations (PDE).

Appendix A. Deduction of the Weight Function

The relation obeyed by the weight function that makes the Liouville operator self-adjoint can be deduced by performing a direct substitution of Equation (1) into (5) and using Green's: $\int_{\mathcal{V}} \phi(\nabla^2 \psi)\, d\mathbf{r} = \int_{\mathcal{V}} \psi(\nabla^2 \phi)\, d\mathbf{r} + \oint_{\partial\mathcal{V}} \left[\phi(\vec{\nabla}\psi) - \psi(\vec{\nabla}\phi)\right] \cdot \mathbf{n}\, dS$ and the Divergence: $\int_{\mathcal{V}} \mathbf{a} \cdot (\vec{\nabla}\psi)\, d\mathbf{r} = \oint_{\partial\mathcal{V}} \psi \mathbf{a} \cdot \mathbf{n}\, dS - \int_{\mathcal{V}} \psi(\vec{\nabla} \cdot \mathbf{a})\, d\mathbf{r}$ theorems. After writing it conveniently, the result of this operation is

$$
\begin{aligned}
\psi(\mathbf{r}) = \int_{\mathbf{r}'} & G(\mathbf{r}',\mathbf{r})\Big[w(\mathbf{r}',\mathbf{r})\big[\nabla^2_{\{\mathbf{r}'\}}\psi(\mathbf{r}')\big] \\
& + \big[\vec{\nabla}_{\{\mathbf{r}'\}}w(\mathbf{r},\mathbf{r}')\big]\cdot\big[\vec{\nabla}_{\{\mathbf{r}'\}}\psi(\mathbf{r}')\big] + w(\mathbf{r}',\mathbf{r})g(\mathbf{r}')\psi(\mathbf{r}')\Big]\mathrm{d}\mathbf{r}' + \\
\int_{\mathbf{r}'} & \Big\{\big[\vec{\nabla}_{\{\mathbf{r}'\}}w(\mathbf{r}',\mathbf{r}) - w(\mathbf{r}',\mathbf{r})\vec{f}(\mathbf{r}')\big]\cdot\vec{\nabla}_{\{\mathbf{r}'\}}\psi(\mathbf{r}') \\
& + \vec{\nabla}_{\{\mathbf{r}'\}}\cdot\big[\vec{\nabla}_{\{\mathbf{r}'\}}w(\mathbf{r}',\mathbf{r}) - w(\mathbf{r}',\mathbf{r})\vec{f}(\mathbf{r}')\big]\psi(\mathbf{r}')\Big\}\mathrm{d}\mathbf{r}' + \\
\oint_{\partial\mathbf{r}'} & \Big[w(\mathbf{r}',\mathbf{r})\big[\psi(\mathbf{r}')\vec{\nabla}_{\{\mathbf{r}'\}}G(\mathbf{r}',\mathbf{r}) - G(\mathbf{r}',\mathbf{r})\vec{\nabla}_{\{\mathbf{r}'\}}\psi(\mathbf{r}')\big] \\
& - G(\mathbf{r}',\mathbf{r})\psi(\mathbf{r}')\big[\vec{\nabla}_{\{\mathbf{r}'\}}w(\mathbf{r}',\mathbf{r}) - w(\mathbf{r}',\mathbf{r})\vec{f}(\mathbf{r}')\big]\Big]\cdot\mathbf{n}\,dS'.
\end{aligned}
\tag{A1}
$$

Notice that under the choice $\vec{\nabla}_{\{\mathbf{r}'\}}w(\mathbf{r}',\mathbf{r}) - w(\mathbf{r}',\mathbf{r})\vec{f}(\mathbf{r}') = 0$, last equation transforms into Equation (8).

Appendix B. Finite Elements Method, Matrix Elements

The elements of matrices $\mathbf{A}^{(n)}$ introduced in Section 3.1 depend on the required level of accuracy and the central site η that we choose; a general algorithm to deduce such elements is shown in [42]. In the simplest case, as we choose $\eta = 0$ as the central point in conjunction with the two closets neighbors—three-point stencil approximation—we have the following relations [42,43]

$$
\mathbf{A}^{(1)} = \begin{pmatrix}
0 & 1 & 0 & \cdots & 0 & 0 & 0 \\
-1 & 0 & 1 & \cdots & 0 & 0 & 0 \\
0 & -1 & 0 & \cdots & 0 & 0 & 0 \\
\vdots & \vdots & \vdots & \ddots & \vdots & \vdots & \vdots \\
0 & 0 & 0 & \cdots & 0 & 1 & 0 \\
0 & 0 & 0 & \cdots & -1 & 0 & 1 \\
0 & 0 & 0 & \cdots & 0 & -1 & 0
\end{pmatrix}_{N+1\times N+1}, \tag{A2}
$$

$$
\mathbf{A}^{(2)} = \begin{pmatrix}
-2 & 1 & 0 & \cdots & 0 & 0 & 0 \\
1 & -2 & 1 & \cdots & 0 & 0 & 0 \\
0 & 1 & -2 & \cdots & 0 & 0 & 0 \\
\vdots & \vdots & \vdots & \ddots & \vdots & \vdots & \vdots \\
0 & 0 & 0 & \cdots & -2 & 1 & 0 \\
0 & 0 & 0 & \cdots & 1 & -2 & 1 \\
0 & 0 & 0 & \cdots & 0 & 1 & -2
\end{pmatrix}_{N+1\times N+1}. \tag{A3}
$$

Notice how the matrices $\mathbf{A}^{(n)}$ must be truncated at the boundaries; this is a natural consequence of the FEM, coming from the boundary conditions.

Appendix C. Derivatives at the Boundaries for DBC

If the Green function is used to find a non-homgeneous function with DBC, the derivatives of the Green function at the borders are needed—see Equations (8) and (14). Combining Equation (44) with the boundary conditions stated in Equations (37), (39), (41) and (43), we deduce the following two relations ($j = 0$ and $j = N$ refer to the two possible boundaries)

$$
\begin{aligned}
G'^{(0,N),k}_{\theta,\theta'} &= \frac{1}{2\pi}\sum_{\lambda,\mu} e^{i\lambda\theta}e^{-i\mu\theta'}\mathbb{B}^{(0,N),k}_{\lambda,\mu}, \text{ where} \\
\mathbb{B}^{(0,N),k}_{\lambda,\mu} &= \mp P^{0,N}\sum_{\nu}\big[\mathbb{S}^{(0,N)}\big]^{-1}_{\lambda,\nu}\mathbb{A}^{(1,N-1),k}_{\nu,\mu}.
\end{aligned}
\tag{A4}
$$

The matrix elements associated with $\mathbb{S}^{(0,N)}$ are $\mathbb{S}^{(0,N)}_{\lambda,\lambda} = p^{0,N} \mp \frac{h}{2} Q^{0,N}_0$ and $\mathbb{S}^{(0,N)}_{\lambda,\lambda-\mu} = \mp\frac{h}{2} Q^{0,N}_{\mu}$. Since ψ is known at the boundaries, the derivatives $G'^{0,0}_{\theta,\theta'}$ and $G'^{N,N}_{\theta,\theta'}$ are irrelevant; additionally, a disk only requires the calculation of $G'^{N,k}_{\theta,\theta'}$. The symmetric elements $G'^{j(0,N)}_{\theta,\theta'}$ can be found similarly, in terms of the transpose elements $\mathbb{B}^{j,(0,N)}_{\lambda,\mu}$, which are defined according to last expression by performing the index change and transposition $\mathbb{A}^{(1,N-1),k}_{\nu,\mu} \to \mathbb{A}^{j,(1,N-1)}_{\nu,\mu}$. In one dimension the derivatives are $G'^{(0,N)k} = \mp \frac{p^{0,N} \mathbb{A}^{(1,N-1),k}}{p^{0,N} \mp \frac{h}{2} Q^{0,N}}$.

Appendix D. Symmetry Properties of Some Matrix Elements

Expanding Equation (48) to eliminate the negative modes, we can write the Green function as

$$
\begin{aligned}
G^{j,k}_{\theta,\theta'} = -\frac{h}{2\pi}\Bigg[& \mathbb{A}^{j,k}_{0,0} + \sum_{\lambda\geq 1}\Big\{ [\mathbb{A}^{j,k}_{-\lambda,0} + \mathbb{A}^{j,k}_{\lambda,0}] \cos(\lambda\theta) + i[-\mathbb{A}^{j,k}_{-\lambda,0} + \mathbb{A}^{j,k}_{\lambda,0}] \sin(\lambda\theta) \Big\} \\
& + \sum_{\mu\geq 1}\Big\{ [\mathbb{A}^{j,k}_{0,-\mu} + \mathbb{A}^{j,k}_{0,\mu}] \cos(\mu\theta') + i[\mathbb{A}^{j,k}_{0,-\mu} - \mathbb{A}^{j,k}_{0,\mu}] \sin(\mu\theta) \Big\} \\
& + \sum_{\lambda,\mu\geq 1}\Big\{ [\mathbb{A}^{j,k}_{-\lambda,-\mu} + \mathbb{A}^{j,k}_{-\lambda,\mu} + \mathbb{A}^{j,k}_{\lambda,-\mu} + \mathbb{A}^{j,k}_{\lambda,\mu}] \cos(\lambda\theta)\cos(\mu\theta') \\
& + i[\mathbb{A}^{j,k}_{\lambda,-\mu} + \mathbb{A}^{j,k}_{\lambda,\mu} - \mathbb{A}^{j,k}_{-\lambda,-\mu} - \mathbb{A}^{j,k}_{-\lambda,\mu}] \sin(\lambda\theta)\cos(\mu\theta') \\
& + i[\mathbb{A}^{j,k}_{-\lambda,-\mu} - \mathbb{A}^{j,k}_{-\lambda,\mu} + \mathbb{A}^{j,k}_{\lambda,-\mu} - \mathbb{A}^{j,k}_{\lambda,\mu}] \cos(\lambda\theta)\sin(\mu\theta') \\
& + [\mathbb{A}^{j,k}_{-\lambda,-\mu} - \mathbb{A}^{j,k}_{-\lambda,\mu} - \mathbb{A}^{j,k}_{\lambda,-\mu} + \mathbb{A}^{j,k}_{\lambda,\mu}] \sin(\lambda\theta)\sin(\mu\theta') \Big\}\Bigg].
\end{aligned} \tag{A5}
$$

Since the Green function must be real for real Liouville operators, we demand that the imaginary contributions of last expression must vanish. Hence, we have the restrictions stated in Equation (49).

Appendix E. Expansion of the Green Function as Sines and Cosines

This expansion allows us to write the Green function as a sum of real elements, explicitly showing that the Green function is real. Using the properties stated in Equation (49) into Equation (A5), we find that

$$
\begin{aligned}
G^{jk}_{\theta\theta'} = & -\frac{h}{2\pi}\mathrm{Re}(\mathbb{A}^{j,k}_{0,0}) - \frac{h}{\pi}\sum_{\lambda\geq 1}\Big[\mathrm{Re}(\mathbb{A}^{j,k}_{\lambda,0})\cos(\lambda\theta) + \mathrm{Re}(\mathbb{A}^{j,k}_{0,\lambda})\cos(\lambda\theta') \\
& \qquad - \mathrm{Im}(\mathbb{A}^{j,k}_{\lambda,0})\sin(\lambda\theta) + \mathrm{Im}(\mathbb{A}^{j,k}_{0,\lambda})\sin(\lambda\theta')\Big] \\
& - \frac{h}{\pi}\sum_{\lambda,\mu\geq 1}\Big[\mathrm{Re}(\mathbb{A}^{j,k}_{\lambda,\mu})\cos(\lambda\theta - \mu\theta') + \mathrm{Re}(\mathbb{A}^{j,k}_{\lambda,-\mu})\cos(\lambda\theta + \mu\theta')\Big] \\
& + \frac{h}{\pi}\sum_{\lambda,\mu\geq 1}\Big[\mathrm{Im}(\mathbb{A}^{j,k}_{\lambda,\mu})\sin(\lambda\theta - \mu\theta') + \mathrm{Im}(\mathbb{A}^{j,k}_{\lambda,-\mu})\sin(\lambda\theta + \mu\theta')\Big].
\end{aligned} \tag{A6}
$$

In the presence of angular symmetry, $A^{jk}_{\lambda\mu} = A^{jk}_{\lambda\mu}\delta_{\lambda\mu}$, so last equation reduces to

$$
\begin{aligned}
G^{jk}_{\theta\theta'} = & -\frac{h}{2\pi}\mathrm{Re}(\mathbb{A}^{j,k}_{0,0}) \\
& - \frac{h}{\pi}\sum_{\lambda\geq 1}\Big[\mathrm{Re}(\mathbb{A}^{j,k}_{\lambda,\lambda})\cos[\lambda(\theta-\theta')] - \mathrm{Im}(\mathbb{A}^{j,k}_{\lambda,\lambda})\sin[\lambda(\theta-\theta')]\Big].
\end{aligned} \tag{A7}
$$

Appendix F. Computation of $\psi(\mathbf{r})$ as an Exponential Expansion

In this section, we will derive expressions for Equations (8) and (14) for both DBC and NBC. Although both approaches must lead to the same results, it is worthwhile to show how both relations can be found through the formalism we have described.

For convenience, we will split $\psi(r,\theta)$ into a *volume* (V) and *surface* (S) contribution—the *volume* contribution is the term containing the integral over $\mathbf{r}'$ in Equations (8) and (14); the *surface* contribution is the one containing the integral over the closed surface $\partial\mathbf{r}'$ in the same equations. For DBC and NBC, ψ can be written in discrete coordinates as

$$(\psi_\theta^j)^{\rm DBC} = (\psi_\theta^j)_V + (\psi_\theta^j)_S^{\rm DBC}\,, \tag{A8a}$$

$$(\psi_\theta^j)^{\rm NBC} = (\psi_\theta^j)_V + (\psi_\theta^j)_S^{\rm NBC}\,. \tag{A8b}$$

There are many ways to evaluate numerically an integral. We will use one of the simplest, however, very efficient, ways to do so, the so called trapezoid rule. Due to the discretization we have used, this rule will be applied to evaluate the the radial integrals, appearing in the *volume* contributions; the integrals over angular coordinates will be evaluated directly using the Fourier expansions of the functions involved.

Using the weight function

Having adopted the convention described in Equation (8), we start performing a Fourier expansions of the external field: $\phi(\mathbf{r}') \to \phi_{\theta'}^k = \sum_\lambda \phi_\lambda^k e^{i\lambda\theta'}$, the weight function: $w(\mathbf{r}',\mathbf{r}) \to \frac{w_{\theta'}^k}{w(r^j,\theta)} = \frac{1}{w(r^j,\theta)}\sum_\lambda w_\lambda^k e^{i\lambda\theta'}$—and something similar for the boundary conditions $\psi_{\theta'}^{(0,N)}$ and $\psi'^{(0,N)}_{\theta'}$. Now, we will define the function

$$\begin{aligned}\xi_w(k, M^{k,j}, \eta^k, \theta) &= \frac{1}{2\pi}\int_0^{2\pi} d\theta' \sum_{\lambda,\mu} e^{i\lambda\theta'} M_{\lambda,\mu}^{k,j}\, e^{-i\mu\theta} \sum_\nu \eta_\nu^k e^{i\nu\theta'} \sum_\rho w_\rho^k e^{i\rho\theta'} \\ &= \sum_{\lambda,\mu,\nu} e^{-i\mu\theta} M_{\lambda,\mu}^{k,j}\, \eta_\nu^k\, w_{-\lambda-\nu}^k\,. \end{aligned} \tag{A9}$$

This definition will be used to define the *volume*- and *surface*-terms.

Since the *volume*-term can be written as $\int_{r^0}^{r^N} r'dr' \int_0^{2\pi} w(\mathbf{r}',\mathbf{r})G(\mathbf{r}',\mathbf{r})\phi(\mathbf{r}')d\theta'$ $(r^0 = R_{\rm int},\, r^N = R_{\rm ext})$, we can say that

$$\begin{aligned}(\psi_\theta^j)_V = -\frac{h^2}{w(r^j,\theta)}\Big[&\sum_{k=1}^{N-1} r^k \xi_w(k, \mathbb{A}^{k,j}, \phi^k, \theta) + \frac{1}{2} r^0 \xi_w(0, \mathbb{A}^{0,j}, \phi^0, \theta) \\ &+ \frac{1}{2} r^N \xi_w(N, \mathbb{A}^{N,j}, \phi^0, \theta)\Big]\,. \end{aligned} \tag{A10}$$

The *surface*-term arising in DBC is written as $r'\int_0^{2\pi} w(\mathbf{r}',\mathbf{r})\psi(\mathbf{r}')\partial_{r'}G(\mathbf{r}',\mathbf{r})d\theta'\big|_{r^0}^{r^N}$. Similarly as shown above, in discrete coordinates it is given by

$$(\psi_\theta^j)_S^{\rm DBC} = \frac{1}{w(r^j,\theta)}\Big[r^N \xi_w(N, \mathbb{B}^{N,j}, \psi^N, \theta) - r^0 \xi_w(0, \mathbb{B}^{0,j}, \psi^0, \theta)\Big]\,. \tag{A11}$$

Finally, the *surface*-term $-\oint_{\partial\mathbf{r}'} w(\mathbf{r}',\mathbf{r})G(\mathbf{r}',\mathbf{r})\vec{\nabla}_{\{\mathbf{r}'\}}\psi(\mathbf{r}') \cdot \mathbf{n}dS'$ that appears in NBC can now be expanded in the form $-r'\int_0^{2\pi} w(\mathbf{r}',\mathbf{r})G(\mathbf{r}',\mathbf{r})\partial_{r'}\psi(\mathbf{r}')d\theta'\big|_{r^0}^{r^N}$; it now becomes

$$(\psi_\theta^j)_S^{\rm NBC} = \frac{h}{w(r^j,\theta)}\Big[r^N \xi_w(N, \mathbb{A}^{N,j}, \psi^N, \theta) - r^0 \xi_w(0, \mathbb{A}^{0,j}, \psi^0, \theta)\Big]\,. \tag{A12}$$

Remark A1. *The matrix elements of matrices $\mathbb{A}$ and $\mathbb{B}^{(0,N)}$ are given by Equations (48) and Equation (A4), respectively—the indices associated to the position in the blocks have been omitted by convenience. The function ψ_θ^j is defined in the interval $1 \leq j \leq N-1$; in DBC the terms ψ_θ^0 and ψ_θ^N are given, in NBC the function at the borders is not accurate enough due to the discontinuity of the Green function at the borders.*

Using no weight function

When we adapt the convention stated in Equation (14), Equations (A10)–(A12) are slightly modified. We now define the function ξ as

$$\xi(k, M^{j,k}, \eta^k, \theta) = \int_0^{2\pi} \frac{d\theta'}{2\pi} \sum_{\lambda,\mu} e^{i\lambda\theta} M^{j,k}_{\lambda,\mu} e^{-i\mu\theta'} \sum_{\nu} \eta^k_\nu e^{i\nu\theta'} = \sum_{\lambda,\mu} e^{i\lambda\theta} M^{j,k}_{\lambda,\mu} \eta^k_\mu . \tag{A13}$$

We can now conclude that

$$(\psi_\theta^j)_V = -h^2 \sum_{k=1}^{N-1} \left[r^k \xi(k, \mathbb{A}^{j,k}, \phi^k, \theta) + \frac{1}{2} r^0 \xi(0, \mathbb{A}^{j,0}, \phi^0, \theta) \right. \tag{A14}$$

$$\left. + \frac{1}{2} r^N \xi(N, \mathbb{A}^{j,N}, \phi^N, \theta) \right], \tag{A15}$$

$$(\psi_\theta^j)_S^{\mathrm{DBC}} = r^N \xi(N, \mathbb{B}^{j,N}, \psi^N, \theta) - r^0 \xi(0, \mathbb{B}^{j,0}, \psi^0, \theta), \tag{A16}$$

$$(\psi_\theta^j)_S^{\mathrm{NBC}} = h r^N \left[\xi(N, \mathbb{A}^{j,N}, f_r^N, \theta) + \xi(N, \mathbb{A}^{j,N}, \psi'^N, \theta) \right]$$
$$- h r^0 \left[\xi(0, \mathbb{A}^{j,0}, f_r^0, \theta) + \xi(0, \mathbb{A}^{j,0}, \psi'^0, \theta) \right]. \tag{A17}$$

Appendix G. Computation of the Inhomogeneous Function as Expansion of Trigonometric Functions

It is now useful to expand the relations shown in previous section as trigonometric functions. Although the expressions found are much longer, this allows us to use the symmetry properties, Equation (49), to get rid of irrelevant terms and explicitly express $\psi(\mathbf{r})$ as a real function. In addition, the exponential expansion defined in Appendix F might introduce some spurious imaginary contributions, which may arise by as a consequence of the truncating process of matrix $\mathbb{U}$—the complex conjugate counterparts of some modes may be discarded in this process. Taking advantage of the definitions used in Appendix F, Equations (A10) to (A12) are still valid when we adopt the convention stated in Equation (8); similarly, when the convention Equation (14) is adopted, Equations (A14) to (A17) are also valid. Now, we only need to expand ξ_w and ξ eliminating the negative complex modes to express them as sum of real modes. By doing so, Equation (A9) becomes

$$
\begin{aligned}
&\xi_w(k, M^{k,j}, \eta^k, \theta) = \mathrm{Re}(M^{k,j}_{0,0})\mathrm{Re}(\eta^k_0)\mathrm{Re}(w^k_0) + 2\sum_{\lambda\geq 1}\mathrm{Re}(\eta^k_0)\left[\mathrm{Re}(M^{k,j}_{0,0})X^k_\lambda + Y^{k,j}_\lambda\right] \\
&+2\sum_{\lambda\geq 1}\mathrm{Re}(\eta^k_0)\mathrm{Re}(w^k_0)\left[\mathrm{Re}(M^{k,j}_{0,\lambda})\cos(\lambda\theta) + \mathrm{Im}(M^{k,j}_{0,\lambda})\sin(\lambda\theta)\right] \\
&+4\sum_{\lambda,\mu\geq 1} X^k_\mu\left[\mathrm{Re}(M^{k,j}_{0,\lambda})\cos(\lambda\theta) + \mathrm{Im}(M^{k,j}_{0,\lambda})\sin(\lambda\theta)\right] \\
&+2\sum_{\lambda,\mu\geq 1}\mathrm{Re}(\eta^k_0)\left[\mathrm{Re}(w^k_\lambda)M^{(1)k,j}_{(+)\lambda,\mu} + \mathrm{Im}(w^k_\lambda)M^{(2)k,j}_{(+)\lambda,\mu}\right]\cos(\mu\theta) \\
&-2\sum_{\lambda,\mu\geq 1}\mathrm{Re}(\eta^k_0)\left[\mathrm{Im}(w^k_\lambda)M^{(1)k,j}_{(-)\lambda,\mu} - \mathrm{Re}(w^k_\lambda)M^{(2)k,j}_{(-)\lambda,\mu}\right]\sin(\mu\theta) \\
&+2\sum_{\lambda,\mu\geq 1}\mathrm{Re}(\eta^k_\mu)\left[\mathrm{Re}(M^{k,j}_{\lambda,0})w^{(1)k}_{+(\lambda,\mu)} + \mathrm{Im}(M^{k,j}_{\lambda,0})w^{(2)k}_{+(\lambda,\mu)}\right] \\
&+2\sum_{\lambda,\mu\geq 1}\mathrm{Im}(\eta^k_\mu)\left[\mathrm{Re}(M^{k,j}_{\lambda,0})w^{(2)k}_{-(\lambda,\mu)} - \mathrm{Im}(M^{k,j}_{\lambda,0})w^{(1)k}_{-(\lambda,\mu)}\right] \\
&+2\sum_{\lambda,\mu,\nu\geq 1}\left[M^{(1)k,j}_{(+)\lambda,\mu}[Z^{(1)k}_{(\lambda,\nu)} + Z^{(2)k}_{(\lambda,\nu)}] + M^{(2)k,j}_{(+)\lambda,\mu}[Z^{(3)k}_{(\lambda,\nu)} + Z^{(4)k}_{(\lambda,\nu)}]\right]\cos(\mu\theta) \\
&+2\sum_{\lambda,\mu,\nu\geq 1}\left[M^{(2)k,j}_{(-)\lambda,\mu}[Z^{(1)k}_{(\lambda,\nu)} + Z^{(2)k}_{(\lambda,\nu)}] - M^{(1)k,j}_{(-)\lambda,\mu}[Z^{(3)k}_{(\lambda,\nu)} - Z^{(4)k}_{(\lambda,\nu)}]\right]\sin(\mu\theta),
\end{aligned}
\tag{A18}
$$

where we used the definitions

$$X^k_\lambda = \mathrm{Re}(\eta^k_\lambda)\mathrm{Re}(w^k_\lambda) + \mathrm{Im}(\eta^k_\lambda)\mathrm{Im}(w^k_\lambda) \tag{A19}$$

$$Y^{k,j}_\lambda = \mathrm{Re}(M^{k,j}_{\lambda,0})\mathrm{Re}(w^k_\lambda) + \mathrm{Im}(M^{k,j}_{\lambda,0})\mathrm{Im}(w^k_\lambda); \tag{A20}$$

$$M^{(1)k,j}_{(\pm)\lambda,\mu} = \mathrm{Re}(M^{k,j}_{\lambda,\mu}) \pm \mathrm{Re}(M^{k,j}_{\lambda,-\mu}),\ M^{(2)k,j}_{(\pm)\lambda,\mu} = \mathrm{Re}(M^{k,j}_{\lambda,\mu}) \pm \mathrm{Re}(M^{k,j}_{\lambda,-\mu}); \tag{A21}$$

$$w^{(1)k}_{\pm(\lambda,\nu)} = \mathrm{Re}(w^k_{\lambda+\nu}) \pm \mathrm{Re}(w^k_{\lambda-\nu}),\ w^{(2)k}_{\pm(\lambda,\nu)} = \mathrm{Im}(w^k_{\lambda+\nu}) \pm \mathrm{Im}(w^k_{\lambda-\nu}); \tag{A22}$$

$$
\begin{aligned}
&Z^{(1)k}_{(\lambda,\nu)} = \mathrm{Re}(\eta^k_\nu)w^{(1)k}_{+(\lambda,\nu)},\ Z^{(2)k}_{(\lambda,\nu)} = \mathrm{Im}(\eta^k_\nu)w^{(2)k}_{-(\lambda,\nu)}, \\
&Z^{(3)k}_{(\lambda,\nu)} = \mathrm{Re}(\eta^k_\nu)w^{(2)k}_{+(\lambda,\nu)},\ Z^{(4)k}_{(\lambda,\nu)} = \mathrm{Im}(\eta^k_\nu)w^{(1)k}_{-(\lambda,\nu)}.
\end{aligned}
\tag{A23}
$$

Similarly, Equation (A13) is now written as

$$
\begin{aligned}
\xi(k, M^{j,k}, \eta^k, \theta) = {} & \mathrm{Re}(M^{j,k}_{0,0})\mathrm{Re}(\eta^k_0) + \\
& 2\sum_{\lambda\geq 1}\left[R^{j,k}_\lambda + \mathrm{Re}(\eta^k_0)[\mathrm{Re}(M^{j,k}_{\lambda,0})\cos(\lambda\theta) - \mathrm{Im}(M^{j,k}_{\lambda,0})\sin(\lambda\theta)]\right] + \\
& 2\sum_{\lambda,\mu\geq 1}[M^{(1)j,k}_{(+)\lambda,\mu}\mathrm{Re}(\eta^k_\mu) - M^{(2)j,k}_{(-)\lambda,\mu}\mathrm{Im}(\eta^k_\mu)]\cos(\lambda\theta) - \\
& 2\sum_{\lambda,\mu\geq 1}[M^{(2)j,k}_{(+)\lambda,\mu}\mathrm{Re}(\eta^k_\mu) + M^{(1)k,j}_{(-)\lambda,\mu}\mathrm{Im}(\eta^k_\mu)]\sin(\lambda\theta),
\end{aligned}
\tag{A24}
$$

with $R^{j,k}_\lambda = \mathrm{Re}(M^{j,k}_{0,\lambda})\mathrm{Re}(\eta^k_\lambda) - \mathrm{Im}(M^{j,k}_{0,\lambda})\mathrm{Im}(\eta^{\mathbb{I}k}_\lambda)$.

The one-dimensional case

The function ψ, satisfying the equation $\mathcal{L}_x\psi(x) = \phi(x)$, where $\mathcal{L}_x$ is defined according to Equation (52), can be found by means of the relations below. For DBC with either weight function or not

$$\psi^j = -h^2\Big[\sum_{k=1}^{N-1} w^{k,j}A^{k,j}\phi^k + \frac{1}{2}w^{0,j}A^{0,j}\phi^0 + \frac{1}{2}w^{N,j}A^{N,j}\phi^N\Big] + \frac{P^N w^{N,j}\psi^N A^{N-1,j}}{1+\frac{h}{2}\frac{1}{Q^N}} + \frac{P^0 w^{0,j}\psi^0 A^{1,j}}{1-\frac{h}{2}\frac{1}{Q^0}}; \tag{A25a}$$

$$= -h^2\Big[\sum_{k=1}^{N-1} A^{j,k}\phi^k + \frac{1}{2}A^{j,0}\phi^0 + \frac{1}{2}A^{j,N}\phi^N\Big] + \frac{q^N\psi^N A^{j,N-1}}{1+\frac{h}{2}\frac{1}{Q^N}} + \frac{P^0\psi^0 A^{j,1}}{1-\frac{h}{2}\frac{1}{Q^0}}. \tag{A25b}$$

For NBC

$$\psi^j = -h^2\Big[\sum_{k=1}^{N-1} w^{k,j}A^{k,j}\phi^k + \frac{1}{2}w^{0,j}A^{0,j}\phi^0 + \frac{1}{2}w^{N,j}A^{Nj}\phi^N\Big] + hP^k w^{k,j}\psi'^k A^{k,j}\Big|_{k=0}^{N}; \tag{A26a}$$

$$= -h^2\Big[\sum_{k=1}^{N-1} A^{j,k}\phi^k + \frac{1}{2}A^{j,0}\phi^0 + \frac{1}{2}A^{j,N}\phi^N\Big] + hP^k A^{j,k}\big[\psi'^k + \psi^k f^k\big]\Big|_{k=0}^{N}. \tag{A26b}$$

Appendix H. Notation and List of Used Parameters

Table A1 shows a list of most parameters that have been used in this document specifying their notation

Table A1. Notation used in this document. For additional information, please see Table 1.

Parameter	Notation	Parameter	Notation
Liouville operator	$\hat{\mathcal{L}}_{\{\mathbf{r}\}}$	Arbitrary scalar field	$\square$
Vector field	$\vec{f}(\mathbf{r})$	Scalar field	$g(\mathbf{r})$
Unknown scalar function	$\psi(\mathbf{r})$	Non-homogeneous scalar function	$\phi(\mathbf{r})$
Green function	$G(\mathbf{r},\mathbf{r}')$	Weight function	$w(\mathbf{r},\mathbf{r}')$
Internal radius	R_{int}, r^0	External radius	R_{ext}, r^N
Polar coordinates	r, θ, r', θ'	Fourier modes	Indexed by λ or μ
Min. radius	ϵ (cutoff)	Max. Fourier mode	L (cutoff)
Grid size	h	Matrix size	N
Full "Green matrix"	$\mathbb{G}_{\theta'}$	Blocks of $\mathbb{G}_{\theta'}$	$\mathbf{G}_{\lambda\mid\theta'}$
Convenient matrices	$\mathbf{P}$, $\mathbf{Q}_\mu$, $\mathbf{R}_{\lambda,\mu}$	Matrix to be inverted	$\mathbb{U}$
Temporary matrices	$\mathbb{V}$, $\mathbb{E}_{\theta'}$, $\mathbb{A} = \mathbb{U}^{-1}\cdot\mathbb{V}$	Matrices used in FEM	$\mathbf{A}^{(n)}$

References

1. Schwinger, J. Brownian motion of a quantum oscillator. *J. Math. Phys.* **1961**, *2*, 407–432. [CrossRef]
2. Wang, J.S.; Agarwalla, B.K.; Li, H.; Thingna, J. Nonequilibrium green's function method for quantum thermal transport. *Front. Phys.* **2014**, *9*, 673–697. [CrossRef]
3. Foster, S.; Neophytou, N. Effectiveness of nanoinclusions for reducing bipolar effects in thermoelectric materials. *Comput. Mater. Sci.* **2019**, *164*, 91–98. [CrossRef]
4. Moulhim, A.; Tripathi, B.; Kumar, M. Nonequilibrium green function technique for analyzing electron transport through single and two levels of interacting quantum dot. *Phys. Scr.* **2021**, *96*, 125802. [CrossRef]
5. Kadanoff, L.P.; Baym, G. *Quantum Statistical Mechanics: Green's Function Methods in Equilibrium and Nonequilibrium Problems*; W. A. Benhamin, Inc. XI: New York, NY, USA, 1962; p. 203.
6. Hidaka, Y.; Pu, S.; Wang, Q.; Yang, D. Foundations and applications of quantum kinetic theory. *Prog. Part. Nucl. Phys.* **2022**, *127*, 103989. [CrossRef]
7. Alkofer, R.; von Smekal, L. The infrared behaviour of qcd green's functions: Confinement, dynamical symmetry breaking, and hadrons as relativistic bound states. *Phys. Rep.* **2001**, *353*, 281–465. [CrossRef]

8. Lucarini, V. Revising and extending the linear response theory for statistical mechanical systems: Evaluating observables as predictors and predictands. *J. Stat. Phys.* **2018**, *173*, 1698–1721. [CrossRef]
9. Chen, Z.; de Gier, J.; Hiki, I.; Sasamoto, T. Exact confirmation of 1d nonlinear fluctuating hydrodynamics for a two-species exclusion process. *Phys. Rev. Lett.* **2018**, *120*, 240601. [CrossRef]
10. Brevik, I.; Parashar, P.; Shajesh, K.V. Casimir force for magnetodielectric media. *Phys. Rev. A* **2018**, *98*, 032509. [CrossRef]
11. Xu, F.; Wang, J.Statistical properties of electrochemical capacitance in disordered mesoscopic capacitors. *Phys. Rev. B* **2014**, *89*, 245430. [CrossRef]
12. Lenzi, E.; Mendes, R.; Rajagopal, A. Green functions based on tsallis nonextensive statistical mechanics: Normalized q-expectation value formulation. *Phys. Stat. Mech. Its Appl.* **2000**, *286*, 503–517. [CrossRef]
13. Lapolla, A.; Vossel, M.; Godec, A. Time- and ensemble-average statistical mechanics of the Gaussian network model. *J. Phys. Math. Theor.* **2021**, *54*, 355601. [CrossRef]
14. Cornu, F.; Jancovici, B. The electrical double layer: A solvable model. *J. Chem. Phys.* **1989**, *90*,2444–2452. [CrossRef]
15. Ferrero, A.; Téllez, G. Two-dimensional two-component plasma with adsorbing impurities. *J. Stat. Phys.* **2007**, *129*, 759–786. [CrossRef]
16. Ferrero, A.; Téllez, G. Screening of an electrically charged particle in a two-dimensional two-component plasma at $\gamma = 2$. *J. Stat. Mech. Theory Exp.* **2014**, *2014*, P11021. [CrossRef]
17. Joost, J.P.; Schlünzen, N.; Hese, S.; Bonitz, M.; Verdozzi, C.; Schmitteckert, P.; Hopjan, M. Löwdin's symmetry dilemma within Green functionstheory for the one-dimensional Hubbard model. *Contrib. Plasma Phys.* **2021**, *62*, e202000220.
18. David, G.; Mayboroda, S. Approximation of Green functions and domains with uniformly rectifiable boundaries of all dimensions. *Adv. Math.* **2022**, *410*, 108717. [CrossRef]
19. . On the Minimality of Extra Critical Points of Green Functions on Flat Tori. *Int. Math. Res. Not.* **2017**, *18*, 5591–5608.
20. Nomura, Y.; Darmawan, A.S.; Yamaji, Y.; Imada, M. Restricted boltzmann machine learning for solving strongly correlated quantum systems. *Phys. Rev. B* **2017**, *96*, 205152. [CrossRef]
21. Salazar, D.S.P. Nonequilibrium thermodynamics of restricted boltzmann machines. *Phys. Rev. E* **2017**, *96*,022131. [CrossRef]
22. Novoselov, K.S.; Geim, A.K.; Morozov, S.V.; Jiang, D.; Zhang, Y.; Dubonos, S.V.; Grigorieva, I.V.; Firsov, A.A. Electric field effect in atomically thin carbon films. *Science* **2004**, *306*, 666–669. [CrossRef] [PubMed]
23. Fiori, G.; Bonaccorso, F.; Iannaccone, G.; Palacios, T.; Neumaier, D.; Seabaugh, A.; Banerjee, S.; Colombo, L. Electronics based on two-dimensional materials. *Nat. Nanotechnol.* **2014**, *9*, 768–779. [CrossRef] [PubMed]
24. Schwierz, F.; Pezoldt, J.; Granzner, R. Two-dimensional materials and their prospects in transistor electronics. *Nanoscale* **2015**, *7*, 8261–8283. [CrossRef] [PubMed]
25. Sterling, R.; Rattanasonti, H.; Weidt, S.; Lake, K.; Srinivasan, P.; Webster, S.; Kraft, M.; Hensinger, W. Fabrication and operation of a two-dimensional ion-trap lattice on a high-voltage microchip. *Nat. Commun.* **2014**, *5*, 3637. [CrossRef] [PubMed]
26. Flindt, C.; Mortensen, N.A.; Jauho, A.-P. Quantum computing via defect states in two-dimensional antidot lattices. *Nano Lett.* **2005**, *5*, 2515–2518. [CrossRef]
27. Sugino, F. Super yang-mills theories on the two-dimensional lattice with exact supersymmetry. *JHEP* **2004**, *403*. [CrossRef]
28. Saraví, R.G.; Schaposnik, F.; Solomin, J. Path-integral formulation of two-dimensional gauge theories with massless fermions. *Nucl. Phys. B* **1981**, *185*, 239–253. [CrossRef]
29. Perera, A.; Urbic, T. Clustering in complex ionic liquids in two dimensions. *J. Mol. Liq.* **2018**, *265*, 307–315. [CrossRef]
30. Rañada, M.F.; Santander, M. Superintegrable systems on the two-dimensional sphere s2 and the hyperbolic plane h2. *J. Math. Phys.* **1999**, *40*, 5026–5057. [CrossRef]
31. Kalnins, E.G.; Kress, J.M.; Miller, W. Second-order superintegrable systems in conformally flat spaces. i. two-dimensional classical structure theory. *J. Math. Phys.* **2005**, *46*, 053509. [CrossRef]
32. Speight, J.M. Static intervortex forces. *Phys. Rev. D* **1997**, *55*, 3830–3835. [CrossRef]
33. Mitrea, D.; Mitrea, I. On the regularity of green functions in lipschitz domains. *Commun. Partial. Differ. Equ.* **2010**, *36*, 304–327. [CrossRef]
34. Truhlar, D.G. Finite difference boundary value method for solving one-dimensional eigenvalue equations. *J. Comput. Phys.* **1972**, *10*, 123–132. [CrossRef]
35. Jomaa, Z.; Macaskill, C. The embedded finite difference method for the poisson equation in a domain with an irregular boundary and dirichlet boundary conditions. *J. Comput. Phys.* **2005**, *202*, 488–506. [CrossRef]
36. Steger, J.L. Coefficient matrices for implicit finite difference solution of the inviscid fluid conservation law equations. *Comput. Methods Appl. Mech. Eng.* **1978**, *13*, 175–188. [CrossRef]
37. Ozis, T.; Aksan, E.; Özdeş, A. A finite element approach for solution of burgers' equation. *Appl. Math. Comput.* **2003**, *139*, 417–428.
38. Lin, Y.; Xu, C. Finite difference/spectral approximations for the time-fractional diffusion equation. *J. Comput. Phys.* **2007**, *225*, 1533–1552. [CrossRef]
39. Izadian, J.; Ranjbar, N.; Jalili, M. The generalized finite difference method for solving elliptic equation on irregular mesh. *World Appl. Sci. J.* **2013**, *21*, 95–100.
40. Jo, G.; Kwak, D. Geometric multigrid algorithms for elliptic interface problems using structured grids. *Numer. Algorithms* **2018**, *81*, 211–235. [CrossRef]
41. Kwak, D.Y.; Kwon, H.J.; Lee, S. Multigrid algorithm for cell centered finite difference on triangular meshes. *Appl. Math. Comput.* **1999**, *105*, 77–85. [CrossRef]

42. Fornberg, B. Generation of finite difference formulas on arbitrarily spaced grids. *Math. Comput.* **1988**, *51*, 699–706. [CrossRef]
43. Forsythe, G.; Wasow, W.; *Finite Difference Methods for Partial Differential Equations: Applied Mathematics Series*; Literary Licensing, LLC: Whitefish, MT, USA, 2013.

mathematics

MDPI

Article

Generalized Thermoelastic Interaction in Orthotropic Media under Variable Thermal Conductivity Using the Finite Element Method

Aatef Hobiny [1,*] **and Ibrahim Abbas** [1,2]

[1] Mathematics Department, Faculty of Science, King Abdulaziz University, Jeddah 21589, Saudi Arabia
[2] Mathematics Department, Faculty of Science, Sohag University, Sohag 82524, Egypt
* Correspondence: ahobany@kau.edu.sa

Abstract: This article addresses a thermoelastic problem under varying thermal conductivity with and without Kirchhoff's transforms. The temperature increment, displacement, and thermal stresses in an orthotropic material with spherical cavities are studied. The inner surface of the hole is constrained and heated by thermal shock. The numerical solutions are derived using the finite element technique in the setting of the generalized thermoelasticity model with one thermal delay time. The thermal conductivity of the material is supposed to be temperature-dependent without Kirchhoff's transformation. Due to the difficulty of nonlinear formulations, the finite element approach is used to solve the problem without using Kirchhoff's transformation. The solution is determined using the Laplace transform and the eigenvalues technique when employing Kirchhoff's transformation in a linear example. Variable thermal conductivity is addressed and compared with and without Kirchhoff's transformation. The numerical result for the investigated fields is graphically represented. According to the numerical analysis results, the varying thermal conductivity provides a limited speed for the propagations of both mechanical and thermal waves.

Keywords: finite element method; orthotropic medium; spherical hole; thermal relaxation time; variable thermal conductivity

MSC: 65L60

1. Introduction

Anisotropic media have material characteristics at specific places that differ from the three perpendicular axes, each of which has a twofold rotationally symmetry in solid mechanics and materials science. Over the last four decades, several researchers have shown a strong interest in generalized thermoelastic models, both technically and mathematically. Due to their realistic implications in various fields, such as nuclear engineering, acoustics, continuum mechanics, high-energy particle accelerators, and aeronautics, these theories are gaining popularity. In this theorem, the concepts of heat transport and elasticity are coupled. Many generalizations of the thermoelasticity hypothesis were established by Lord–Shulman [1]. The Lord–Shulman hypothesis was improved by Dhaliwal and Sherief [2] in 1980 so that it could account for anisotropic examples.

When temperatures rise, it is possible that the material's properties may decrease. In most materials, the thermal conductive K decreases almost linearly with increasing absolute temperature. A mapping approach (Kirchhoff's transformation) [3] is applied to obtain a solution to the problem under varying thermal conductivity in [4]. For a one-dimensional problem with variable material parameters, [5] used a finite difference approach. Because it varies with temperature, varying thermal conductivity is critical to better understand the study of thermal loads of specific materials, primarily semiconducting devices. The LS theory on generalized magneto-thermoelastics under varying thermal conductivity for indefinitely long annular cylinders was examined in [6]. The effect of thermal relaxations on thermal and elastic interactions in an unbounded orthotropic material with a cylindrical cavity were investigated by Abbas and Abd-alla [7]. Yasein et al. [8] discussed the effects of varying thermal conductivity in a one-dimension semiconducting material subjected to photothermal stimulation. Abbas and Zenkour [9] applied the finite element scheme to study the magnetothermoelastic interactions in unbounded FG thermoelasticity cylinders. Sharma et al. [10] discussed the thermal conduction and diffusion of two-temperature thermo-elastic diffusion plates under variable thermal conductivity. Hobiny and Abbas [11] studied generalized thermoelastic interaction due to a pulse heat transfer in two-dimension orthotropic materials. Song et al. [12] investigated the vibrations of optically activated semiconductors and micro conductors using the extended thermoelastic theorem. Mondal and Sur [13] investigated photothermoelastic wave propagations and memory response in an orthotropic semiconductor medium with a spherical cavity. Said [14] used the eigenvalues technique to compare three theories on the problem of magneto-thermoelasticity spinning medium with varying thermal conductivity. Lata and Himanshi [15] discussed the fractional effects in an orthotropic magneto-thermoelasticity rotating solid due to normal forces under the Green–Naghdi model. Singh et al. [16] studied the magneto-thermoelastic interactions under memory responses due to laser pulse in an orthotropic material based on the Green–Naghdi model. Many studies are conducted under the broad thermoelastic models described in the following types of literature [17–41]. In the scientific literature, exact solutions of the linear or nonlinear governing equations for the problems of generalized thermoelasticity theories only exist for certain circumstances. To calculate complex problems, a numerical solution method must be used. Therefore, the finite-element approach is selected. The technique of weighted residuals produces the most accurate approximation of linear and nonlinear ordinary and partial differential equations when applied to the formulation of finite-element equations. Applying this method involves three steps. The first step is to assume that the general behaviour of the unknown field variables can be described in a form that satisfies the differential equations that have been provided. Then, when these approximation functions are substituted into the differential equations and boundary conditions, it leads to certain inaccuracies that are referred to as the residual. On average, across the solution domain, this residue must disappear completely. The next stage, which is the second one, is the integration of time. It is necessary to use the previous results in order to calculate the time derivatives of the variables that are unknown. Applying a finite-element solution method to the equations that have been generated as a consequence of the first and second processes is the third step in the process as in [42–51].

This work studies the influence of varying thermal conductivity and thermal relaxation time in orthotropic media with a spherical cavity. The material's thermal conductivity is supposed to be temperature-dependent, which gives the nonlinear and complex problems. The nonlinear problem (without Kirchhoff's Transform) has been studied in this work. Due to the difficulty of nonlinear formulations, the finite element method is used to solve this problem without using Kirchhoff's transformations. In addition, Kirchhoff's transformations are applied to obtain the linear problem, and then the solution is obtained using the Laplace transforms and the eigenvalue technique. Variable thermal conductivity has been addressed and compared with and without Kirchhoff's transformations. According to the numerical analysis results, the varying thermal conductivity provides limited speed for the propagation of both mechanical and thermal waves.

2. Mathematical Model

The basic equations in an orthotropic material in the absence of body forces and thermal source are presented as [2]:

$$\sigma_{ij,j} = \rho \frac{\partial^2 u_i}{\partial t^2}, \tag{1}$$

$$\frac{\partial T_{,ii}}{\partial t}(K_{ii}T_{,i})_{,i} = \left(\frac{\partial}{\partial t} + \tau_o\frac{\partial^2}{\partial t^2}\right)\left(\rho c_e T + \beta_{ii}T_o\partial u_{j,j}\right), \tag{2}$$

$$\sigma_{ij} = c_{ijkl}e_{kl} - \beta_{ij}(T - T_o)\delta_{ij}, \tag{3}$$

$$e_{ij} = \frac{1}{2}(u_{i,j} + u_{j,i}), \tag{4}$$

where T points to the temperature increments, c_e points to the specific heat, β_{ij} are the thermal moduli, ρ is the density of mass, K_{ii} are the thermal conductivity components that are temperature-dependent and variable, e_{kl} are the strain tensor components and c_{ijkl} are the elastic constants, T_o is the reference temperature, σ_{ij} are the stresses components and u_i are the components of displacement. Consider an unbounded elastic body involving spherical cavities occupying the area $a \leq r < \infty$, whose states are defined in terms of space variable r and the time variable t. The only non-vanishing component of displacement is the radial one $u_r = u(r,t)$, which is related to the spherical coordinates (r,θ,φ) as in Figure 1. The nonvanishing strain tensor components are as follows:

$$e_{rr} = \frac{\partial u}{\partial r}, e_{\theta\theta} = \frac{u}{r}, \; e_{\varphi\varphi} = \frac{u}{r}, \tag{5}$$

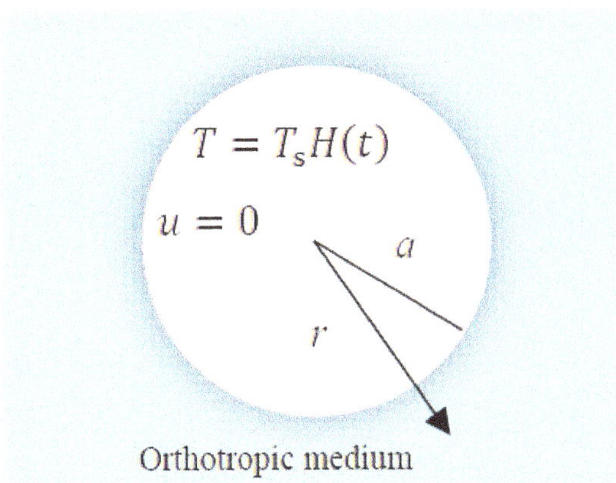

Figure 1. The diagram of an unbounded medium with a spherical hole.

Substituting for e_{rr}, $e_{\theta\theta}$ and $e_{\varphi\varphi}$ into the basic equations can be given by

$$\frac{\partial \sigma_{rr}}{\partial r} + \frac{1}{r}(2\sigma_{rr} - \sigma_{\theta\theta} - \sigma_{\varphi\varphi}) = \rho\frac{\partial^2 u}{\partial t^2}, \tag{6}$$

$$\frac{1}{r^2}\frac{\partial}{\partial r}\left(r^2 K(T)\frac{\partial T}{\partial r}\right) = \left(\frac{\partial}{\partial t} + \tau_o\frac{\partial^2}{\partial t^2}\right)\left(\rho c_e T + \beta_{11}T_o\frac{\partial u}{\partial r} + \beta_{22}T_o\frac{2u}{r}\right), \tag{7}$$

$$\sigma_{rr} = c_{11}\frac{\partial u}{\partial r} + c_{12}\frac{2u}{r} - \beta_{11}T, \sigma_{\theta\theta} = \sigma_{\varphi\varphi} = c_{12}\frac{\partial u}{\partial r} + (c_{22} + c_{23})\frac{u}{r} - \beta_{22}T, \tag{8}$$

$$e = \frac{\partial u}{\partial r} + \frac{2u}{r}, \tag{9}$$

In this case, the varying thermal conductivity of orthotropic media that may be chosen as in [52]

$$K(T) = K_o(1 + K_n T), \tag{10}$$

where K_o are the thermal conductivity when $T = T_o$ and $K_n \leq 0$ identifies the negative parameter.

3. Application

The initial condition can be given by:

$$u(r,0) = 0, \quad \frac{\partial u(r,0)}{\partial t} = 0, \quad T(r,0) = 0, \quad \frac{\partial T(r,0)}{\partial t} = 0, \tag{11}$$

whereas the following constitute the requirements of the boundaries:

$$u(a,t) = 0, \quad T(a,t) = T_s H(t), \tag{12}$$

where $H(t)$ is the Heaviside function and T_s is constant. Consequently, the nondimensionality of variables may be stated as follows:

$$T^* = \frac{T - T_o}{T_o}, \quad (r^*, u^*) = \mu c(r,u), \quad (t^*, \tau_o^*) = \omega c^2(t, \tau_o), \quad (\sigma_{rr}^*, \sigma_{\theta\theta}^*) = \frac{(\sigma_{rr}, \sigma_{\theta\theta},)}{c_{11}}, \tag{13}$$

where $\mu = \frac{\rho c_e}{K_o}$ and $c = \sqrt{\frac{c_{11}}{\rho}}$. Equation (13)'s non-dimensional governing equations are written as (after the superscript * has been removed for appropriateness)

$$\frac{\partial^2 u}{\partial r^2} + \frac{2}{r}\frac{\partial u}{\partial r} - \frac{2(s_3 - s_1)u}{r^2} - s_2\frac{\partial T}{\partial r} + \frac{2(s_4 - s_2)}{r}T = \frac{\partial^2 u}{\partial t^2}, \tag{14}$$

$$(1 + K_n T)\frac{\partial^2 T}{\partial r^2} + K_n\left(\frac{\partial T}{\partial r}\right)^2 + \frac{2(1 + K_n T)}{r}\frac{\partial T}{\partial r} = \left(\frac{\partial}{\partial t} + \tau_o\frac{\partial^2}{\partial t^2}\right)\left(T + \varepsilon_1\frac{\partial u}{\partial r} + \varepsilon_2\frac{2u}{r}\right), \tag{15}$$

$$\sigma_{rr} = \frac{\partial u}{\partial r} + 2s_1\frac{u}{r} - s_2 T, \sigma_{\theta\theta} = \sigma_{\varphi\varphi} = s_1\frac{\partial u}{\partial r} + s_3\frac{u}{r} - s_4 T, \tag{16}$$

where $s_1 = \frac{c_{12}}{c_{11}}$, $s_2 = \frac{T_o\beta_{11}}{c_{11}}$, $s_3 = \frac{(c_{22}+c_{23})}{c_{11}}$, $s_4 = \frac{T_o\beta_{22}}{c_{11}}$, $\varepsilon_1 = \frac{\beta_{11}}{\rho c_e}$, $\varepsilon_2 = \frac{\beta_{22}}{\rho c_e}$.

4. Numerical Scheme

The standard techniques may be used to generate the finite element method (FEM) for thermoelasticity problems. The finite element scheme is the preferred method for complex systems in numerous domains since it is a powerful and most sophisticated way to obtain numerical solutions to complicated problems. The solutions of the governing relations (14) and (15) under the boundary condition (12) and the use of the initial condition (11) are obtained using a finite element diagram. The displacement u and the temperature T are linked to the corresponding nodal values in finite element techniques by

$$u = \sum_{j=1}^{n} N_j u_j(t), T = \sum_{j=1}^{n} N_j T_j(t), \tag{17}$$

where n refers to the number of nodes per element, and N refers to the shape functions. For the unknown displacement u and the unknown temperature T, the same shape function is used in Galerkin methods to approximate the corresponding test functions.

$$\delta u = \sum_{j=1}^{n} N_j \delta u_j, \ \delta T = \sum_{j=1}^{n} N_j \delta T_j, \tag{18}$$

We assume that the master elements local coordinates fall between [1 and −1]. In this situation, one-dimension quadratic components are used, and they are written as follows:

$$N_1 = \tfrac{1}{2}(\chi^2 + \chi), \quad N_1 = 1 - \chi^2, \quad N_3 = \tfrac{1}{2}(\chi^2 - \chi), \tag{19}$$

The weak formulation of finite element method that correspond to the nonlinear formulations (14) and (15) may be written by:

$$\int_a^L \delta u\left(\frac{\partial^2 u}{\partial t^2} - \frac{2}{r}\frac{\partial u}{\partial r} + \frac{2(s_3 - s_1)u}{r^2} + s_2\frac{\partial T}{\partial r} - \frac{2(s_4 - s_2)}{r}T\right)dr + \int_a^L \frac{\partial \delta u}{\partial r}\left(\frac{\partial u}{\partial r}\right)dr = \delta u\left(\frac{\partial u}{\partial r}\right)_a^L, \tag{20}$$

$$\int_a^L \delta T\left((\frac{\partial}{\partial t} + \tau_o \frac{\partial^2}{\partial t^2})(T + \varepsilon_1 \frac{\partial u}{\partial r} + \varepsilon_2 \frac{2u}{r}) - \frac{2(1+K_n T)}{r} \frac{\partial T}{\partial r} \right) dr + \int_a^L \frac{\partial \delta T}{\partial r} \left((1+K_n T) \frac{\partial T}{\partial r} \right) dr = \delta T \left((1+K_n T) \frac{\partial T}{\partial r} \right)_a^L. \tag{21}$$

Implicit approaches can be employed to determine the time derivatives of unknown variables. For example, the time derivatives of the unknown variables must be determined using the Newmark time integration method or the central finite difference method by time step 0.0001 [53]. The grid size was changed until the values of the fields under examination were stable. Further increasing the mesh size over 25,000 elements has no discernible effect on the results. Therefore, for this investigation, a grid size of 25,000 was chosen.

5. Special Cases and the Validation of the Numerical Approach

Analytical solutions for homogeneous and isotropic material are being provided to validate the finite element approach. Moreover, when $K_n = 0$, the analytical and numerical solutions are compared with each other to validate the numerical solutions. For homogeneous and isotropic material $c_{11} = c_{22} = \lambda + 2\mu$, $c_{12} = c_{23} = \lambda$, $\beta_{11} = \beta_{22} = \gamma$ and $K_n = 0$. As a consequence of this, Equations (14)–(16) with the initial and boundary conditions may be expressed as follows:

$$\frac{\partial^2 u}{\partial r^2} + \frac{2}{r}\frac{\partial u}{\partial r} - \frac{2u}{r^2} - a_2 \frac{\partial T}{\partial r} = \frac{\partial^2 u}{\partial t^2}, \tag{22}$$

$$\frac{\partial^2 T}{\partial r^2} + \frac{2}{r}\frac{\partial T}{\partial r} = \left(\frac{\partial}{\partial t} + \tau_o \frac{\partial^2}{\partial t^2}\right)\left(T + \varepsilon_1\left(\frac{\partial u}{\partial r} + \frac{2u}{r}\right)\right), \tag{23}$$

$$\sigma_{rr} = \frac{\partial u}{\partial r} + 2a_1 \frac{u}{r} - a_2 T, \sigma_{\theta\theta} = \sigma_{\varphi\varphi} = a_1 \frac{\partial u}{\partial r} + (1 + a_1)\frac{u}{r} - a_2 T, \tag{24}$$

$$u(r,0) = 0, \frac{\partial u(r,0)}{\partial t} = 0, T(r,0) = 0, \frac{\partial T(r,0)}{\partial t} = 0, \tag{25}$$

$$T(a,t) = T_s H(t),\ u(a,t) = 0, \tag{26}$$

where $a_1 = \frac{\lambda}{\lambda+2\mu}$, $a_2 = \frac{T_o\gamma}{\lambda+2\mu}$, $\varepsilon = \frac{\gamma}{\rho c_e}$. Applying Laplace transforms in order to find solutions to Equations (22)–(26):

$$\overline{f}(x,s) = L[f(x,t)] = \int_0^\infty f(x,t)e^{-st}dt. \tag{27}$$

As a consequence of this, we can deduce the following:

$$\frac{d^2\overline{u}}{dr^2} + \frac{2}{r}\frac{d\overline{u}}{dr} - \frac{2\overline{u}}{r^2} = s^2\overline{u} + a_2 \frac{d\overline{T}}{dr}, \tag{28}$$

$$\frac{d^2\overline{T}}{dr^2} + \frac{2}{r}\frac{d\overline{T}}{dr} = \left(s + s^2\tau_o\right)\left(\overline{T} + \varepsilon_1\left(\frac{d\overline{u}}{dr} + \frac{2\overline{u}}{r}\right)\right), \tag{29}$$

$$\overline{\sigma}_{rr} = \frac{d\overline{u}}{dr} + 2a_1\frac{\overline{u}}{r} - a_2\overline{T}, \overline{\sigma}_{\theta\theta} = \overline{\sigma}_{\varphi\varphi} = a_1\frac{d\overline{u}}{dr} + (1 + a_1)\frac{\overline{u}}{r} - a_2\overline{T}, \tag{30}$$

$$\overline{T}(a,s) = \frac{T_s}{s}, \overline{u}(a,s) = 0, \tag{31}$$

Using Equation (28) with the differentiating Equation (29) with respect to r, we obtain

$$\frac{d^2}{dr^2}\left(\frac{d\overline{T}}{dr}\right) + \frac{2}{r}\frac{d}{dr}\left(\frac{d\overline{T}}{dr}\right) - \frac{2}{r^2}\left(\frac{d\overline{T}}{dr}\right) = \left(s + s^2\tau_o\right)\left(\varepsilon_1 s^2 \overline{u} + (1 + a_2\varepsilon_1)\frac{d\overline{T}}{dr}\right) \tag{32}$$

It is possible to write Equations (28) and (32) in the form of a vector–matrix differential equation as follows:

$$DV = AV, \tag{33}$$

where $\frac{d^2}{dr^2}+\frac{2}{r}\frac{d}{dr}-\frac{2}{r^2}$, $V=\left(\overline{u}\ \ \frac{d\overline{T}}{dr}\right)^T$ and $A=\begin{pmatrix}a_{11} & a_{12}\\ a_{21} & a_{22}\end{pmatrix}$, $a_{11}=s^2$, $a_{12}=a_2$, $a_{21}=\varepsilon_1 s^2(s+s^2\tau_o)$ and $a_{22}=(1+a_2\varepsilon_1)(s+s^2\tau_o)$,

The using of eigenvalue approach [54,55] to solve the Equation (33), the characteristic relation of matrix A can be written as

$$a_{11}a_{22}-a_{12}a_{21}-(a_{11}+a_{22})\zeta+\zeta^2=0, \tag{34}$$

where $\zeta=\zeta_1$, $\zeta=\zeta_2$ are the roots of the characteristic Equation (34) which have the corresponding eigenvectors $X_1=a_{12}$ and $X_2=\zeta-a_{11}$. Thus, the solution of Equation (34) can be expressed by

$$\overline{u}(r,s)=r^{-1/2}U_1A_1I_{3/2}\left(r\sqrt{\zeta_1}\right)+r^{-1/2}U_2A_2I_{3/2}\left(r\sqrt{\zeta_2}\right), \tag{35}$$

$$\overline{T}(r,s)=\frac{T_1}{\sqrt{r\zeta_1}}A_1I_{1/2}\left(r\sqrt{\zeta_1}\right)+\frac{T_2}{\sqrt{r\zeta_2}}A_2I_{1/2}\left(r\sqrt{\zeta_2}\right) \tag{36}$$

where A_1 and A_2 are constants that can be calculated from the boundary condition of the problem, and $I_{3/2}, I_{1/2}$ are the modified of Bessel's functions with order $\frac{3}{2}$ and $\frac{1}{2,}$ respectively. It is possible to use the Stehfest [56] method as a numerical inversion technique in order to obtain the final solutions of temperature, displacement and stresses distributions.

6. Numerical Outcomes and Discussions

Numerical results for a single crystal of magnesium medium using the following physical parameters are computed to demonstrate the theoretical findings derived in the previous sections [57]:

$$\begin{gathered}c_{11}=5.974\times10^{10}(\mathrm{N})(\mathrm{m}^{-2}), \beta_{11}=\beta_{22}=2.68\times10^{6}(\mathrm{N})\ (\mathrm{m}^{-2})\left(\mathrm{k}^{-1}\right), T_o=298(k),\ a=1,\\ c_{22}=6.17\times10^{10}(\mathrm{N})\ (\mathrm{m}^{-2}),\ K_o=170\ (\mathrm{W})(\mathrm{m}^{-1})\left(\mathrm{k}^{-1}\right), c_{12}=2.624\times10^{10}(\mathrm{N})(\mathrm{m}^{-2}),\\ \rho=1470(\mathrm{kg})(\mathrm{m}^{-3}),\ c_e=1040\ (\mathrm{J})\left(\mathrm{kg}^{-1}\right)\left(\mathrm{k}^{-1}\right), \tau_o=0.05, t=0.25,\\ c_{23}=2.17\times10^{10}(\mathrm{N})(\mathrm{m}^{-2}).\end{gathered}$$

Figures 2–21 show the calculated physical values (numerical) under generalized thermoelastic theory with one thermal delay time based on the previous set of parameters. The computation is carried out for the time $t=0.25$. The temperature variations, radial displacement, and the variation in the radial and shear stress distributions along the radial distances r under variable thermal conductivity are determined numerically. Figure 2 shows the variation in temperature along the radial distance r. It is clear that the temperature has maximums value $T=1$ at the internal surface of hole $a=1$ to accept the boundary condition of the problem, and then steadily falls when the radial distance r is increased to close to zero. Figure 3 shows the variations in radial displacement via the radial distances. It is seen that the radial displacement starts at zero, which meets the boundary condition of the problem, and lowers steadily up to peak values before decreasing to near zero. Figure 4 depicts the variations of radial stress σ_{rr} versus the radial distances r. The radial stress has maximum negative values before gradually diminishing to near zero. The variations in shear stress $\sigma_{\theta\theta}$ along the radial distance r are displayed in Figure 5. It is noted that it has negative maximums before steadily rising to zero. Under the variable thermal conductivity, there are big significant variances in the values of all considering variables, according to the results. The varying thermal conductivity has a remarkable impact on the values of all considering variables, as predicted. Figures 6–9 show the impact of thermal delay time in all physical quantities, whereas Figures 10–13 show the variation of physical quintettes along the distance for different time values. The variations in temperature, the radial displacement, the radial stress and the shear stress under comparisons between the isotropic and orthotropic materials under varying thermal conductivity and with one relaxation time are shown in Figures 14–17. The analytical results for isotropic elastic material have been presented to verify that the suggested approach is accurate as in Figures 14–17. Additionally, the variations of temperature, the radial displacement, the radial stress and the shear stress under the comparisons between the elastic and orthotropic materials under varying thermal conductivity and with one relaxation time are shown in Figures 18–21. Finally, based on the numerical results, it is possible to infer that utilizing a generalized thermoelastic theory under the changing thermal conductivity is a major phenomenon with a considerable effect on the physical quantity distributions.

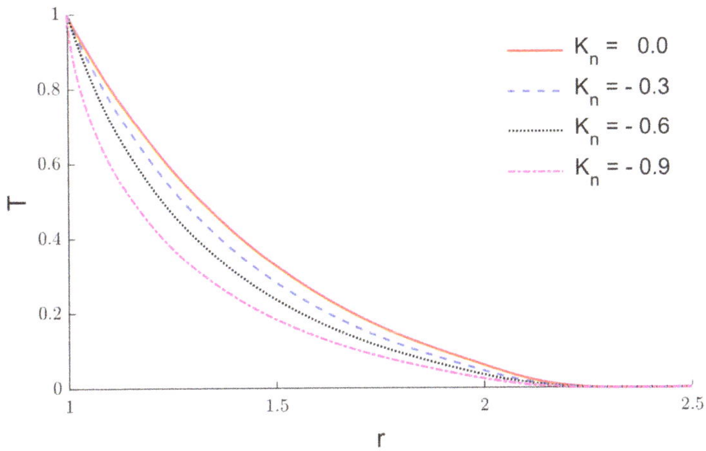

Figure 2. The temperature variations T via r when $\tau_o = 0.05$ under varying thermal conductivity.

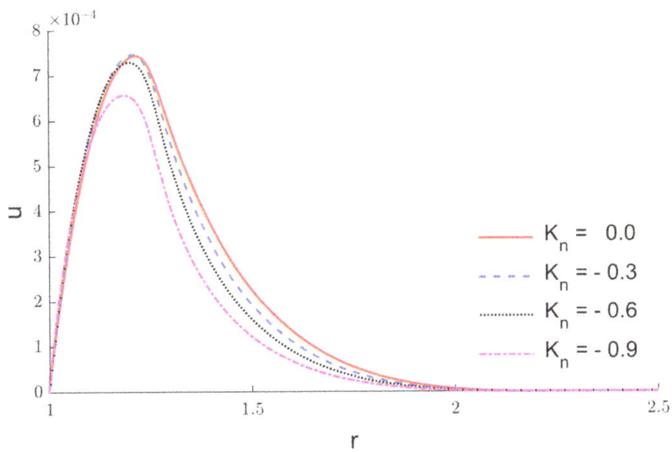

Figure 3. The variation of radial displacement u via r when $\tau_o = 0.05$ under varying thermal conductivity.

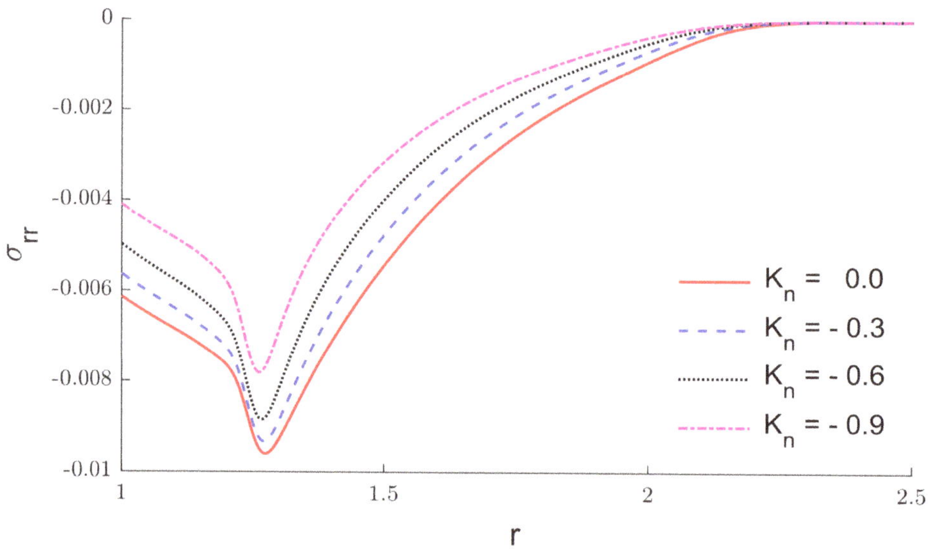

Figure 4. The variations of radial stress σ_{rr} via r when $\tau_o = 0.05$ under varying thermal conductivity.

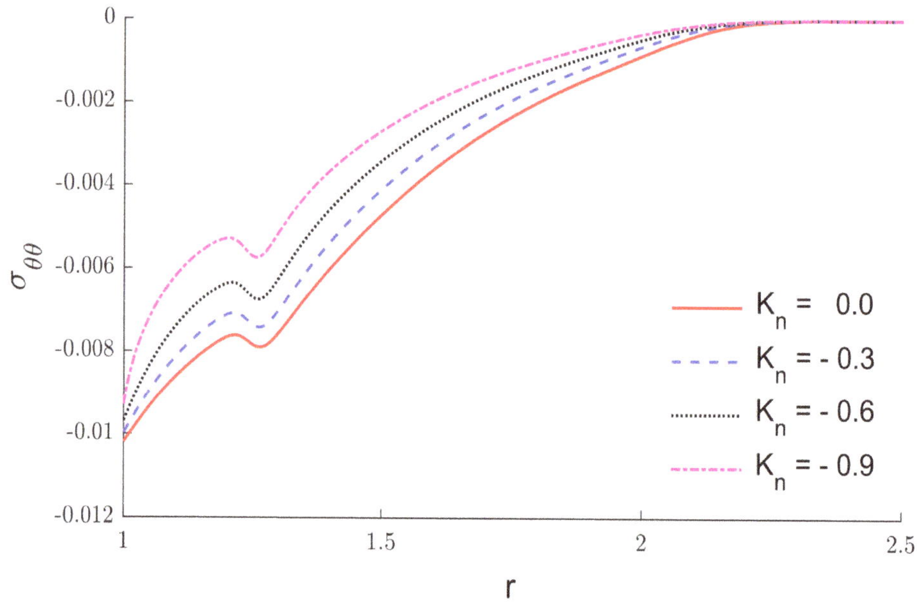

Figure 5. The variation of sheer stress $\sigma_{\theta\theta}$ via r when $\tau_o = 0.05$ under varying thermal conductivity.

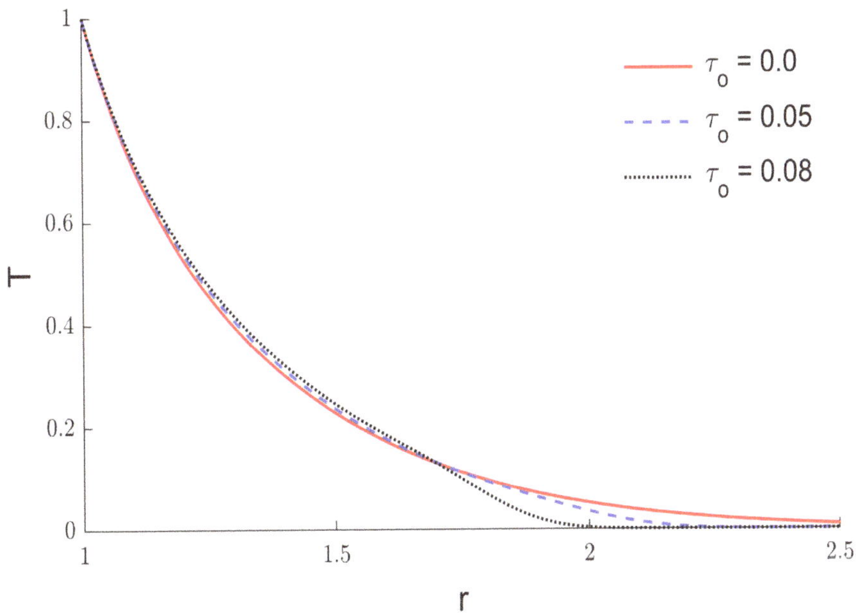

Figure 6. The impacts of thermal delay time τ_o in the temperature variations T, when $K_n = -0.6$.

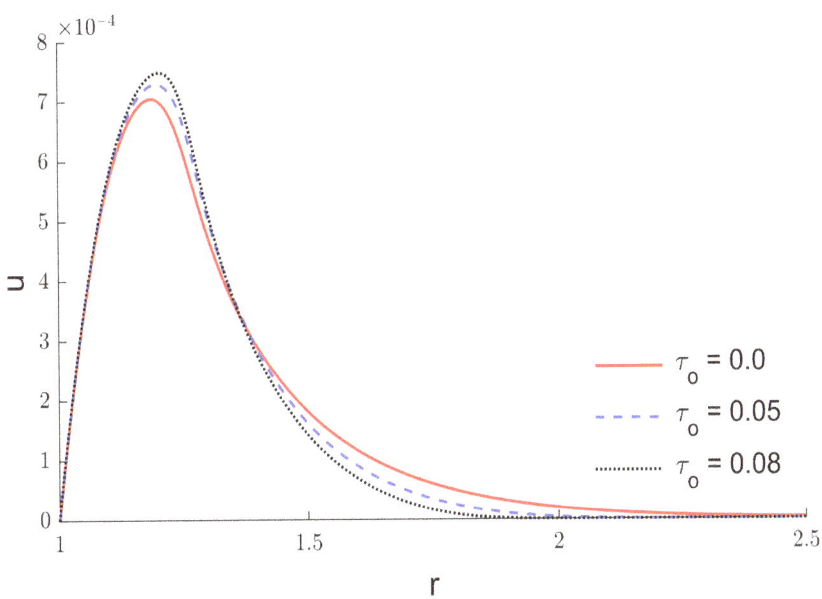

Figure 7. The impacts of thermal relaxation time τ_o in the variation of radial displacement u when $K_n = -0.6$.

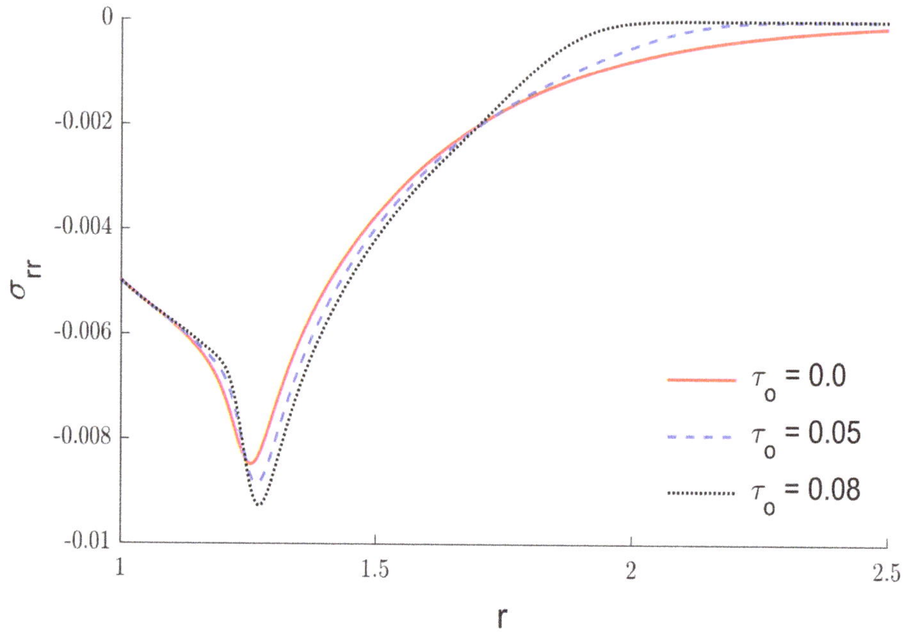

Figure 8. The impacts of thermal delay time τ_o in the variations of radial stress σ_{rr}, when $K_n = -0.6$.

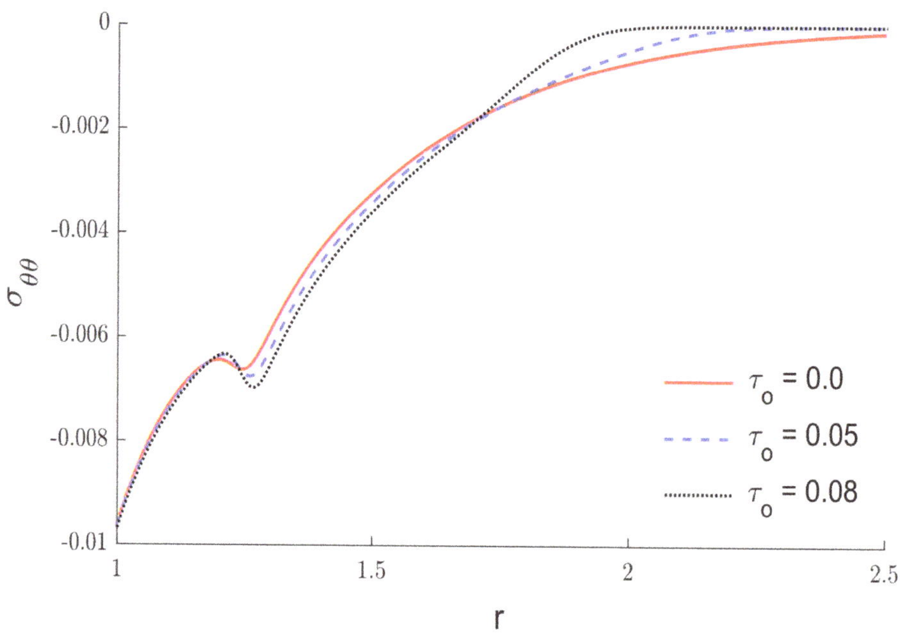

Figure 9. The impacts of thermal relaxation time τ_o in the variation of shear stress $\sigma_{\theta\theta}$, when $K_n = -0.6$.

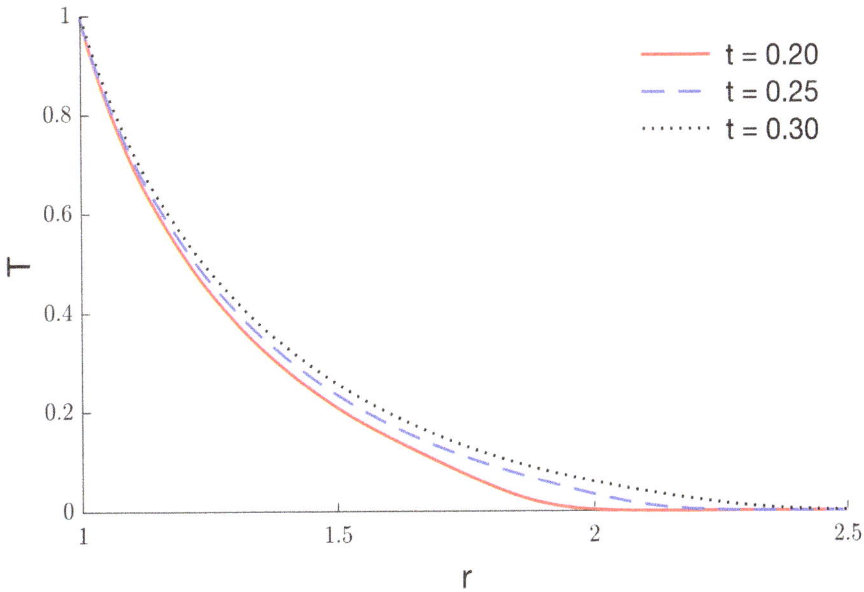

Figure 10. The temperature variation T for different values of time.

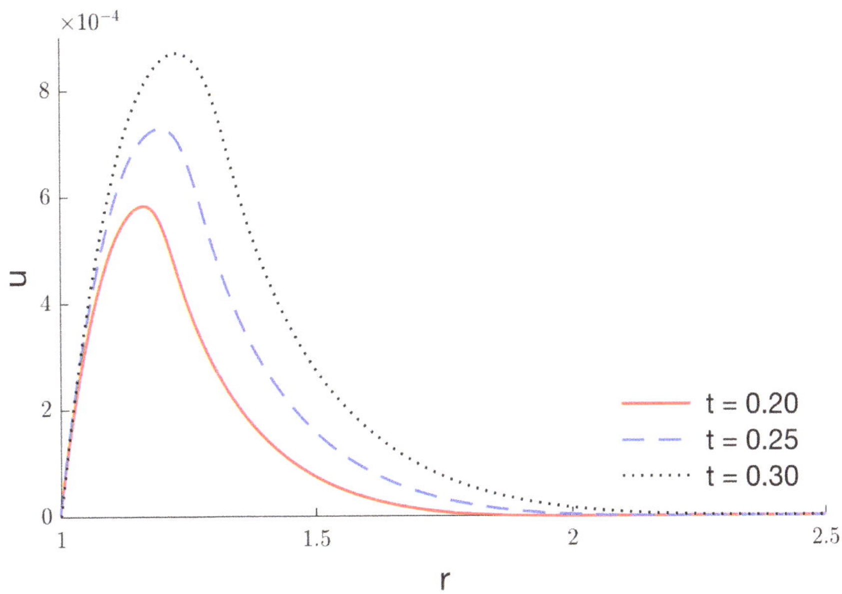

Figure 11. The radial displacement variation u for different values of time.

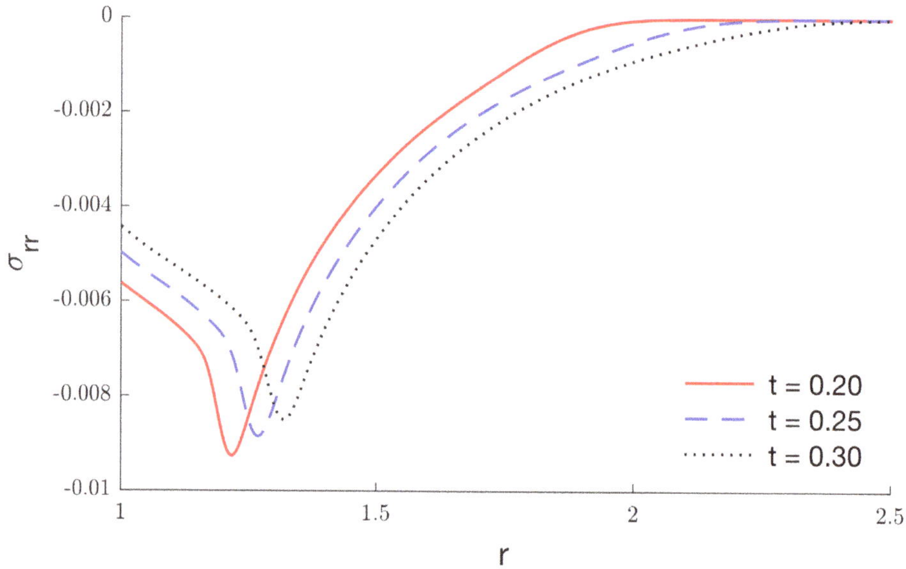

Figure 12. The radial stress variation σ_{rr} for different values of time.

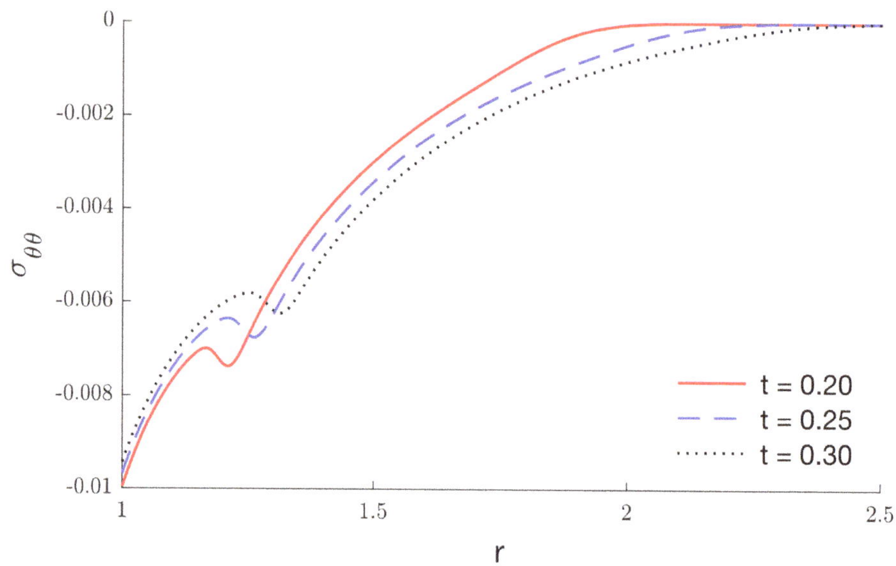

Figure 13. The shear stress variation $\sigma_{\theta\theta}$ for different values of time.

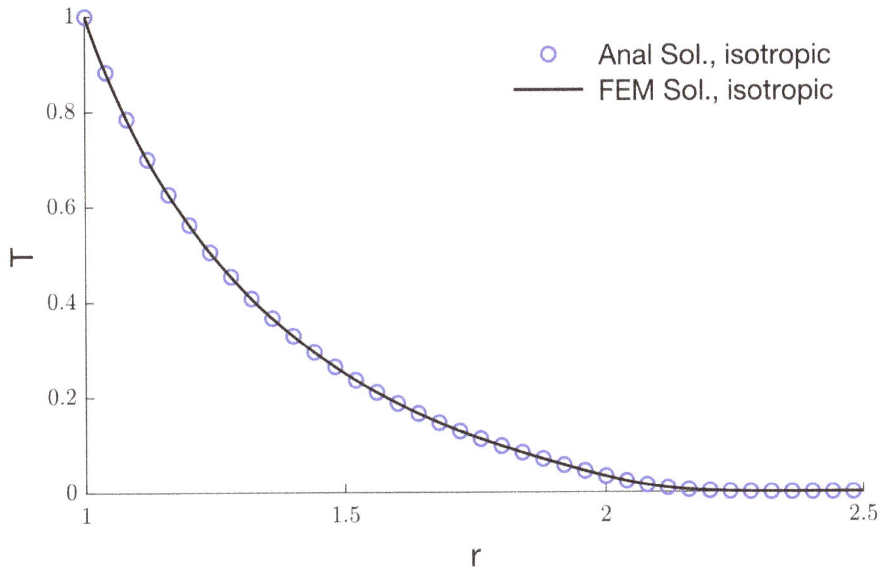

Figure 14. The temperature variation T for isotropic material.

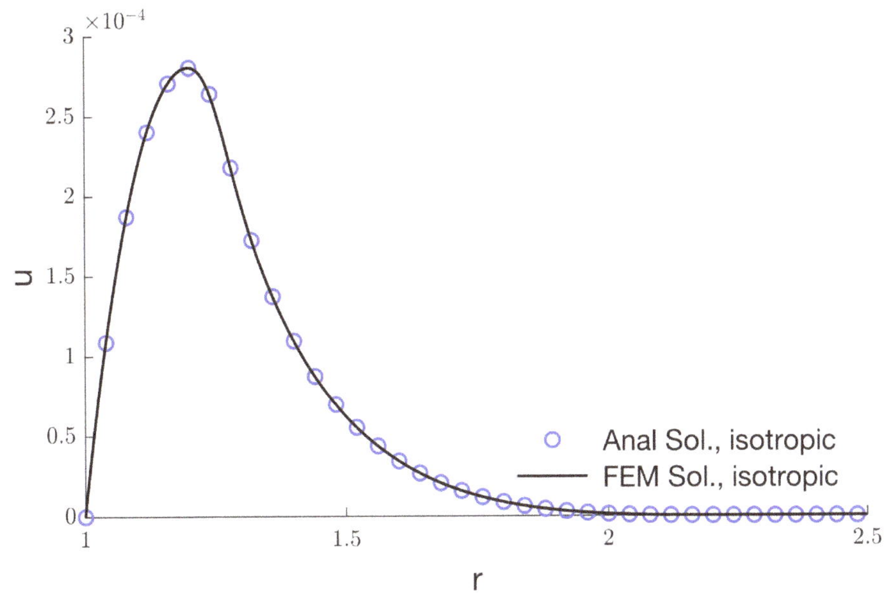

Figure 15. The radial displacement variation u for isotropic material.

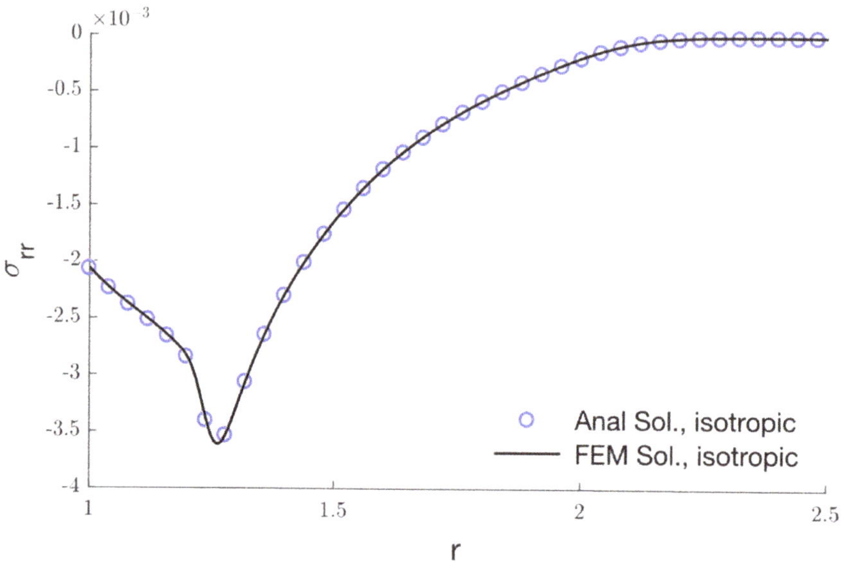

Figure 16. The radial stress variation σ_{rr} for isotropic material.

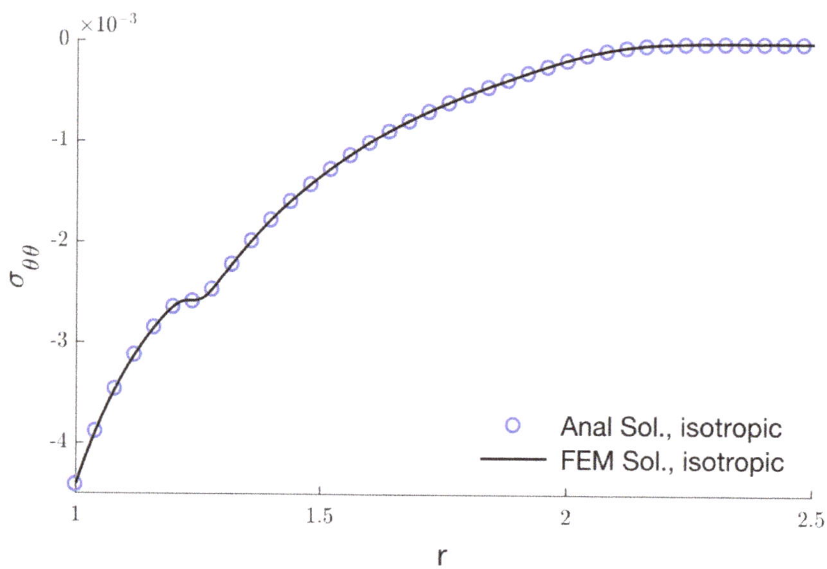

Figure 17. The shear stress variation $\sigma_{\theta\theta}$ for isotropic material.

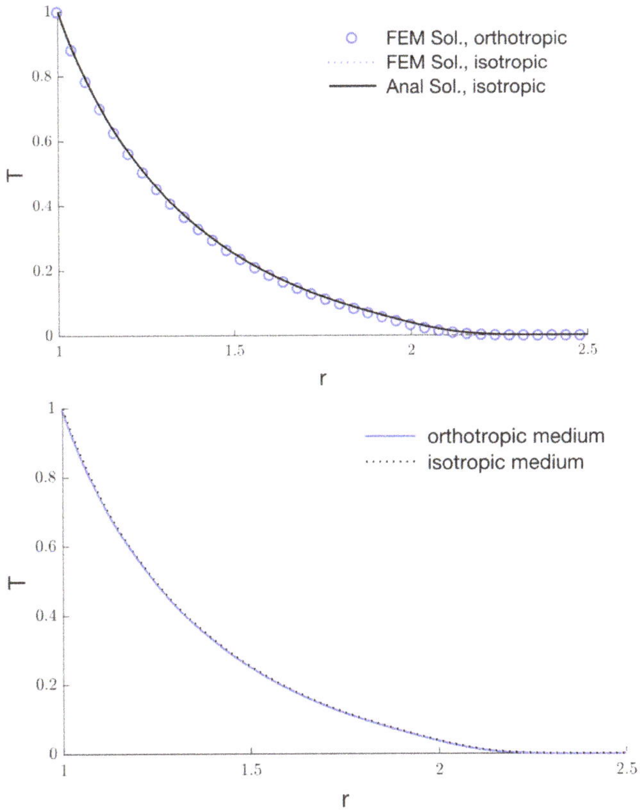

Figure 18. The temperature variation T for different materials.

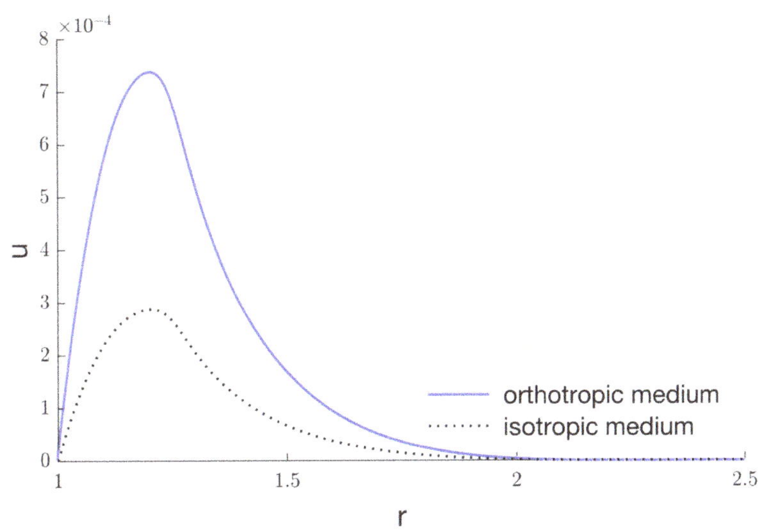

Figure 19. The redial displacement variation u for different materials.

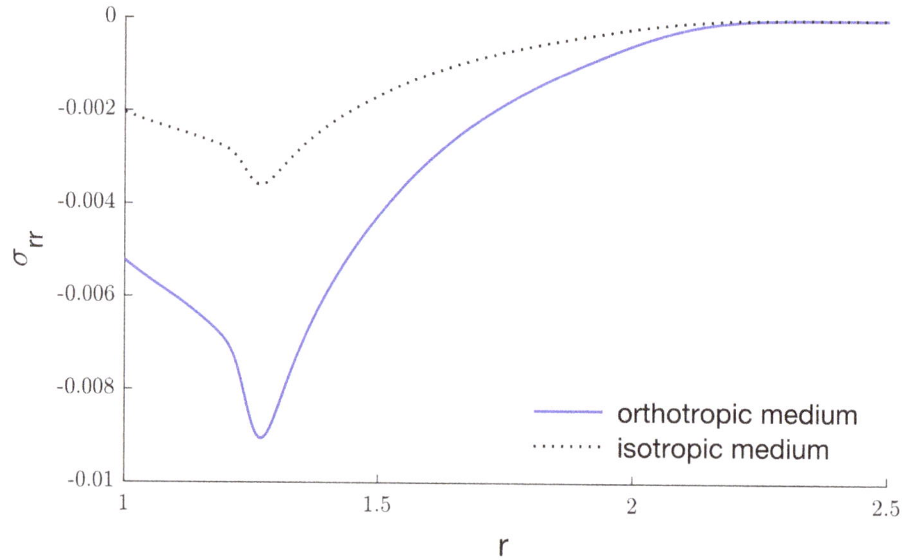

Figure 20. The redial stress variation σ_{rr} for different materials.

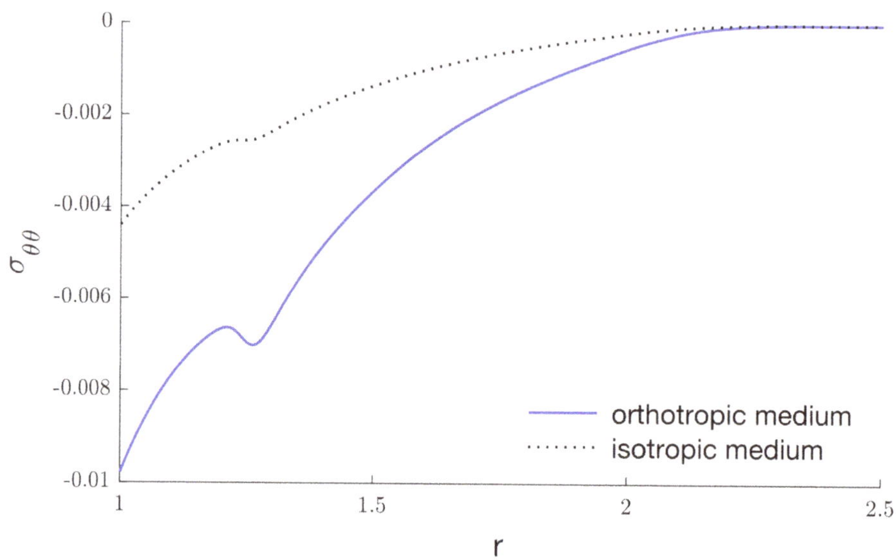

Figure 21. The shear stress variation $\sigma_{\theta\theta}$ for different materials.

7. Conclusions

This work presents a mathematical analysis of the effect of variable thermal conductivity in an orthotropic medium including a spherical hole. The distributions of temperature, radial displacement, radial stress, and shear stress in a thermoelastic orthotropic medium with one thermal relaxation time have been given. To provide a numerical solution for nonlinear equations, the finite element technique is used. It was discovered that the varying thermal conductivity has significant effects and influences how various physical field components behave as they deform. The effects of thermal delay time are presented. It was shown that the deformation behaviour of different components of physical fields is significantly affected by the thermal relaxation time. The impact of time is shown. It was shown that time has a considerable impact on the deformation behavior of several physical field components. There are comparisons shown between the orthotropic and isotropic materials. To verify that the suggested approach is accurate, numerical solutions and analytical solutions have been compared for isotropic elastic material.

Author Contributions: Methodology, A.H. and I.A.; Validation, A.H. and I.A.; Formal analysis, A.H.; Investigation, I.A.; Writing—review & editing, I.A.; Funding acquisition, A.H. All authors have read and agreed to the published version of the manuscript.

Funding: This research work was funded by Institutional Fund Projects under grant no. (IFPIP: 63-130-1443). The authors gratefully acknowledge technical and financial support provided by the Ministry of Education and King Abdulaziz University, DSR, Jeddah, Saudi Arabia.

Institutional Review Board Statement: Not applicable.

Informed Consent Statement: Not applicable.

Data Availability Statement: Not applicable.

Conflicts of Interest: The authors declare no conflict of interest.

References

1. Lord, H.W.; Shulman, Y. A generalized dynamical theory of thermoelasticity. *J. Mech. Phys. Solids* **1967**, *15*, 299–309. [CrossRef]
2. Dhaliwal, R.S.; Sherief, H.H. Generalized thermoelasticity for anisotropic media. *Q. Appl. Math.* **1980**, *38*, 1–8. [CrossRef]
3. Hetnarski, R.B. *Thermal Stresses IV*; Elsevier: Amsterdam, The Netherlands, 1996.
4. Sherief, H.; Abd El-Latief, A.M. Effect of variable thermal conductivity on a half-space under the fractional order theory of thermoelasticity. *Int. J. Mech. Sci.* **2013**, *74*, 185–189. [CrossRef]
5. Mukhopadhyay, S.; Kumar, R. Solution of a Problem of Generalized Thermoelasticity of an Annular Cylinder with Variable Material Properties by Finite Difference Method. *Comput. Methods Sci. Technol.* **2009**, *15*, 169–176. [CrossRef]
6. Abo-Dahab, S.M.; Abbas, I.A. LS model on thermal shock problem of generalized magneto-thermoelasticity for an infinitely long annular cylinder with variable thermal conductivity. *Appl. Math. Model.* **2011**, *35*, 3759–3768. [CrossRef]
7. Abbas, I.A.; Abd-Alla, A.-E.N. Effects of thermal relaxations on thermoelastic interactions in an infinite orthotropic elastic medium with a cylindrical cavity. *Arch. Appl. Mech.* **2007**, *78*, 283–293. [CrossRef]
8. Yasein, M.d.; Mabrouk, N.; Lotfy, K.; EL-Bary, A. The influence of variable thermal conductivity of semiconductor elastic medium during photothermal excitation subjected to thermal ramp type. *Results Phys.* **2019**, *15*, 102766. [CrossRef]
9. Zenkour, A.M.; Abbas, I.A. Magneto-thermoelastic response of an infinite functionally graded cylinder using the finite element method. *J. Vib. Control* **2013**, *20*, 1907–1919. [CrossRef]
10. Sharma, P.K.; Bajpai, A.; Kumar, R. Analysis of two temperature thermoelastic diffusion plate with variable thermal conductivity and diffusivity. *Waves Random Complex Media* **2021**, 1–19. [CrossRef]
11. Hobiny, A.; Abbas, I. Generalized thermoelastic interaction in a two-dimensional orthotropic material caused by a pulse heat flux. *Waves Random Complex Media* **2021**, 1–18. [CrossRef]
12. Song, Y.; Todorovic, D.M.; Cretin, B.; Vairac, P. Study on the generalized thermoelastic vibration of the optically excited semiconducting microcantilevers. *Int. J. Solids Struct.* **2010**, *47*, 1871–1875. [CrossRef]
13. Mondal, S.; Sur, A. Photo-thermo-elastic wave propagation in an orthotropic semiconductor with a spherical cavity and memory responses. *Waves Random Complex Media* **2020**, *31*, 1835–1858. [CrossRef]
14. Said, S.M. Eigenvalue approach on a problem of magneto-thermoelastic rotating medium with variable thermal conductivity: Comparisons of three theories. *Waves Random Complex Media* **2021**, *31*, 1322–1339. [CrossRef]
15. Lata, P.; Himanshi. Fractional effect in an orthotropic magneto-thermoelastic rotating solid of type GN-II due to normal force. *Struct. Eng. Mech.* **2022**, *81*, 503–511. [CrossRef]
16. Singh, B.; Pal, S. Magneto-thermoelastic interaction with memory response due to laser pulse under Green-Naghdi theory in an orthotropic medium. *Mech. Based Des. Struct. Mach.* **2020**, *50*, 3105–3122. [CrossRef]
17. Hobiny, A.; Abbas, I.A. Analytical solutions of photo-thermo-elastic waves in a non-homogenous semiconducting material. *Results Phys.* **2018**, *10*, 385–390. [CrossRef]
18. Zenkour, A.M.; Abbas, I.A. Nonlinear Transient Thermal Stress Analysis of Temperature-Dependent Hollow Cylinders Using a Finite Element Model. *Int. J. Struct. Stab. Dyn.* **2014**, *14*, 1450025. [CrossRef]
19. Vlase, S.; Marin, M.; Öchsner, A.; Scutaru, M.L. Motion equation for a flexible one-dimensional element used in the dynamical analysis of a multibody system. *Contin. Mech. Thermodyn.* **2018**, *31*, 715–724. [CrossRef]
20. Marin, M.; Vlase, S.; Paun, M. Considerations on double porosity structure for micropolar bodies. *AIP Adv.* **2015**, *5*, 037113. [CrossRef]
21. Marin, M. An evolutionary equation in thermoelasticity of dipolar bodies. *J. Math. Phys.* **1999**, *40*, 1391–1399. [CrossRef]

22. Lata, P.; Singh, S. Stoneley wave propagation in nonlocal isotropic magneto-thermoelastic solid with multi-dual-phase lag heat transfer. *Steel Compos. Struct.* **2021**, *38*, 141–150. [CrossRef]
23. Kaur, H.; Lata, P. Effect of thermal conductivity on isotropic modified couple stress thermoelastic medium with two temperatures. *Steel Compos. Struct.* **2020**, *34*, 309–319. [CrossRef]
24. Lata, P.; Kumar, R.; Sharma, N. Plane waves in an anisotropic thermoelastic. *Steel Compos. Struct.* **2016**, *22*, 567–587. [CrossRef]
25. Lataa, P.; Kaur, I. Effect of time harmonic sources on transversely isotropic thermoelastic thin circular plate. *Geomach. Eng.* **2019**, *19*, 29–36. [CrossRef]
26. Marin, M.; Baleanu, D.; Vlase, S. Effect of microtemperatures for micropolar thermoelastic bodies. *Struct. Eng. Mech.* **2017**, *61*, 381–387. [CrossRef]
27. Abbas, I.A.; Alzahrani, F.S.; Elaiw, A. A DPL model of photothermal interaction in a semiconductor material. *Waves Random Complex Media* **2018**, *29*, 328–343. [CrossRef]
28. Abbas, I.A. Eigenvalue approach on fractional order theory of thermoelastic diffusion problem for an infinite elastic medium with a spherical cavity. *Appl. Math. Model.* **2015**, *39*, 6196–6206. [CrossRef]
29. Lata, P.; Himanshi. Orthotropic magneto-thermoelastic solid with higher order dual-phase-lag model in frequency domain. *Struct. Eng. Mech.* **2021**, *77*, 315–327. [CrossRef]
30. Hobiny, A.; Abbas, I.A. A GN model of thermoelastic interaction in a 2D orthotropic material due to pulse heat flux. *Struct. Eng. Mech.* **2021**, *80*, 669–675. [CrossRef]
31. Said, S.M.; Othman, M.I.A. The effect of gravity and hydrostatic initial stress with variable thermal conductivity on a magneto-fiber-reinforced. *Struct. Eng. Mech.* **2020**, *74*, 425–434. [CrossRef]
32. Lata, P.; Kaur, H. Effect of length scale parameters on transversely isotropic thermoelastic medium using new modified couple stress theory. *Struct. Eng. Mech.* **2020**, *76*, 17–26. [CrossRef]
33. Sheokand, S.K.; Kumar, R.; Kalkal, K.K.; Deswal, S. Propagation of plane waves in an orthotropic magneto-thermodiffusive rotating half-space. *Struct. Eng. Mech.* **2019**, *72*, 455–468. [CrossRef]
34. Kumar, R.; Sharma, N.; Lata, P. Effects of Hall current in a transversely isotropic magnetothermoelastic with and without energy dissipation due to normal force. *Struct. Eng. Mech.* **2016**, *57*, 91–103. [CrossRef]
35. Kumar, R.; Devi, S. Thermomechanical deformation in porous generalized thermoelastic body with variable material properties. *Struct. Eng. Mech.* **2010**, *34*, 285–300. [CrossRef]
36. Abbas, I.A.; Abdalla, A.-E.-N.N.; Alzahrani, F.S.; Spagnuolo, M. Wave propagation in a generalized thermoelastic plate using eigenvalue approach. *J. Therm. Stress.* **2016**, *39*, 1367–1377. [CrossRef]
37. Lata, P.; Himanshi, H. Inclined load effect in an orthotropic magneto-thermoelastic solid with fractional order heat transfer. *Struct. Eng. Mech.* **2022**, *81*, 529–537.
38. Sharifi, H. Generalized coupled thermoelasticity in an orthotropic rotating disk subjected to thermal shock. *J. Therm. Stress.* **2022**, *45*, 695–719. [CrossRef]
39. Sharifi, H. Analytical Solution for Thermoelastic Stress Wave Propagation in an Orthotropic Hollow Cylinder. *Eur. J. Comput. Mech.* **2022**, 239–274. [CrossRef]
40. Cesarini, G.; Antonelli, M.; Anulli, F.; Bauce, M.; Biagini, M.E.; Blanco-García, O.R.; Boscolo, M.; Casaburo, F.; Cavoto, G.; Ciarma, A.; et al. Theoretical Modeling for the Thermal Stability of Solid Targets in a Positron-Driven Muon Collider. *Int. J.* **2021**, *42*, 163. [CrossRef]
41. Jamari, J.; Ammarullah, M.I.; Saad, A.P.; Syahrom, A.; Uddin, M.; van der Heide, E.; Basri, H. The Effect of Bottom Profile Dimples on the Femoral Head on Wear in Metal-on-Metal Total Hip Arthroplasty. *J. Funct. Biomater.* **2021**, *12*, 38. [CrossRef]
42. Vasilyeva, M.; Ammosov, D.; Vasil'ev, V. Finite Element Simulation of Thermo-Mechanical Model with Phase Change. *Computation* **2021**, *9*, 5. [CrossRef]
43. El Harti, K.; Sanbi, M.; Saadani, R.; Bentaleb, M.; Rahmoune, M. Dynamic Analysis and Active Control of Distributed Piezothermoelastic Fgm Composite Beam with Porosities Modeled by the Finite Element Method. *Compos. Mech. Comput. Appl. Int. J.* **2021**, *12*, 57–74. [CrossRef]
44. Qiao, Y.J.; Ciavarella, M.; Yi, Y.B.; Wang, T. Effect of wear on frictionally excited thermoelastic instability: A finite element approach. *J. Therm. Stress.* **2020**, *43*, 1564–1576. [CrossRef]
45. Sur, A.; Pal, P.; Mondal, S.; Kanoria, M. Finite element analysis in a fiber-reinforced cylinder due to memory-dependent heat transfer. *Acta Mech.* **2019**, *230*, 1607–1624. [CrossRef]
46. Sharma, D.; Kaur, R. Finite element solution for stress and strain in FGM circular disk. In Proceedings of the International Conference on Advances in Basic Sciences, ICABS 2019, Bhiwani, India, 7–9 February 2019.
47. Hirwani, C.K.; Panda, S.K. Nonlinear finite element solutions of thermoelastic deflection and stress responses of internally damaged curved panel structure. *Appl. Math. Model.* **2019**, *65*, 303–317. [CrossRef]
48. Alzahrani, F.; Hobiny, A.; Abbas, I.; Marin, M. An Eigenvalues Approach for a Two-Dimensional Porous Medium Based Upon Weak, Normal and Strong Thermal Conductivities. *Symmetry* **2020**, *12*, 848. [CrossRef]
49. Abbas, I.A. Analytical solution for a free vibration of a thermoelastic hollow sphere. *Mech. Based Des. Struct. Mach.* **2015**, *43*, 265–276. [CrossRef]
50. Goyal, R.; Bhargava, R. FEM simulation of EM field effect on body tissues with bio-nanofluid (blood with nanoparticles) for nanoparticle mediated hyperthermia. *Math Biosci* **2018**, *300*, 76–86. [CrossRef]

51. Tian, X.; Shen, Y.; Chen, C.; He, T. A direct finite element method study of generalized thermoelastic problems. *Int. J. Solids Struct.* **2006**, *43*, 2050–2063. [CrossRef]
52. Youssef, H. State-space approach on generalized thermoelasticity for an infinite material with a spherical cavity and variable thermal conductivity subjected to ramp-type heating. *Can. Appl. Math. Quaterly* **2005**, *13*, 4.
53. Wriggers, P. *Nonlinear Finite Element Methods;* Springer Science & Business Media: Berlin/Heidelberg, Germany, 2008.
54. Das, N.C.; Lahiri, A.; Giri, R.R. Eigenvalue approach to generalized thermoelasticity. *Indian J. Pure Appl. Math.* **1997**, *28*, 1573–1594.
55. Hobiny, A.; Abbas, I. A GN model on photothermal interactions in a two-dimensions semiconductor half space. *Results Phys.* **2019**, *15*. [CrossRef]
56. Stehfest, H. Algorithm 368: Numerical inversion of Laplace transforms [D5]. *Commun. ACM* **1970**, *13*, 47–49. [CrossRef]
57. Abouelregal, A.E.; Abo-Dahab, S.M. Dual Phase Lag Model on Magneto-Thermoelasticity Infinite Non-Homogeneous Solid Having a Spherical Cavity. *J. Therm. Stress.* **2012**, *35*, 820–841. [CrossRef]

mathematics

Article

A Two-Step Lagrange–Galerkin Scheme for the Shallow Water Equations with a Transmission Boundary Condition and Its Application to the Bay of Bengal Region—Part I: Flat Bottom Topography

Md Mamunur Rasid [1,2], Masato Kimura [3], Md Masum Murshed [4], Erny Rahayu Wijayanti [5] and Hirofumi Notsu [3,*]

1 Division of Mathematical and Physical Sciences, Kanazawa University, Kakuma, Kanazawa 920-1192, Japan; mamun.math@stu.kanazawa-u.ac.jp
2 Institute of Education and Research, University of Rajshahi, Rajshahi 6205, Bangladesh
3 Faculty of Mathematics and Physics, Kanazawa University, Kakuma, Kanazawa 920-1192, Japan; mkimura@se.kanazawa-u.ac.jp
4 Faculty of Mathematics, University of Rajshahi, Rajshahi 6205, Bangladesh; mmmurshed82@ru.ac.bd
5 Department of Mechanical and Industrial Engineering, Gadjah Mada University, Yogyakarta 55281, Indonesia; erny.wijayanti@ugm.ac.id
* Correspondence: notsu@se.kanazawa-u.ac.jp

Abstract: A two-step Lagrange–Galerkin scheme for the shallow water equations with a transmission boundary condition (TBC) is presented. First, we show the experimental order of convergence to see the second-order accuracy in time realized by the two-step methods for conservative and non-conservative material derivatives along the trajectory of fluid particles. Second, we observe the effect of the TBC in a simple domain, and the artificial reflection is removed significantly when the wave touches the TBC. Third, we apply the scheme to a practical domain with islands, namely, the Bay of Bengal region, and observe the effect of the TBC again for the practical domain; the artificial reflections are removed significantly from the transmission boundaries on open sea boundaries. We also study the effect of a position of an open sea boundary with the TBC and reveal that it is sufficiently small to neglect. The numerical results in this study show that the scheme has the following properties: (i) the same advantages of Lagrange–Galerkin methods (the CFL-free robustness for convection-dominated problems and the symmetry of the matrices for the system of linear equations); (ii) second-order accuracy in time by the two-step methods; (iii) mass preservation of the function for the water level from the reference height (until the contact with the transmission boundaries of the wave); and (iv) no significant artificial reflection from the transmission boundaries. The numerical results by the scheme presented in this paper are for the flat bottom topography of the domain. In the next part of this work, Part II, the scheme will be applied to rapidly varying bottom surfaces and a real bottom topography of the Bay of Bengal region.

Keywords: shallow water equations; two-step Lagrange–Galerkin scheme; second order in time; transmission boundary condition; Bay of Bengal; bottom topography

MSC: 65M25; 65M60; 76D05; 76B15

1. Introduction

The system of shallow water equations (SWEs) is one of the most common models for describing fluid flow in rivers, channels, estuaries, and coastal areas, and is often used for simulating tsunamis and storm surges in oceanic phenomena. Natural disasters like tsunamis, cyclones, and storm surges cause a tremendous loss of lives and properties in the coastal areas in several regions. According to [1], statistics show that about 5% of the global tropical cyclones form over the Bay of Bengal, and, on average, five to six storms form in this region every year, but with 80% of the global casualties. The significant factors behind the heavy casualties are the shallow coastal water, thickly populated low-lying islands, highly curved coastal and island boundaries, river discharge, high astronomical tidal range, and favorable cyclone track, cf. [2] and Figure 1. That is why an effective storm surge prediction model and method are highly desired for the coastal region of Bangladesh to minimize the resulting damage from storm surges.

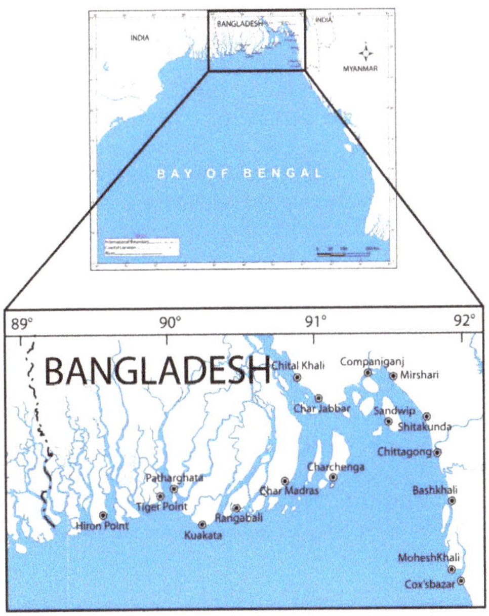

Figure 1. The Bay of Bengal region.

Studies focusing on the Bay of Bengal region are found in [1–8] and references therein. Almost all the researchers implemented SWEs with a radiation-type boundary condition for open sea boundaries. Although for real problems, the finite element method is more suitable than the finite difference method because of the advantages of handling complex physical domains, geometries, or boundary conditions, as far as we know, there is no study to solve SWEs employing a transmission boundary condition (TBC) for the Bay of Bengal region using the finite element method except [9,10].

Since a bounded computational domain is needed to compute the SWEs in a practical coastal region, e.g., the Bay of Bengal, we set an artificial boundary in the open sea, called the open boundary, which is a part of the boundary of the domain. Let $u = (u_1, u_2)^\top$ be the velocity (averaged in x_3-direction), $\phi\ (= \eta + \zeta)$ the total wave height, η the water level from the reference height, and ζ (>0) the depth of the water level from the reference height. On the coastal boundary, it is natural to have the reflection, which is realized by the Dirichlet boundary condition, $u = 0$, and, on the open boundary, an artificial boundary condition is required so that the wave passes through the boundary without any reflection, as the boundary is set artificially on the open sea. Most open boundary conditions proposed in the literature are based on or modifications of the Sommerfeld radiation boundary condition (RBC) [11] whose typical form is

$$u = \sqrt{g/\zeta}\,\eta n \tag{1}$$

for the gravity constant g (>0) and the outward unit normal vector n. The condition (1) is derived by considering the SWEs in one-dimensional space essentially and assuming that the velocity u on the open boundary is $u = V\eta/\zeta\, n$ for the wave propagation speed V and that V is given by $V = \sqrt{g\zeta}$. Due to some limitations of the RBC for oblique flows, many researchers suggested and implemented modified boundary conditions for open boundaries similar to the RBC, cf., e.g., [12–14]. Kanayama and Dan [15] also employed an open boundary condition of the form,

$$u = c_0\sqrt{g\zeta}\,\eta/\phi\, n \tag{2}$$

for a constant c_0 (>0), which removes the artificial reflection from the open boundary significantly. The condition (2) is comparable to the RBC as Equation (2) is obtained by replacing ζ with ϕ^2/ζ in Equation (1), where the relation $\zeta \approx \phi^2/\zeta \approx \phi$ holds if $|\eta| \ll \zeta$ is satisfied. In fact, the numerical results by the TBC and the RBC are similar, cf. Appendix B. On the other hand, the TBC is more reasonable than the RBC for the theoretical stability study of the system of the SWEs from the viewpoint of energy as presented in Murshed et al. [9] and Murshed [10], while it is still a partial study (but practically useful), cf. Remark 6 for a brief review of the theoretical results. Based on the stability study, we employ the TBC in this paper and observe the effect of the TBC (or the RBC) for the passing wave in addition to the effect of the Dirichlet boundary condition for the reflection wave. These observations are basic but necessary for the development of a scheme for SWEs.

The system of the SWEs consists of two equations, a pure convection equation for the total wave height and a modified Navier–Stokes momentum equation for the velocity derived by taking the average of function values in x_3-direction, cf. [9,16], which include the material derivatives in conservative and non-conservative forms, respectively. For a time step size $\Delta t > 0$, let $t^n := n\Delta t$. The so-called Lagrange–Galerkin method is the finite element method combined with the idea of the method of characteristics; the non-conservative and conservative material derivatives are discretized as, for a scalar-valued function ϕ and a velocity u, cf., e.g., [17–20],

$$\left[\frac{\partial\phi}{\partial t} + u\cdot\nabla\phi\right](x,t^n) = \frac{\phi^n(x) - \phi^{n-1}(x - u^n(x)\Delta t)}{\Delta t} + O(\Delta t),$$

$$\left[\frac{\partial\phi}{\partial t} + \nabla\cdot(u\phi)\right](x,t^n) = \frac{\phi^n(x) - \phi^{n-1}(x - u^n(x)\Delta t)\gamma^n(x)}{\Delta t} + O(\Delta t),$$

respectively, which are first-order approximations in time, where $x - u^n(x)\Delta t$ is an upwind point of x with respect to $u^n(x)$ and γ^n is the Jacobian determinant of the mapping $x - u^n(x)\Delta t$. In general, the Lagrange–Galerkin method has two advantages; (i) the CFL-free robustness for convection-dominated problems and (ii) the symmetry of the resulting coefficient matrices for the system of linear equations. In addition to the four pioneering works above, many authors have proposed the ideas of this type of approximation in the context of the finite element method, cf. [21–48] and references therein. When we focus on the SWEs, to the best of our knowledge, Murshed et al. [9] and Murshed [10] firstly solved the SWEs with a TBC by a (single-step) Lagrange–Galerkin scheme of first-order in time for a flat bottom topography. Recently, a two-step mass-preserving Lagrange–Galerkin scheme of second order in time for conservative convection-diffusion problems has been proposed and analyzed with error estimates in [49].

In this paper, we present a new two-step Lagrange–Galerkin scheme to solve the SWEs together with a TBC, which is of second order in time and maintains the two advantages of the Lagrange–Galerkin methods, i.e., the CFL-free robustness and the symmetry of the resulting matrices. The two material derivatives are discretized based on the ideas of two-step methods proposed for the non-conservative form in [17,21,24,40] and the conservative form in [49]. Firstly, preparing an artificial exact solution, we observe our scheme's experimental order of convergence (EOC) to see the second-order accuracy in time on a simple (square) domain. Since long (real-)time computations on a mesh refined locally are needed in practical problems, the CFL-free second-order accuracy in time of our scheme is a significant advantage, enabling us to employ a more extensive time increment compared with first-order numerical methods. Secondly, we observe the effect of the TBC on a simple (square) domain, and the artificial reflections are kept from the Dirichlet boundaries and removed significantly from the transmission boundaries. Thirdly, our scheme is applied to the Bay of Bengal region, which is non-convex, includes islands, and is, therefore, a complex domain. We again observe the effect of the TBC for this realistic domain. The artificial reflections are removed significantly from the transmission boundaries, which are set on open sea boundaries. We also study the effect of a position of an open sea boundary with the TBC and reveal that it is sufficiently small to neglect. In [9], energy estimates for the SWEs were given, where the L^2-norm of the water level from the reference height was an important value related to the potential energy. Focusing on the energy and the mass of the water level function, we observe the L^2-norm and the mass of the water level function, which show the effectiveness of the TBC.

From the computations, we show that our new scheme has the following properties; (i) the same advantages of Lagrange–Galerkin methods; (ii) second-order accuracy in time; (iii) mass preservation of the function of the water level from the reference height (until the contact with the transmission boundaries of the wave); and (iv) no significant artificial reflection from the transmission boundaries. We mention again that the TBC is employed in this paper based on the theoretical stability study in [9,10], while the numerical results by the TBC and the RBC are similar.

All of the numerical results in this paper, Part I, are for the flat bottom topography, and the non-homogeneous bottom topography will be studied in our forthcoming paper, Part II.

The outline of this paper is as follows. Section 2 presents a two-step Lagrange–Galerkin scheme for the SWEs together with a TBC, which is of second order in time. In Section 3, numerical results for simple square domains are shown to observe the second-order accuracy in time and the effect of TBC. In Section 4, our scheme is applied to the Bay of Bengal region, where the domain is non-convex and complex. In Section 5, conclusions are given. The data for choosing the constant c_0 required in the TBC and a comparison of the TBC with the RBC are given in Appendixes A and B, respectively.

2. A Two-Step Lagrange–Galerkin Scheme

We introduce some notations to be used in this paper. Ω is a bounded spatial domain in $\mathbb{R}^2$, $\Gamma := \partial\Omega$ is the boundary of Ω, and $(0,T)$ is a temporal domain in $\mathbb{R}_+$ $(:= \{x \in \mathbb{R}; x > 0\})$ for a positive constant T. We use the Lebesgue space $L^p(\Omega)$ $(p \in [1,\infty])$ and the Sobolev space $H^1(\Omega)$. For any normed space X with its norm $\|\cdot\|_X$, we define function spaces $C^0([0,T];X)$ and $L^\infty(0,T;X)$ consisting of X-valued functions in $C^0([0,T])$ and $L^\infty(0,T)$, respectively. Let $(\cdot,\cdot)$ be the inner product in $L^2(\Omega)$, i.e., $(f,g) := \int_\Omega f(x)g(x)dx$ for $f,g \in L^2(\Omega)$. We employ the same notation $(\cdot,\cdot)$ to represent the $L^2(\Omega)$ inner product for scalar-, vector-, and matrix-valued functions. Let $A : B$ be the tensor product defined by $A : B := \sum_{i,j=1}^2 A_{ij}B_{ij} = \mathrm{tr}(AB^\top)$ for $A, B \in \mathbb{R}^{2\times 2}$.

2.1. Statement of the Problem

Our problem is to find $(\phi, u)\colon \Omega \times (0,T) \to \mathbb{R} \times \mathbb{R}^2$ such that

$$\frac{\partial \phi}{\partial t} + \nabla\cdot(u\phi) = f \qquad \text{in } \Omega\times(0,T), \tag{3a}$$

$$\rho\phi\Big[\frac{\partial u}{\partial t} + (u\cdot\nabla)u\Big] - 2\mu\nabla\cdot(\phi D(u)) + \rho g\phi\nabla\eta = F \qquad \text{in } \Omega\times(0,T), \tag{3b}$$

$$\phi = \eta + \zeta \qquad \text{in } \Omega\times(0,T), \tag{3c}$$

$$u = 0 \qquad \text{on } \Gamma_{\mathrm{D}}\times(0,T), \tag{3d}$$

$$u = c_0\sqrt{g\zeta}\,\frac{\eta}{\phi}\,n \qquad \text{on } \Gamma_{\mathrm{T}}\times(0,T), \tag{3e}$$

$$(\phi, u) = (\phi^0, u^0) \qquad \text{in } \Omega,\ \text{at } t = 0, \tag{3f}$$

where the total wave height and the velocity are denoted by ϕ and $u = (u_1, u_2)^\top$, respectively, the water level from the reference height and the depth of water level from the reference height, i.e., bottom topography, are represented by $\eta\colon \Omega \times (0,T) \to \mathbb{R}$ and $\zeta\colon \Omega \to \mathbb{R}_+$, respectively, a pair of external forces is given by $(f, F)\colon \Omega \times (0,T) \to \mathbb{R} \times \mathbb{R}^2$, a pair of initial values is given by $(\phi^0, u^0)\colon \Omega \to \mathbb{R} \times \mathbb{R}^2$, density and viscosity constants of water are denoted by $\rho > 0$ and $\mu > 0$, the gravity constant is given by $g > 0$, the strain-rate tensor $D(u)$ is defined by

$$D(u) := \frac{1}{2}\Big[\nabla u + (\nabla u)^\top\Big],$$

and the outward unit normal vector is denoted by $n\colon \Gamma \to \mathbb{R}^2$, cf. Figure 2. We suppose that the boundary Γ is divided into two non-overlapping parts, Γ_{D} and Γ_{T}, i.e., $\overline{\Gamma} = \overline{\Gamma}_{\mathrm{D}} \cup \overline{\Gamma}_{\mathrm{T}}$ and $\Gamma_{\mathrm{D}} \cap \Gamma_{\mathrm{T}} = \emptyset$, where the subscripts "D" and "T" imply Dirichlet and transmission boundaries, respectively. A positive constant c_0 is chosen suitably to remove the artificial reflection, and, throughout this paper, we employ $c_0 = 0.9$, which is determined based on numerical experiments given in Appendix A. We consider homogeneous flat bottom topography in this paper, Part I, and non-homogeneous bottom topography in our forthcoming paper, Part II.

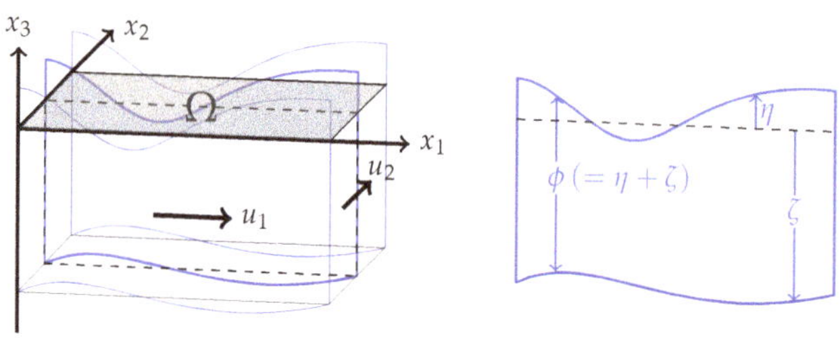

Figure 2. Diagrams for the problem; left: the domain Ω and the velocity $u = (u_1, u_2)^\top$; right: the total wave height $\phi = \eta + \zeta$.

2.2. *Presentation of the Scheme*

Let $\Psi := L^2(\Omega)$, $Y := H^1(\Omega)^2$,

$$V(G) := \big\{v \in Y;\ v = 0 \text{ on } \Gamma_{\mathrm{D}} \text{ and } v = G \text{ on } \Gamma_{\mathrm{T}}\big\}$$

for a function $G\colon \Gamma_{\mathrm{T}} \to \mathbb{R}^2$, and $V := V(0)$. We introduce a ϕ-dependent function, $G(\phi) = G(\phi;\eta)\colon \Gamma_{\mathrm{T}} \to \mathbb{R}^2$, defined by

$$G(\phi) = G(\phi;\eta) := c_0\sqrt{g\zeta}\,\frac{\eta}{\phi}\,n.$$

Assume $\phi^0 \in \Psi$, $\eta^0 := \phi^0 - \zeta \in \Psi$ and $u^0 \in V(G(\phi^0)) = V(G(\phi^0;\eta^0))$. A weak formulation to problem (3) is to find $\{(\phi,u)(t) \in \Psi \times V(G(\phi(t);\eta(t)));\ t \in (0,T)\}$ such that, for $t \in (0,T)$,

$$\Big(\frac{\partial \phi}{\partial t} + \nabla\cdot(u\phi), \psi\Big) = (f, \psi) \qquad \forall \psi \in \Psi, \tag{4a}$$

$$\rho\bigg(\phi\Big[\frac{\partial u}{\partial t} + (u\cdot\nabla)u\Big], v\bigg) + a(u,v;\phi) + b(\eta,v;\phi) = (F,v) \qquad \forall v \in V, \tag{4b}$$

$$\phi = \eta + \zeta, \tag{4c}$$

with the initial condition $(\phi,u)(0) = (\phi^0,u^0) \in \Psi \times V(G(\phi^0;\eta^0))$, where the bilinear forms $a(\cdot,\cdot;\phi)\colon Y \times Y \to \mathbb{R}$ and $b(\cdot,\cdot;\phi)\colon \Psi \times Y \to \mathbb{R}$ are defined by

$$a(u,v;\phi) := 2\mu(\phi D(u), D(v)), \qquad b(\eta,v;\phi) := \rho g(\phi\nabla\eta, v).$$

Now, we present our scheme for solving problem (3). Let $\mathcal{T}_h = \{K\}$ be a partition of $\overline{\Omega}$ by triangular elements, h be the maximum diameter of $K \in \mathcal{T}_h$, and $\Omega_h := \mathrm{int}(\cup_{K\in\mathcal{T}_h} K)$ be an approximated domain. Although it holds that $\Omega \neq \Omega_h$ in general, we assume $\Omega = \Omega_h$ throughout the paper to avoid the complexity of introducing many symbols. We define finite element spaces, Ψ_h, Y_h and $V_h(G)$, corresponding to Ψ, Y and $V(G)$ by

$$\begin{aligned}
\Psi_h &:= \{\psi_h \in C^0(\overline{\Omega});\ \psi_{h|K} \in P_k(K)\ \forall K \in \mathcal{T}_h\},\\
Y_h &:= \{v_h \in C^0(\overline{\Omega})^2;\ v_{h|K} \in P_\ell(K)^2\ \forall K \in \mathcal{T}_h\},\\
V_h(G) &:= \{v_h \in Y_h;\ v_h = 0 \text{ on } \Gamma_{\mathrm{D}} \text{ and } v_h = G \text{ on } \Gamma_{\mathrm{T}}\},
\end{aligned}$$

for $k, \ell \in \mathbb{N}$, and set $V_h := V_h(0)$, where $P_k(K)$ is the space of polynomial functions of degree $k \in \mathbb{N}$ on $K \in \mathcal{T}_h$. In this paper, we employ $k = \ell = 1$, and the function $G\colon \Gamma_{\mathrm{T}} \to \mathbb{R}^2$ is assumed to be a piecewise linear function.

Let Δt be a time increment, $N_T := \lfloor T/\Delta t \rfloor$ a total number of time steps, and $t^n := n\Delta t$ a time at n-th time step. For $v\colon \Omega \to \mathbb{R}^2$, we define mappings $X_1[v], \tilde{X}_1[v]\colon \Omega \to \mathbb{R}^2$ and $\gamma_1[v], \tilde{\gamma}_1[v]\colon \Omega \to \mathbb{R}$ by

$$\begin{aligned}
X_1[v](x) &:= x - \Delta t\, v(x), & \tilde{X}_1[v](x) &:= x - 2\Delta t\, v(x),\\
\gamma_1[v](x) &:= \det\left(\frac{\partial X_1[v]}{\partial x}(x)\right), & \tilde{\gamma}_1[v](x) &:= \det\left(\frac{\partial \tilde{X}_1[v]}{\partial x}(x)\right).
\end{aligned}$$

For $\{\phi^n\}_{n=0}^{N_T}$ and $\{u^n\}_{n=0}^{N_T}$, we define an operator $\mathcal{A}_{\Delta t}[u]\phi^n$ by, for $n = 1, \ldots, N_T$,

$$\mathcal{A}_{\Delta t}[u]\phi^n := \begin{cases} \mathcal{A}_{\Delta t}^{(1)}[u]\phi^n & (n = 1),\\ \mathcal{A}_{\Delta t}^{(2)}[u]\phi^n & (n \geq 2), \end{cases}$$

where

$$\begin{aligned}
\mathcal{A}_{\Delta t}^{(1)}[u]\phi^n &:= \frac{\phi^n - \phi^{n-1} \circ X_1[u^{n-1}]\gamma_1[u^{n-1}]}{\Delta t},\\
\mathcal{A}_{\Delta t}^{(2)}[u]\phi^n &:= \frac{3\phi^n - 4\phi^{n-1} \circ X_1[u^{n*}]\gamma_1[u^{n*}] + \phi^{n-2} \circ \tilde{X}_1[u^{n*}]\tilde{\gamma}_1[u^{n*}]}{2\Delta t}.
\end{aligned}$$

The composition of functions is represented by the symbol $\circ$, i.e.,

$$(\psi \circ X_1[v])(x) = \psi(X_1[v](x)),$$

and the function $u^{n*}\colon \Omega \to \mathbb{R}^2$ is defined by

$$u^{n*} := 2u^{n-1} - u^{n-2},$$

which is a second-order temporal approximation of u^n if u is sufficiently smooth. We also define, for $\{w^n\}_{n=0}^{N_T}$,

$$\mathcal{B}_{\Delta t}[w]u^n := \begin{cases} \mathcal{B}_{\Delta t}^{(1)}[w]u^n & (n = 1),\\ \mathcal{B}_{\Delta t}^{(2)}[w]u^n & (n \geq 2), \end{cases}$$

where

$$\begin{aligned}
\mathcal{B}_{\Delta t}^{(1)}[w]u^n &:= \frac{u^n - u^{n-1} \circ X_1[w^{n-1}]}{\Delta t},\\
\mathcal{B}_{\Delta t}^{(2)}[w]u^n &:= \frac{3u^n - 4u^{n-1} \circ X_1[w^{n*}] + u^{n-2} \circ \tilde{X}_1[w^{n*}]}{2\Delta t}.
\end{aligned}$$

The two-step Lagrange–Galerkin scheme is to find $\{(\phi_h^n, u_h^n) \in \Psi_h \times V_h(G(\phi_h^n; \eta_h^n));\ n = 1, \dots, N_T\}$ such that, for $n = 1, 2, \dots, N_T$,

$$(\mathcal{A}_{\Delta t}[u_h]\phi_h^n, \psi_h) = (f^n, \psi_h) \qquad \forall \psi_h \in \Psi_h, \tag{5a}$$

$$\rho(\phi_h^n \mathcal{B}_{\Delta t}[u_h]u_h^n, v_h) + a(u_h^n, v_h; \phi_h^n) + b(\eta_h^n, v_h; \phi_h^n) = (F^n, v_h) \qquad \forall v_h \in V_h, \tag{5b}$$

$$\phi_h^n = \eta_h^n + \Pi_h \zeta, \tag{5c}$$

with an initial condition

$$(\phi_h^0, u_h^0) = (\Pi_h \phi^0, \Pi_h u^0) \in \Psi_h \times Y_h, \tag{5d}$$

where the Lagrange interpolation operator is denoted by $\Pi_h \colon C(\overline{\Omega}) \to \Psi_h$, which is also used for the vector-valued function u^0, i.e., $\Pi_h u^0 \in Y_h$.

Remark 1. *Scheme* (5) *is equivalent to*

$$\begin{aligned}
\left(\frac{\phi_h^n - \phi_h^{n-1} \circ X_1[u_h^{n-1}] \gamma_1[u_h^{n-1}]}{\Delta t}, \psi_h \right) &= (f^n, \psi_h) \qquad \forall \psi_h \in \Psi_h, \\
\rho\left(\phi_h^n \frac{u_h^n - u_h^{n-1} \circ X_1[u_h^{n-1}]}{\Delta t}, v_h \right) + 2\mu(\phi_h^n D(u_h^n), D(v_h)) & \\
+ \rho g(\phi_h^n \nabla \eta_h^n, v_h) &= (F^n, v_h) \qquad \forall v_h \in V_h, \\
\phi_h^n &= \eta_h^n + \Pi_h \zeta,
\end{aligned}$$

for the first step $n = 1$, *and*

$$\begin{aligned}
\left(\frac{3\phi_h^n - 4\phi_h^{n-1} \circ X_1[u_h^{n*}] \gamma_1[u_h^{n*}] + \phi_h^{n-2} \circ \tilde{X}_1[u_h^{n*}] \tilde{\gamma}_1[u_h^{n*}]}{2\Delta t}, \psi_h \right) &= (f^n, \psi_h) \qquad \forall \psi_h \in \Psi_h, \\
\rho\left(\phi_h^n \frac{3u_h^n - 4u_h^{n-1} \circ X_1[u_h^{n*}] + u_h^{n-2} \circ \tilde{X}_1[u_h^{n*}]}{2\Delta t}, v_h \right) & \\
+ 2\mu(\phi_h^n D(u_h^n), D(v_h)) + \rho g(\phi_h^n \nabla \eta_h^n, v_h) &= (F^n, v_h) \qquad \forall v_h \in V_h, \\
\phi_h^n &= \eta_h^n + \Pi_h \zeta,
\end{aligned}$$

for general steps $n \geq 2$.

Remark 2. *We have the following notes.*

(i) *At each time step, we obtain* $\phi_h^n \in \Psi_h$ *from Equation* (5a) *and* $u_h^n \in V_h(G(\phi_h^n; \eta_h^n))$ *from Equation* (5b) *combined with Equation*(5c), *where both of the resulting coefficient matrices of the systems of linear equations derived from Equations* (5a) *and* (5b) *are symmetric.*

(ii) *We need* $\mathcal{A}_{\Delta t}^{(1)}[u]$ *and* $\mathcal{B}_{\Delta t}^{(1)}[w]$ *due to the lack of the functions* ϕ_h^{n-2} *and* u_h^{n-2} *for* $n = 1$, *which are used for* $\mathcal{A}_{\Delta t}^{(2)}[u_h]\phi_h^n$ *and* $\mathcal{B}_{\Delta t}^{(2)}[u_h]u_h^n$ *for* $n \geq 2$.

(iii) *The two-step methods in conservative and non-conservative forms,* $\mathcal{A}_{\Delta t}^{(2)}[u_h]\phi_h^n$ *and* $\mathcal{B}_{\Delta t}^{(2)}[u_h]u_h^n$, *are developed and analyzed for convection-diffusion problems in [17,49].*

(iv) *It is discussed in [40,49] that the one-time use of first-order single-step methods,* $\mathcal{A}_{\Delta t}^{(1)}[u_h]\phi_h^n$ *and* $\mathcal{B}_{\Delta t}^{(1)}[u_h]u_h^n$, *has no loss of convergence order in discrete version of* $L^\infty(0, T; L^2(\Omega))$*-norm for a conservative convection-diffusion equation and the Navier–Stokes equations, respectively.*

(v) *The so-called quadrilateral elements* $Q_k(K)$, *e.g., bilinear* ($k = 1$) *and biquadratic* ($k = 2$) *elements, with a partition of* $\overline{\Omega}$, $\mathcal{T}_h = \{K\}$, *by rectangles are also available for* Ψ_h *and* Y_h.

Remark 3. *Suppose that the pair* $(\phi, u) \colon \Omega \times (0, T) \to \mathbb{R} \times \mathbb{R}^d$ *is a smooth solution to Equation* (3) *and that* $n \geq 2$. *Then, the truncation errors of the Equations* (5a) *and* (5b) *are of second order in time, i.e.,*

$$\left\| \mathcal{A}_{\Delta t}[u]\phi^n - f^n \right\|_{L^\infty(\Omega)} = O(\Delta t^2),$$

$$\|\rho\phi^n \mathcal{B}_{\Delta t}[u]u^n - 2\mu\nabla\cdot(\phi D(u^n)) + \rho g\phi^n\nabla\eta^n - F^n\|_{L^\infty(\Omega)} = O(\Delta t^2),$$

as $\mathcal{A}_{\Delta t}[u]\phi^n$ and $\mathcal{B}_{\Delta t}[u]u^n$ are second-order approximations of the conservative and non-conservative material derivatives, respectively, i.e.,

$$\big[\mathcal{A}_{\Delta t}[u]\phi^n\big](x) = \Big[\frac{\partial\phi}{\partial t} + \nabla\cdot(u\phi)\Big](x,t^n) + O(\Delta t^2),$$
$$\big[\mathcal{B}_{\Delta t}[u]u^n\big](x) = \Big[\frac{\partial u}{\partial t} + (u\cdot\nabla)u\Big](x,t^n) + O(\Delta t^2),$$

and the evaluation point is $(x,t^n) \in \Omega\times(0,T)$, cf. [40,49].

Remark 4. *Suppose that Ω is convex and $\Gamma = \Gamma_D$, that ϕ is known and smooth, that there exist positive constants $\underline{c}_+$ and $\overline{c}_+$ such that $(0 <)\,\underline{c}_+ \le \phi(x,t) \le \overline{c}_+$ for any $(x,t) \in \overline{\Omega}\times[0,T]$, and $\ell = 1$. Then, the unknown function of problem* (3) *is only u, and we can prove stability and error estimates for the velocity if u is smooth enough, i.e., there exist positive constants h_* and c_* independent of h and Δt such that, for any pair $(h,\Delta t)$ with $h \in (0,h_*]$ and $\Delta t \le c_* h^{2/5}$, the solution $\{u_h^n\}_{n=1}^{N_T} \subset V_h$ to scheme* (5) *whose ϕ_h^n is replaced with ϕ^n satisfies $\|u_h\|_{\ell^\infty(L^\infty(\Omega))} \le \|u\|_{C^0(L^\infty(\Omega))} + 1$ and $\|u_h - u\|_{\ell^\infty(L^2)} = O(\Delta t^2 + h^2)$ by induction argument similar to the proof of the stability and error estimates of a scheme for the Navier–Stokes equations in [40].*

3. Numerical Results in Square Domains

In this section, numerical results via FreeFem++ [50] with $k = \ell = 1$ (piecewise linear, P1-element) are presented to see the experimental order of convergence (EOC) and the effect of the TBC in square domains, where both of the systems of linear equations for Equations (5a) and (5b) are solved by the LU decomposition method in FreeFem++. We call scheme (5) LG2, and also call scheme (5) replacing $\mathcal{A}_{\Delta t}$ and $\mathcal{B}_{\Delta t}$ with $\mathcal{A}_{\Delta t}^{(1)}$ and $\mathcal{B}_{\Delta t}^{(1)}$, respectively, LG1 [9,10], which is a (single-step) Lagrange–Galerkin scheme of first order in time.

3.1. Experimental Order of Convergence

We solve Examples 1 and 2 below by LG1 and LG2 and compare the experimental orders of convergence (EOCs).

Example 1 ($\Gamma = \Gamma_D$). *In problem* (3)*, we set $\Omega = (0,1)^2$, $\Gamma = \Gamma_D$ ($\Gamma_T = \emptyset$), $T = 1$, $g = \rho = \mu = \zeta = 1$, and the function η^0, u^0, f and F are given so that the exact solution is*

$$\phi(x,t) = 1 + \frac{\sin\pi x_1 \sin\pi x_2(2+\sin\pi t)}{8}, \quad u(x,t) = \frac{\sin\pi x_1 \sin\pi x_2(2+\sin\pi t)}{3}\begin{bmatrix}1\\1\end{bmatrix}.$$

Example 2 ($\Gamma = \overline{\Gamma}_D \cup \overline{\Gamma}_T$). *In Example 1, we replace Γ_T and Γ_D with $\Gamma_T = \{x \in \Gamma;\ x_2 = 0\}$ and $\Gamma_D = \Gamma \setminus \overline{\Gamma}_T$, respectively.*

For a numerical solution $z_h = \{z_h^n\}_{n=0}^{N_T}$ and its exact solution $z = \{z^n\}_{n=0}^{N_T}$, we introduce notations of errors, $E_i(z)$, $i = 0,1$, defined by

$$E_0(z) := \frac{\|z_h - z\|_{\ell^\infty(L^2)}}{\|z\|_{\ell^\infty(L^2)}}, \qquad E_1(z) := \frac{\|\nabla(z_h - z)\|_{\ell^\infty(L^2)}}{\|\nabla z\|_{\ell^\infty(L^2)}},$$

where $\|\cdot\|_{\ell^\infty(L^2)}$ is a norm given by

$$\|z\|_{\ell^\infty(L^2)} := \max\{\|z^n\|_{L^2(\Omega)};\ n = 0,\ldots,N_T\}.$$

Let N be a division number of each side of the unit square domain Ω and $h := 1/N$ a representative mesh size. We prepare non-uniform triangulations of Ω, $\mathcal{T}_h$, for $N = 8, 16, 32, 64, 128$ and 256, cf. Figure 3 for $N = 32$.

Choosing $\Delta t = 0.25\sqrt{h}$, we compute the errors, $E_i(\eta)$ and $E_i(u)$, $i = 0,1$, by LG1 and LG2. Figures 4 and 5 show graphs of the errors of $E_0(\cdot)$ and $E_1(\cdot)$, respectively, in logarithmic scale by LG1 for Example 1 (i) and Example 2 (ii), and by LG2 for Example 1 (iii) and Example 2 (iv), and the values of errors and their EOCs are given in Tables 1 and 2. We observe that LG2 is of second order in time numerically and that the order is higher than that of LG1. Although $E_1(\eta)$ is not of second order in time, it is natural as Equation (3a) for ϕ $(= \eta + \zeta)$ does not include any diffusion term.

Remark 5. *Lagrange–Galerkin schemes are basically CFL-free, and our scheme also has this property. In fact, the CFL number in this computation is* $U\Delta t/h = 1/(4\sqrt{h}) = 4$ *for* $N = 256$ *as the maximum velocity* U *is* 1 *and the* Δt *is chosen as* $\Delta t = 0.25\sqrt{h}$.

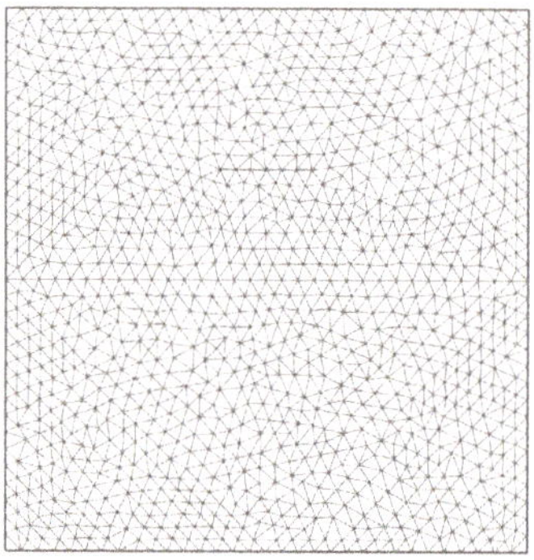

Figure 3. A sample mesh with $N = 32$ for Example 1.

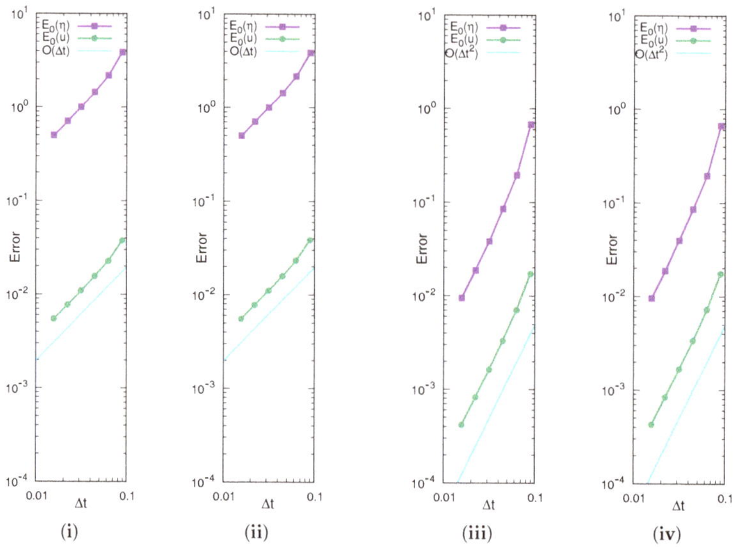

Figure 4. Graphs of errors $E_0(\eta)$ and $E_0(u)$ in logarithmic scale by LG1 for Example 1 (**i**) and Example 2 (**ii**), and by LG2 for Example 1 (**iii**) and Example 2 (**iv**).

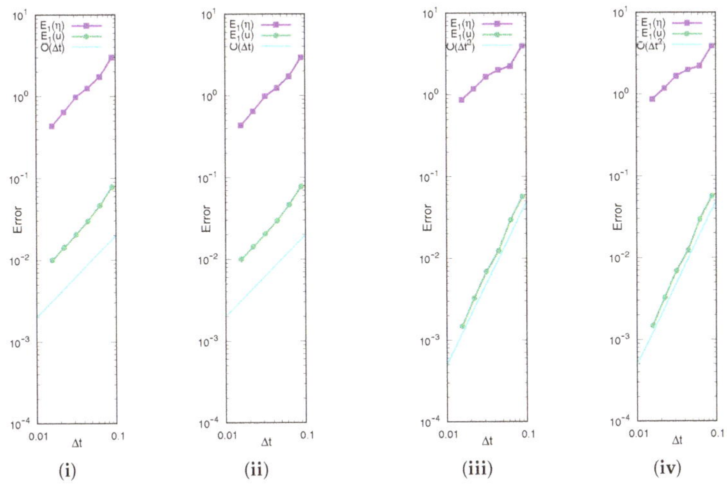

Figure 5. Graphs of errors $E_1(\eta)$ and $E_1(u)$ in logarithmic scale by LG1 for Example 1 **(i)** and Example 2 **(ii)**, and by LG2 for Example 1 **(iii)** and Example 2 **(iv)**.

Table 1. Values of $E_i(\eta)$ and $E_i(u)$, $i = 0, 1$, by schemes LG1 and LG2 for Example 1 ($\Gamma = \Gamma_D$).

		LG1			
N	Δt	$E_0(\eta)$	EOC	$E_0(u)$	EOC
8	8.84×10^{-2}	3.89×10^{0}	-	3.78×10^{-2}	-
16	6.25×10^{-2}	2.20×10^{0}	1.65	2.28×10^{-2}	1.45
32	4.42×10^{-2}	1.45×10^{0}	1.19	1.57×10^{-2}	1.09
64	3.13×10^{-2}	1.01×10^{0}	1.05	1.10×10^{-2}	1.03
128	2.21×10^{-2}	7.11×10^{-1}	1.01	7.77×10^{-3}	1.00
256	1.56×10^{-2}	5.02×10^{-1}	1.00	5.51×10^{-3}	0.99
		LG1			
N	Δt	$E_1(\eta)$	EOC	$E_1(u)$	EOC
8	8.84×10^{-2}	3.00×10^{0}	-	7.78×10^{-2}	-
16	6.25×10^{-2}	1.73×10^{0}	1.59	4.63×10^{-2}	1.49
32	4.42×10^{-2}	1.25×10^{0}	0.93	2.95×10^{-2}	1.31
64	3.13×10^{-2}	9.78×10^{-1}	0.71	2.04×10^{-2}	1.06
128	2.21×10^{-2}	6.42×10^{-1}	1.22	1.42×10^{-2}	1.04
256	1.56×10^{-2}	4.35×10^{-1}	1.12	1.00×10^{-2}	1.01
		LG2			
N	Δt	$E_0(\eta)$	EOC	$E_0(u)$	EOC
8	8.84×10^{-2}	6.81×10^{-1}	-	1.71×10^{-2}	-
16	6.25×10^{-2}	1.96×10^{-1}	3.60	7.03×10^{-3}	2.57
32	4.42×10^{-2}	8.53×10^{-2}	2.40	3.32×10^{-3}	2.16
64	3.13×10^{-2}	3.82×10^{-2}	2.32	1.64×10^{-3}	2.04
128	2.21×10^{-2}	1.87×10^{-2}	2.05	8.20×10^{-4}	1.99
256	1.56×10^{-2}	9.46×10^{-3}	1.97	4.17×10^{-4}	1.95
		LG2			
N	Δt	$E_1(\eta)$	EOC	$E_1(u)$	EOC
8	8.84×10^{-2}	3.97×10^{0}	-	5.68×10^{-2}	-
16	6.25×10^{-2}	2.24×10^{0}	1.65	2.90×10^{-2}	1.94
32	4.42×10^{-2}	2.00×10^{0}	0.33	1.20×10^{-2}	2.54
64	3.13×10^{-2}	1.64×10^{0}	0.57	6.72×10^{-3}	1.67
128	2.21×10^{-2}	1.17×10^{0}	0.97	3.23×10^{-3}	2.11
256	1.56×10^{-2}	8.64×10^{-1}	0.88	1.47×10^{-3}	2.28

Table 2. Values of $E_i(\eta)$ and $E_i(u)$, $i = 0, 1$, by schemes LG1 and LG2 for Example 2 ($\Gamma = \overline{\Gamma}_{\mathrm{D}} \cup \overline{\Gamma}_{\mathrm{T}}$).

		LG1			
N	Δt	$E_0(\eta)$	EOC	$E_0(u)$	EOC
8	8.84×10^{-2}	3.88×10^{0}	-	3.86×10^{-2}	-
16	6.25×10^{-2}	2.19×10^{0}	1.65	2.33×10^{-2}	1.46
32	4.42×10^{-2}	1.45×10^{0}	1.19	1.58×10^{-2}	1.11
64	3.13×10^{-2}	1.01×10^{0}	1.05	1.11×10^{-2}	1.03
128	2.21×10^{-2}	7.09×10^{-1}	1.01	7.82×10^{-3}	1.01
256	1.56×10^{-2}	5.01×10^{-1}	1.00	5.53×10^{-3}	1.00

		LG1			
N	Δt	$E_1(\eta)$	EOC	$E_1(u)$	EOC
8	8.84×10^{-2}	2.95×10^{0}	-	7.80×10^{-2}	-
16	6.25×10^{-2}	1.71×10^{0}	1.57	4.64×10^{-2}	1.50
32	4.42×10^{-2}	1.24×10^{0}	0.94	2.95×10^{-2}	1.31
64	3.13×10^{-2}	9.78×10^{-1}	0.67	2.03×10^{-2}	1.07
128	2.21×10^{-2}	6.42×10^{-1}	1.21	1.41×10^{-2}	1.04
256	1.56×10^{-2}	4.34×10^{-1}	1.13	9.96×10^{-3}	1.01

		LG2			
N	Δt	$E_0(\eta)$	EOC	$E_0(u)$	EOC
8	8.84×10^{-2}	6.70×10^{-1}	-	1.75×10^{-2}	-
16	6.25×10^{-2}	1.95×10^{-1}	3.56	7.23×10^{-3}	2.55
32	4.42×10^{-2}	8.58×10^{-2}	2.37	3.37×10^{-3}	2.20
64	3.13×10^{-2}	3.97×10^{-2}	2.22	1.67×10^{-3}	2.03
128	2.21×10^{-2}	1.87×10^{-2}	2.17	8.37×10^{-4}	2.00
256	1.56×10^{-2}	9.54×10^{-3}	1.94	4.25×10^{-4}	1.96

		LG2			
N	Δt	$E_1(\eta)$	EOC	$E_1(u)$	EOC
8	8.84×10^{-2}	3.89×10^{0}	-	5.70×10^{-2}	-
16	6.25×10^{-2}	2.21×10^{0}	1.63	2.93×10^{-2}	1.92
32	4.42×10^{-2}	1.98×10^{0}	0.32	1.24×10^{-2}	2.49
64	3.13×10^{-2}	1.65×10^{0}	0.54	6.90×10^{-3}	1.69
128	2.21×10^{-2}	1.17×10^{0}	0.97	3.26×10^{-3}	2.16
256	1.56×10^{-2}	8.62×10^{-1}	0.89	1.48×10^{-3}	2.27

3.2. Effect of the TBC

We consider the following example to see the effect of the TBC.

Example 3. *In problem* (3), *we set* $\Omega = (0, 10)^2$, $T = 100$, $g = \rho = \mu = \zeta = 1$, $(f, F) = (0, 0)$, $\eta^0 = c\exp(-100\,|x - p|^2)$, $c = 10^{-3}$, $p = (5, 5)^{\top}$, *and* $u^0 = 0$. *We consider five cases of* Γ_{T},

(a) $\Gamma_{\mathrm{T}} = \emptyset$, *i.e.*, $\Gamma = \Gamma_{\mathrm{D}}$,

(b) $\Gamma_{\mathrm{T}} = \{x \in \Gamma;\ x_2 = 0\}$ *(bottom)*, $\Gamma_{\mathrm{D}} = \Gamma \setminus \overline{\Gamma}_{\mathrm{T}}$,

(c) $\Gamma_{\mathrm{T}} = \{x \in \Gamma;\ x_1 = 10, x_2 = 0\}$ *(right and bottom)*, $\Gamma_{\mathrm{D}} = \Gamma \setminus \overline{\Gamma}_{\mathrm{T}}$,

(d) $\Gamma_{\mathrm{T}} = \{x \in \Gamma;\ x_1 = 10, x_2 = 0, 10\}$ *(right, bottom and top)*, $\Gamma_{\mathrm{D}} = \Gamma \setminus \overline{\Gamma}_{\mathrm{T}}$,

(e) $\Gamma_{\mathrm{T}} = \Gamma$.

We solve Example 3 by LG2. Figure 6 shows the color contours of η_h^n for $t = 25k$, $k = 0, \ldots, 4$, cf. (i)–(v), for the five cases, (a)–(e). We can see the effect of the boundary conditions; the artificial reflection is observed and removed significantly when the wave touches the Dirichlet (Γ_{D}) and the transmission (Γ_{T}) boundaries, respectively. Thus, LG2 works well for the SWEs with and without the TBC in the simple square domain.

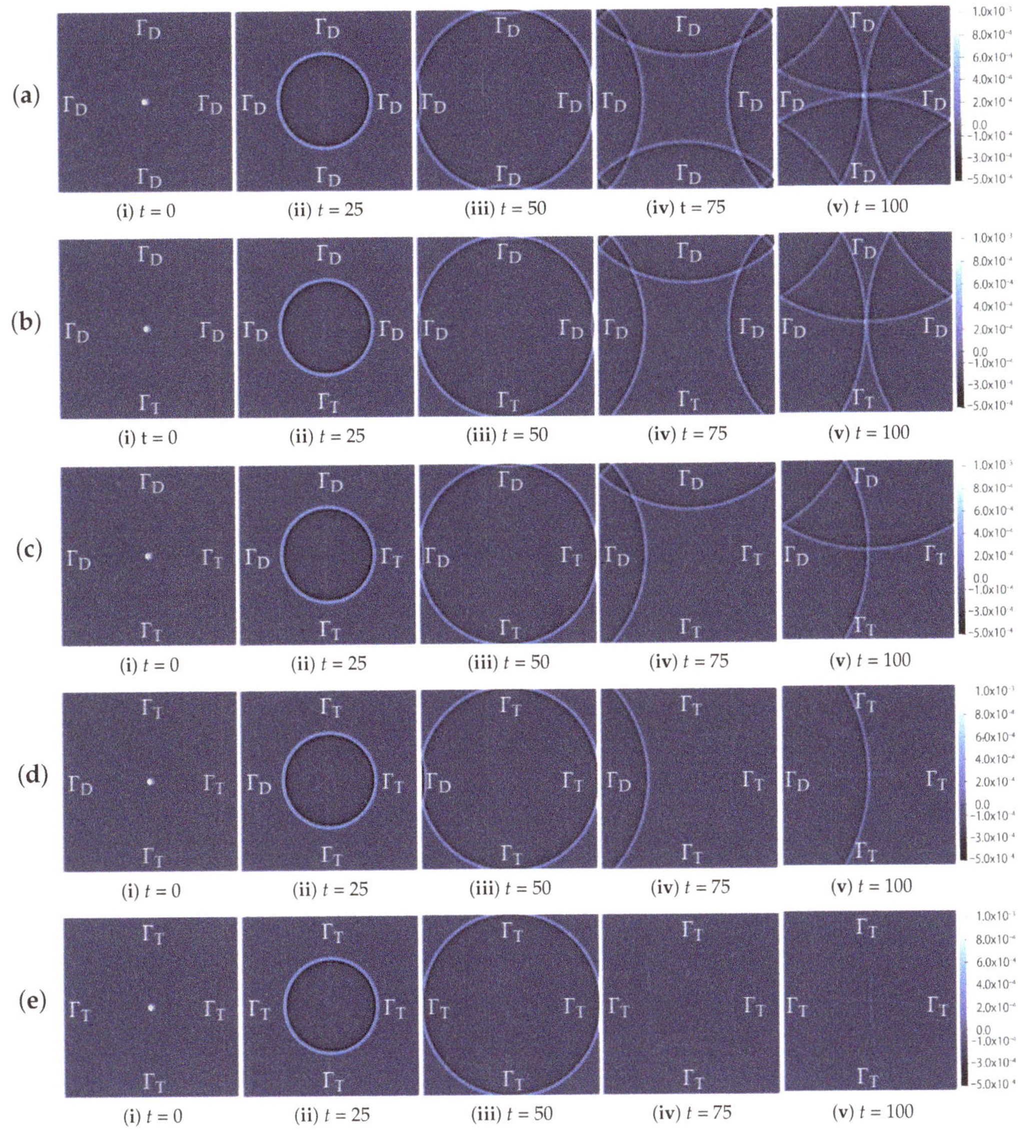

Figure 6. Color contours of η_h^n by LG2 with and without the TBC for the five cases, (**a**–**e**), in Example 3.

4. Application to the Bay of Bengal

In this section, we apply LG2, i.e., scheme (5) discussed in Section 2.2, to a computational domain of the Bay of Bengal region, cf. Figure 7, which is an approximate domain of the original, cf. Figure 1. All the computations are performed via FreeFem++ [50].

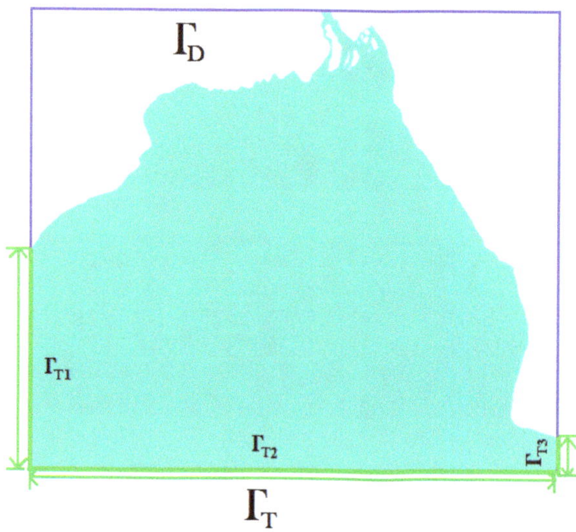

Figure 7. The domain for the Bay of Bengal region with the information of boundaries, Γ_D and Γ_T $(= \Gamma_{T1} \cup \Gamma_{T2} \cup \Gamma_{T3})$ used in Example 4.

4.1. Numerical Simulation with and without the TBC

We set the following example.

Example 4. *Let Ω be the domain shown in Figure 7. The domain is considered from 0 to 1051.4 [km] in the horizontal direction and 0 to 889.59 [km] in the vertical direction. We employ two boundary conditions, the Dirichlet boundary condition on Γ_D and the TBC on Γ_T, cf. Figure 7. We set Γ_D on the coastal and island boundaries and Γ_T on the artificial boundaries for the open sea. As shown in Figure 7, there are three artificial boundaries on the open sea, i.e., $\Gamma_T = \Gamma_{T1} \cup \Gamma_{T2} \cup \Gamma_{T3}$. In problem (3), we set $T = 5000$ [s], $\zeta = 2$ [km], $\eta^0(x) = c_1 \exp(-0.04|x-p|^2)$ [km], $c_1 = 0.01$ [–], $p = (559.56, 430.02)^\top$, $u^0 = 0$, $\mu = 1$ [Pa · s], $\rho = 10^{12}$ [kg/km^3], $g = 9.8 \times 10^{-3}$ [km/s^2] and $(f, F) = (0, 0)$.*

We prepare a triangular mesh of the domain as shown in Figure 8, where the numbers of elements and nodal points are 60,619 and 31,120, respectively. Then, a numerical simulation is done by LG2 with $\Delta t = 0.2$ [s]. The results at $t = 0, 2500, 3000, 4000, 4500$ and 5000 [s] are presented in Figures 9 and 10. In the figures, for comparison to see the effect of the TBC, we compute Example 4 by replacing Γ_T with Γ_D and put it on the left. From Figure 9, we can see that a circular wave is created at around the point p, that it propagates towards the boundary over time, that reflections are found when the wave touches Γ_D, and that the results with $\Gamma = \Gamma_D$ (left) and $\Gamma = \Gamma_D \cup \Gamma_T$ (right) are similar. From Figure 10, we can observe that artificial reflections on the open sea boundaries are significantly removed when the wave touches Γ_T, cf. the right figures. Thus, LG2 works well for a simple (square) domain and this complex domain, the Bay of Bengal region, which is non-convex and includes islands.

For any (smooth) solution to problem (3), we define the total energy $\mathcal{E}(t)$ by

$$\mathcal{E}(t) := \mathcal{E}_1(t) + \mathcal{E}_2(t) := \int_\Omega \frac{\rho}{2}\phi|u|^2 dx + \int_\Omega \frac{\rho g|\eta|^2}{2} dx, \tag{6}$$

where $\mathcal{E}_1(t)$ is the kinetic energy, and $\mathcal{E}_2(t)$ is the potential energy. Then, it is worthy to note that the following energy estimate holds, cf. ([9] Corollary 3.3-(i)),

$$\frac{d}{dt}\mathcal{E}(t) = -\frac{\rho}{2}\int_{\Gamma_T} \phi|u|^2 u \cdot n \, ds - \rho g \int_{\Gamma_T} \phi\eta u \cdot n \, ds$$

$$+2\mu \int_{\Gamma_T} \phi[D(u)n] \cdot u\, ds - 2\mu \int_{\Omega} \phi |D(u)|^2\, dx. \tag{7}$$

Here, focusing on $\mathcal{E}_2(t)$ $(= \frac{1}{2} \int_\Omega \rho g |\eta|^2 dx)$ and the mass of η, i.e., $\int_\Omega \eta\, dx$, we present the values of the $L^2(\Omega)$-norm of η_h^n, i.e, $\|\eta_h^n\|_{L^2(\Omega)}$, and the mass of η_h^n, i.e., $\int_\Omega \eta_h^n\, dx$, in Figures 11 and 12, respectively. In principle, we can say that the TBC works well numerically if $\|\eta_h^n\|_{L^2(\Omega)}$ and $\int_\Omega \eta_h^n\, dx$ decrease around the time that the wave touches the transmission boundaries. Figure 11 shows graphs of $\|\eta_h^n\|_{L^2(\Omega)}$ for the two cases, with and without the transmission boundaries, i.e., $\Gamma = \Gamma_D \cup \Gamma_T$ and $\Gamma = \Gamma_D$ $(\Gamma_T = \emptyset)$, respectively. Figure 12 shows the graphs of $\int_\Omega \eta_h^n\, dx$ for the four cases of (transmission) boundaries, (i) no transmission boundary, i.e., $\Gamma_T = \emptyset$, (ii) one transmission boundary, i.e., $\Gamma_T = \Gamma_{T2}$, (iii) two transmission boundaries, i.e., $\Gamma_T = \Gamma_{T1} \cup \Gamma_{T3}$, and (iv) three transmission boundaries, i.e., $\Gamma_T = \Gamma_{T1} \cup \Gamma_{T2} \cup \Gamma_{T3}$. From Figures 11 and 12, we can see that there are decreasing phenomena of the value of $L^2(\Omega)$-norm as well as the value of the mass when the TBC is imposed. From Figure 9, we can see that the wave touches the transmission boundary Γ_{T2} at time around $t = 3000$ [s]; that is why, the mass of η_h^n decreases drastically from around 3000 [s] to 3200 [s], cf. Figure 12 (yellow and green lines). Again, the mass started to decrease between the period from around 4000 [s] to 4500 [s], cf. Figure 12, since the wave reached the transmission boundary Γ_{T1} and Γ_{T3}, cf. Figure 10.

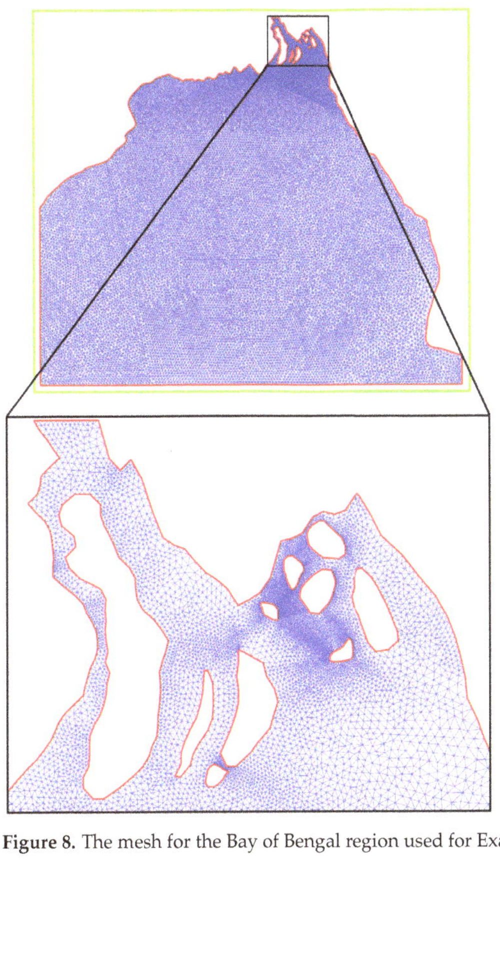

Figure 8. The mesh for the Bay of Bengal region used for Example 4.

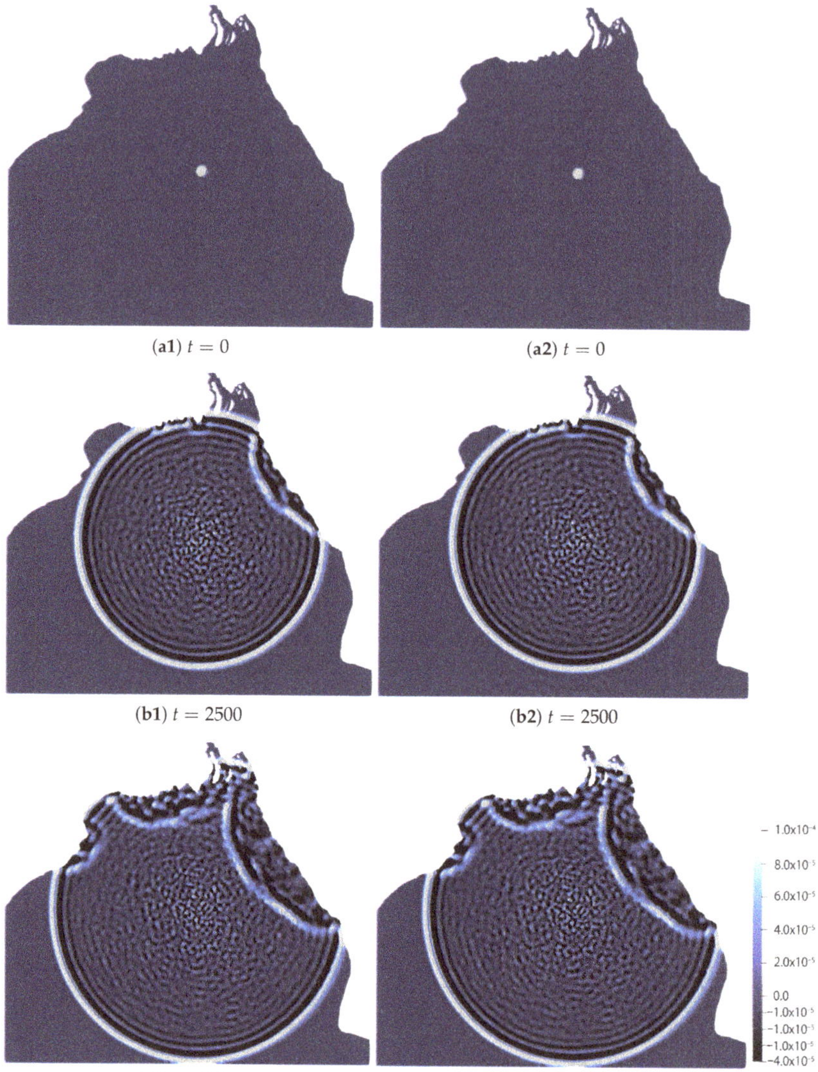

(**a1**) $t = 0$ (**a2**) $t = 0$

(**b1**) $t = 2500$ (**b2**) $t = 2500$

(**c1**) $t = 3000$ (**c2**) $t = 3000$

Figure 9. Contour plot of η_h^n by LG2 with $\Gamma = \Gamma_D$ (**left**) and $\Gamma = \Gamma_D \cup \Gamma_T$ (**right**) on the Bay of Bengal for $t = 0, 2500$ and 3000.

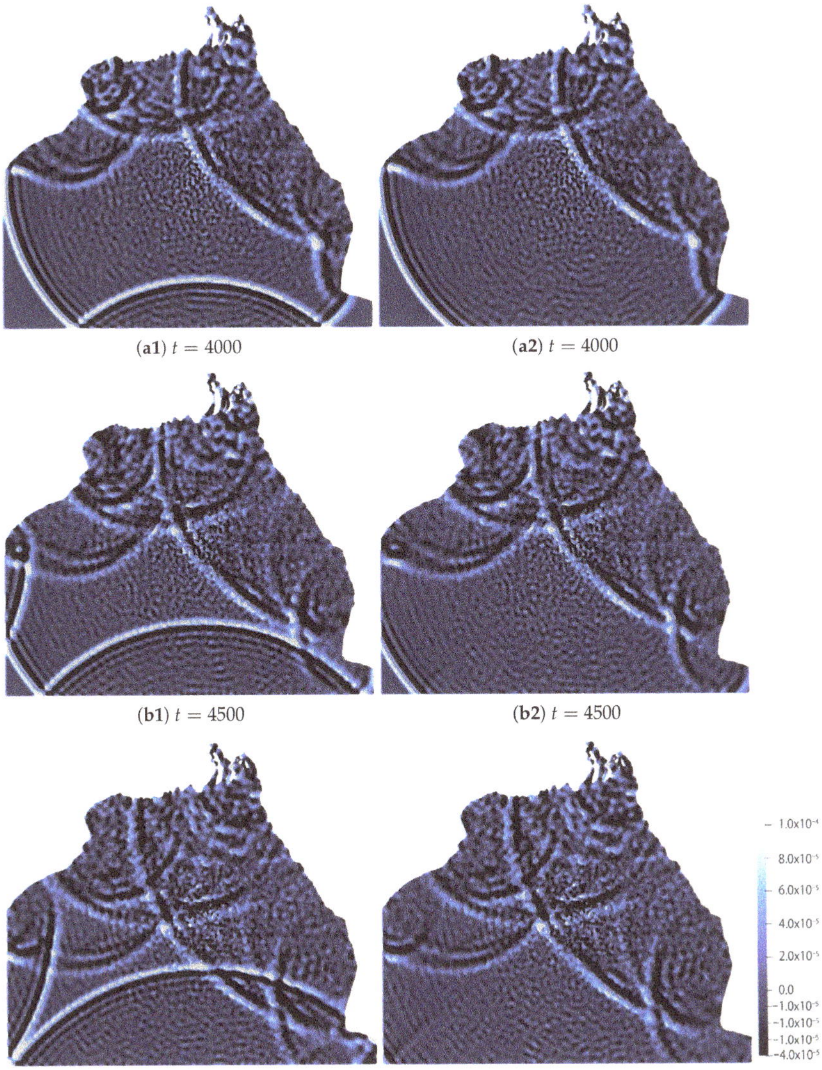

(**a1**) $t = 4000$ (**a2**) $t = 4000$

(**b1**) $t = 4500$ (**b2**) $t = 4500$

(**c1**) $t = 5000$ (**c2**) $t = 5000$

Figure 10. Contour plot of η_h^n by LG2 with $\Gamma = \Gamma_D$ (**left**) and $\Gamma = \bar{\Gamma}_D \cup \bar{\Gamma}_T$ (**right**) on the Bay of Bengal for $t = 4000, 4500$ and 5000.

Remark 6. *We recall the results in [9] and mention the advantage of the TBC Equation* (3e) *on the stability under the assumption* $\phi > 0$ *on* $\Gamma_T \times [0, T]$.

(i) *The last term in the RHS of* (7) *is obviously non-positive. From the TBC Equation* (3e), *i.e.,* $\phi u = c_0\sqrt{g\zeta}\eta n$, *we observe that the second term in the RHS of Equation* (7) *is non-positive:*

$$-\rho g \int_{\Gamma_T} \phi\eta u \cdot n \, ds = -\rho g \int_{\Gamma_T} c_0\sqrt{g\zeta}\,\eta^2 \, ds \le 0.$$

Since it is numerically observed in [9] that the second term is dominant from the viewpoint of the energy $\mathcal{E}(t)$, *cf. ([9] (Remark 3.5)), we can expect that this non-positivity derived from the TBC Equation* (3e) *improves the stability of the SWEs Equation* (3).

(ii) *Let us additionally introduce a theorem ([9] (Theorem 3.4)). Suppose that there exists* $\alpha \in (0,1)$ *such that*

$$\begin{aligned} \eta(x,t) &\geq -\alpha\zeta(x) \quad (x \in \overline{\Gamma}_{\mathrm{T}},\ t \in [0,T]), \\ 0 < c_0 &\leq \sqrt{2/\alpha}\,(1-\alpha). \end{aligned} \tag{8}$$

Then, the summation of the first and second terms in the RHS of Equation (7) *is non-positive, i.e.,*

$$-\frac{\rho}{2}\int_{\Gamma_{\mathrm{T}}} \phi|u|^2 u \cdot n\, ds - \rho g \int_{\Gamma_{\mathrm{T}}} \phi\eta u \cdot n\, ds \leq 0,$$

in particular,

$$\frac{d}{dt}\mathcal{E}(t) \leq 2\mu \int_{\Gamma_{\mathrm{T}}} \phi[D(u)n] \cdot u\, ds.$$

(iii) *As mentioned in ([9] (Remark 3.6)), the condition* (8) *is not strict in the practical computation, where* α *and* c_0 *are chosen typically as, e.g.,* $\alpha = 0.01$ *and* $c_0 = 0.9$*. These satisfy condition* (8) *since* $\sqrt{2/\alpha}\,(1-\alpha) \approx 14$.

(iv) *We have compared our results by the TBC* ($c_0 = 0.9$) *and a modified TBC* ($c_0 = 1$) *with those by the RBC:*

$$u = \sqrt{g/\zeta}\,\eta n \qquad \text{on } \Gamma_{\mathrm{T}} \times (0,T). \tag{9}$$

The results by the three boundary conditions are not significantly different as presented in Appendix B. We note that condition (9) *is the well-known RBC, cf., e.g., [8], and that the modified TBC is obtained by replacing* ζ *with* ϕ^2/ζ *in Equation* (9)*, where the relation* $\zeta \approx \phi^2/\zeta \approx \phi$ *holds if* $|\eta| \ll \zeta$ *is satisfied.*

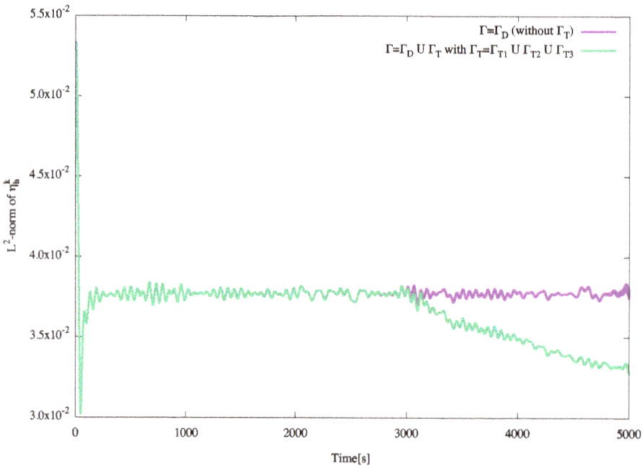

Figure 11. Graphs of $\|\eta_h^n\|_{L^2(\Omega)}$ with respect to time ($t = t^n$) for Example 4 with Γ_{T} ($\Gamma = \Gamma_{\mathrm{D}} \cup \Gamma_{\mathrm{T}}$) and without Γ_{T} ($\Gamma = \Gamma_{\mathrm{D}}$).

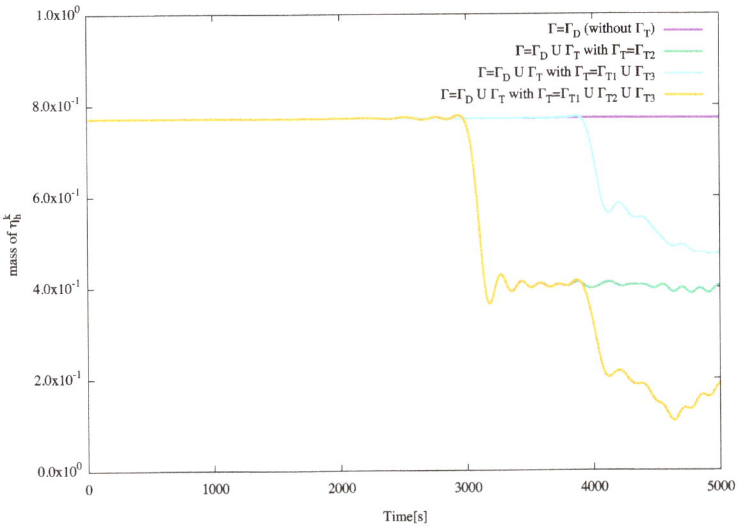

Figure 12. Graphs of the mass of η_h^n with respect to time ($t = t^n$) for Example 4 with the following four settings; no transmission boundary, i.e., $\Gamma_T = \emptyset$ (purple), one transmission boundary, i.e., $\Gamma_T = \Gamma_{T2}$ (green), two transmission boundaries, i.e., $\Gamma_T = \Gamma_{T1} \cup \Gamma_{T3}$ (blue), and three transmission boundaries, i.e., $\Gamma_T = \Gamma_{T1} \cup \Gamma_{T2} \cup \Gamma_{T3}$ (yellow).

4.2. Effect of Position of a Transmission Boundary

We consider Example 4 again to see the effect of the TBC with an extension of the domain (Ω), where the size of the domain in the vertical direction is extended from 889.59 [km] to 989.59 [km], i.e., 100 [km] extension. We employ the same boundary conditions on $\Gamma = \Gamma_D \cup \Gamma_T$ for both original and extended domains, where $\Gamma_T = \Gamma_{T1} \cup \Gamma_{T2} \cup \Gamma_{T3}$. We compare the numerical results for the extended domain with the ones for the original domain, cf. Figures 13 and 14, where the left and right figures show the results for the extended and original domains, respectively. It is observed that there is no significant effect of the vertical position of the bottom transmission boundary Γ_{T2}. We also computed the mass of η for both domains, cf. Figure 15. From Figure 15, we can see that the mass of η_h^k started to decrease at time $t = 3000$ for the original domain, cf. Figure 13c2, while the mass of η_h^k started to decrease at time $t = 4000$ for the extended domain, cf. Figure 14b1, because the wave touches the boundary Γ_{T2} at these times ($t = 3000$ and $t = 4000$) for the original and extended domains, respectively. A similar decreasing property of mass of η_h^k can be observed from Figure 15 when the wave touches the transmission boundaries. The results confirm that the TBC works well numerically and that we can choose the vertical position of the bottom transmission boundary Γ_{T2} without significant effect.

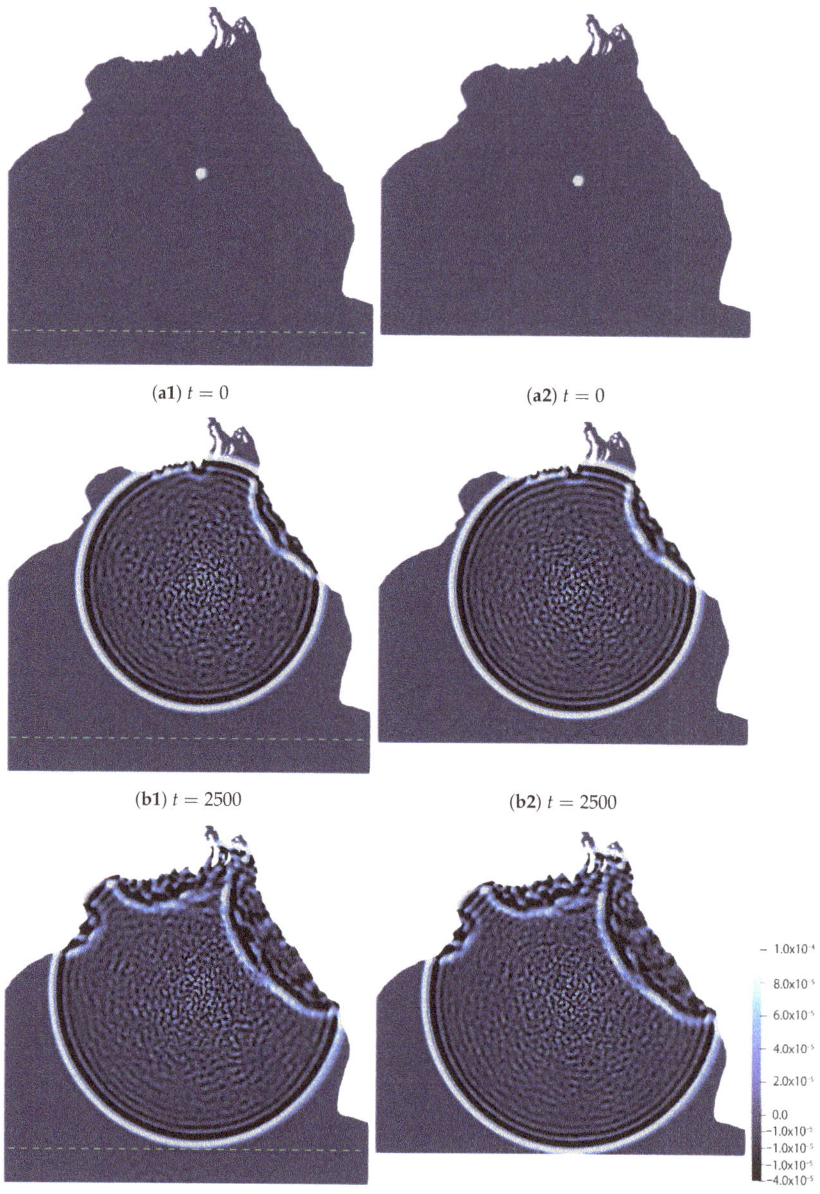

Figure 13. Contour plot of η_h^n by LG2 with $\Gamma = \bar{\Gamma}_D \cup \bar{\Gamma}_T$ for the extended domain (**left**) and for the original domain (**right**) on the Bay of Bengal for $t = 0, 2500$ and 3000. The green dotted lines in the left figures indicate the position of the bottom boundary of the original domain.

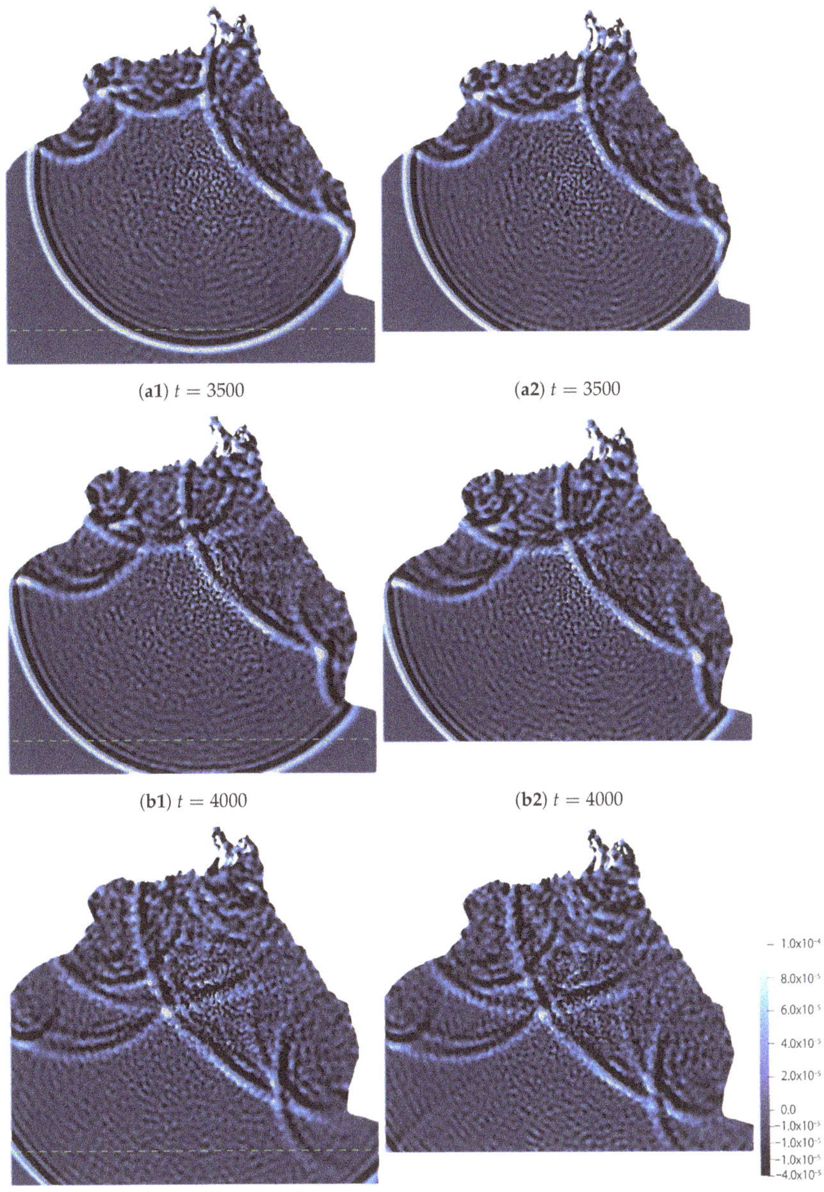

(**a1**) $t = 3500$ (**a2**) $t = 3500$

(**b1**) $t = 4000$ (**b2**) $t = 4000$

(**c1**) $t = 5000$ (**c2**) $t = 5000$

Figure 14. Contour plot of η_h^n by LG2 with $\Gamma = \bar{\Gamma}_D \cup \bar{\Gamma}_T$ for the extended domain (**left**) and for the original domain (**right**) on the Bay of Bengal for $t = 3500, 4000$ and 5000.

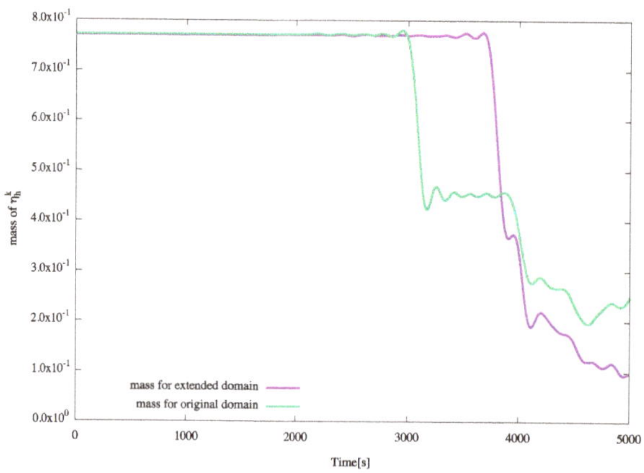

Figure 15. Graphs of the mass of η_h^n for the extended and original domain with a TBC.

5. Conclusions

We have presented a two-step Lagrange–Galerkin scheme for the shallow water equations with a TBC. For the scheme, the EOCs have been computed (cf. Examples 1 and 2 in Section 3.1) and the second-order accuracy in time has been confirmed. From numerical experiments on a simple square domain (cf. Example 3 in Section 3.2), it has been observed that the effect of the TBC works well. Our scheme has been applied to a realistic domain, the Bay of Bengal, and numerical experiments have been performed for two different types of boundary conditions, i.e., with and without the TBC (cf. Section 4.1). There have been no significant reflections from Γ_T and the wave has passed through Γ_T while reflections have been observed from Γ_D, and, in the graphs of $\|\eta_h^n\|_{L^2(\Omega)}$ and the mass of η_h^n (cf. Figures 11 and 12), natural decays of the values of $\|\eta_h^n\|_{L^2(\Omega)}$ as well as the mass of η_h^n have been observed when the TBC is imposed. In addition, for the domain extended by 100 [km] in the vertical direction, it has been confirmed that there is no significant effect of changing the position of the transmission boundary (cf. Section 4.2). From these numerical experiments, we conclude that our two-step Lagrange–Galerkin scheme, cf. Equation (5), works well numerically not only for a simple domain but also for a complex domain with the TBC if the bottom topography is flat. We note that the TBC is employed in this paper based on the theoretical stability study in [9,10], while the numerical results by the TBC and the RBC are similar (cf. Appendix B). In our forthcoming paper, Part II, the scheme will be applied to rapidly varying bottom surfaces and a real bottom topography of the Bay of Bengal region to investigate the effect of non-homogeneity of the bottom topography. In addition to the effect of the non-homogeneous bottom topography, there are other effects for developing an accurate storm surge prediction, e.g., the Coriolis and the bottom friction forces and the wind stresses, which will be the future work.

Author Contributions: M.M.R. and H.N. wrote the main manuscript text. M.M.M., M.K. and H.N. contributed to the study conceptualization. M.M.R., E.R.W. and H.N. contributed to the development and implementation of the high-order scheme. All authors have read and agreed to the published version of the manuscript.

Funding: M.M.R. is supported by the Japanese Government (Monbukagakusho: MEXT) Scholarship. This work is partially supported by JSPS KAKENHI Grant Numbers JP20KK0058, JP21H00999, JP20H00117, JP20H01812, JP18H01135, JP21H04431, and JP20H01823, and JST CREST Grant Number JPMJCR2014.

Data Availability Statement: Data can be available on request.

Conflicts of Interest: The authors declare no conflict of interest.

Abbreviations

The following abbreviations are used in this manuscript:

RBC	Radiation boundary condition
TBC	Transmission boundary condition
SWEs	Shallow water equations
EOC	Experimental order of convergence
LG1	Single-step Lagrange–Galerkin scheme of first order in time
LG2	Two-step Lagrange–Galerkin scheme of second order in time

Appendix A. Choice of c_0

Based on [9], focusing on the potential energy $\mathcal{E}_2(t)$, cf. Equation (6), we perform numerical experiments for the choice of c_0 for two cases with the following settings:

- Case I (the square domain). In problem (3), we set $\Omega = (0,10)^2$, $T = 100$, $g = 9.8 \times 10^{-3}$, $\rho = 10^{12}$, $\mu = \zeta = 1$, $(f,F) = (0,0)$, $c = 10^{-3}$, $\eta^0 = c\exp(-100|x-p|^2)$, $p = (5,5)^\top$, $u^0 = 0$ and $\Gamma = \Gamma_T$ ($\Gamma_D = \emptyset$). We employ discretization parameters, $N = 200$ ($h = 1/N$), and $\Delta t = 0.25\sqrt{h}$.
- Case II (the Bay of Bengal). The parameters are the same as Example 4 except the value of c_0. We employ the same mesh and Δt (=0.2) in Section 4.

For $\eta_h = \{\eta_h^n\}_{n=1}^{N_T}$, let $\|\eta_h\|_{\ell^2(L^2)}$ be a norm of η_h defined by

$$\|\eta_h\|_{\ell^2(L^2)} := \sqrt{\Delta t \sum_{n=1}^{N_T} \|\eta_h^n\|_{L^2(\Omega)}^2} \quad (\approx \|\eta\|_{L^2(0,T;L^2(\Omega))}).$$

We compute the two cases for $c_0 = 0.5, 0.6, \ldots,$ and 1.2. The results are shown in Table A1 and imply that, for both cases, we have minimum values of $\|\eta_h\|_{\ell^2(L^2)}$ for $c_0 = 0.9$.

Table A1. Values of c_0 and $\|\eta_h\|_{\ell^2(L^2)}$.

	$\|\eta_h\|_{\ell^2(L^2)}$	
Value of c_0	**Case I (the Square Domain)**	**Case II (the Bay of Bengal)**
0.5	8.16×10^{-2}	13.55
0.6	8.08×10^{-2}	13.54
0.7	8.03×10^{-2}	13.5342
0.8	8.002×10^{-2}	13.5323
0.9	7.997×10^{-2}	13.5319
1.0	8.006×10^{-2}	13.5328
1.1	8.02×10^{-2}	13.5354
1.2	8.05×10^{-2}	13.5375

Appendix B. Comparison with Radiation Type Open Boundary Condition

For the comparison, we consider the same problem settings of Case I and Case II in Appendix A. We compare the TBC (with $c_0 = 0.9$) and a modified TBC (with $c_0 = 1$) with the RBC Equation (9) used for the Bay of Bengal in [1–8] by focusing on the values of $\|\eta_h\|_{\ell^2(L^2)}$. Table A2 shows the values, which are all similar, while the smallest value is obtained by the TBC (with $c_0 = 0.9$) employed in this paper. Figure A1 shows the graphs of $\|\eta_h^n\|_{L^2(\Omega)}$ ($\approx \|\eta(\cdot,t^n)\|_{L^2(\Omega)}$) for further information.

Table A2. Valuesof $\|\eta_h\|_{\ell^2(L^2)}$ for different boundary conditions for Case I and Case II.

	$\|\eta_h\|_{\ell^2(L^2)}$	
Boundary Condition	**Case I (the Square Domain)**	**Case II (the Bay of Bengal)**
TBC	7.997×10^{-2}	13.5316
modified TBC with $c_0 = 1$	8.006×10^{-2}	13.5328
RBC	8.007×10^{-2}	13.5334

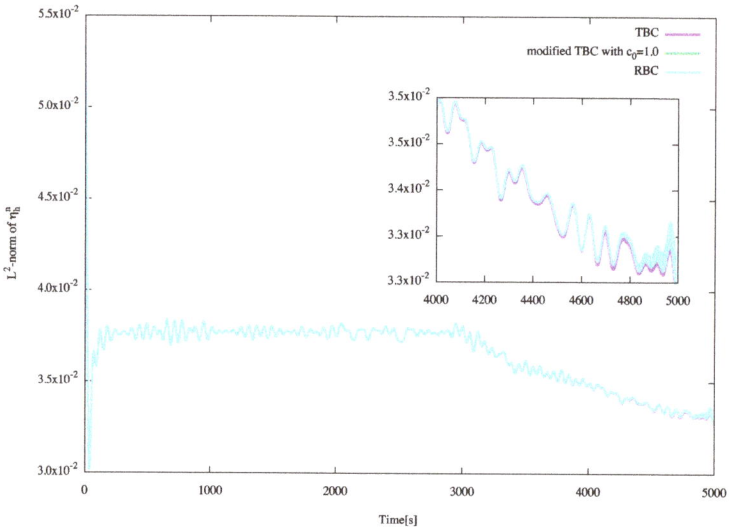

Figure A1. Graphs of $L^2(\Omega)$-norm of η_h^n for different boundary conditions for Case II (the Bay of Bengal).

References

1. Debsarma, S.K. Simulations of storm surges in the Bay of Bengal. *Mar. Geod.* **2009**, *32*, 178–198. [CrossRef]
2. Das, P.K. Prediction Model for Storm Surges in the Bay of Bengal. *Nature* **1972**, *239*, 211–213. [CrossRef]
3. Johns, B. Numerical simulation of storm surges in the Bay of Bengal. In *Monsoon Dynamics*; Cambridge University Press: Cambridge, UK, 1981; pp. 689–706.
4. Roy, G.; Kabir, A.H.; Mandal, M.; Haque, M. Polar coordinates shallow water storm surge model for the coast of Bangladesh. *Dyn. Atmos. Ocean.* **1999**, *29*, 397–413. [CrossRef]
5. Paul, G.C.; Ismail, A.I.M. Tide–surge interaction model including air bubble effects for the coast of Bangladesh. *J. Frankl. Inst.* **2012**, *349*, 2530–2546. [CrossRef]
6. Paul, G.C.; Ismail, A.I.M. Contribution of offshore islands in the prediction of water levels due to tide–surge interaction for the coastal region of Bangladesh. *Nat. Hazards* **2013**, *65*, 13–25. [CrossRef]
7. Paul, G.C.; Senthilkumar, S.; Pria, R. Storm surge simulation along the Meghna estuarine area: An alternative approach. *Acta Oceanol. Sin.* **2018**, *37*, 40–49. [CrossRef]
8. Dube, S.; Sinha, P.; Roy, G. Numerical simulation of storm surges in Bangladesh using a bay-river coupled model. *Coast. Eng.* **1986**, *10*, 85–101. [CrossRef]
9. Murshed, M.M.; Futai, K.; Kimura, M.; Notsu, H. Theoretical and numerical studies for energy estimates of the shallow water equations with a transmission boundary condition. *Discret. Contin. Dyn. Syst.-S* **2021**, *14*, 1063–1078. [CrossRef]
10. Murshed, M.M. Theoretical and Numerical Studies of the Shallow Water Equations with a Transmission Boundary Condition. Ph.D. Thesis, Kanazawa University, Kanazawa, Japan, 2019.
11. Sommerfeld, A. *Partial Differential Equations: Lectures in Theoretical Physics;* Academic Press: Cambridge, MA, USA, 1949; Volume 6.
12. Orlanski, I. A simple boundary condition for unbounded hyperbolic flows. *J. Comput. Phys.* **1976**, *21*, 251–269. [CrossRef]
13. Røed, L.P.; Cooper, C.K. Open Boundary Conditions in Numerical Ocean Models. *Adv. Phys. Oceanogr. Numer. Model.* **1986**, *186*, 411–436.
14. Jensen, T.G. Open boundary conditions in stratified ocean models. *J. Mar. Syst.* **1998**, *16*, 297–322. [CrossRef]
15. Kanayama, H.; Dan, H. Tsunami Propagation from the open sea to the coast. In *Tsunami*; IntechOpen: London, UK, 2016.

16. Kanayama, H.; Dan, H. A finite element scheme for two-layer viscous shallow-water equations. *Jpn. J. Ind. Appl. Math.* **2006**, *23*, 163–191. [CrossRef]
17. Ewing, R.; Russell, T. Multistep Galerkin methods along characteristics for convection-diffusion problems. In *Advances in Computer Methods for Partial Differential Equations IV*; Vichnevetsky, R., Stepleman, R., Eds.; IMACS : New Brunswick, NJ, USA, 1981; pp. 28–36.
18. Douglas, J.J.; Russell, T.F. Numerical Methods for Convection-Dominated Diffusion Problems Based on Combining the Method of Characteristics with Finite Element or Finite Difference Procedures. *SIAM J. Numer. Anal.* **1982**, *19*, 871–885. [CrossRef]
19. Pironneau, O. On the transport-diffusion algorithm and its applications to the Navier-Stokes equations. *Numer. Math.* **1982**, *38*, 309–332. [CrossRef]
20. Rui, H.; Tabata, M. A mass-conservative characteristic finite element scheme for convection-diffusion problems. *J. Sci. Comput.* **2010**, *43*, 416–432. [CrossRef]
21. Ewing, R.; Russell, T.; Wheeler, M. Simulation of miscible displacement using mixed methods and a modified method of characteristics. In *Proceedings of the Seventh Reservoir Simulation Symposium*; Society of Petroleum Engineers of AIME: San Francisco, CA, USA, 1983; pp. 71–81.
22. Süli, E. Convergence and nonlinear stability of the Lagrange-Galerkin method for the Navier-Stokes equations. *Numer. Math.* **1988**, *53*, 459–483. [CrossRef]
23. Pironneau, O. *Finite Element Methods for Fluids*; John Wiley & Sons: Chichester, UK, 1989.
24. Boukir, K.; Maday, Y.; Métivet, B.; Razafindrakoto, E. A high-order characteristics/finite element method for the incompressible Navier–Stokes equations. *Int. J. Numer. Methods Fluids* **1997**, *25*, 1421–1454. [CrossRef]
25. Achdou, Y.; Guermond, J.L. Convergence analysis of a finite element projection/Lagrange–Galerkin method for the incompressible Navier–Stokes equations. *SIAM J. Numer. Anal.* **2000**, *37*, 799–826. [CrossRef]
26. Rui, H.; Tabata, M. A second order characteristic finite element scheme for convection-diffusion problems. *Numer. Math.* **2002**, *92*, 161–177. [CrossRef]
27. Bermúdez, A.; Nogueiras, M.R.; Vázquez, C. Numerical analysis of convection-diffusion-reaction problems with higher order characteristics/finite elements. Part I: Time Discretization. *SIAM J. Numer. Anal.* **2006**, *44*, 1829–1853. [CrossRef]
28. Bermúdez, A.; Nogueiras, M.R.; Vázquez, C. Numerical analysis of convection-diffusion-reaction problems with higher order characteristics/finite elements. Part II: Fully discretized scheme and quadrature formulas. *SIAM J. Numer. Anal.* **2006**, *44*, 1854–1876. [CrossRef]
29. Chrysafinos, K.; Walkington, N.J. Lagrangian and moving mesh methods for the convection diffusion equation. *ESAIM Math. Model. Numer. Anal.* **2008**, *42*, 25–55. [CrossRef]
30. Notsu, H. Numerical computations of cavity flow problems by a pressure stabilized characteristic-curve finite element scheme. *Trans. Jpn. Soc. Comput. Eng. Sci.* **2008**, *2008*, 20080032.
31. Pironneau, O.; Tabata, M. Stability and convergence of a Galerkin-characteristics finite element scheme of lumped mass type. *Int. J. Numer. Methods Fluids* **2010**, *64*, 1240–1253. [CrossRef]
32. Benítez, M.; Bermúdez, A. A second order characteristics finite element scheme for natural convection problems. *J. Comput. Appl. Math.* **2011**, *235*, 3270–3284. [CrossRef]
33. Benítez, M.; Bermúdez, A. Numerical analysis of a second order pure Lagrange–Galerkin method for convection-diffusion problems. Part I: Time discretization. *SIAM J. Numer. Anal.* **2012**, *50*, 858–882. [CrossRef]
34. Benítez, M.; Bermúdez, A. Numerical analysis of a second order pure Lagrange–Galerkin method for convection-diffusion problems. Part II: Fully discretized scheme and numerical results. *SIAM J. Numer. Anal.* **2012**, *50*, 2824–2844. [CrossRef]
35. Bermejo, R.; Saavedra, L. Modified Lagrange–Galerkin methods of first and second order in time for convection-diffusion problems. *Numer. Mathematik* **2012**, *120*, 601–638. [CrossRef]
36. Bermejo, R.; Gálan del Sastre, P.; Saavedra, L. A second order in time modified Lagrange–Galerkin finite element method for the incompressible Navier–Stokes equations. *SIAM J. Numer. Anal.* **2012**, *50*, 3084–3109. [CrossRef]
37. Notsu, H.; Rui, H.; Tabata, M. Development and L2-Analysis of a Single-Step Characteristics Finite Difference Scheme of Second Order in Time for Convection-Diffusion Problems. *J. Algorithms Comput. Technol.* **2013**, *7*, 343–380. [CrossRef]
38. Notsu, H.; Tabata, M. Error Estimates of a Pressure-Stabilized Characteristics Finite Element Scheme for the Oseen Equations. *J. Sci. Comput.* **2015**, *65*, 940–955. [CrossRef]
39. Notsu, H.; Tabata, M. Error estimates of a stabilized Lagrange–Galerkin scheme for the Navier–Stokes equations. *ESAIM Math. Model. Numer. Anal.* **2016**, *50*, 361–380. [CrossRef]
40. Notsu, H.; Tabata, M. Error Estimates of a Stabilized Lagrange–Galerkin Scheme of Second-Order in Time for the Navier–Stokes Equations. In *Mathematical Fluid Dynamics, Present and Future Springer Proceedings in Mathematics & Statistics*; Springer: Berlin, Germany, 2016; pp. 497–530.
41. Tabata, M.; Uchiumi, S. A genuinely stable Lagrange–Galerkin scheme for convection-diffusion problems. *Jpn. J. Ind. Appl. Math.* **2016**, *33*, 121–143. [CrossRef]
42. Lukáčová-Medvid'ová, M.; Notsu, H.; She, B. Energy dissipative characteristic schemes for the diffusive Oldroyd-B viscoelastic fluid. *Int. J. Numer. Methods Fluids* **2015**, *81*, 523–557. [CrossRef]

43. Lukáčová-Medvid'ová, M.; Mizerová, H.; Notsu, H.; Tabata, M. Numerical analysis of the Oseen-type Peterlin viscoelastic model by the stabilized Lagrange–Galerkin method, Part I: A linear scheme. *ESAIM Math. Model. Numer. Anal.* **2017**, *51*, 1637–1661. [CrossRef]
44. Lukáčová-Medvid'ová, M.; Mizerová, H.; Notsu, H.; Tabata, M. Numerical analysis of the Oseen-type Peterlin viscoelastic model by the stabilized Lagrange–Galerkin method, Part II: A nonlinear scheme. *ESAIM Math. Model. Numer. Anal.* **2017**, *51*, 1663–1689. [CrossRef]
45. Tabata, M.; Uchiumi, S. An exactly computable Lagrange–Galerkin scheme for the Navier–Stokes equations and its error estimates. *Math. Comput.* **2018**, *87*, 39–67. [CrossRef]
46. Uchiumi, S. A viscosity-independent error estimate of a pressure-stabilized Lagrange–Galerkin scheme for the Oseen problem. *J. Sci. Comput.* **2019**, *80*, 834–858. [CrossRef]
47. Colera, M.; Carpio, J.; Bermejo, R. A nearly-conservative high-order Lagrange–Galerkin method for the resolution of scalar convection-dominated equations in non-divergence-free velocity fields. *Comput. Methods Appl. Mech. Eng.* **2020**, *372*, 113366. [CrossRef]
48. Colera, M.; Carpio, J.; Bermejo, R. A nearly-conservative, high-order, forward Lagrange–Galerkin method for the resolution of scalar hyperbolic conservation laws. *Comput. Methods Appl. Mech. Eng.* **2021**, *376*, 113654. [CrossRef]
49. Futai, K.; Kolbe, N.; Notsu, H.; Suzuki, T. A mass-preserving two-step Lagrange–Galerkin scheme for convection-diffusion problems. *J. Sci. Comput.* **2022**, *92*, 37. [CrossRef]
50. Hecht, F. New development in FreeFem++. *J. Numer. Math.* **2012**, *20*, 251–265. [CrossRef]

Σ mathematics

MDPI

Article

Simulation of Electromagnetic Forming Process and Optimization of Geometric Parameters of Perforated Al Sheet Using RSM

Nilesh Satonkar [1] **and Venkatachalam Gopalan** [2,*]

[1] School of Mechanical Engineering, Vellore Institute of Technology, Chennai 600127, India; nilesh.nandkumar2016@vitstudent.ac.in
[2] Centre for Innovation and Product Development, Vellore Institute of Technology, Chennai 600127, India
* Correspondence: g.venkatachalam@vit.ac.in

Abstract: Electromagnetic forming (EMF) is a kind of high-speed forming technology that can be useful for materials like aluminum. EMF helps to overcome the limitations of traditional forming. Due to this ability, the use of EMF in automotive applications has risen in recent years. The application of finite element software packages such as ANSYS 22 gives numerical modelling capabilities to simulate the EMF process and to design the forming process. Hence, the aim of this research work is to build and study the three-dimensional finite element model for the electromagnetic forming process and analyze the geometric parameters influencing the deformation of the perforated sheet with a design of experiments (DOE) approach. The finite element simulation is used in two stages. In the first stage, the electromagnetic force or Lorentz force striking the workpiece (i.e., Al sheet) is predicted using the ANSYS 22 Emag module. In the second stage, the predicted Lorentz force is then applied on an Al sheet to calculate the sheet deformation. The deformation of the sheet is predicted for different combinations of the geometric parameters of the sheet, such as open area percentage, ligament ratio (LR) and size of the hole, using ANSYS 22 Structural. In the DOE, response surface methodology (RSM) is used by considering the geometric parameters of perforated sheet such as open area percentage, ligament ratio (LR) and size of the hole. To minimize the number of experiments, an RSM model named central composite design (CCD) is employed. Further, the optimization study finds that the maximum deformation 0.0435 mm is calculated for the optimized combination of 25% open area, 0.14 LR and 4 mm hole size.

Keywords: electromagnetic forming; finite element method; numerical simulation; Lorentz force; design of experiments

MSC: 65-04; 65-11; 65K10

1. Introduction

In the electromagnetic forming (EMF) process, metal sheets are deformed by using repulsive force created between the opposite magnetic fields in adjacent conductors. When a pulsed current passes through the coil, it generates transient magnetic field which in turn induces eddy currents in the metallic workpiece opposite to the direction of the current passing through the coil. Due to the induced eddy current, a repulsive force is generated between the work piece and the forming coil, which causes the deformation of the workpiece.

This repulsive force causes the workpiece to stress beyond its yield limit, so that the workpiece is shaped permanently at high strain rates. In order to design an EMF system successfully and analyze its performance, appropriate numerical methods must be used in order to have cost effective industrial applications. For calculating the magnetic forces, a three-dimensional (3D) finite element model is created. To determine the deformation, this generated magnetic force is applied to a perforated aluminum 5052 sheet.

1.1. Working Principle of EMF

In electromagnetic forming, Lorentz forces (magnetic forces) are used to deform metallic sheets at high speeds. Figure 1a,b shows the set-up of the EMF process, consisting of a low inductance electrical circuit with large capacitance, which supplies electric current through a (forming) coil tool. Therefore, by Faraday's law of induction, the current induces a magnetic flux in the nearby conductor (workpiece), which generates eddy current. This eddy current induces magnetic forces, causing the deformation of the metal sheet (workpiece) beyond its elastic limit. The impulse electromagnetic system is used for different applications, including welding, compression or expansion of sheet metal tubes, and the forming of flat metal sheets (e.g., Figure 2) such as panels used in the automotive industry. The arrangement of an impulse electromagnetic forming system depends on the geometries of the forming coils and the geometry of the workpiece to be modified.

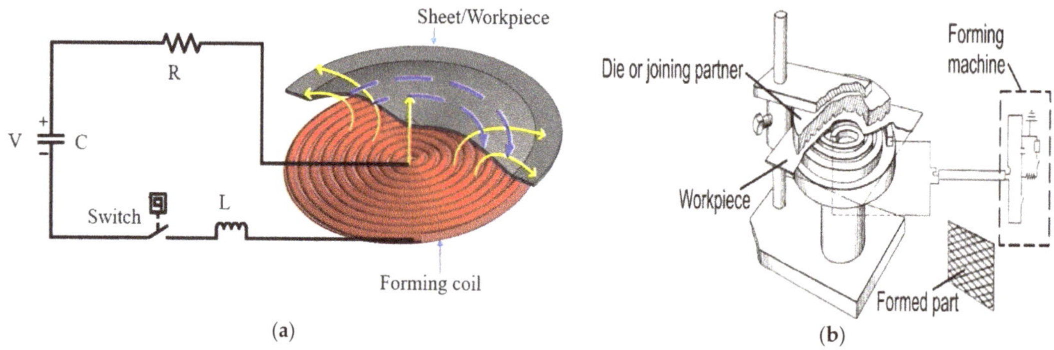

Figure 1. (**a**) Schematic representation of the EMF process (**b**) Set- up of the EMF process.

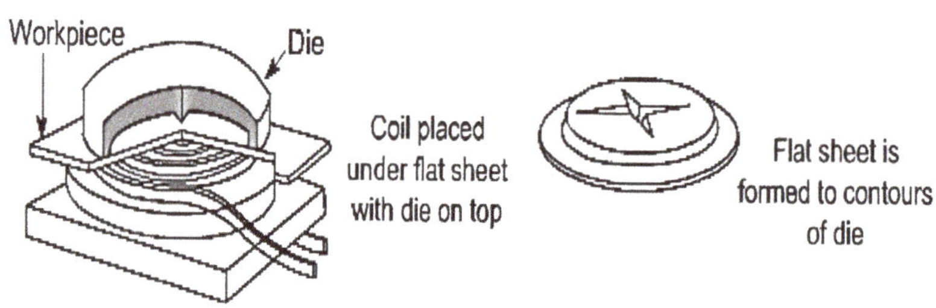

Figure 2. Electromagnetic flat sheet forming.

The fundamental equations representing the electromagnetic fields are governed by Maxwell, as given in Equations (1)–(5) [1].

$$\Delta \times \overline{E} = -\frac{d\overline{B}}{\mathrm{dt}} \tag{1}$$

$$\Delta \times \overline{H} = \overline{J} \tag{2}$$

$$\Delta \cdot \overline{B} = 0 \tag{3}$$

$$\overline{B} = \mu \overline{H} \tag{4}$$

$$\Delta \cdot \overline{J} = 0 \tag{5}$$

where, $\overline{E}$ is the electric field, $\overline{H}$ is the magnetic field intensity, $\overline{B}$ is the magnetic field density, μ is the permeability, $\overline{F}$ is the Lorentz force, and $\overline{J}$ is the current density.

The current density dependence can be represented per Equation (6):

$$\bar{J} = \sigma\bar{E}, \tag{6}$$

in which σ is the electrical conductivity of workpiece.

In 1895, Lorentz stated that the force density ($\bar{F}$) acting on the workpiece depends upon the magnetic flux density ($\bar{B}$), generated due to the supplied current density ($\bar{J}$), given as:

$$\bar{F} = \bar{J} \times \bar{B} \tag{7}$$

1.2. Existing Research Efforts

Furth and Waniek [2] first introduced the electromagnetic forming by which the workpiece is pushed away from the tool coil. The authors suggested using two different coils to establish pulling forces, which in turn allow the formation of bulges on hollow workpieces or large sheets.

Kleiner et al. [3] analyzed the effects of process parameters such as strain rate and magnetic pressure on workpiece deformation for tubular as well as flat sheet workpieces. Meriched et al.'s [4] investigation developed a numerical technique to solve the three coupled problems: electric circuit analysis, electromagnetic force and the deformation of a circular thin sheet using a flat spiral coil. Fenton et al. [5] used a computer code ALE (Arbitrary Lagrangian–Eulerian) to simulate the EMF process. They validated the simulation results of deformation of a thin aluminum sheet using two dimensional axi-symmetric models with experimental results. Zhang et al. [6] simulated a 2D axi-symmetric model in the COMSOL Multiphysics software package, and analyzed the dynamic behavior of a sheet metal workpiece. Reese et al. [7] focused on the use of coarse mesh, with which the accuracy of the numerical solution can be increased. It also reduced the computational time by reducing the gauss points. This reduced integration and hourglass stabilization method may be used to couple the mechanical and electromagnetic fields more efficiently. Mamalis et al. [8] used the ANSYS finite element code and LS-DYNA software to model a 2D axi-symmetric aluminum alloy sheet using a loose coupling approach. The authors also validated the current numerical model with experimental results using an equivalent circuit method.

Another 2D finite element model was developed by Luca [9], using FLUX2D software. The stresses and strains on the AlMn0.5Mg0.5 sheet are calculated using the ALGOR software. These numerical simulation results were compared with the EMF experiment and found to be in good agreement with each other.

Siddiqui et al. [10] considered the simulation of the electromagnetic forming process as two separate problems, i.e., an electromagnetic problem and a mechanical problem. The magnetic forces were predicted with the help of a finite element code named FEMM4.0. These forces were taken as the input boundary condition, and by a subroutine VDLOAD, were then applied to a finite element model with commercial FE software ABAQUS/Explicit. Unger et al. [11] investigated the coupled multi-field formulation of the electromagnetic forming process with which a thermo-magneto-mechanical model was developed, and simulation was performed on an aluminum alloy (AA 6005) plate. Denga et al. [12] studied electromagnetic attractive force forming, in which ANSYS software was used to simulate a 2D axisymmetric model. Along the flat coil, magnetic flux was distributed and validated with the experiment results, indicating that the workpiece was attracted to the coil and moved quickly.

Khandelwal et al. [13] performed experimental and numerical analyses of EMF on aluminum tubes. They considered discharge energy, standoff distance (gap between workpiece and coil) and workpiece thickness as influencing parameters on the workpiece's deformation using an ANOVA approach. Imbert et al. [14] employed a commercial FEA package LS-DYNA to carry out numerical simulation of EMF process on conical and V-shaped AA 5754 sheets. For both models, the numerical and experimental results were compared and found to be in good agreement. The authors concluded that the formability of the sheets was improved due to the reduction in tool–sheet interaction. To explore the numerical approaches to the EMF process, Parez et al. [15] used software such as Maxwell 3D, Sysmagna® and Pam-Stamp2G. These pieces of software were used to model sequential coupling and loose coupling, and their results were validated with experimental results carried out on an Al 1050 sheet.

Siddiqui et al. [16] carried out numerical simulation of an Al 1050 aluminum tube, with the help of FE code FORTRAN and FEA software FEMM. The results were compared with experimental results from earlier literature. Then, these numerical results were introduced in FEA software ABAQUS/Explicit to predict the electromagnetic tube expansion process. Bahmani et al. [17] used field shapers to concentrate the magnetic field at required points of metal sheet. They concluded that in 3D modeling of the EMF process, the magnitude of magnetic flux density generated is greater than 2D axisymmetric simulation by 15%. Haiping et al. [18] formulated a sequential coupling approach to model a 2D axisymmetric electromagnetic model in ANSYS for the process of electromagnetic tube compression. They analyzed the effect of tube deformation on electromagnetic geometry so that accuracy of simulation would be improved.

Xu et al. [19] focused on using various meshing types in the simulation of the EMF process in order to reduce the computational time and increase the accuracy of numerical simulation. They also concluded that due to the use of a regular progressive meshing method, there is a reduction in the computational time. Ahmed et al. [20] placed emphasis on the design of the forming coil, which helped to distribute the magnetic forces properly along the workpiece. The authors used ANSYS software to perform electromagnetic simulation. Additionally, they investigated the current density and distribution of magnetic forces.

Psyk et al. [21] reviewed various aspects of electromagnetic forming such as the process principle, influential process parameters, workpiece deformation and various industrial applications. The authors also reviewed the various research articles on process analysis, analytical analysis, numerical analysis and experimental analysis of electromagnetic forming.

Bhole et al. [22] studied the stress and strain generated in tool–sheet interactions, as well as the formability improvement of ALU5754MF and ALU5182MF metal sheets. The authors created a numerical model for the EMF process using LS-DYNA explicit finite element code. They calculated the strain distributions on workpieces at various levels of discharge energy, which produced points of failure. Qiu et al. [23] used pieces of finite element software such as COMSOL multiphysics and FLUX to develop numerical models of the EMF process. The authors concluded that when the workpiece velocity is above 200 m/s, the effect of workpiece motion on forming velocity should be taken into account.

Since a loosely coupled approach gives accurate simulation results within short period of time, Abdelhafeez et al. [24] focused on using it to simulate the electromagnetic forming process. The authors developed two material hardening models named the Steinberg model and the rate-dependent power law model. The numerical simulation results of these models were compared with the experimental results of Takatsu et al. [25]/Fenton and Daehn [5], and found to be in good agreement. Deng et al. [26] proposed the electromagnetic punching–flanging (EMPF) process for 6061 Al alloy sheets, along with electromagnetic-mechanical-fracture numerical simulation of them. This numerical model predicted the electromagnetic punching–flanging process. It also established the relationship between flange deformations and discharge energies. Xu et al. [27] focused on electromagnetic blanking's ability to make high-quality, no-burr diaphragm parts. In conclusion, electromagnetically driven loading was used to finish both the punching and the flanging. In order to achieve precise control of the forming process, Yan et al. [28] investigated the impact of the induced eddy current in electromagnetic forming (EMF). To forecast the current-carrying dynamic deformation behaviors of aluminum alloy bands, they created a semi-phenomenological model.

From the literature, it can be concluded that very few researchers have attempted three-dimensional finite element modeling of the EMF process. In this research work, the study and analysis of perforated aluminum sheet metals is carried out by applying the electromagnetic forming process in two stages. In the first stage (electromagnetic analysis), the magnetic force (also called the Lorentz force) is generated by applying current density to the forming coil. In the second stage (structural analysis), the generated Lorentz force is applied to an aluminum 5052 perforated sheet to study deformation.

2. Modeling and Finite Element Simulation

To simulate the electromagnetic forming process, the result of Asati et al. [29] is referred to. Firstly, a two-dimensional (2D) finite element (FE) model is created axi-symmetrically. In order to validate this finite element model, it is compared with the results of Asati et al. [29]. Based on these results, the authors developed a three-dimensional (3D) simulation of the EMF process and calculated the deformation of a perforated aluminum sheet workpiece. Figure 3 shows the flow chart of steps followed.

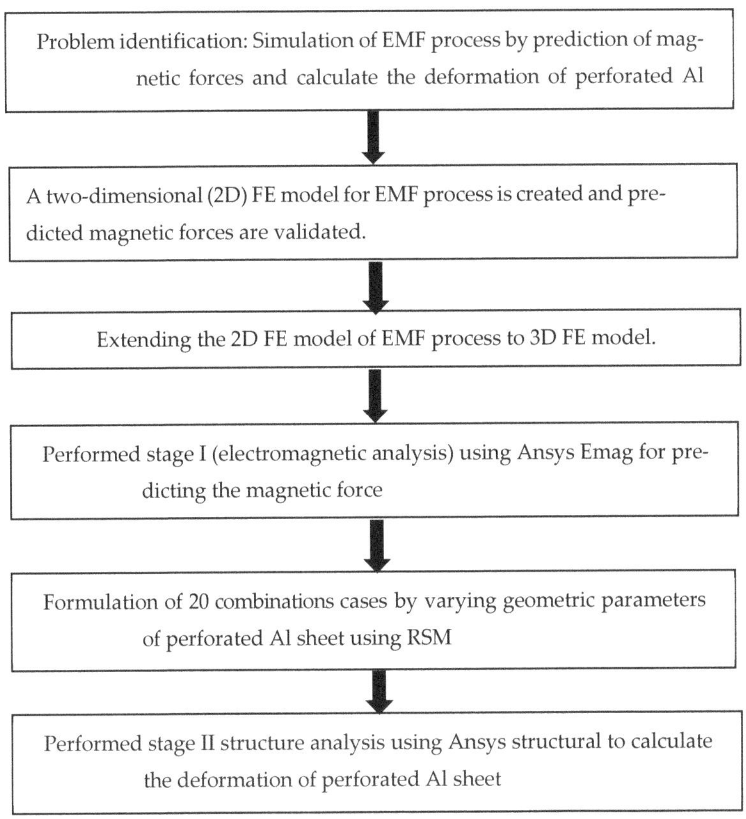

Figure 3. Flow chart of the research work.

2.1. Geometric Parameters of the Perforated Sheet

Perforated sheets (dimension 156 mm × 156 mm × 1.5 mm) of a rectangular shape with circular holes are considered for the structural analysis. The modeled commercial aluminum 5052 sheet for the sample (Run 1) is shown in Figure 4. The sheet has a Poisson's ratio and Young's modulus of 0.27 and 70 GPa, respectively. Venkatachalam et al. [30] studied the influential geometrical parameters of the perforated sheet, such as the open area percentage, ligament ratio and hole size. The open area is a ratio that reflects how much of the sheet is occupied by holes, normally expressed by a percentage. The ligament ratio is the ratio of ligament width to perforation pitch. Ligament width is the distance between the boundaries of two successive holes, whereas the perforation pitch is the distance between the center points of two successive holes. The open areas considered are 5%, 10%, 15%, 20% and 25%. For the study, ligament ratios of 0.14, 0.2, 0.25, 0.29 and 0.33 are used. The third geometrical measure is the diameter of a circular hole, which is taken as 4 mm, 8 mm, 12 mm, 16 mm and 20 mm.

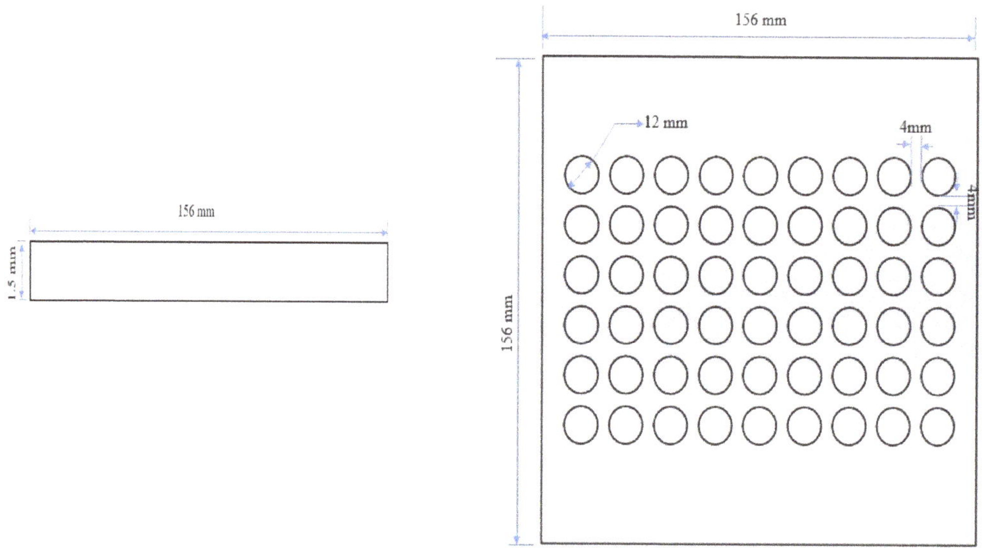

Figure 4. Perforated sheet (for Run 1).

2.2. Two-Dimensional (2D) Finite Element Model

The electromagnetic forming process simulation and computation of Lorentz force (magnetic force) is achieved using commercial FEA software ANSYS 22 Emag. With reference to literature results from Asati et al. [29], a two-dimensional (2D) FE model is created axi- symmetrically, as shown in Figure 5. The geometric parameters are given in Table 1. Four noded axi-symmetric elements (PLANE13) are used to simulate the mesh coil, workpiece (Sheet) and air region. The material properties that are assigned to simulate the electromagnetic forming process are given in Table 2. In this simulation, the model is discretized into 12,480 elements, with a total number of 12,717 nodes.

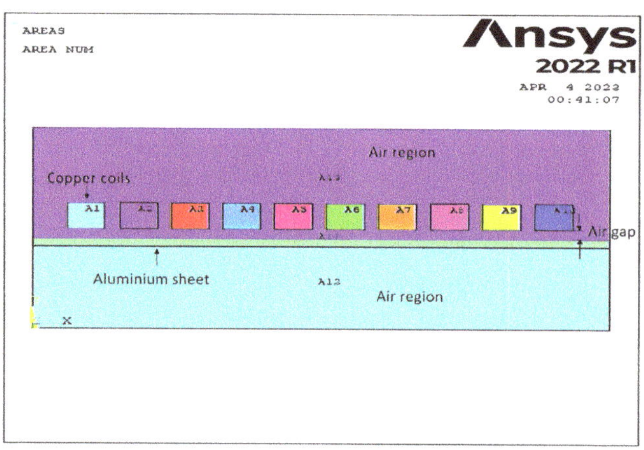

Figure 5. Finite element model.

Table 1. Geometric parameters for 2D model.

Geometric Parameters	Values
Length of the sheet (mm)	156
Thickness of the sheet (mm)	1.5
Number of coils	10
Size of the square coil (mm^2)	5×5

Table 2. Material properties of finite element model.

Material	Relative Permeability (μ)
Air	1
Copper (for forming coil)	0.999
Aluminum (for metal sheet)	1.003

The flux parallel boundary conditions are used, and current density (equal to 8000 A/m^2) is given as an input to the square-shaped copper coil with 10 turns, which induces a magnetic field. The magnetic force generated due to the forming coil is calculated. Figure 6 shows the meshed model. Figures 7–9 illustrate the magnetic force vector sum, a 2D flux line plot and a Vector plot, respectively. In order to validate this finite element model, it is compared with the results of Asati et al. [29], as shown in Table 3. The error percentage is 0.19%, which shows the accuracy of the present model.

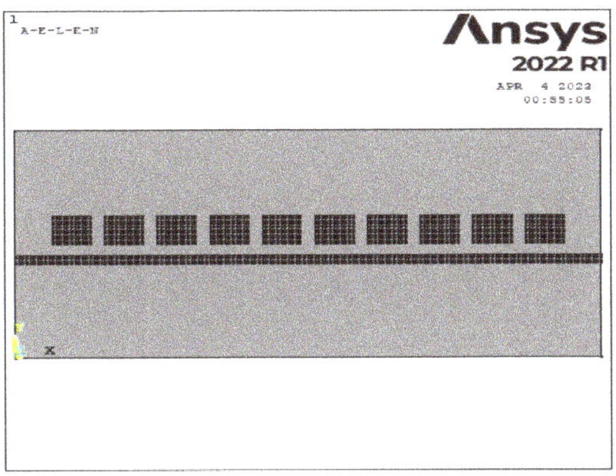

Figure 6. 2D Meshed model.

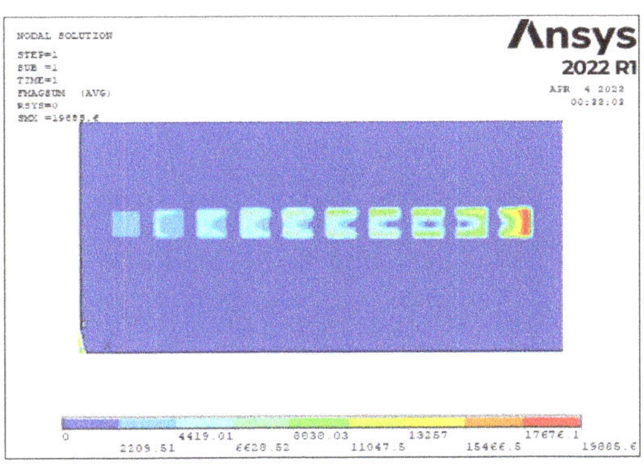

Figure 7. The magnetic force vector sum.

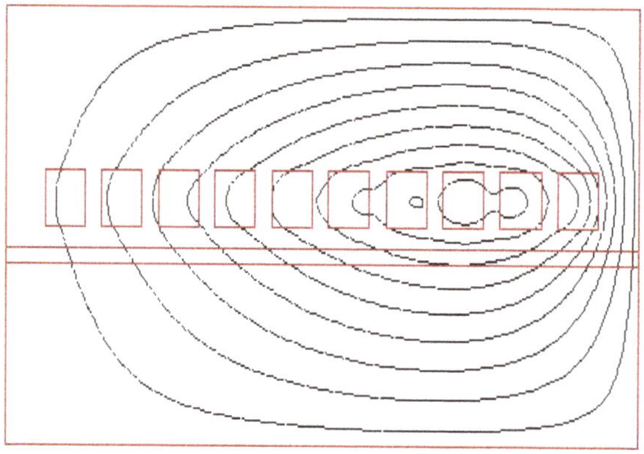

Figure 8. 2D flux lines.

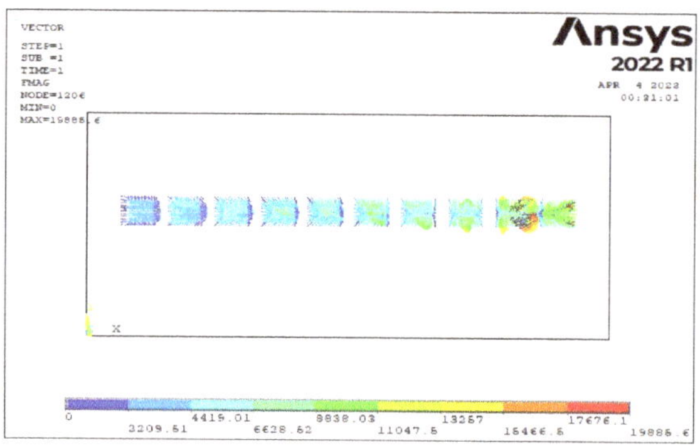

Figure 9. Vector plot.

Table 3. Comparison of the present finite element model with Asati et al. [29].

Process Parameters	Input Values	Magnetic Force Generated (N)		Error Percentage (%)
		Asati et al. [29]	Present 2D model	
Current density (A/m^2)	8000	19,923.9	19,885.6	0.192
Gap between sheet and coil (mm)	2			
Size of square coil (Length × Height) (mm^2)	5			

2.3. *Three-Dimensional (3D) Finite Element Model*

After the validation of the 2D finite element model, the same approach is extended to develop a three-dimensional simulation of the EMF process. The three-dimensional (3D) setup of the EMF system, as shown in Figure 10, is modelled in Solidworks 2021 and imported into ANSYS 22 Emag. The geometry details are given in Table 4. The material properties used are given in Table 5.

ANSYS 22 Emag software is used to simulate the 3D electromagnetic simulation. The electromagnetic force is generated after the current excitation of the forming coil. Figure 11 represents the finite element model of the EMF process. A SOLID97 element is used for meshing the forming coil, the Al sheet and the air region so that a magnetic field is propagated in the region. Over the outer surface area, the flux parallel boundary condition is provided. As shown in Figure 12, a magnetic field is created when a square-shaped copper coil with 10 turns is subjected to a current density of 13.75×10^6 A/m^2, which produces a Lorentz force of 300 N in the area. This force is given to a perforated aluminum sheet in the structural analysis to determine the sheet's deformation.

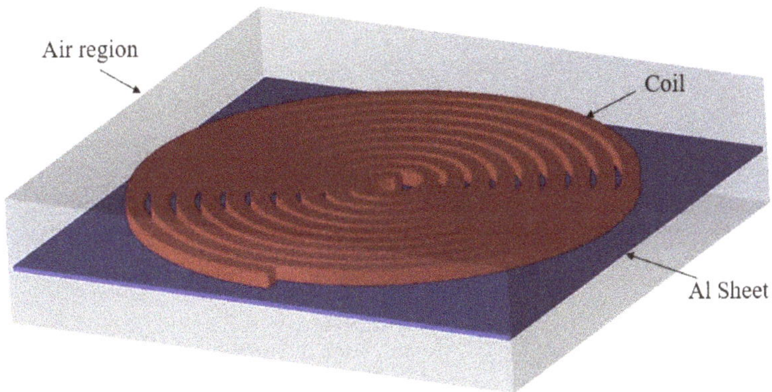

Figure 10. Three-dimensional setup of the Al sheet, forming the coil and air regions.

Table 4. Geometric parameters for 3D model.

Geometric Parameters	Values
Length of the sheet (mm)	156
Thickness of the sheet (mm)	1.5
Number of turns of coil	10
Cross-section of the square coil (mm^2)	5×5

Table 5. Material properties of the 3D finite element model.

Material	Relative Permeability (μ)
Air	1
Copper (for forming coil)	0.999
Aluminum (for metal sheet)	1.003

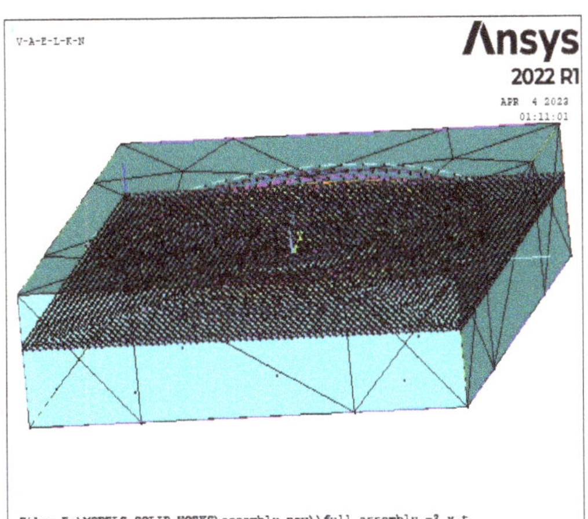

Figure 11. 3D Meshed model.

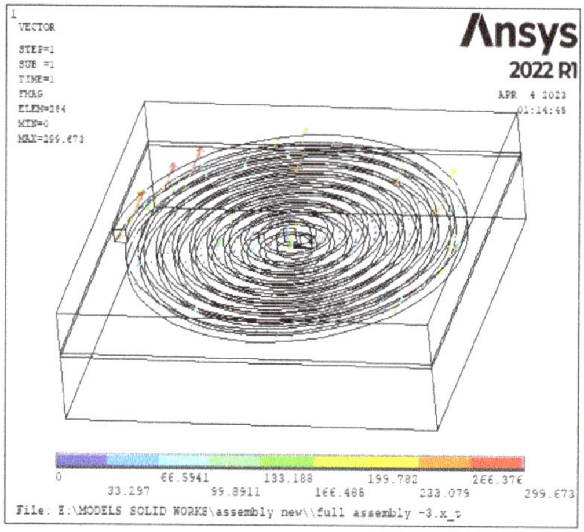

Figure 12. Magnetic force generated.

3. Structural Analysis

3.1. Design of Experiments and Optimization

In the RSM designs, the CCD (central composite design) is the most widely used design. In a minimum number of runs, it provides much information on variable effects and overall error. It consists of 20 points with 6 axial and 8 corner points. Five different levels of all three parameters are set. The levels of all three parameters are categorized as −2, −1, 0, 1 and 2 (Table 6). In Figure 13, the CCD with 20 simulation runs is shown. The influential geometric parameters of the perforated sheet are considered to be the open area percentage, ligament ratio and size of the hole. To perform the simulation, 20 different combinations (Runs) of open area percentage, ligament ratio and size of hole are found with the help of the DOE method. For each of these open area percentage, ligament ratio and size of the hole parameters, five different levels are considered. As depicted in Figure 13, the response surface methodology's central composite design (CCD) is employed.

After the end of stage I (electromagnetic analysis), the Lorentz force is obtained, and stage II (structural analysis) is used to determine the deformation and stresses in the sheet following the forming process. The generated Lorentz force from stage I is then applied to a perforated sheet to determine the deformation. The outcomes for Run 1 are shown in Figure 14.

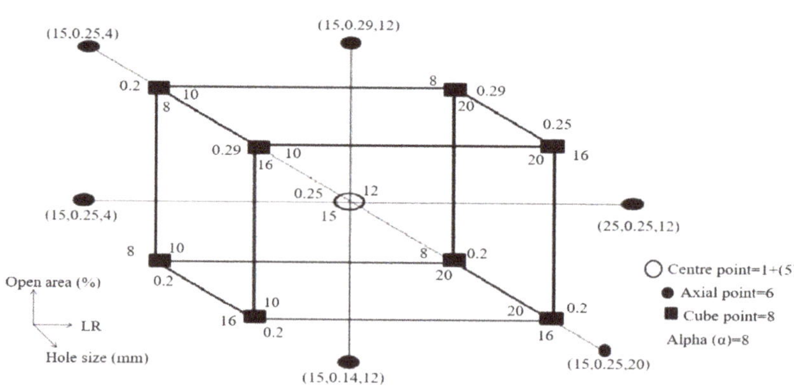

Figure 13. Central composite design.

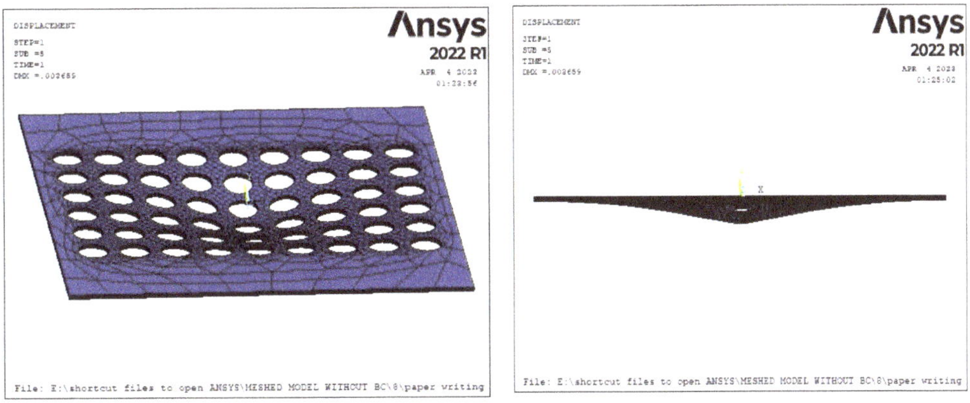

Figure 14. Deformed sheet.

Table 6. Geometric parameter levels.

Factors	Levels				
	−2	−1	0	1	2
Open area (%)	5	10	15	20	25
Ligament Ratio	0.14	0.2	0.25	0.29	0.33
Hole size (mm)	4	8	12	16	20

Figure 15 depicts the three-dimensional finite element model of the perforated aluminum sheet for Run 1. Solidworks 2021 software is used to build the geometric model, which is then imported into ANSYS 22 software. The nonlinear material properties of an Al 5052 sheet with a Poisson's ratio of 0.27 are included in numerical model.

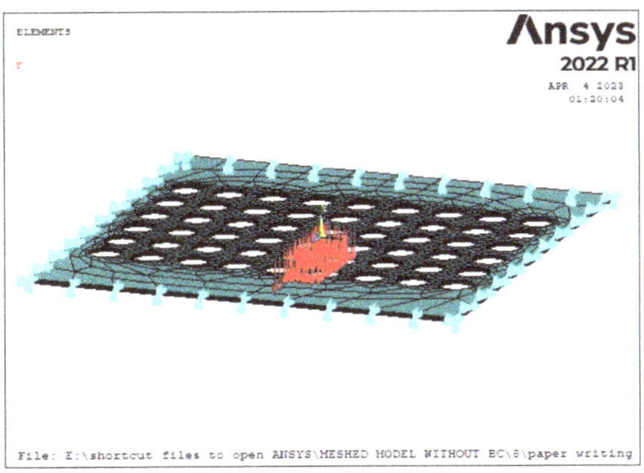

Figure 15. 3D finite element model (for Run 1).

The DOE table, i.e., Table 7, gives the number of simulations to be performed, and accordingly, the geometric models are created. With the help of ANSYS structural, the obtained Lorentz force (i.e., 300 N) from stage I (electromagnetic analysis) is applied, and the corresponding deformation is calculated for each sample model (combinations or runs). To determine the impact of three input geometrical parameters, namely the open area percentage, ligament ratio, and hole size, on the response parameter, i.e., deformation, the analysis of variance (ANOVA) technique is used. Table 8 displays the ANOVA findings. A regression equation that describes the connection between the response parameter and the input parameters is produced from the ANOVA. It also shows the relationships between the variables of the model. The ANOVA is performed with the help of MINITAB 19 software.

Table 7. DOE table representing different combinations and corresponding sheet deformation.

Run	Open Area (%)	Ligament Ratio	Hole Size (mm)	Deformation (mm) × (10^{-3})
1	25	0.25	12	3.6
2	15	0.25	20	0.75
3	5	0.25	12	0.61
4	10	0.29	8	1.7
5	15	0.25	12	1.4
6	15	0.25	12	1.4
7	15	0.14	12	5.8
8	10	0.2	8	2.2
9	15	0.25	12	1.4
10	15	0.25	4	5.4
11	15	0.25	12	1.4
12	10	0.29	16	0.53
13	15	0.25	12	1.4
14	20	0.2	8	18.5
15	15	0.33	12	1.1
16	15	0.25	12	1.4
17	20	0.29	16	1
18	20	0.29	8	5.7
19	10	0.2	16	0.9
20	20	0.2	16	1.6

Table 8. ANOVA results.

Source	DF	Adj SS	Adj MS	F-Value	*p*-Value
Model	9	0.000255	0.000028	5.14	0.009
Linear	3	0.000078	0.000026	4.72	0.027
Open area (%)	1	0.000041	0.000041	7.53	0.021
Ligament ratio	1	0.000005	0.000005	0.96	0.351
Hole size (mm)	1	0.000008	0.000008	1.44	0.257
Square	3	0.000010	0.000003	0.62	0.616
Open area (%) × Open area (%)	1	0.000002	0.000002	0.40	0.543
Ligament ratio × Ligament ratio	1	0.000005	0.000005	0.87	0.373
Hole size (mm) × Hole size (mm)	1	0.000007	0.000007	1.31	0.278
2-Way interaction	3	0.000090	0.000030	5.41	0.018
Open area (%) × Ligament ratio	1	0.000022	0.000022	4.04	0.072
Open area (%) × Hole size (mm)	1	0.000046	0.000046	8.30	0.016
Ligament ratio × Hole size (mm)	1	0.000021	0.000021	3.90	0.077
Error	10	0.000055	0.000006		
Lack-of-Fit	5	0.000055	0.000011		
Pure error	5	0.000000	0.000000		
Total	19	0.000310			

Where Adj SS—adjusted some of squares, DF–degrees of freedom, Adj MS—adjusted mean squares, with *p*-value guides to find the significance of results. The F-value helps to decide whether to "accept or reject" the hypothesis.

3.2. Regression Equation

The regression equation (Equation (8)) is a second-order polynomial equation obtained through MINITAB software. In this regression equation, the deformation of the Al sheet is calculated by substituting the corresponding values of open area percentage, ligament ratio and size of the hole for different samples, as shown in Table 9. Table 9 also contains the error percentage between the sheet deformation calculated from the finite element simulation (ANSYS Emag) and the regression equation.

$$\text{Deformation (mm)} = 0.0077 + 0.00325\,A - 0.124\,B - 0.00178\,C + 0.000012\,A^2 + 0.196\,B^2 + 0.000034\,C^2 - 0.00739\,AB - 0.000120\,AC + 0.00908\,BC \quad (8)$$

where A = percentage of open area, B = ligament ratio, and C = hole size.

Table 9. DOE table showing different combinations and deformation and error percentage.

Run	Open Area (%)	Ligament Ratio	Hole Size (mm)	Deformation (mm) × (10^{-3})		Error (%)
				Finite Element Simulation	Regression Equation	
1	25	0.25	12	3.6	3.98	9.54
2	15	0.25	20	0.75	0.714	3.46
3	5	0.25	12	0.61	0.624	2.24
4	10	0.29	8	1.7	1.68	1.17
5	15	0.25	12	1.4	1.51	7.28
6	15	0.25	12	1.4	1.51	7.28
7	15	0.14	12	5.8	6.3	8.62
8	10	0.2	8	2.2	2.5	1.01
9	15	0.25	12	1.4	1.51	7.28
10	15	0.25	4	5.4	6.1	10
11	15	0.25	12	1.4	1.51	7.28
12	10	0.29	16	0.53	0.49	9.43
13	15	0.25	12	1.4	1.51	7.28
14	20	0.2	8	18.5	17.2	7.02
15	15	0.33	12	1.1	1	9.03
16	15	0.25	12	1.4	1.51	7.28
17	20	0.29	16	1	0.98	2
18	20	0.29	8	5.7	5.91	9.98
19	10	0.2	16	0.9	0.89	1.9
20	20	0.2	16	1.6	1.75	9.3

Regression model compatibility is tested by comparing it with FEA findings. The error calculated between the regression model and the finite element simulation pertaining to the deformation value is less than 10%, which shows the legitimacy of regression model.

Figure 16 shows the influence of different parameters on sheet deformation. Figure 17 shows the maximum deformation generated when the percentage of open area ranges from 20 to 25%, with respect to a variation of ligament ratio from 0.2 to 0.25.

In Figure 18, the contour plot helps to identify the effect of open area (%) and hole size on deformation. Figure 19 shows that maximum deformation is generated for hole sizes ranging from 4 to 8 mm.

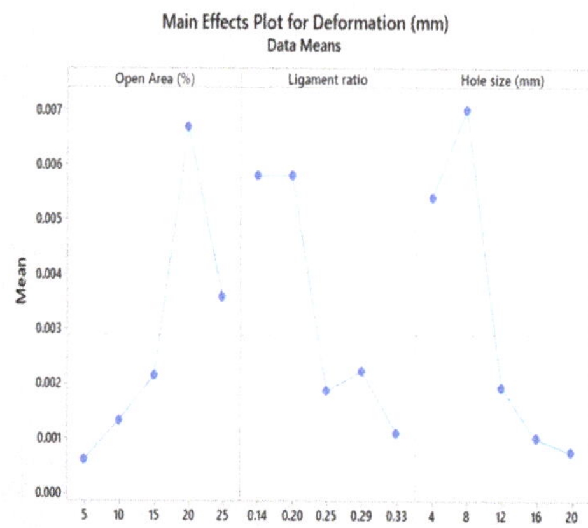

Figure 16. Main effects plot showing influences of different parameters on the sheet deformation.

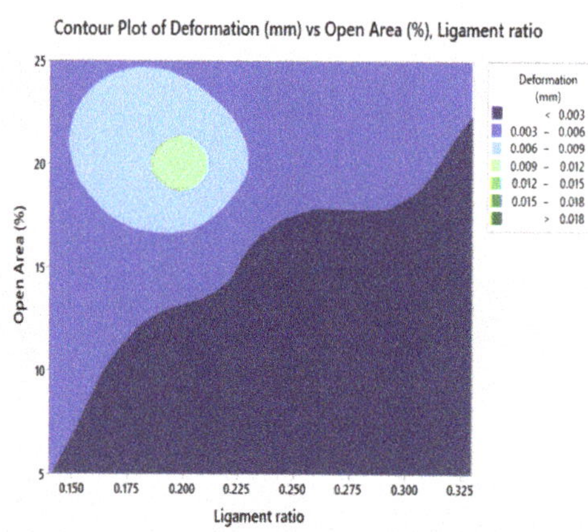

Figure 17. Influence of percentage of open area and ligament ratio.

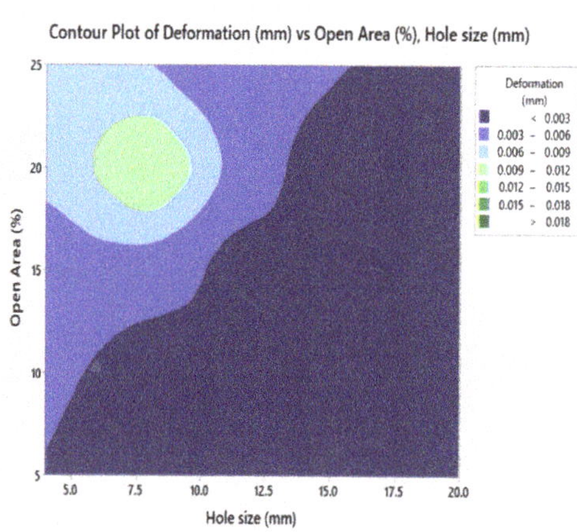

Figure 18. Influence of percentage of open area and hole size.

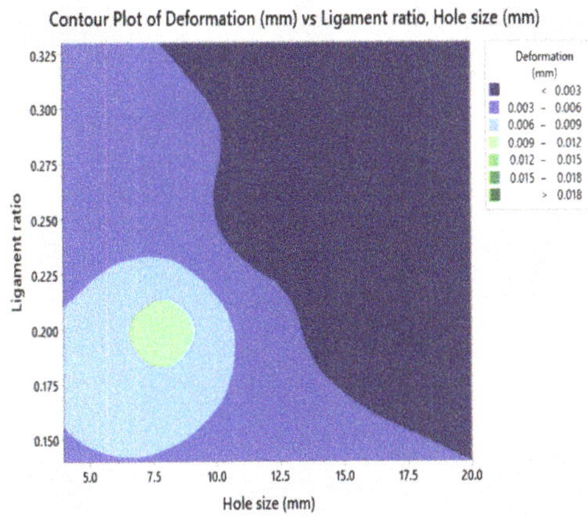

Figure 19. Influence of ligament ratio and hole size.

3.3. Response Optimization

The MINITAB software is used to carry out study on response optimization. It predicts the optimized combination of variables that optimizes a single or multiple responses. As shown in Figure 20, it helps to observe the effect of multiple variables on response. After the optimized values are obtained from MINITAB, they are again checked and validated with finite element simulation. The maximum deformation (equal to 0.0435 mm) is calculated for the optimized combination of 25% open area, 0.14 LR and 4 mm hole size, as shown in Table 10. The deformation is also calculated for this optimized combination in ANSYS Emag, and is equal to 0.0419 mm. The error for deformation calculated by optimized combination in MINITAB (0.0435 mm) and FE simulation (0.0419 mm) is 4%, which shows worthiness of optimized model (Figure 21).

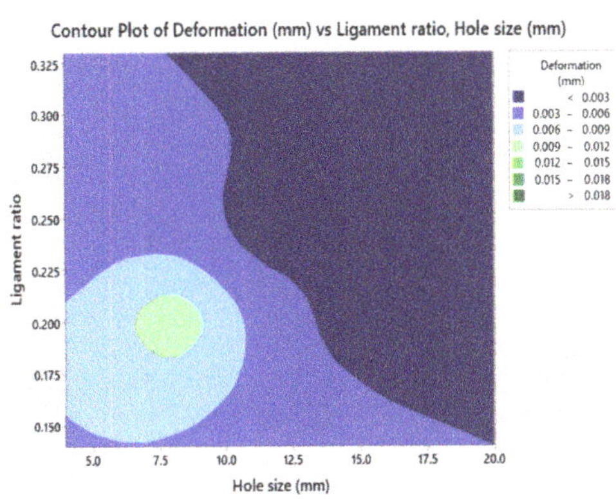

Figure 20. Influence of ligament ratio and hole size (for optimized model).

Table 10. Response optimization results.

Variable			Setting	
Open area (%)			25	
Ligament ratio			0.14	
Hole size (mm)			4	
Response	Fit	SE Fit	95% CI	95% PI
Deformation (mm)	0.04351	0.00757	(0.02664, 0.06038)	(0.02585, 0.06118)

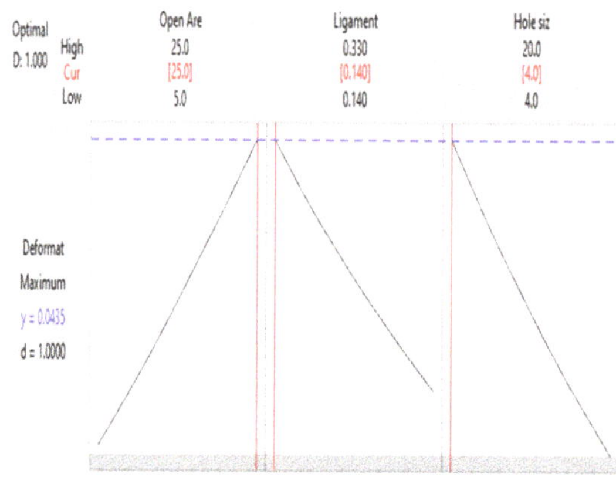

Figure 21. Response optimization of different parameters.

4. Conclusions

In this research work, a three-dimensional (3D) model for the EMF process is developed by extending a validated 2D axisymmetric model to three dimensions. In terms of the EMF process, experimental studies are usually very expensive, whereas numerical analyses are much more cost-effective and enable a wider range of parameters to be investigated quickly. The deformation of the perforated Al sheet is caused due to the magnetic force generated, which is then calculated by finite element simulation of the EMF process. The DOE/RSM approach is used to investigate the influences of the geometric parameters of the perforated sheet (i.e., the open area percentage, ligament ratio and size of the hole). For 20 different combinations, finite element simulations are performed, and the corresponding deformation is calculated. These finite element results are compared with the deformation calculated by a regression equation developed through ANOVA, which gives less than 10% error, showing the accuracy of the regression model. It is concluded that the optimized combination of 25% open area, 0.14 LR and 4 mm hole size gives the maximum deformation of the sheet, equal to 0.0435 mm. The confirmation simulation is carried out to validate the optimization study, showing good agreement (error percentage = 4%) with the optimized regression model, which will help by saving lot of time in future designs.

Author Contributions: Methodology, V.G.; Investigation, N.S.; Writing—review & editing, V.G. All authors have read and agreed to the published version of the manuscript.

Funding: The authors received no financial support for the research.

Institutional Review Board Statement: Not applicable.

Informed Consent Statement: Not applicable.

Data Availability Statement: Not applicable.

Acknowledgments: The authors are very grateful to the Vellore Institute of Technology, Chennai, India for providing facilities.

Conflicts of Interest: The authors declare no conflict of interest.

References

1. Daehn, G.S. *High Velocity Metal Forming, ASM Handbook of Forming and Forging*; ASM International: Materials Park, OH, USA, 2003.
2. Furth, H.; Waniek, R. New ideas on magnetic forming. *Am. Mach. Metalwork. Manuf.* **1962**, *106*, 92–95.
3. Kleiner, M.; Beerwald, C.; Homberg, W. Analysis of Process Parameters and Forming Mechanisms within the Electromagnetic Forming Process. *CIRP Ann. Manuf. Technol.* **2005**, *54*, 225–228. [CrossRef]
4. Meriched, A.H.; Feliachi, M.; Mohellebi, H. Electromagnetic Forming of Thin Metal Sheets. *IEEE Trans. Magn.* **2000**, *36*, 1804–1807. [CrossRef]
5. Fenton, G.; Deahn, G.S. Modeling of electromagnetically formed sheet metal. *J. Mater. Process Technol.* **1998**, *75*, 6–16. [CrossRef]
6. Cao, Q.; Li, L.; Lai, Z.; Zhou, Z.; Xiong, Q.; Zhang, X.; Han, X. Dynamic analysis of electromagnetic sheet metal forming process using finite element method. *Int. J. Adv. Manuf. Technol.* **2014**, *74*, 361–368. [CrossRef]
7. Reese, S.; Svendsen, B.; Stiemer, M.; Unger, J.; Schwarze, M.; Blum, H. On a new finite element technology for electromagnetic metal forming processes. *Arch. Appl. Mech.* **2005**, *74*, 834–845. [CrossRef]
8. Mamalis, A.G.; Manolakos, D.E.; Kladas, A.G.; Koumoutsos, A.K. On the electromagnetic sheet metal forming: Numerical simulation. *AIP Conf. Proc. Am. Inst. Phys.* **2004**, *712*, 778–783.
9. Luca, D. Finite element modeling and experiment for behavior estimation of AlMn0.5Mg0.5 sheet during electromagnetic forming. *Trans. Nonferrous Met. Soc. China* **2015**, *25*, 2331–2341. [CrossRef]
10. Siddiqui, M.A.; Correia, J.P.M.; Ahzi, S.; Belouettar, S. A numerical model to simulate electromagnetic sheet metal forming process. *Int. J. Mater. Form.* **2008**, *1* (Suppl. S1), 1387–1390. [CrossRef]
11. Unger, J.; Stiemer, M.; Svendsen, B.; Blum, H. Multifield modeling of electromagnetic metal forming processes. *J. Mater. Process. Technol.* **2006**, *177*, 270–273. [CrossRef]
12. Deng, J.; Li, C.; Zhao, Z.; Tu, F.; Yu, H. Numerical simulation of magnetic flux and force in electromagnetic forming with attractive force. *J. Mater. Process. Technol.* **2007**, *184*, 190–194. [CrossRef]
13. Khandelwal, R.; Dabade, U.A. *Performance Analysis of Electromagnetic Forming Process*; GRIN Verlag: München, Germany, 2015.
14. Imbert, J.M.; Winkler, S.L.; Worswick, M.J.; Golovashchenko, S. Formability and Damage in Electromagnetically Formed AA5754 and AA6111. In Proceedings of the 1st International Conference on High Speeding Forming, Dortmund, Germany, 31 March–1 April 2004; pp. 201–210.
15. Parez, I.; Aranguren, I.; Gonzlez, B.; Eguia, I. Electromagnetic forming: A new coupling method. *Int. J. Mater. Form.* **2009**, *2*, 637–640. [CrossRef]
16. Siddiqui, M.A.; Correia, J.P.M.; Ahzi, S.; Belouettar, S. Electromagnetic forming process: Estimation of magnetic pressure in tube expansion and numerical simulation. In Proceedings of the 12th ESAFORM Conference on Material Forming, Enschede, The Netherlands, 27–29 April 2009; pp. 27–29.
17. Bahmani, M.A.; Niayesh, K.; Karimi, A. 3D Simulation of magnetic field distribution in electromagnetic forming systems with field-shaper. *J. Mater. Process. Technol.* **2009**, *209*, 2295–2301. [CrossRef]
18. Haiping, Y.U.; Chunfeng, L.I.; Jianghua, D.E.N.G. Sequential coupling simulation for electromagnetic mechanical tube compression by finite element analysis. *J. Mater. Process. Technol.* **2009**, *209*, 707–713. [CrossRef]
19. Xu, W.; Liu, X.S.; Yang, J.G.; Fang, H.Y.; Xu, D.; Xu, W.L. Meshing and choice of evaluating parameters of results in simulation of electromagnetic force for forming of sheet metal. *J. Mater. Process. Technol.* **2009**, *209*, 3320–3324. [CrossRef]
20. Ahmed, M.; Panthi, S.K.; Ramakrishnan, N.; Jha, A.K.; Yegneswaran, A.H.; Dasgupta, R. Alternative flat coil design for electromagnetic forming using FEM. *Trans. Nonferrous Met. Soc. China* **2011**, *21*, 618–625. [CrossRef]
21. Psyk, V.; Risch, D.; Kinsey, B.L.; Tekkaya, A.E.; Kleiner, M. Electromagnetic forming—A review. *J. Mater. Process. Technol.* **2011**, *211*, 787–829. [CrossRef]
22. Bhole, K.S.; Kale, B.S.; Deshmukh, P.D.; Sonare, O.G. Numerical Analysis and Investigation of Aluminum Alloys in Electromagnetic Metal Forming Process. *Int. J. Technol. Eng. Syst.* **2011**, *2*, 98–102.
23. Qiu, L.; Han, X.; Xiong, Q.; Zhou, Z.; Li, L. Effect of Workpiece Motion on Forming Velocity in Electromagnetic Forming. In Proceedings of the 5th International Conference on High-Speed Forming, Dortmund, Germany, 24–26 April 2012; Volume 12800, pp. 103–112.
24. Abdelhafeez Ali, M.; Nemat-Alla, M.M.; El-Sebaie, M.G. Finite element analysis of electromagnetic bulging of sheet metal. *Int. J. Sci. Eng. Res.* **2012**, *3*, 1–7.
25. Takatsu, N.; Kato, M.; Sato, K.; Tobe, T. High-speed forming of metal sheets by electromagnetic force. *JSME Int. J. Vib. Control. Eng. Eng. Ind.* **1988**, *31*, 142–148. [CrossRef]
26. Zhang, X.; Huang, Y.; Wang, Y.; Shen, W.; Cui, J.; Li, G.; Deng, H. Numerical simulation and experimental study on electromagnetic punching-flanging process of 6061 aluminum alloy sheets. *J. Manuf. Process.* **2022**, *84*, 902–912. [CrossRef]
27. Xu, J.; Huang, L.; Hong, X.; Liu, X.; Su, H.; Ma, F.; Li, J. Research on the electromagnetic blanking based on force-free region deformation: Simulation and experiments. *Int. J. Adv. Manuf. Technol.* **2020**, *108*, 1751–1766. [CrossRef]

28. Li, H.W.; Yan, S.L.; Zhan, M.; Zhang, X. Eddy current induced dynamic deformation behaviors of aluminum alloy during EMF: Modeling and quantitative characterization. *J. Mater. Process. Technol.* **2019**, *263*, 423–439. [CrossRef]
29. Asati, R.; Pradhan, S.K. Two-stage Finite Element simulation to predict deformation and stresses in Electromagnetic Formed component. *Procedia Manuf.* **2017**, *12*, 42–58. [CrossRef]
30. Venkatachalam, G.; Narayanan, S.; Sathiyanarayanan, C. A finite element method-based formability analysis of triangular pattern of square hole perforated commercial pure aluminium sheets. *Int. J. Mech. Mater. Eng.* **2012**, *7*, 209–213.

mathematics

Article

Concurrent Topology Optimization of Multi-Scale Composite Structures Subjected to Dynamic Loads in the Time Domain

Xudong Jiang [1,*], Wei Zhang [1], Xiaoyan Teng [2] and Xiangyang Chen [2]

[1] Key Laboratory of Advanced Manufacturing Intelligent Technology, Ministry of Education, Harbin University of Science and Technology, Harbin 150080, China; 18342852628@163.com
[2] Key Laboratory of Ship Special Auxiliary and Underwater Equipment, Ministry of Industry and Information, Harbin Engineering University, Harbin 150001, China; tengxiaoyan@hrbeu.edu.cn (X.T.); 18845135118@163.com (X.C.)
* Correspondence: jxd_2023@163.com

Abstract: This paper presents a concurrent topology optimization of multi-scale composite structures subjected to general time-dependent loads for minimizing dynamic compliance. A three-field density-based method is adopted to implement the concurrent topological design, with macroscopic effective properties of the microstructure evaluated through energy-based homogenization method (EBHM). Transient response is obtained from the two-scale finite element analysis with the HHT-α approach as an implicit time integration procedure. Design sensitivities are formulated employing the adjoint variable method (AVM) based on two main philosophies: "discretize-then-differentiate" and "differentiate-then-discretize" approaches, respectively. The method of moving asymptotes is adopted to update the design variables at two scales. Several benchmark examples are presented to demonstrate that the "discretize-then-differentiate" AVM attains consistent sensitivities in an inherent manner such that the resulting optimal topology is more efficient when compared with the "differentiate-then-discretize" AVM. Moreover, the potential of the proposed method for concurrent dynamic topology optimization problems under general time-dependent loads is also highlighted.

Keywords: concurrent topology optimization; multi-scale composite structure; compliance minimization; elastodynamics; adjoint sensitivity analysis; energy-based homogenization method

MSC: 57R18

1. Introduction

Additive manufacturing process enables the fabrication of structures in the light of an expected macrostructure layout along with underlying microstructures. This offers significant design space for designers to create lighter and more efficient structures. Concurrent topology optimization provides a rigorous mathematical framework for seeking optimized material distribution at macro and micro scales to achieve superior structural performances. Therefore, they are of great interest for exploring multi-scale modeling and design methodology in this exciting field [1–3].

The two-scale concurrent topology optimization framework simultaneously optimizes two sets of design variables representing respective layout of the macrostructure and periodic unit cell. This framework is widely applied to two-scale hierarchical structural design issues, such as static compliance [4–6], eigenfrequency [7–9], structural modal damping ratio [10], as well as thermomechanical behavior [11,12]. Bai et al. [4] introduced a two-step Helmholtz filtering/projection scheme to describe the shell interface, whereby a multi-scale topology optimization model for shell-infill structure is developed for minimizing the static compliance. Gangwar et al. [6] presented a concurrent material and a structure design framework considering shape and orientation of various phrases in a hierarchical system across multiple various length scales. Xiao et al. [7] designed graded lattice sandwich structures in terms of maximal natural frequency through multi-scale topology optimization, which is employed to integrate the optimization of thickness of two solid face-sheets and layout of lattice cells into a core layer. Zhang et al. [8] extended the work of Xiao et al. [7] to inhomogeneous cellular structures for maximizing the eigenfrequencies of desired modes based on mode-tracking strategy. Hu et al. [9] performed the multi-scale topology optimization of coated structures with multiple layers of graded lattice infill for maximization of the fundamental eigenfrequency. Ni et al. [10] proposed an optimization strategy to maximize the structural damping performance, where the damping material layout and its microstructural configuration are concurrently optimized. Ali et al. [11] formulated the concurrent multi-scale and multiphysics topology optimization for minimization of the thermal and mechanical compliances. Zhou et al. [12] designed lightweight channel-cooling cellular structures with eminent heat barrier and load-carrying capacity via metamodel-assisted concurrent multi-scale and multi-material topology optimization. For a comprehensive review on concurrent multi-scale topology optimization, one can refer to the published literature [13].

Despite this, certain challenges still remain in some efficient cumbersome sensitivity analysis and dynamic response analysis across multiple scalers for hierarchical structures under dynamic load. Concurrent topology optimization for dynamic response was investigated in both the frequency domain [14–20] and the time domain [21,22]. This work concentrates on a transient response optimization problem for minimizing the dynamic compliance of multi-scale composite structures under general time-dependent load. Millions of design variables for transient problems of multi-scale structures pose great significance to efficient sensitivity analysis when gradient-based topology optimization algorithm is implemented. Therefore, the adjoint variable method (AVM) is essential for sensitivity analysis. There are two dominant philosophies to implement the AVM in terms of the order of discretization and differentiation regarding the time variable, i.e., differentiate-then-discretize method and discretize-then-differentiate approach. Zhao et al. [22] adopted the AVM based on a differentiate-then-discretize approach to conduct the sensitivity analysis for transient concurrent topology optimization of two-scale hierarchical structures. Majority of investigations adopted the differentiate-then-discretize approach for linear transient problems due to its relative simplicity in formulation and implementation [22–26]. Nevertheless, Jensen et al. [27], Zhang et al. [28] and Ding et al. [29] demonstrated that the differentiate-then-discretize AVM can cause consistency errors representing differences between the calculated and accurate sensitivities through investigating a single DOF damping system. Alternatively, AVM based on a discretize-then-differentiate approach can diminish resulting consistency errors associated with the differentiate-then-discretize approach. Giraldo-Londono et al. [30] proposed a transient topology optimization implementation of an elastodynamic system employing the discretize-then-differentiate AVM, whereafter their work was further extended to local stress-constrained topology optimization problem with arbitrary dynamic loads [31]. Other studies, such as microstructural layout optimization of viscoelastical component under time-dependent loading and transient thermomechanical coupling problems have also been based on the differentiate-then-discretize AVM [32,33]. Recently, Kristiansen [34] developed a completely parallel framework to address the large-scale transient topology optimization employing the fully discretized adjoint sensitivity analysis in [35]. Nevertheless, to the author's knowledge, very few investigations on multi-scale concurrent topology optimization adopting the differentiate-then-discretize AVM are focused on linear transient problems due to comparatively cumbersome sensitivity analysis.

This work intends to construct an efficient two-scale concurrent topology optimization framework for minimizing the dynamic compliance of composite structures under transient loading. A three-field density-based method is exploited for multi-scale concurrent topology optimization to achieve material-structure integrated designs. The major contributions of this study consists of three aspects: (1) to formulate an efficient sensitivity computation for transient response optimization of two-scale hierarchical structures; (2) to demonstrate and discuss some findings in concurrent topology optimization aiming at the dynamic compliance minimization in the context of linear transient problems; and (3) to indicate the capabilities of the proposed concurrent topology optimization approach to design composite structures suffering from general transient loads.

The remainder of this paper is organized as follows. Section 2 briefly reviews the problem formulation of concurrent topology optimization for minimizing dynamic compliance of two-scale composite structures in the time domain. We present the HHT-α method in Section 2, followed by the adjoint sensitivity analysis via the discretize-then-differentiate approach in Section 3. Next, the inconsistent sensitivity via the differentiate-then-discretize approach is formulated in Section 4. Section 6 explains that the order of differentiation and discretization plays a critical role in the consistency of adjoint sensitivity analysis, and demonstrates the potential of the proposed approach to address a wide variety of concurrent topology optimization problems under general transient loading, with four numerical examples. Finally, the conclusions of this work are presented in Section 7.

2. Concurrent Topology Optimization for Dynamic Compliance Minimization

The concurrent topology optimization framework is presented to simultaneously achieve the optimal macrostructure and material microstructure for minimal dynamic compliance in the time domain. Material microstructure is assumed to be uniform in the composition of a macrostructure for convenient manufacturing. This framework is briefly outlined to comprehend the fundamental procedure of performing concurrent topology optimization in this section.

2.1. Three-Field Density-Based Approach

We adopt the three-field density-based approach [36,37] to guarantee clear topologies in two scales. Two sets of design variables are separately defined, namely macroscopic design density in structural design domain and microscopic design density in a unit cell. Each design variable ranges from 0 to 1. To diminish the chessboard pattern and mesh-independence, the original design variables are regulated with a smooth regularization filter [38] and expressed as follows:

$$\bar{\xi}_i = \frac{\sum_{k\in\Phi_i} w_{ki}^{\mathrm{mac}} v_k^{\mathrm{mac}} \xi_k}{\sum_{k\in\Phi_i} w_{ki}^{\mathrm{mac}} v_k^{\mathrm{mac}}} \tag{1}$$

$$\bar{\eta}_j = \frac{\sum_{l\in\Psi_j} w_{lj}^{\mathrm{mic}} v_l^{\mathrm{mic}} \eta_l}{\sum_{l\in\Psi_j} w_{lj}^{\mathrm{mic}} v_l^{\mathrm{mic}}} \tag{2}$$

where Φ_i is the neighboring set of elements within a specified filter radius R in the macroscopic design domain that have a center located at the centroid of the ith element and Ψ_i is the neighboring set of elements within a specified filter radius r in the unit cell that have a center located at the centroid of the jth element. v_k^{mac} is the volume of element k in the macroscopic design domain and v_l^{mic} is the volume of element l in the unit cell. The weighting factors w_{ki}^{mac} and w_{lj}^{mic} are defined using a linearly decaying function:

$$w_{ki}^{\mathrm{mac}} = R - \|\mathbf{x}_k - \mathbf{x}_i\| \tag{3}$$

$$w_{lj}^{\mathrm{mic}} = r - \|\mathbf{y}_l - \mathbf{y}_j\| \tag{4}$$

where $\mathbf{x}$ and $\mathbf{y}$ denote the center position of elements in both macro and micro design domains, respectively.

To achieve the clear black-white design, Wang et al. [39] modified the linearly filtered design densities in Equations (1) and (2) employing a threshold projection function:

$$\tilde{\xi}_i = \xi_{\min} + (1-\xi_{\min}) \frac{\tanh(\beta^{\mathrm{mac}}\xi_{\mathrm{th}}) + \tanh(\beta^{\mathrm{mac}}(\bar{\xi}_i - \xi_{\mathrm{th}}))}{\tanh(\beta^{\mathrm{mac}}\xi_{\mathrm{th}}) + \tanh(\beta^{\mathrm{mac}}(1-\xi_{\mathrm{th}}))} \tag{5}$$

$$\widetilde{\eta}_j = \eta_{\min} + (1 - \eta_{\min})\frac{\tanh(\beta^{\mathrm{mic}}\eta_{\mathrm{th}}) + \tanh\left(\beta^{\mathrm{mic}}\left(\overline{\eta}_j - \eta_{\mathrm{th}}\right)\right)}{\tanh(\beta^{\mathrm{mic}}\eta_{\mathrm{th}}) + \tanh(\beta^{\mathrm{mic}}(1 - \eta_{\mathrm{th}}))} \quad (6)$$

where the physical design variables, $\widetilde{\xi}_i$ and $\widetilde{\eta}_j$, use the Ersatz parameters much less than one denoted by $\xi_{\min}$ and $\eta_{\min}$, respectively, to inhibit numerical instabilities of the stiffness and mass matrices when $\overline{\xi} \to 0$ and $\overline{\eta} \to 0$. β^{mac} and β^{mic} are exploited to regulate the aggressiveness of the projection function. ξ_{th} and η_{th} are the threshold density specified as 0.5 in this work.

2.2. Numerical Homogenization

To attain the clear configuration at both scales, the material interpolation schemes with penalization are employed. At the microscale, the modulus matrix of an element within the cellular microstructure is interpolated via SIMP [40]. At the macro-scale, the modulus matrix of an element within the macrostructure with porous material is interpolated with RAMP [41].

$$\mathbf{D}_j^{\mathrm{mic}} = \widetilde{\eta}_j^p \mathbf{D}^{\mathrm{B}} \quad (7)$$

$$\mathbf{D}_i^{\mathrm{mac}} = g\left(\widetilde{\xi}_i\right)\mathbf{D}^{\mathrm{H}} \quad (8)$$

where $\mathbf{D}^{\mathrm{B}}$ is the elastic constitutive matrix of base material and $\mathbf{D}^{\mathrm{H}}$ is the effective macroscopic constitutive matrix, which is computed as follows:

$$\mathbf{D}^{\mathrm{H}} = \frac{1}{|\Omega_m|}\int_{\Omega_m} \mathbf{D}_j^{\mathrm{mic}}(\mathbf{I} - \mathbf{b}\mathbf{u}_m)\mathrm{d}\Omega_m \quad (9)$$

where $\mathbf{I}$ denotes a unit matrix, $\mathbf{b}$ denotes the strain matrix at the microscale and $\mathbf{u}_m$ denotes the unknown displacement field excited by the unit test strains in the microstructural domain Ω_m.

The resultant displacement matrix $\mathbf{u}_m$ is obtained through resolving the following unit cell equilibrium problem with periodic boundary conditions:

$$\mathbf{k}^{\mathrm{mic}}\mathbf{u}_m = \int_{\Omega_m} \mathbf{b}^{\mathrm{T}}\mathbf{D}_j^{\mathrm{mic}}\mathrm{d}\Omega_m \quad (10)$$

where the stiffness matrix $\mathbf{k}^{\mathrm{mic}}$ is given by the following:

$$\mathbf{k}^{\mathrm{mic}} = \int_{\Omega_m} \mathbf{b}^{\mathrm{T}}\mathbf{D}_j^{\mathrm{mic}}\mathbf{b}\mathrm{d}\Omega_m \quad (11)$$

To prohibit the local eigenmodes occurring in regions with low densities, the polynomial function, as suggested by [42], is selected to penalize the macroscopic element stiffness matrix via the RAMP model:

$$g\left(\widetilde{\xi}_i\right) = \left(15\widetilde{\xi}_i^p + \widetilde{\xi}_i\right)/16 \quad (12)$$

where the penalization exponent p is set to be 3.

In addition, the effective mass density of corresponding periodic cellular material is represented as follows:

$$\rho^{\mathrm{H}} = \frac{1}{|\Omega_m|}\int_{\Omega_m} \rho^{\mathrm{B}}\widetilde{\eta}_j\mathrm{d}\Omega_{mj} \quad (13)$$

where ρ^{B} is the physical mass density of the base material. The energy-based homogenization method (EBHM) was employed to calculate the macroscopic effective properties of the porous material [43].

2.3. Formulation of Compliance Minimization

When a two-scale hierarchical structure is excited by a transient external load, the finite element equation used to solve the boundary value problem for this elastodynamic system is expressed as follows:

$$\mathbf{M}\ddot{\mathbf{u}}_t + \mathbf{C}\dot{\mathbf{u}}_t + \mathbf{K}\mathbf{u}_t = \mathbf{f}_t \ (t = 0, \cdots, \overline{N}) \tag{14}$$

where $\mathbf{M}$, $\mathbf{C}$, and $\mathbf{K}$ represent the global mass, damping, and stiffness matrices, respectively. $\ddot{\mathbf{u}}_t$, $\dot{\mathbf{u}}_t$, and $\mathbf{u}_t$ are the respective acceleration, velocity, and displacement vectors in response to the force vector $\mathbf{f}_t$ at time step t. $\overline{N}$ is the number of analysis steps. The global mass and stiffness matrices are assembled using the penalized macroscopic element matrix:

$$\mathbf{K} = \sum_{i=1}^{N^{\text{mac}}} g\left(\tilde{\xi}_i\right)\mathbf{k}_i^0 \tag{15}$$

$$\mathbf{M} = \sum_{i=1}^{N^{\text{mac}}} \tilde{\xi}_i \mathbf{m}_i^0 \tag{16}$$

where

$$\mathbf{k}_i^0 = \int_{\Omega_i} \mathbf{B}^{\text{T}}\mathbf{D}^{\text{H}}\mathbf{B}\text{d}\Omega_i \tag{17}$$

$$\mathbf{m}_i^0 = \rho^{\text{H}} \int_{\Omega_i} \mathbf{N}^{\text{T}}\mathbf{N}\text{d}\Omega_i \tag{18}$$

where $\mathbf{N}$ is the matrix of shape functions and $\mathbf{B}$ is the first derivative of $\mathbf{N}$.

We employ the Rayleigh damping to compute the damping matrix as linear combination of mass and stiffness matrices, such that

$$\mathbf{C} = \alpha_{\text{r}}\mathbf{M} + \beta_{\text{r}}\mathbf{K} \tag{19}$$

where α_{r} and β_{r} are the respective mass and stiffness proportional damping coefficients, which are assumed to be design-independent in this work.

This work aims to minimize the dynamic compliance for a two-scale hierarchical structure with the limited available amount of material in the time domain. Mathematically, we formulate this two-scale concurrent topology optimization problem as follows:

$$\begin{aligned}
\min_{\xi,\eta} \quad & f(\boldsymbol{\xi}, \boldsymbol{\eta}, \mathbf{u}(t)) = \sum_{t=0}^{\overline{N}} \mathbf{f}_t^{\text{T}}\mathbf{u}_t \\
s.t. \quad & \mathbf{M}\ddot{\mathbf{u}}_t + \mathbf{C}\dot{\mathbf{u}}_t + \mathbf{K}\mathbf{u}_t = \mathbf{f}_t \ (t = 0, \cdots, \overline{N}) \\
& G_1 = \Big(\sum_{i=1}^{N^{\text{mac}}} \tilde{\xi}_i v_i^{\text{mac}}\Big)/V^{\text{mac}} - \varsigma \leq 0 \\
& G_2 = \Big(\sum_{j=1}^{N^{\text{mic}}} \tilde{\eta}_j v_j^{\text{mic}}\Big)/V^{\text{mic}} - \vartheta \leq 0 \\
& 0 \leq \xi_i \leq 1, \ 1 \leq i \leq N^{\text{mac}} \\
& 0 \leq \eta_j \leq 1, \ 1 \leq j \leq N^{\text{mic}}
\end{aligned} \tag{20}$$

where $f(\boldsymbol{\xi}, \boldsymbol{\eta}, \mathbf{u}(t))$ is the concerned objective function, V^{mac} and V^{mic} are the respective volumes of macroscopic and microscopic design domains. ς and ϑ are the volume fraction upper bounds associated with macroscopic and microscopic constraints of G_1 and G_2, respectively. Here, the macroscopic design domain is discretized into N^{mac} elements, while the unit cell is discretized into N^{mic} elements.

3. HHT-α Method

We apply the HHT-α method, a well-developed implicit time integration scheme, to solve the second-order initial value problems stated as Equation (14). Due to an unconditional stability along with a second-order convergence [44,45], the HHT-α method have been used for linear and nonlinear structural dynamic analysis [46,47]. The HHT-α method is characteristic of superior numerical dispersion and energy dissipation by introducing a parameter α into the Newmark method to control the numerical damping. Accordingly, the motion Equation (14) representing the dynamic equilibrium is modified as follows:

$$\begin{aligned}\mathbf{M}\ddot{\mathbf{u}}_t + (1-\alpha)\mathbf{C}\dot{\mathbf{u}}_t + \alpha\mathbf{C}\dot{\mathbf{u}}_{t-1} + (1-\alpha)\mathbf{K}\mathbf{u}_t + \alpha\mathbf{K}\mathbf{u}_{t-1} \\ = (1-\alpha)\mathbf{f}_t + \alpha\mathbf{f}_{t-1},\ t = 1,\ldots,\overline{N}\end{aligned} \tag{21}$$

The HHT-α method adopts finite difference relationships from the Newmark-β method and hence the recursive formula of displacement and velocity is determined with the following:

$$\mathbf{u}_t = \mathbf{u}_{t-1} + \Delta t\dot{\mathbf{u}}_{t-1} + \Delta t^2\left[(1/2-\beta)\ddot{\mathbf{u}}_{t-1} + \beta\ddot{\mathbf{u}}_t\right] \tag{22}$$

$$\dot{\mathbf{u}}_t = \dot{\mathbf{u}}_{t-1} + \Delta t\left[(1-\gamma)\ddot{\mathbf{u}}_{t-1} + \gamma\ddot{\mathbf{u}}_t\right] \tag{23}$$

where the Newmark parameters β and γ are constants which control the integration accuracy and stability, respectively, by satisfying the following relationship:

$$0 \le \alpha \le 1/3,\ \beta = \left(1+\alpha^2\right)/4,\ \gamma = (1+2\alpha)/2 \tag{24}$$

By substitution of Equations (22) and (23) into Equation (21), the time-discretized motion equation in residual form is derived as follows:

$$\mathbf{R}_t = \mathbf{M}_1\ddot{\mathbf{u}}_t + \mathbf{M}_0\ddot{\mathbf{u}}_{t-1} + \mathbf{C}_0\dot{\mathbf{u}}_{t-1} + \mathbf{K}\mathbf{u}_{t-1} - (1-\alpha)\mathbf{f}_t - \alpha\mathbf{f}_{t-1} = 0 \tag{25}$$

where

$$\mathbf{M}_1 = \mathbf{M} + (1-\alpha)\gamma\Delta t\mathbf{C} + (1-\alpha)\beta\Delta t^2\mathbf{K} \tag{26}$$

$$\mathbf{M}_0 = (1-\alpha)(1-\gamma)\Delta t\mathbf{C} + (1-\alpha)\left(\frac{1}{2}-\beta\right)\Delta t^2\mathbf{K} \tag{27}$$

$$\mathbf{C}_0 = \mathbf{C} + (1-\alpha)\Delta t\mathbf{K} \tag{28}$$

Following a standard HHT-α scheme, we can obtain the dynamic response at each time step. We resolve Equation (25) for $\ddot{\mathbf{u}}_t$ and thereupon compute $\mathbf{u}_t$ and $\dot{\mathbf{u}}_t$ by applying the Newmark-β Formulas (22) and (23), respectively. As for $\ddot{\mathbf{u}}_0$, by assuming $\dot{\mathbf{u}}_0$ and $\mathbf{u}_0$ to be design-independent, it can be computed using the following residual equation:

$$\mathbf{R}_0 = \mathbf{M}\ddot{\mathbf{u}}_0 + \mathbf{C}\dot{\mathbf{u}}_0 + \mathbf{K}\mathbf{u}_0 - \mathbf{f}_0 = 0 \tag{29}$$

4. Adjoint Sensitivity Analysis Using Discretize-Then-Differentiate

We apply the discretize-then-differentiate AVM to construct the corresponding adjoint equation on the discretized elastodynamic system in space and time. The standard AVM sensitivity analysis is performed following two essential procedure. First, some residual equations are added into the objective function to develop an augmented function. Then, this augmented function is differentiated and the adjoint variables are derived by vanishing the derivative terms of state variables regarding design variables.

In terms of the chain rule, the sensitivities of both the objective and constraint functions with respect to the original design variables can be calculated as follows:

$$\frac{\partial f}{\partial \xi_i} = \sum_{k \in \Phi_i} \frac{\partial f}{\partial \tilde{\xi}_k} \frac{\partial \tilde{\xi}_k}{\partial \overline{\xi}_k} \frac{\partial \overline{\xi}_k}{\partial \xi_i} \tag{30}$$

$$\frac{\partial G_1}{\partial \xi_i} = \sum_{k \in \Phi_i} \frac{\partial G_1}{\partial \tilde{\xi}_k} \frac{\partial \tilde{\xi}_k}{\partial \overline{\xi}_k} \frac{\partial \overline{\xi}_k}{\partial \xi_i} \tag{31}$$

$$\frac{\partial f}{\partial \eta_i} = \sum_{l \in \Psi_j} \frac{\partial f}{\partial \tilde{\eta}_l} \frac{\partial \tilde{\eta}_l}{\partial \overline{\eta}_l} \frac{\partial \overline{\eta}_l}{\partial \eta_j} \tag{32}$$

$$\frac{\partial G_2}{\partial \eta_i} = \sum_{l \in \Psi_j} \frac{\partial G_2}{\partial \tilde{\eta}_l} \frac{\partial \tilde{\eta}_l}{\partial \overline{\eta}_l} \frac{\partial \overline{\eta}_l}{\partial \eta_j} \tag{33}$$

where

$$\frac{\partial \tilde{\xi}_k}{\partial \overline{\xi}_k} = (1 - \xi_{\min}) \frac{\beta^{\mathrm{mac}} \left(\mathrm{sech}\left(\beta^{\mathrm{mac}} (\overline{\xi}_k - \xi_{\mathrm{th}})\right)\right)^2}{\tanh(\beta^{\mathrm{mac}} \xi_{\mathrm{th}}) + \tanh(\beta^{\mathrm{mac}} (1 - \xi_{\mathrm{th}}))} \tag{34}$$

$$\frac{\partial \tilde{\eta}_l}{\partial \overline{\eta}_l} = (1 - \eta_{\min}) \frac{\beta^{\mathrm{mic}} \left(\mathrm{sech}\left(\beta^{\mathrm{mic}} (\overline{\eta}_l - \eta_{\mathrm{th}})\right)\right)^2}{\tanh(\beta^{\mathrm{mic}} \eta_{\mathrm{th}}) + \tanh(\beta^{\mathrm{mic}} (1 - \eta_{\mathrm{th}}))} \tag{35}$$

$$\partial \overline{\xi}_k / \partial \xi_i = w_{ki} v_i^{\mathrm{mac}} \Big/ \sum\nolimits_{i \in \Phi_k} w_{ki} v_i^{\mathrm{mac}} \tag{36}$$

$$\partial \overline{\eta}_l / \partial \eta_j = w_{lj} v_j^{\mathrm{mic}} \Big/ \sum\nolimits_{j \in \Psi_l} w_{lj} v_j^{\mathrm{mic}} \tag{37}$$

The sensitivity of f with respect to the arbitrary design variable $x(\xi_i, \eta_i)$ is also written as follows:

$$\frac{\mathrm{d}f}{\mathrm{d}x} = \frac{\partial f}{\partial x} + \sum_{t=0}^{\overline{N}} \frac{\partial f}{\partial \mathbf{u}_t} \frac{\partial \mathbf{u}_t}{\partial x} \tag{38}$$

In order to facilitate the sensitivity analysis, we transform Equations (22) and (23) into the following residual form:

$$\mathbf{P}_t = -\mathbf{u}_t + \mathbf{u}_{t-1} + \Delta t \dot{\mathbf{u}}_{t-1} + \Delta t^2 [(\frac{1}{2} - \beta) \ddot{\mathbf{u}}_{t-1} + \beta \ddot{\mathbf{u}}_t] = 0 \quad t = 1, \ldots, \overline{N} \tag{39}$$

$$\mathbf{Q}_t = -\dot{\mathbf{u}}_t + \dot{\mathbf{u}}_{t-1} + \Delta t [(1 - \gamma) \ddot{\mathbf{u}}_{t-1} + \gamma \ddot{\mathbf{u}}_t] = 0 \quad t = 1, \ldots, \overline{N} \tag{40}$$

Sequentially, we add adjoint variables $\boldsymbol{\lambda}_t$, $\boldsymbol{\mu}_t$ and $\boldsymbol{\zeta}_t$ and rewrite Equation (38) as follows:

$$\frac{\mathrm{d}f}{\mathrm{d}x} = \frac{\partial f}{\partial x} + \sum_{t=0}^{\overline{N}} \frac{\partial f}{\partial \mathbf{u}_t} \frac{\partial \mathbf{u}_t}{\partial x} + \sum_{t=0}^{\overline{N}} \boldsymbol{\lambda}_t^{\mathrm{T}} \frac{\mathrm{d}\mathbf{R}_t}{\mathrm{d}x} + \sum_{t=1}^{\overline{N}} \boldsymbol{\mu}_t^{\mathrm{T}} \frac{\mathrm{d}\mathbf{P}_t}{\mathrm{d}x} + \sum_{t=1}^{\overline{N}} \boldsymbol{\zeta}_t^{\mathrm{T}} \frac{\mathrm{d}\mathbf{Q}_t}{\mathrm{d}x} \tag{41}$$

From Equations (39) and (40), it is obvious that $\partial \mathbf{P}_t / \partial x = \mathbf{0}$ and $\partial \mathbf{Q}_t / \partial x = \mathbf{0}$. Due to the design-independence of the initial conditions, $\partial \mathbf{u}_0 / \partial x = \mathbf{0}$ and $\partial \dot{\mathbf{u}}_0 / \partial x = \mathbf{0}$. We employ these simplifications and eliminate all implicit terms including $\partial \mathbf{u} / \partial x$, $\partial \dot{\mathbf{u}} / \partial x$ and $\partial \ddot{\mathbf{u}} / \partial x$ in Equation (41), such that the following adjoint equations can be obtained:

$$\boldsymbol{\lambda}_0^{\mathrm{T}} \frac{\partial \mathbf{R}_0}{\partial \ddot{\mathbf{u}}_0} + \boldsymbol{\lambda}_1^{\mathrm{T}} \frac{\partial \mathbf{R}_1}{\partial \ddot{\mathbf{u}}_0} + \boldsymbol{\mu}_1^{\mathrm{T}} \frac{\partial \mathbf{P}_1}{\partial \ddot{\mathbf{u}}_0} + \boldsymbol{\zeta}_1^{\mathrm{T}} \frac{\partial \mathbf{Q}_1}{\partial \ddot{\mathbf{u}}_0} = \mathbf{0} \tag{42}$$

$$\begin{cases} \sum_{\ell=1}^{\overline{N}} \left(\boldsymbol{\lambda}_\ell^{\mathrm{T}} \frac{\partial \mathbf{R}_\ell}{\partial \mathbf{u}_t} + \boldsymbol{\mu}_\ell^{\mathrm{T}} \frac{\partial \mathbf{P}_\ell}{\partial \mathbf{u}_t} + \boldsymbol{\zeta}_\ell^{\mathrm{T}} \frac{\partial \mathbf{Q}_\ell}{\partial \mathbf{u}_t} + \frac{\partial f}{\partial \mathbf{u}_t} \right) = \mathbf{0} \\ \sum_{\ell=1}^{\overline{N}} \left(\boldsymbol{\lambda}_\ell^{\mathrm{T}} \frac{\partial \mathbf{R}_\ell}{\partial \dot{\mathbf{u}}_t} + \boldsymbol{\mu}_\ell^{\mathrm{T}} \frac{\partial \mathbf{P}_\ell}{\partial \dot{\mathbf{u}}_t} + \boldsymbol{\zeta}_\ell^{\mathrm{T}} \frac{\partial \mathbf{Q}_\ell}{\partial \dot{\mathbf{u}}_t} \right) = \mathbf{0} \\ \sum_{\ell=1}^{\overline{N}} \left(\boldsymbol{\lambda}_\ell^{\mathrm{T}} \frac{\partial \mathbf{R}_\ell}{\partial \ddot{\mathbf{u}}_t} + \boldsymbol{\mu}_\ell^{\mathrm{T}} \frac{\partial \mathbf{P}_\ell}{\partial \ddot{\mathbf{u}}_t} + \boldsymbol{\zeta}_\ell^{\mathrm{T}} \frac{\partial \mathbf{Q}_\ell}{\partial \ddot{\mathbf{u}}_t} \right) = \mathbf{0} \end{cases} \tag{43}$$

By substituting the residual Equations of (25), (29), (39) and (40) into the adjoint Equations of (42) and (43), we obtain the solution of the adjoint problem as follows:

$$\boldsymbol{\mu}_{\overline{N}} = \frac{\partial f}{\partial \mathbf{u}_{\overline{N}}},\ \boldsymbol{\zeta}_{\overline{N}} = \mathbf{0},\ \mathbf{M}_1 \boldsymbol{\lambda}_{\overline{N}} = -\beta \Delta t^2 \boldsymbol{\mu}_{\overline{N}} - \gamma \Delta t \boldsymbol{\zeta}_{\overline{N}} \tag{44}$$

$$\boldsymbol{\mu}_{t-1} = \frac{\partial f}{\partial \mathbf{u}_{t-1}} + \mathbf{K}\boldsymbol{\lambda}_t + \boldsymbol{\mu}_t,\ \boldsymbol{\zeta}_{t-1} = \mathbf{C}_0 \boldsymbol{\lambda}_t + \Delta t \boldsymbol{\mu}_t + \boldsymbol{\zeta}_t \tag{45}$$

$$\mathbf{M}_1 \boldsymbol{\lambda}_{t-1} = \mathbf{M}_0 \boldsymbol{\lambda}_t - \Delta t^2 \left[\beta \boldsymbol{\mu}_{t-1} + \left(\frac{1}{2} - \beta \right) \boldsymbol{\mu}_t \right] - \Delta t [\gamma \boldsymbol{\zeta}_{t-1} + (1-\gamma) \boldsymbol{\zeta}_t] \tag{46}$$

$$\mathbf{M}\boldsymbol{\lambda}_0 = \mathbf{M}_0 \boldsymbol{\lambda}_1 - \left(\frac{1}{2} - \beta \right) \Delta t^2 \boldsymbol{\mu}_1 - (1-\gamma) \Delta t \boldsymbol{\zeta}_1 \tag{47}$$

Using the adjoint solution from Equations (44)–(47), we rewrite Equation (38) as follows:

$$\frac{\mathrm{d}f}{\mathrm{d}x} = \frac{\partial f}{\partial x} + \sum_{t=0}^{\overline{N}} \boldsymbol{\lambda}_t^{\mathrm{T}} \frac{\partial \mathbf{R}_t}{\partial x} \tag{48}$$

4.1. Sensitivity Analysis for Design Variables at the Macroscale

Provided that the concurrent optimization problem (20) applies macrostructural density relevant information via the stiffness interpolation function, $\mathbf{E} = [E_i] = \left[g\left(\tilde{\xi}_i \right) \right]$, and the volume interpolation function, $\mathbf{V} = [V_i] = \left[\tilde{\xi}_i \right]$, it facilitates recasting the sensitivity information of macroscopic design variables according to these fields. Therefore, we compute the sensitivity of f with respect to $\boldsymbol{\xi}$ by chain rule as follows:

$$\frac{\mathrm{d}f}{\mathrm{d}\boldsymbol{\xi}} = \frac{\mathrm{d}f}{\mathrm{d}\mathbf{E}} \frac{\partial \mathbf{E}}{\partial \boldsymbol{\xi}} + \frac{\mathrm{d}f}{\mathrm{d}\mathbf{V}} \frac{\partial \mathbf{V}}{\partial \boldsymbol{\xi}} \tag{49}$$

where the sensitivities of f regarding the macroscopic element volume fractions and stiffness parameters can be attained as demonstrated in Equation (48).

$$\mathrm{d}f/\mathrm{d}E_i = \partial f/\partial E_i + \sum_{t=0}^{\overline{N}} \boldsymbol{\lambda}_t^{\mathrm{T}} \partial \mathbf{R}_t / \partial E_i \tag{50}$$

$$\mathrm{d}f/\mathrm{d}V_i = \partial f/\partial V_i + \sum_{t=0}^{\overline{N}} \boldsymbol{\lambda}_t^{\mathrm{T}} \partial \mathbf{R}_t / \partial V_i \tag{51}$$

The terms, $\partial \mathbf{R}_t / \partial E_i$ and $\partial \mathbf{R}_t / \partial V_i$, are evaluated in terms of Equations (25) and (29), respectively. There is a case for $t = 0$.

$$\frac{\partial \mathbf{R}_t}{\partial E_i} = \frac{\partial \mathbf{K}}{\partial E_i} (\mathbf{u}_0 + \beta_{\mathrm{r}} \dot{\mathbf{u}}_0) = \mathbf{k}_i (\mathbf{u}_{i,0} + \beta_{\mathrm{r}} \dot{\mathbf{u}}_{i,0}) \tag{52}$$

$$\frac{\partial \mathbf{R}_t}{\partial V_i} = \frac{\partial \mathbf{M}}{\partial E_i} (\ddot{\mathbf{u}}_0 + \alpha_{\mathrm{r}} \dot{\mathbf{u}}_0) = \mathbf{m}_i (\ddot{\mathbf{u}}_{i,0} + \alpha_{\mathrm{r}} \dot{\mathbf{u}}_{i,0}) \tag{53}$$

and for $t = 1, \cdots, \overline{N}$

$$\begin{aligned}\frac{\partial \mathbf{R}_t}{\partial E_i} &= \frac{\partial \mathbf{K}}{\partial E_i}\left[(1-\alpha)\left(\mathbf{u}_t + \beta_r \dot{\mathbf{u}}_t\right) + \alpha\left(\mathbf{u}_{t-1} + \beta_r \dot{\mathbf{u}}_{t-1}\right)\right] \\ &= \mathbf{k}_i\left[(1-\alpha)\left(\mathbf{u}_{i,t} + \beta_r \dot{\mathbf{u}}_{i,t}\right) + \alpha\left(\mathbf{u}_{i,t-1} + \beta_r \dot{\mathbf{u}}_{i,t-1}\right)\right]\end{aligned} \tag{54}$$

$$\begin{aligned}\frac{\partial \mathbf{R}_t}{\partial V_i} &= \frac{\partial \mathbf{M}}{\partial E_i}\left[\ddot{\mathbf{u}}_t + \alpha_r\left((1-\alpha)\dot{\mathbf{u}}_t + \alpha \dot{\mathbf{u}}_{t-1}\right)\right] \\ &= \mathbf{m}_i\left[\ddot{\mathbf{u}}_{i,t} + \alpha_r\left((1-\alpha)\dot{\mathbf{u}}_{i,t} + \alpha \dot{\mathbf{u}}_{i,t-1}\right)\right]\end{aligned} \tag{55}$$

where subscript (i, t) denotes the field vector of element i at time step t and subscript (i, $t-1$) denotes the field vector at time step $t-1$.

From Equation (12), the partial derivative of E_i with respect to $\tilde{\xi}_i$ is computed as follows:

$$\frac{\partial E_i}{\partial \tilde{\xi}_i} = \frac{1}{16}\left(15p\tilde{\xi}_i^{p-1} + 1\right) \tag{56}$$

As such, the sensitivity of the objective function regarding the macroscopic design variables can be obtained by substituting Equations (50)–(56) into Equation (49), where the adjoint variables are solved using Equations (44)–(47).

4.2. Sensitivity Analysis for Design Variables at the Microscale

Due to the effective material properties as a bridge between macro and microstructures, it is convenient to obtain the sensitivity information for the microscale design variables in the light of these homogenized parameters. For transient response problems, the sensitivity of f regarding the microscale design variables is recast via chain rule as follows:

$$\frac{\mathrm{d}f}{\mathrm{d}\eta_j} = \frac{\mathrm{d}f}{\mathrm{d}\mathbf{D}^{\mathrm{H}}}\frac{\partial \mathbf{D}^{\mathrm{H}}}{\partial \eta_j} + \frac{\mathrm{d}f}{\mathrm{d}\rho^{\mathrm{H}}}\frac{\partial \rho^{\mathrm{H}}}{\partial \eta_j} \tag{57}$$

where

$$\frac{\partial \mathbf{D}^{\mathrm{H}}}{\partial \tilde{\eta}_j} = \frac{p\tilde{\eta}_j^{p-1}}{|\Omega_m|}\int_{\Omega_m} \mathbf{D}_j^{\mathrm{mic}}(\mathbf{I} - \mathbf{b}\mathbf{u}_m)\mathrm{d}\Omega_m \tag{58}$$

$$\frac{\partial \rho^{\mathrm{H}}}{\partial \tilde{\eta}_j} = \frac{1}{|\Omega_m|}\int_{\Omega_m} \rho^{\mathrm{B}}\mathrm{d}\Omega_{mj} \tag{59}$$

The sensitivity of f with respect to the effective material properties can be attained from Equation (48), i.e.,

$$\frac{\mathrm{d}f}{\mathrm{d}\mathbf{D}^{\mathrm{H}}} = \frac{\partial f}{\partial \mathbf{D}^{\mathrm{H}}} + \sum_{t=0}^{\overline{N}} \boldsymbol{\lambda}_t^{\mathrm{T}} \frac{\partial \mathbf{R}_t}{\partial \mathbf{D}^{\mathrm{H}}} \tag{60}$$

$$\frac{\mathrm{d}f}{\mathrm{d}\rho^{\mathrm{H}}} = \frac{\partial f}{\partial \rho^{\mathrm{H}}} + \sum_{t=0}^{\overline{N}} \boldsymbol{\lambda}_t^{\mathrm{T}} \frac{\partial \mathbf{R}_t}{\partial \rho^{\mathrm{H}}} \tag{61}$$

where $\partial f/\partial \mathbf{D}^{\mathrm{H}} = \mathbf{0}$ and $\partial f/\partial \rho^{\mathrm{H}} = 0$, according to the objective function as shown in Equation (20).

Similarly, the partial derivatives, $\partial \mathbf{R}_t/\partial \mathbf{D}^{\mathrm{H}}$ and $\partial \mathbf{R}_t/\partial \rho^{\mathrm{H}}$, are evaluated using Equations (25) and (29), and for $i = 0$:

$$\frac{\partial \mathbf{R}_0}{\partial \mathbf{D}^{\mathrm{H}}} = \frac{\partial \mathbf{K}}{\partial \mathbf{D}^{\mathrm{H}}}\left(\mathbf{u}_0 + \beta_r \dot{\mathbf{u}}_0\right) = \sum_{i=1}^{N^{\mathrm{mac}}} g\left(\tilde{\xi}_i\right)\frac{\partial \mathbf{k}_i^0}{\partial \mathbf{D}^{\mathrm{H}}}\left(\mathbf{u}_0 + \beta_r \dot{\mathbf{u}}_0\right) \tag{62}$$

$$\frac{\partial \mathbf{R}_0}{\partial \rho^{\mathrm{H}}} = \frac{\partial \mathbf{M}}{\partial \rho^{\mathrm{H}}}\left(\ddot{\mathbf{u}}_0 + \alpha_r \dot{\mathbf{u}}_0\right) = \sum_{i=1}^{N^{\mathrm{mac}}} \tilde{\xi}_i \frac{\partial \mathbf{m}_i^0}{\partial \rho^{\mathrm{H}}}\left(\ddot{\mathbf{u}}_0 + \alpha_r \dot{\mathbf{u}}_0\right) \tag{63}$$

for $t = 1, \cdots, \overline{N}$:

$$\begin{aligned}\frac{\partial \mathbf{R}_t}{\partial \mathbf{D}^{\mathrm{H}}} &= \frac{\partial \mathbf{K}}{\partial \mathbf{D}^{\mathrm{H}}}\left[(1-\alpha)\left(\mathbf{u}_t + \beta_{\mathrm{r}}\dot{\mathbf{u}}_t\right) + \alpha\left(\mathbf{u}_{t-1} + \beta_{\mathrm{r}}\dot{\mathbf{u}}_{t-1}\right)\right] \\ &= \sum_{i=1}^{N^{\mathrm{mac}}} g\left(\tilde{\xi}_i\right)\frac{\partial \mathbf{k}_i^0}{\partial \mathbf{D}^{\mathrm{H}}}\left[(1-\alpha)\left(\mathbf{u}_t + \beta_{\mathrm{r}}\dot{\mathbf{u}}_t\right) + \alpha\left(\mathbf{u}_{t-1} + \beta_{\mathrm{r}}\dot{\mathbf{u}}_{t-1}\right)\right]\end{aligned} \tag{64}$$

$$\frac{\partial \mathbf{R}_t}{\partial \rho^{\mathrm{H}}} = \frac{\partial \mathbf{M}}{\partial \rho^{\mathrm{H}}}\left[\ddot{\mathbf{u}}_t + \alpha_{\mathrm{r}}\left((1-\alpha)\dot{\mathbf{u}}_t + \alpha\dot{\mathbf{u}}_{t-1}\right)\right] = \sum_{i=1}^{N^{\mathrm{mac}}} \tilde{\xi}_i \frac{\partial \mathbf{m}_i^0}{\partial \rho^{\mathrm{H}}}\left[\ddot{\mathbf{u}}_t + \alpha_{\mathrm{r}}\left((1-\alpha)\dot{\mathbf{u}}_t + \alpha\dot{\mathbf{u}}_{t-1}\right)\right] \tag{65}$$

4.3. Solution Procedure

The flowchart of the proposed concurrent topology optimization for multi-scale structures is depicted in Figure 1.

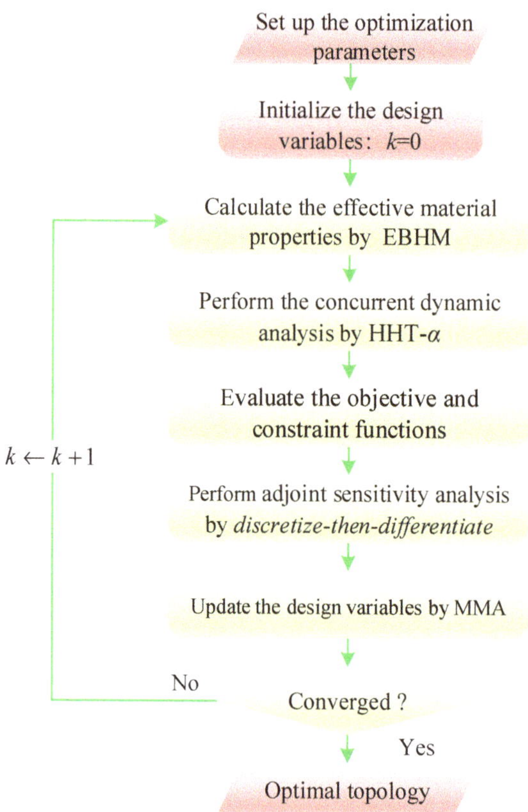

Figure 1. Schematic flowchart profiling the principal procedure to solve the concurrent dynamic compliance minimization problem.

This procedure launches through inputting the FEM information (i.e., the mesh, base material properties and boundary conditions) and the optimization parameters (i.e., the projection parameters, filter radius and penalty parameter), followed by the initialization of design variables. Then, on the basis of the current design variables, the homogenized mass density and the constitutive matrix are obtained via EBHM. The transient response of the multi-scale structure is computed using the HHT-α method whereby the objective function and constraints are directly calculated. Subsequently, the adjoint sensitivity analysis is performed based on the discretize-then-differentiate approach. Finally, the

Method of Moving Asymptotes (MMA) [48] is employed to update the design variables. This optimization process is terminated once a certain convergence criterion is met.

5. Adjoint Sensitivity Analysis Using Differentiate-Then-Discretize

The differentiate-then-discretize AVM constructs the adjoint equation in a semi-discretized dynamic system on the basis of spatial discrete and time continuous field variables, and subsequently the transient response is evaluated at each time step. We rewrite an objective function Φ in the following integral form:

$$\Phi = \int_0^J c(\mathbf{u}, \dot{\mathbf{u}}) \mathrm{d}\bar{t} \tag{66}$$

where J is the duration of the dynamic event and $\bar{t}$ is the continuous time variable.

We introduce the motion Equation (14) into Φ and thereby obtain the sensitivity Φ' by standard AVM:

$$\Phi' = \int_0^J \left(\partial c/\partial \mathbf{u} \mathbf{u}' + \partial c/\partial \dot{\mathbf{u}} \dot{\mathbf{u}}'\right) \mathrm{d}\bar{t} + \int_0^J \boldsymbol{\lambda}^{\mathrm{T}} (\mathbf{M}\ddot{\mathbf{u}} + \mathbf{C}\dot{\mathbf{u}} + \mathbf{K}\mathbf{u} - \mathbf{f})' \mathrm{d}\bar{t} \tag{67}$$

where the prime denotes differentiation regarding the design variables and $\boldsymbol{\lambda}$ denotes the smooth adjoint variable. Through twice integrating-by-parts, we rearrange Φ' as follows:

$$\begin{aligned} \Phi' = & \int_0^J \boldsymbol{\lambda}^{\mathrm{T}} (\mathbf{M}'\ddot{\mathbf{u}} + \mathbf{C}'\dot{\mathbf{u}} + \mathbf{K}'\mathbf{u}) \mathrm{d}\bar{t} \\ & + \int_0^J \mathbf{u}'^{\mathrm{T}} \left(\mathbf{M}\ddot{\boldsymbol{\lambda}} - \mathbf{C}\dot{\boldsymbol{\lambda}} + \mathbf{K}\boldsymbol{\lambda} + \partial c/\partial \mathbf{u} - \mathrm{d}(\partial c/\partial \dot{\mathbf{u}})/\mathrm{d}t\right) \mathrm{d}\bar{t} \\ & + \left[\mathbf{u}'^{\mathrm{T}} \left(-\mathbf{M}\dot{\boldsymbol{\lambda}} + \mathbf{C}\boldsymbol{\lambda} + \partial c/\partial \dot{\mathbf{u}}^{\mathrm{T}}\right) + \dot{\mathbf{u}}'^{\mathrm{T}} \mathbf{M}\boldsymbol{\lambda}\right]\Big|_{\bar{t}=J} \end{aligned} \tag{68}$$

where we employ the assumption that the external load, as well as the initial condition, is design-independent for simplification. To remove the response derivatives $\mathbf{u}'(J)$ and $\dot{\mathbf{u}}'(J)$ at the final time step, we assign the adjoint variables such that the terminal conditions are satisfied as follows:

$$\boldsymbol{\lambda}(J) = 0,\ \mathbf{M}\dot{\boldsymbol{\lambda}}(J) = (\partial c/\partial \mathbf{u})^{\mathrm{T}}\Big|_{\bar{t}=J} \tag{69}$$

To transform the adjoint problem into the initial value problem, we use a variable transformation $\bar{t} = \tau(s) = J - s$ and then construct a composite function $\boldsymbol{\Lambda}$ satisfying $\boldsymbol{\Lambda}(s) = \boldsymbol{\lambda}(\tau(s))$. Accordingly, we rewrite Equation (68) by transforming all the terms including $\mathbf{u}'$ and $\dot{\mathbf{u}}'$:

$$\begin{aligned} \Phi' = & \int_0^J \boldsymbol{\lambda}^{\mathrm{T}} (\mathbf{M}'\ddot{\mathbf{u}} + \mathbf{C}'\dot{\mathbf{u}} + \mathbf{K}'\mathbf{u}) \mathrm{d}\bar{t} + \int_0^J \mathbf{u}'^{\mathrm{T}}(\tau(s)) \left(\partial c/\partial \mathbf{u} - \mathrm{d}(\partial c/\partial \dot{\mathbf{u}})/\mathrm{d}t\right)\big|_{\bar{t}=\tau(s)} \mathrm{d}s \\ & + \int_0^J \mathbf{u}'^{\mathrm{T}}(\tau(s)) \left(\mathbf{M}\ddot{\boldsymbol{\Lambda}}(\tau(s)) + \mathbf{C}\dot{\boldsymbol{\Lambda}}(\tau(s)) + \mathbf{K}\boldsymbol{\Lambda}(\tau(s))\right) \mathrm{d}s \\ & + \left[\mathbf{u}'^{\mathrm{T}}(J) \left(\mathbf{M}\dot{\boldsymbol{\Lambda}}(0) - \mathbf{C}\boldsymbol{\Lambda}(0) + \partial c/\partial \dot{\mathbf{u}}^{\mathrm{T}}\Big|_{\bar{t}=J}\right) + \dot{\mathbf{u}}'^{\mathrm{T}}(J) \mathbf{M}\boldsymbol{\Lambda}(0)\right] \end{aligned} \tag{70}$$

To annul all the terms containing $\mathbf{u}'$ and $\dot{\mathbf{u}}'$, we formulate the adjoint variable $\boldsymbol{\Lambda}$ as follows:

$$\begin{aligned} & \mathbf{M}\ddot{\boldsymbol{\Lambda}}(\tau(s)) + \mathbf{C}\dot{\boldsymbol{\Lambda}}(\tau(s)) + \mathbf{K}\boldsymbol{\Lambda}(\tau(s)) = \left(-\partial c/\partial \mathbf{u} + \mathrm{d}(\partial c/\partial \dot{\mathbf{u}})/\mathrm{d}t\right)\big|_{\bar{t}=\tau(s)} \\ & \boldsymbol{\Lambda}(0) = \mathbf{0},\ \mathbf{M}\dot{\boldsymbol{\Lambda}}(0) = -\partial c/\partial \dot{\mathbf{u}}^{\mathrm{T}}\big|_{\bar{t}=J} \end{aligned} \tag{71}$$

where the sensitivity is simplified as follows:

$$\Phi' = \int_0^J \boldsymbol{\Lambda}^{\mathrm{T}}(J - \bar{t}) (\mathbf{M}'\ddot{\mathbf{u}}(\bar{t}) + \mathbf{C}'\dot{\mathbf{u}}(\bar{t}) + \mathbf{K}'\mathbf{u}(\bar{t})) \mathrm{d}\bar{t} = \boldsymbol{\Lambda}^{\mathrm{T}} * (\mathbf{M}'\ddot{\mathbf{u}} + \mathbf{C}'\dot{\mathbf{u}} + \mathbf{K}'\mathbf{u})\Big|_{\bar{t}=J} \tag{72}$$

where $*$ denotes the convolution operator.

Following the obtained displacement and velocity, $\mathbf{u}_t$ and $\dot{\mathbf{u}}_t$, we approximate the original objective function employing the rectangular formula:

$$\widetilde{\Phi} = \sum_{t=0}^{N} c(\mathbf{u}_t, \dot{\mathbf{u}}_t) \tag{73}$$

Based on the discretized adjoint variables $\mathbf{\Lambda}_n$ solution from Equation (71), the sensitivity of objective function is approximated as follows:

$$\widetilde{\Phi}' = \sum_{t=0}^{N} \mathbf{\Lambda}_{N-t}^{\mathrm{T}} \left(\mathbf{M}'\ddot{\mathbf{u}}_t + \mathbf{C}'\dot{\mathbf{u}}_t + \mathbf{K}'\mathbf{u}_t\right) \tag{74}$$

In virtue of the order of differentiation and discretization, this method is featured as differentiate-then-discretize in that we first differentiate the augmented objective function to achieve Equation (72) and subsequently implement the time discretization to achieve Equation (74). This approach is seemingly elegant since the resultant adjoint transient problem is similar to the primal problem. Nevertheless, the method encounters the notably inconsistent sensitivity, as indicated in the following numerical examples. Since the resultant optimal configuration is based on the objective function sensitivity, gradient-based topology optimization demands the precise sensitivity information to design variables. We examine the efficiency of both discretize-then-differentiate and differentiate-then-discretize approaches for AVM sensitivity analysis by comparing them with the sensitivity evaluated through the finite difference method (FDM).

6. Numerical Examples

This section offers four benchmark cases to validate the proposed approach: a cantilever beam, a clamped beam, a support structure, a building and a simply supported 3D structure. We compare the two-scale optimal results obtained from Zhao et al. [22] based on the differentiate-then-discretize AVM with those from this manuscript, based on the discretize-then-differentiate AVM in the given four examples. For all numerical examples, we adopt the damping coefficient $\alpha = 0.05$ and determine the Newmark constants β and γ by employing the formulas $\beta = (1+\alpha)^2/4$ and $\gamma = (1+2\alpha)/2$, for at least second-order accuracy and unconditional stability, respectively. Moreover, in every example, we first verify the validness of the discretize-then-differentiate method for AVM sensitivity analysis, and then investigate the influence of loading parameters on the optimum solution using the transient concurrent topology optimization based on the discretize-then-differentiate AVM. All the programs in four benchmark cases are written with the available version of MATLAB 2021.

6.1. Cantilever Beam Design under Half-Cycle Sinusoidal Load

As depicted in Figure 2, a cantilever beam is subjected to a concentrated half-sine load vertically exerted at the midpoint of right free edge. The geometrical dimension of the cantilever beam is as follows: length L = 8 m, height H = 4 m and thickness h = 0.01 m. For a composite structure with uniform microstructure, its Young's modulus is 200 GPa, Poisson's ratio is 0.3 and mass density is 7800 kg/m^3. The Rayleigh damping parameters α_r and β_r are assumed to be 10 s^{-1} and 1×10^{-5} s, respectively. The macroscopic and microscopic design domains are discretized into 5000 and 2500 four-node square quadrilateral elements, respectively. The maximal volume fraction for the macrostructure is specified to be 50%, and that for the unit cell is defined as 50%. To solve this problem, we adopt the input parameters listed in Table 1.

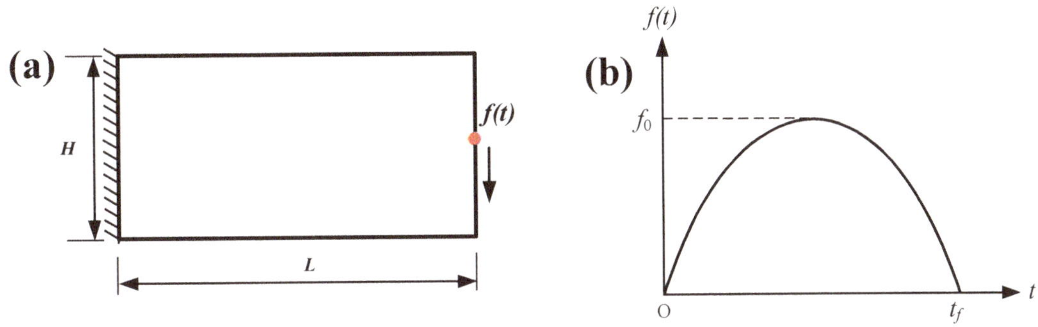

Figure 2. Cantilever beam problem: (**a**) design domain and (**b**) half-cycle sinusoidal load.

Table 1. Input parameters used to solve the cantilever beam problem.

Parameter	Value
Simulation time	0.05 s, 0.03 s, and 0.01 s
Number of time steps	100
Young's modulus of base material	200 GPa
Poisson's ratio of base material	0.3
Mass density of base material	7800 kg/m^3
Rayleigh damping parameters	10 s^{-1} and 1×10^{-5} s
Volume fraction limit of macrostructure and unit cell	0.5 and 0.5
Filter radius in macro/micro design domain and filter exponent	[0.12, 0.002] and 3
Chosen element type	Four-nodes bilateral element
Macroscopic element thickness	0.01 m
Number of elements discretized in macroscopic design domain	5000
Number of elements discretized in microscopic design domain	2500

Table 2 compares the design sensitivity between two AVM approaches, discretize-then-differentiate and differentiate-then-discretize, and FDM for this cantilever beam problem with a load application duration of $t_f = 0.05$ s. We demonstrate the consistency error, namely the relative difference normalized by the exact sensitivity through FDM. It can be found that the sensitivities obtained with discretize-then-differentiate are significantly consistent with those obtained through FDM. However, the differentiate-then-discretize AVM induces significant inconsistent sensitivities. Figure 3 presents the iteration histories of the objective function and the constraint, and the optimized solution obtained using these two AVM-based sensitivity analysis techniques with a load application duration of 0.05 s. Obviously, the optimized configuration via discretize-then-differentiate is more favorable due to a lower value of the objective function. Thus, these results show that the order of differentiation and discretization has obvious effect on the consistency errors, which in turn can produce the inefficient optimum design.

Table 2. Comparison of design sensitivity and optimum for the cantilever beam problem.

Sensitivity Analysis Method	Peak Relative Error (%)		Optimum (Nm)
	Macro Design Domain	Micro Design Domain	
Discretize-then-differentiate	1.8	1.6	1.12
Differentiate-then-discretize	13.6	11.5	1.71

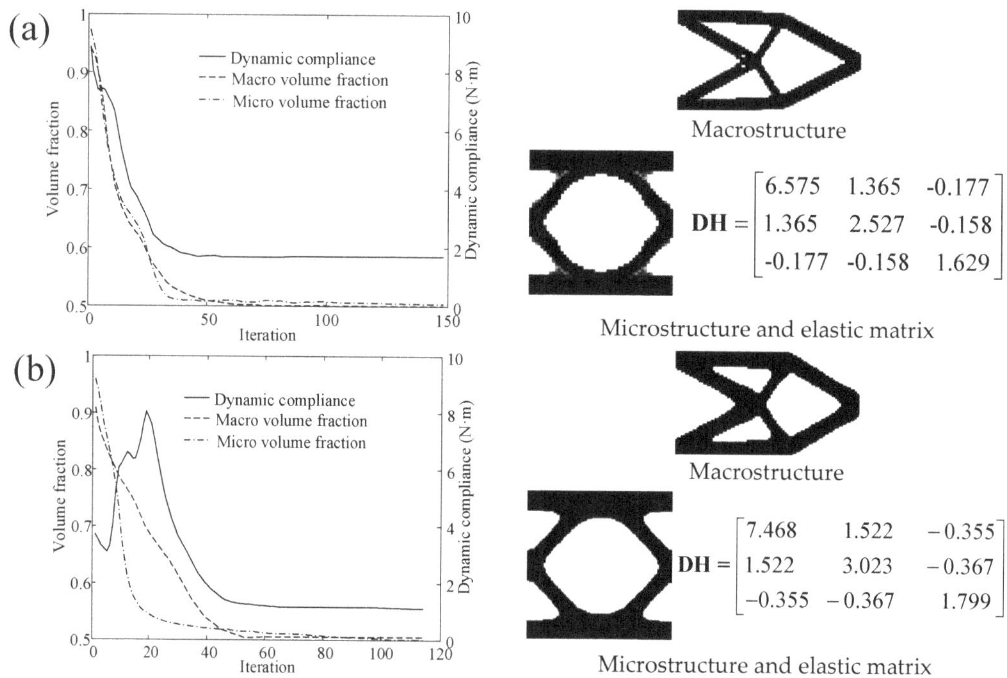

Figure 3. Iterative history (left) and optimized topologies obtained (right) for a cantilever beam with $t_f = 0.05$ s using various adjoint sensitivity analysis. (**a**) Differentiate-then-discretize and (**b**) discretize-then-differentiate.

Figure 4 shows the iterative histories during concurrent optimization and the resulting optimal designs for the load application duration of $t_f = 0.03, 0.01$ s. It is seen that the optimized topologies at two scales for $t_f = 0.05$ s (Figure 3b) and $t_f = 0.03$ s (Figure 4a) are nearly identical to each other. But in the case of $t_f = 0.01$ s (Figure 4b), the optimal configurations greatly distinguish from the counterparts obtained for larger load application duration. When $t_f = 0.01$s, substantial porous material is placed near the free edge of this beam, which produces inertial force to offset the short impulsive loading, which is is subsequently verified with the dynamic response as plotted in Figure 4. Also, the optimized macrostructure links the large mass distributed towards the free edge to the bracing ends by two horizontal beam-like members, which contribute to reducing the vertical bending of the beam.

Figure 5 depicts the vertical displacement history at the load application point and the transient dynamic compliance of the beam. These results demonstrate that the transient responses for $t_f = 0.05$ s resemble those for $t_f = 0.03$ s, while they are significantly different for $t_f = 0.01$ s. Particularly for $t_f = 0.01$ s, the optimal beam continuously deflects downward, although the external load gradually decreases following $t_f = 0.005$ s, which attributes to the fact that the resulting inertial force is sufficiently large to drive the beam downward.

6.2. Clamped Beam Design under Half-Cycle Cosine Load

In this example, we consider a beam fixed at both ends and excited via a concentrated half-cosine load vertically at the center of the bottom edge, as shown in Figure 6. The macroscopic design domain has length $L = 12$ m, height $H = 2$ m and thickness $h = 0.01$ m. We adopt a linear elastic material with a Young's modulus of 200 GPa, Poisson's ratio of 0.3 and mass density of 7800 kg/m^3. The macroscopic design domain and the unit cell are discretized by respective 5000 and 2500 bilinear square elements. The volume fraction limits for both macrostructure and unit cell are set to be 0.5. The Rayleigh damping parameters α_r and β_r are the same as those in the first example. To solve this problem, we adopt the input parameters listed in Table 3.

Table 3. Input parameters used to solve the clamped beam problem.

Parameter	Value
Simulation time	0.5 s and 0.05 s
Number of time steps	100
Young's modulus of base material	200 GPa
Poisson's ratio of base material	0.3
Mass density of base material	7800 kg/m^3
Rayleigh damping parameters	10 s^{-1} and 1×10^{-5} s
Volume fraction limit of macrostructure and unit cell	0.5 and 0.5
Filter radius in macro/micro design domain and filter exponent	[0.10, 0.005] and 3
Chosen element type	Four-nodes bilateral element
Macroscopic element thickness	0.01 m
Number of elements discretized in macroscopic design domain	5000
Number of elements discretized in microscopic design domain	2500

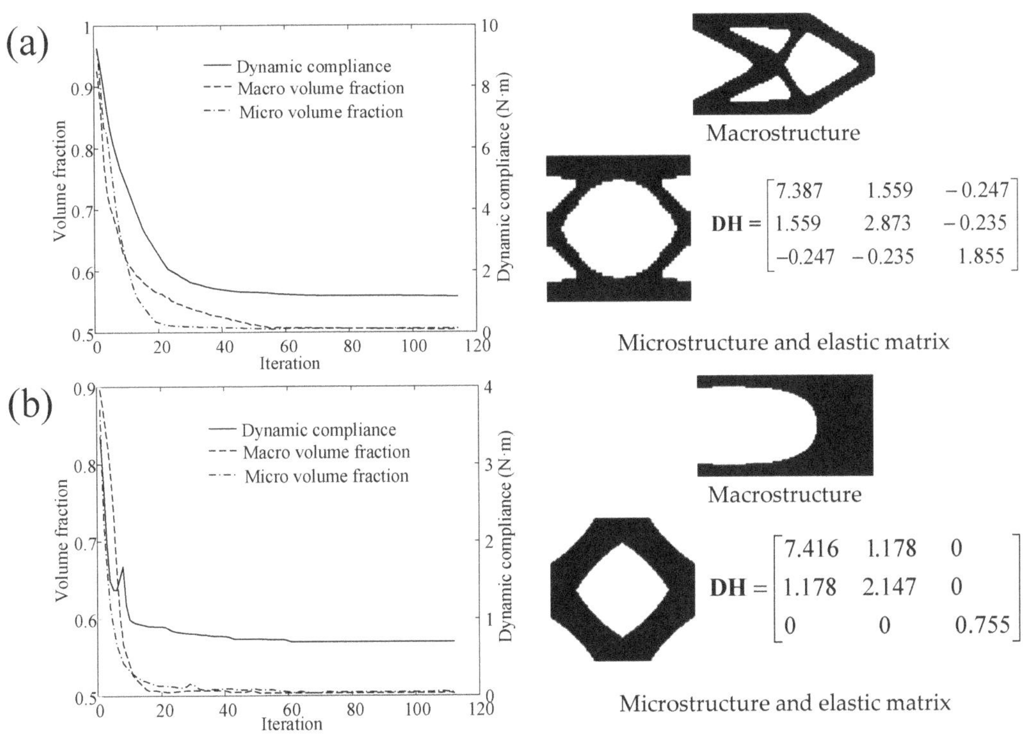

Figure 4. Iterative history (left) and optimized topologies obtained (right) for a cantilever beam. (**a**) $t_f = 0.03$ s and (**b**) $t_f = 0.01$ s.

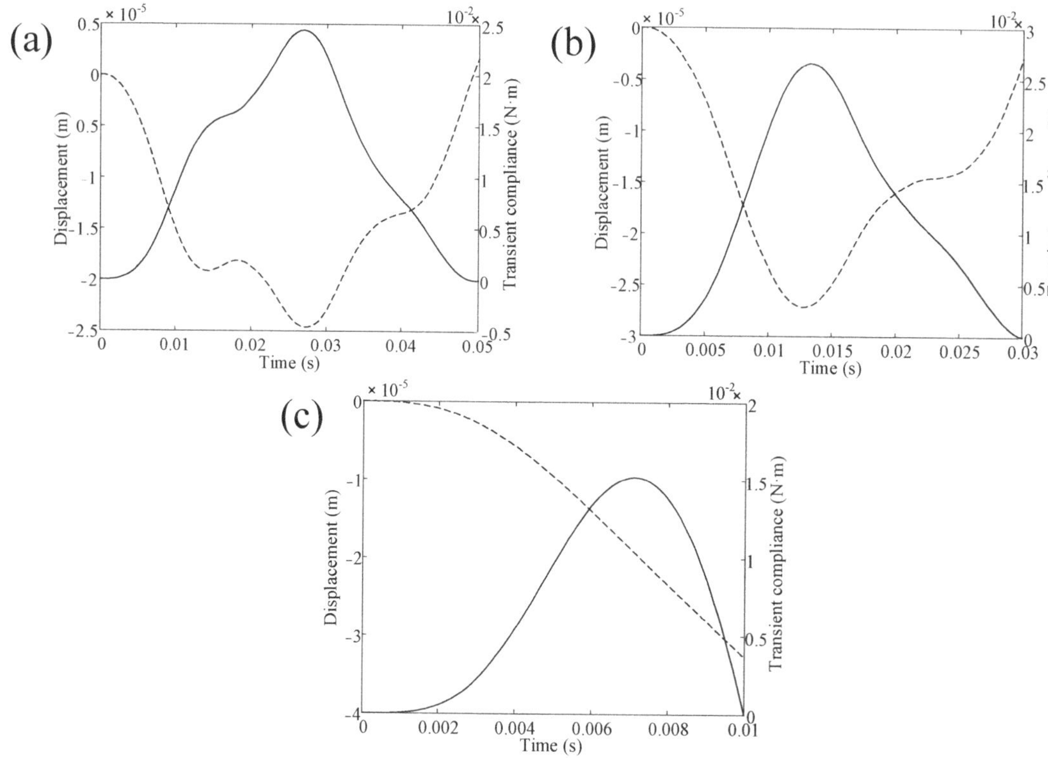

Figure 5. Time histories of deflection at the load application point and structural transient compliance for each design of Figures 4b and 5. (**a**) t_f = 0.05 s, (**b**) t_f = 0.03 s, and (**c**) t_f = 0.01 s. ——— denotes the dynamic compliance and – – – denotes the vertical displacement, respectively.

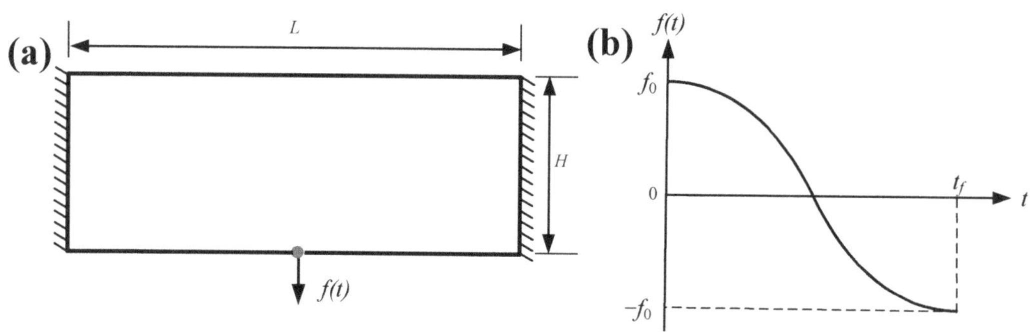

Figure 6. Clamped beam problem. (**a**) Design domain and (**b**) half-cycle cosine load.

Table 4 compares the relative errors of the sensitivity obtained through the discretize-then-differentiate AVM with those of the sensitivity obtained with the differentiate-then-discretize AVM for this clamped beam problem for a load application duration of $t_f = 0.5$ s. The former achieves consistent sensitivities with the FDM, while the latter results in obvious consistency errors. This comparison affirms the efficiency of the discretize-then-differentiate AVM for dynamic problems in the time domain. To verify the discretize-then-differentiate AVM for transient concurrent topology optimization, we apply this approach to solve the clamped beam problem and carry out a comparison of the optimized solution with those obtained via the differentiate-then-discretize AVM. These results, as illustrated in Figure 7, reveal that concurrent topology optimization based on the discretize-then-differentiate AVM is more efficient for the transient problem due to lower optimum value of the dynamic compliance.

Table 4. Comparison of design sensitivity and optimum for the clamped beam problem.

Sensitivity Analysis Method	Peak Relative Error (%)		Optimum (N m)
	Macro Design Domain	Micro Design Domain	
Discretize-then-differentiate	2.1	1.8	0.46
Differentiate-then-discretize	18.9	16.3	0.82

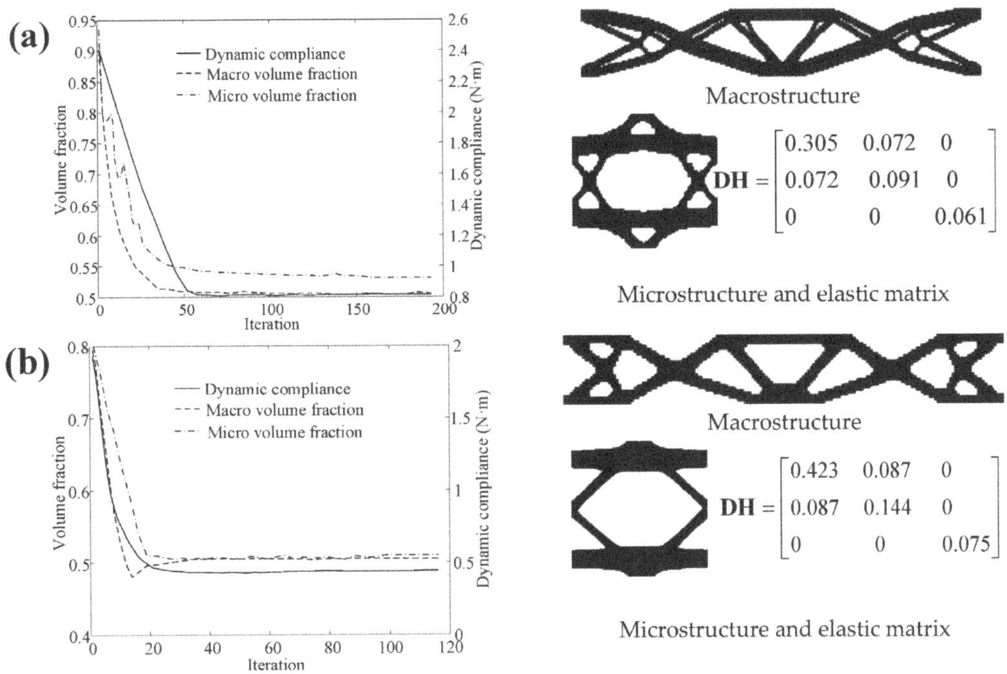

Figure 7. Iterative history (left) and optimized topologies obtained (right) for a clamped beam with $t_f = 0.5$ s using various adjoint sensitivity analysis. (**a**) Differentiate-then-discretize and (**b**) discretize-then-differentiate.

Figure 8 shows the convergence history and the optimal design for $t_f = 0.05$ s. As seen from the results in Figures 7b and 8, the optimal topologies are highly dependent on t_f. For short-term dynamic load, the optimizer assigns less porous material within the neighborhood of load application point and instead adds two beam-like members. That is favorable to endure the increased local deflection near the load application point, which arise as a result of the augmentation of dynamic influence.

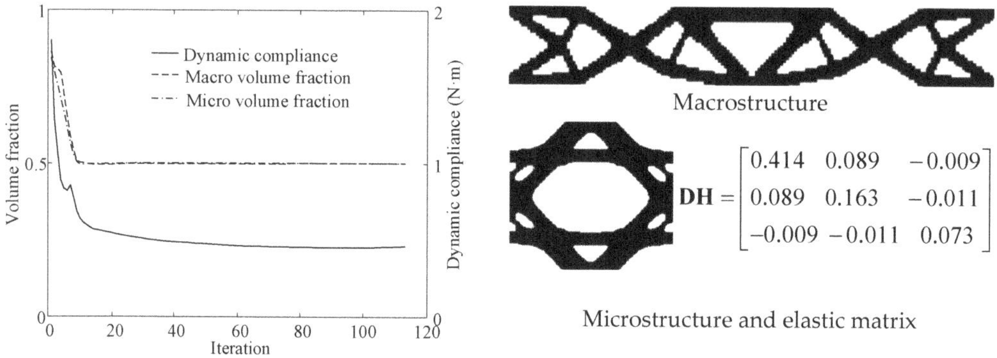

Figure 8. Iterative history (**left**) and optimized topologies obtained (**right**) for a clamped beam with $t_f = 0.05$ s.

Figure 9 depicts the dynamic response of respective optimized design for $t_f = 0.5$ s and $t_f = 0.05$ s, as demonstrated in Figures 7b and 8. The damping effect is obviously identified from the results acquired for $t_f = 0.5$ s, when the amplitude of vertical displacement and transient dynamic compliance decay over the load application duration due to the energy dissipation in the damping material. In contrast to the results for $t_f = 0.5$ s, the dissipation effect of damping attenuates over time for $t_f = 0.05$ s, owing to the shorter load application duration. Therefore, the load application duration directly affects the dissipation of internal energy and the structural vibration. This explains why the optimum designs are susceptible to the load application duration.

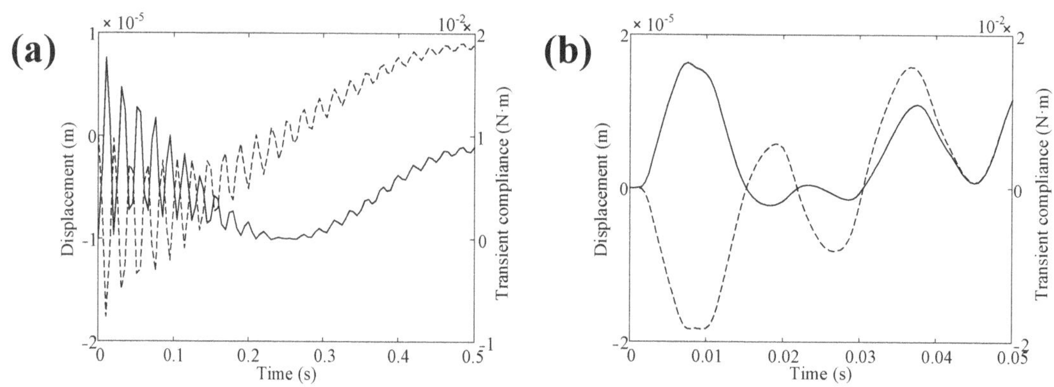

Figure 9. Time histories of deflection at the load application point and structural transient compliance for each design of Figures 9b and 10. (**a**) $t_f = 0.5$ s and (**b**) $t_f = 0.05$ s. ——— denotes the dynamic compliance and — — — denotes the vertical displacement, respectively.

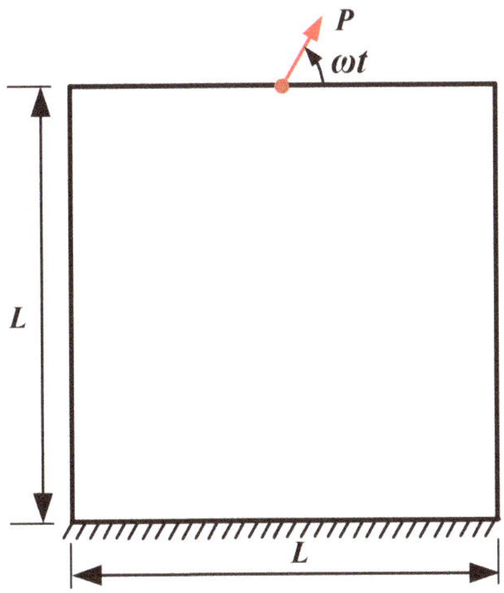

Figure 10. Support structure under rotating load.

6.3. Support Structure Design under Rotating Load

As shown in Figure 10, we use a square structure fixed at the bottom edge, subjected to a rotating load with a specified constant amplitude and angular frequency at the center of upper free edge. The square domain has length L = 3 m and thickness h = 0.05 m. The base material has a Young's modulus of 70 GPa, a Poisson's ratio of 0.3, and a mass density of 7800 kg/m^3. The macroscopic design domain and the unit cell are discretized by respective 5000 and 2500 bilinear square elements. The volume fraction limits of the macrostructure and the unit cell are defined as 0.3 and 0.5, respectively. The Rayleigh damping parameters α_r and β_r are assumed to be 50 s^{-1} and 3×10^{-5} s, respectively. To solve this problem, we adopt the input parameters listed in Table 5.

Table 5. Input parameters used to solve the support structure problem.

Parameter	Value
Simulation time	$10\pi/\omega$, $\omega = 100\pi$ and 25π rad/s
Number of time steps	100
Young's modulus of base material	70 GPa
Poisson's ratio of base material	0.3
Mass density of base material	7800 kg/m^3
Rayleigh damping parameters	50 s^{-1} and 3×10^{-5} s
Volume fraction limit of macrostructure and unit cell	0.3 and 0.5
Filter radius in macro/micro design domain and filter exponent	[0.06, 0.0015] and 3
Chosen element type	Four-nodes bilateral element
Macroscopic element thickness	0.05 m
Number of elements discretized in macroscopic design domain	5000
Number of elements discretized in microscopic design domain	2500

To demonstrate the consistency of adjoint sensitivity analysis for transient concurrent topology optimization, we plot the relative error of the two sensitivities obtained with both differentiate-then-discretize and discretize-then-differentiate through examining this support structure design under a rotating load. These results with angular frequency $\omega = 100\pi$ rad/s, as illustrated in Table 6, confirm that the latter can ensure consistent sensitivities despite more cumbersome implementation. In gradient-based topology optimization, an accurate sensitivity analysis is requisite for the exact optimal solution. As a consequence, the optimized design based on the discretize-then-differentiate approach is necessary to be more effective due to high accuracy in sensitivity computation. Figure 11 demonstrates that the objective function converges to the smaller value acquired with discretize-then-differentiate than the counterpart acquired via differentiate-then-discretize. As such, we prefer the former for a transient multi-scale topology optimization problem. In order to study the influence of angular frequency on the final design for this support structure, we present an additional optimal design for $\omega = 25\pi$ rad/s, as shown in Figure 12. The first design (Figure 11b) adds an extra lateral resistant system in its macroscopic topology to diminish the structural lateral motion, whereas the second (Figure 12) is just composed of two rod-like members in its macroscopic topology. These two designs have a similar microscopic topology.

Table 6. Comparison of design sensitivity and optimum for the support structure problem.

Sensitivity Analysis Method	Peak Relative Error (%)		Optimum (Nm)
	Macro Design Domain	Micro Design Domain	
Discretize-then-differentiate	1.4	0.9	1.96
Differentiate-then-discretize	15.6	14.2	2.91

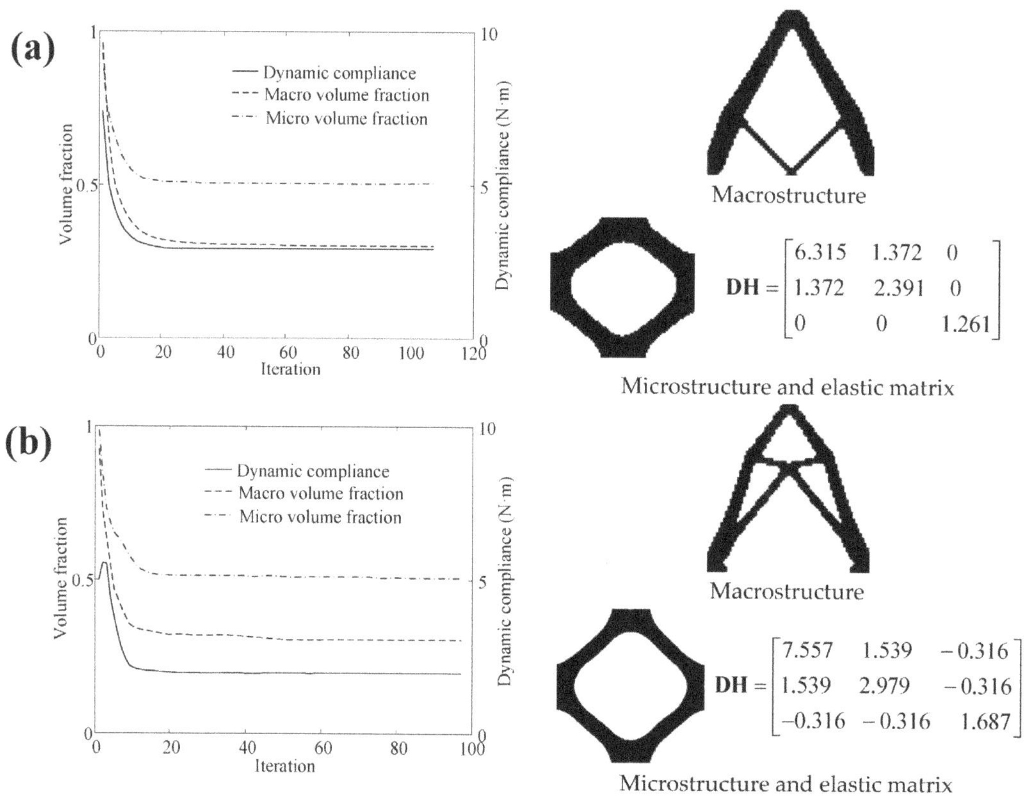

Figure 11. Iterative history (left) and optimized topologies obtained (right) for a support structure with $\omega = 100\pi$ rad/s using various adjoint sensitivity analysis. (**a**) Differentiate-then-discretize and (**b**) discretize-then-differentiate.

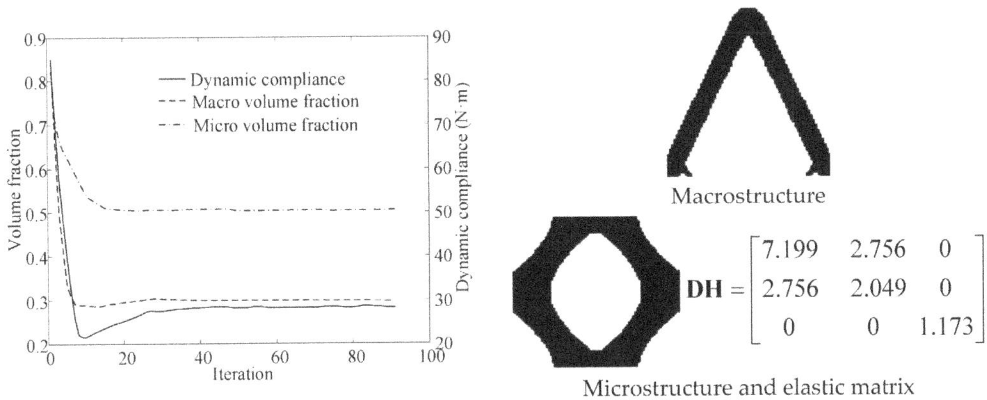

Figure 12. Iterative history (**left**) and optimized topologies obtained (**right**) for a support structure with ω = 25π rad/s.

Figure 13 presents the time history of horizontal displacement at the load application point and transient dynamic compliance for the two optimum designs demonstrated in Figures 11b and 12. The results indicate that the dynamic effect happen through the initial time steps, followed by vibration attenuation owing to damping dissipation. Furthermore, as is expected, the optimal design obtained for $\omega = 100\pi$ rad/s produce the lower vibrational level than the counterpart obtained for $\omega = 25\pi$ rad/s due to the additional lateral resistant system.

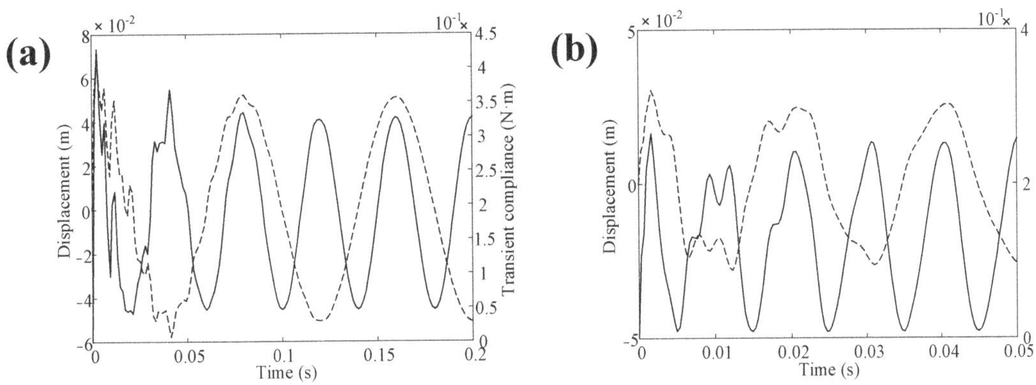

Figure 13. Time histories of deflection at the load application point and structural transient compliance for each design of Figures 4b and 5. (**a**) ω = 25π rad/s and (**b**) ω = 100π rad/s. ——— denotes the dynamic compliance and – – – denotes the displacement along the rotating load, respectively.

6.4. Building Design under Ground Excitation

This example aims to design a building under a time-varying ground acceleration in a sinusoidal function. Figure 14 states this optimization problem with the initial configuration, ground acceleration as well as specified volume constraint at two scales. The building with length L = 75 m, height H = 75 m and thickness h = 0.05 m is clamped at the bottom and a lumped mass mc at the center of top edge is placed. The Young's modulus, Poisson's ratio and mass density of the base material are 35 Gpa, 0.25 and 2400 kg/m^3, respectively. The macroscopic design domain and the unit cell are meshed into respective 10,000 and 2500 square bilateral elements, where volume fraction limits at the two scales are prescribed as 0.5. The Rayleigh damping parameters α_r and β_r are assumed to be 2

s^{-1} and 2×10^{-6} s, respectively. Note that when considering ground accelerations, we replace the external load **f** with $-m_c a_g \mathbf{I}$ in Equation (14). In this example, the frequency of ground acceleration is supposed to be 2.5π rad/s. To solve this problem, we adopt the input parameters listed in Table 7.

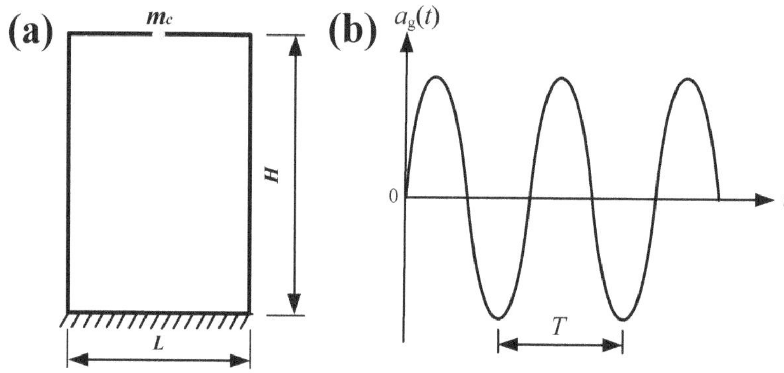

Figure 14. Building design subjected to ground acceleration: (**a**) building domain and (**b**) sinusoidal ground acceleration.

Table 7. Input parameters used to solve the building problem.

Parameter	Value
Simulation time	4.8 s
Number of time steps	100
Young's modulus of base material	35 GPa
Poisson's ratio of base material	0.25
Mass density of base material	2400 kg/m^3
Rayleigh damping parameters	2 s^{-1} and 2×10^{-6} s
Lumped masses	0.1×10^6, 0.3×10^6 and 0.6×10^6 kg
Volume fraction limit of macrostructure and unit cell	0.3 and 0.5
Filter radius in macro/micro design domain and filter exponent	[1.0, 0.02] and 3
Chosen element type	Four-nodes bilateral element
Macroscopic element thickness	0.05 m
Number of elements discretized in macroscopic design domain	10,000
Number of elements discretized in microscopic design domain	2500

Similarly, we first review the consistency of adjoint sensitivity analysis for transient concurrent topology optimization and then demonstrate the influence of sensitivity approximation on the final topology with this building design. These results in sensitivity calculation with a lumped mass $m_c = 0.3 \times 10^6$ kg, as listed in Table 8, indicating that the discretize-then-differentiate AVM can present consistent sensitivity due to high accuracy in nature. However, the differentiate-then-discretize AVM inherently generates inconsistent sensitivities. Consequently, we can obtain a more efficient multi-scale topology optimized via discretize-then-differentiate, as demonstrated in Figure 15. Figure 15 shows the optimal topologies obtained for 2.5π rad/s and $m_c = 0.6 \times 10^6$ kg. As is seen from the results in Figures 15b and 16, the optimum design is greatly susceptible to the lumped mass magnitude. The cross bars conjoined to the lumped mass are slightly thicker with increasing lumped mass. This is due to the larger inertial loads transferred from the lumped mass to the building when m_c is increasing. Additionally, merely a lateral resistant system develops on the upper end of the building for small m_c in Figure 16a, while an additive lateral resistant system develops at the bottom for large m_c in Figures 15b and 16b, which is in favor of incremental inertial forces' transfer to the supports.

Table 8. Comparison of design sensitivity and optimum for the building problem.

Sensitivity Analysis Method	Peak Relative Error (%)		Optimum (Nm)
	Macro Design Domain	Micro Design Domain	
Discretize-then-differentiate	2.0	1.2	23.4
Differentiate-then-discretize	23.6	15.4	31.6

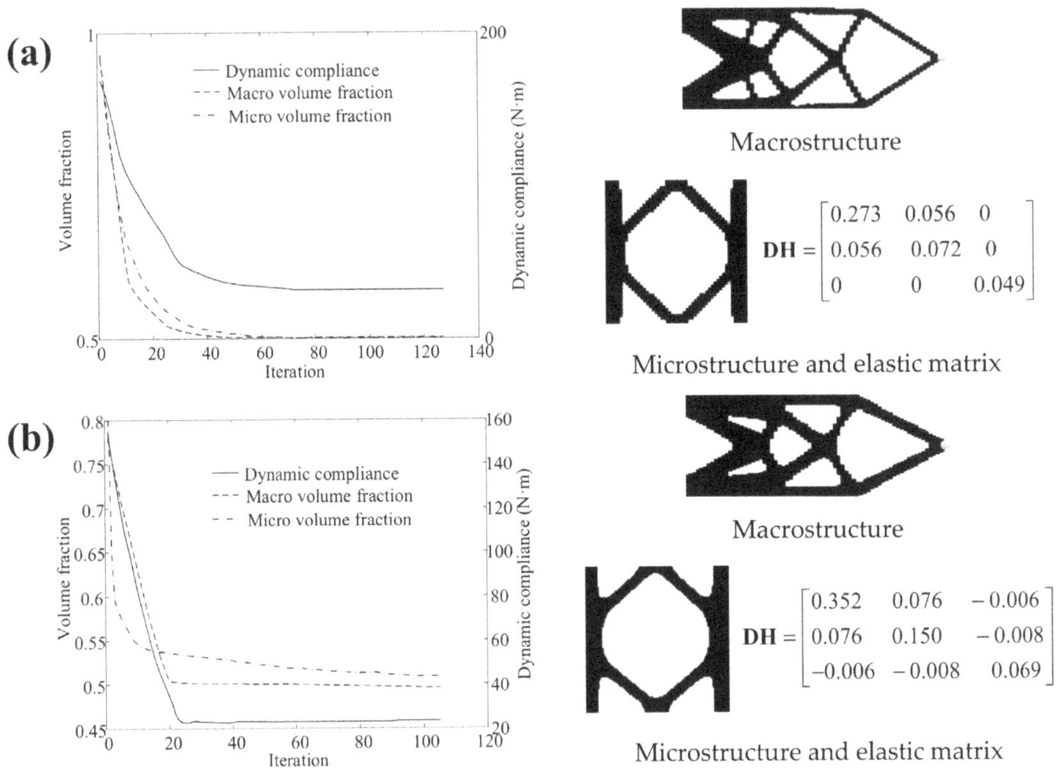

Figure 15. Iterative history (left) and optimized topologies obtained (right) for a building structure with $m_c = 0.3 \times 10^6$ kg using various adjoint sensitivity analysis. (**a**) Differentiate-then-discretize and (**b**) discretize-then-differentiate.

To comprehend the dynamic behavior of the building underground excitation along both horizontal and vertical directions, we plot the dynamic response of the optimum designs for various lumped mass, as illustrated in Figure 17. As observed from these results, the vertical displacement at the load application point is much larger than the horizontal counterpart due to the lateral resistant system regardless of the magnitude of the lumped mass. Note that with increasing lumped mass, the resultant vertical displacements at the load application point increase in the amplitude, such that the corresponding dynamic compliances became slightly larger. This inertial effect obviously influences the optimal topology, which cannot be apprehended with static optimization formulations.

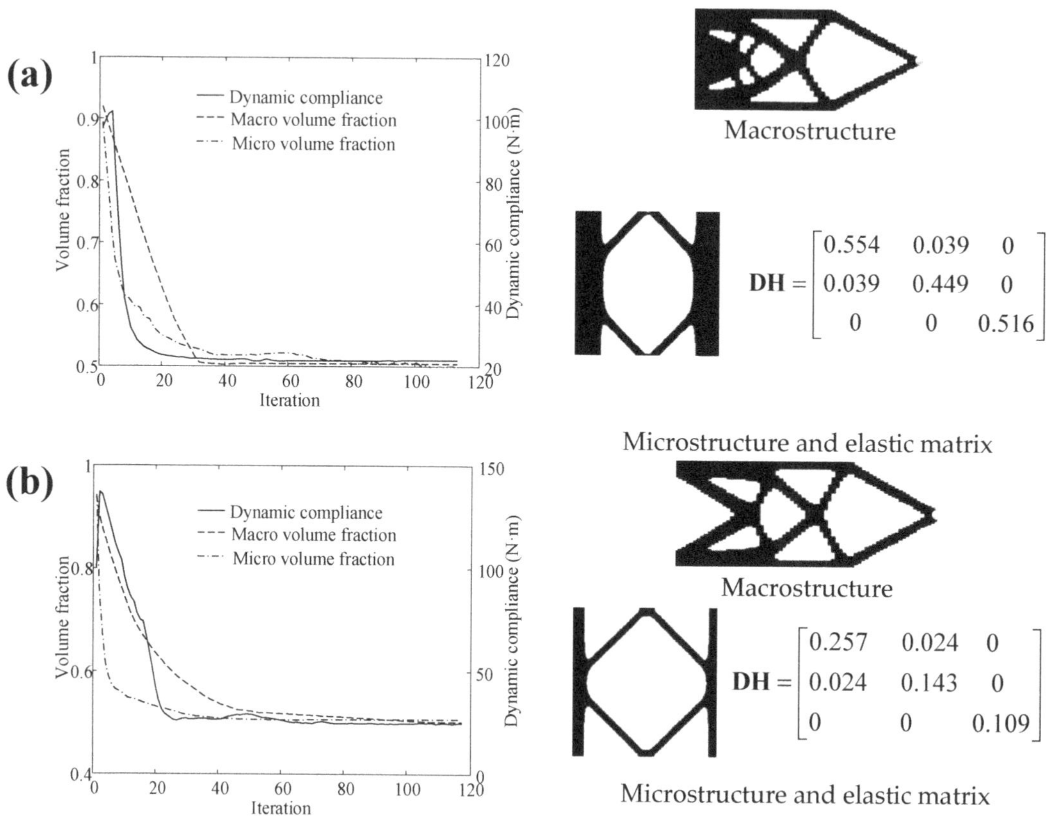

Figure 16. Iterative history (left) and optimized topologies obtained (right) for a building structure. (**a**) $m_c = 0.1 \times 10^6$ kg and (**b**) $m_c = 0.6 \times 10^6$ kg.

6.5. Simply Supported 3D Structure

This example optimizes a 3D structure to examine the capability of the presented algorithm for large-scale transient topology optimization. As shown in Figure 18, this design domain has the following dimensions: length $L = 4.5$ m, height $H = 0.75$ m and thickness $h = 0.5$ m. This structure is supported at the bottom four corners under the same transient load as the first example. The Young's modulus, Poisson's ratio and mass density of base material are 200 Gpa, 0.3 and 7800 kg/m^3, respectively. The macroscopic design domain is discretized with 13,500 eight-nodes brick elements and the unit cell with 8000 eight-nodes brick elements. The volume fraction limits at the two scales are prescribed as 0.5. The Rayleigh damping parameters α_r and β_r are assumed to be 10 s^{-1} and 2×10^{-5} s, respectively. Table 9 offers all the adopted input data to solve the problem.

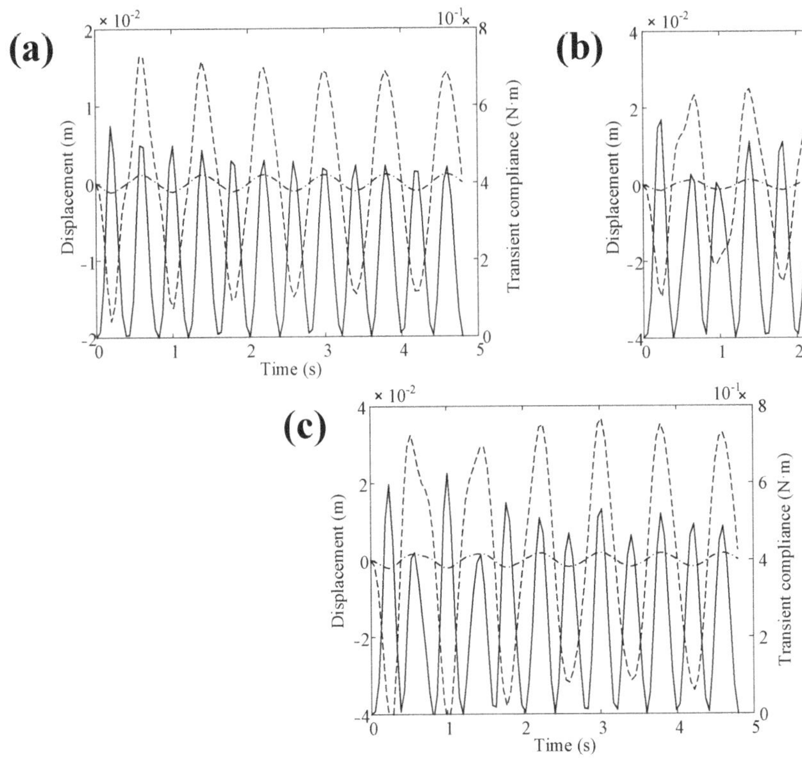

Figure 17. Time histories of deflection at the load application point and structural transient compliance for each design of Figures 15b and 16. (**a**) $m_c = 0.1 \times 10^6$ kg, (**b**) $m_c = 0.3 \times 10^6$ kg and (**c**) $m_c = 0.6 \times 10^6$ kg. denotes the dynamic compliance, denotes the vertical displacement and denotes the horizontal displacement, respectively.

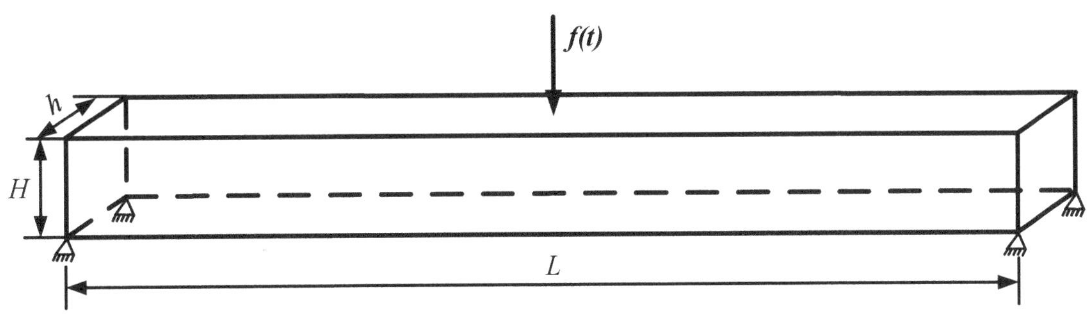

Figure 18. Simply supported 3D structure.

Table 9. Input parameters used to solve the simply supported 3D structure problem.

Parameter	Value
Simulation time	0.05 s
Number of time steps	100
Young's modulus of base material	200 GPa
Poisson's ratio of base material	0.3
Mass density of base material	7800 kg/m^3
Rayleigh damping parameters	10 s^{-1} and 2×10^{-5} s
Volume fraction limit of macrostructure and unit cell	0.5 and 0.5
Filter radius in macro/micro design domain and filter exponent	[0.15, 0.008] and 3
Chosen element type	Eight-nodes brick element
Number of elements discretized in macroscopic design domain	13,500
Number of elements discretized in microscopic design domain	8000

Figure 19 depicts the final designs at macro/micro scales. Compared with the 2D structure, the design space is enlarged by incorporating more freedom and a hollow pattern is generated in the middle domain. For a unit cell, the main microscopic structural members have coincident orientations with the corresponding macroscopic structural counterparts. This is favorable to transfer the load from the loading point to the constrained points. This numerical result demonstrates that the proposed approach has the potential to handle the optimization problem of 3D structures. In the future work, a fully parallelized MPI framework for multi-scale transient topology optimization is proposed to efficiently solve the large-scale transient lattice optimization problems on the basis of [34].

Figure 19. Optimized macroscale (**left**) and microscale (**right**) designs for simply supported 3D structure.

7. Conclusions

This paper develops an efficient concurrent topological design approach for improving the dynamic performance of composite structures. According to the homogenized properties calculated via EBHM, the multi-scale dynamic finite element analysis is accomplished in the composite structure subjected to an impact load with the HHT-α method. Two adjoint sensitivity analysis schemes, differentiate-then-discretize and discretize-then-differentiate, are developed to evaluate the derivatives of dynamic responses regarding design variables at two scales. The consistency errors in the sensitivity calculations obtained from both adjoint sensitivity analysis schemes are compared to analyze how the inconsistent sensitivities influence the optimal solution for linear structural dynamic problems.

The popular AVM based on the differentiate-then-discretize approach encounters significant consistency errors in the sensitivity evaluation as demonstrated using the numerical examples. Alternatively, the discretize-then-differentiate AVM tackles this inconsistent sensitivity problem and achieves the effective optimal solution, whereby the multi-scale topology optimization problems associated with transient response are efficiently resolved. We consider arbitrary loading situations with varying amplitudes, directions, and application durations besides ground acceleration, such that the proposed approach can resolve a wide variety of transient concurrent topology optimization problems. It is noted that the inertial force can play a significant role in the final optimal design at both macrostructure and microstructure levels, particularly when the composite structure suffers from the impact load imposed at a fast rate of speed. In future work, we extend the proposed concurrent topology optimization formulation to multi-material design of composite structures with non-uniform microstructures at macro and micro levels. Furthermore, the clustering-based approach grouping the microscopic unit cells based on a physical quantity, is introduced to implement the multi-scale topology optimization for a considerable reduction in computational cost.

Author Contributions: Conceptualization, X.J. and X.T.; methodology, X.J. and X.T.; software, X.J.; validation, data curation, W.Z.; writing—original draft preparation, X.T.; writing—review and editing, X.C.; supervision, X.J.; project administration, X.J. and X.T.; funding acquisition, X.T. All authors have read and agreed to the published version of the manuscript.

Funding: This research was funded by the National Natural Science Foundation of China under Grant No. 51505096, and the Natural Science Foundation of Heilongjiang Province under Grant No. LH2020E064.

Data Availability Statement: The data presented in this study are available on request from the corresponding author. The data are not publicly available due to lab privacy.

Conflicts of Interest: The authors declare no conflict of interest.

Nomenclature

Φ_i	Neighborhood set of the *i*th macroscopic element	R	Filter radius in the macroscopic design domain
Ψ_j	Neighborhood set of the *j*th microscopic element	r	Filter radius in the microscopic design domain
v_k^{mac}	Volume of the *k*th macroscopic element	v_l^{mic}	Volume of the *l*th microscopic element
$w_{ki}^{\mathrm{mac}}, w_{lj}^{\mathrm{mic}}$	Weighting factors	$\mathbf{x},\mathbf{y}$	Center position of macro/micro elements
$\tilde{\xi}_i, \tilde{\eta}_j$	Physical design variables	ξ_k, η_l	Original design variables
$\xi_{\min}, \eta_{\min}$	Ersatz parameters	$\beta^{\mathrm{mac}}, \beta^{\mathrm{mic}}$	Aggressiveness of the projection function
$\xi_{\mathrm{th}}, \eta_{\mathrm{th}}$	Threshold densities	$\mathbf{D}^{\mathrm{B}}$	Elastic constitutive matrix of base material
$\mathbf{D}^{\mathrm{H}}$	Effective macroscopic constitutive matrix	$\mathbf{I}$	Unit matrix
$\mathbf{b}$	Strain matrix at the microscale	$\mathbf{u}_m$	Microstructural displacement field
Ω_m	Microstructural domain	$\mathbf{k}^{\mathrm{mic}}$	Stiffness matrix of microscopic element
p	Penalization exponent	ρ^{B}	Physical mass density of the base material
t	Time step	$\mathbf{M}$	Global mass matrix
$\mathbf{C}$	Global damping matrix	$\mathbf{K}$	Global stiffness matrix
$\ddot{\mathbf{u}}_t$	Macrostructural acceleration vector	$\dot{\mathbf{u}}_t$	Macrostructural velocity vector
$\mathbf{u}_t$	Macrostructural displacement vector	$\mathbf{f}_t$	External force vector
$\overline{N}$	Number of analysis steps	$\alpha_{\mathrm{r}}, \beta_{\mathrm{r}}$	Rayleigh damping parameters
$\mathbf{N}$	Matrix of shape functions	$\mathbf{B}$	Matrix of shape function derivatives
$f(\boldsymbol{\xi}, \boldsymbol{\eta}, \mathbf{u}(t))$	Objective function	V^{mac}	Volume of macroscopic design domain
V^{mic}	Volume of microscopic design domain	G_1, G_2	Macroscopic and microscopic constraints
ϑ, ς	Upper bounds for G_1 and G_2	$N^{\mathrm{mac}}, N^{\mathrm{mic}}$	Element numbers of macro/micro design domains
α, β, γ	HHT-α parameters	$\mathbf{E},\mathbf{V}$	Stiffness and volume interpolation functions
$\boldsymbol{\lambda}_t, \boldsymbol{\mu}_t, \boldsymbol{\zeta}_t$	Adjoint variables	Φ	Rewritten objective function
J	Duration of the dynamic event	$\bar{t}$	Continuous time variable
$\boldsymbol{\lambda}, \boldsymbol{\Lambda}$	Adjoint variables	Φ'	Sensitivity of Φ
$\widetilde{\Phi}$	Approximated Φ	$\widetilde{\Phi}'$	Sensitivity of $\widetilde{\Phi}$
L	Length of the structure	H	Height of the structure
h	Thickness of the structure	t_{f}	Simulation time
ω	Angular frequency	m_c	Lumped mass

References

1. Wu, J.; Sigmund, O.; Groen, J.P. Topology optimization of multi-scale structures: A review. *Struct. Multidiscip. Optim.* **2021**, *63*, 1455–1480. [CrossRef]
2. Murphy, R.; Imediegwu, C.; Hewson, R.; Santer, M. Multi-scale structural optimization with concurrent coupling between scales. *Struct. Multidiscip. Optim.* **2021**, *63*, 1721–1741. [CrossRef]
3. Bertolino, G.; Montemurro, M. Two-scale topology optimisation of cellular materials under mixed boundary conditions. *Int. J. Mech. Sci.* **2022**, *216*, 106961. [CrossRef]
4. Bai, Y.C.; Jing, W.X. Multi-scale topology optimization method for shell-infill structures based on filtering/projection boundary description. *J. Mech. Eng.* **2021**, *57*, 121–129.
5. Gao, J.; Luo, Z.; Xia, L.; Gao, L. Concurrent topology optimization of multi-scale composite structures in Matlab. *Struct. Multidiscip. Optim.* **2019**, *60*, 2621–2651. [CrossRef]
6. Gangwar, T.; Schillinger, D. Concurrent material and structure optimization of multiphase hierarchical systems within a continuum micromechanics framework. *Struct. Multidiscip. Optim.* **2021**, *64*, 1175–1197. [CrossRef] [PubMed]
7. Mi, X.; Xi, A.; Yan, Z.A.; Liang, G.A.; Jie, G.; Sheng, C.A. Design of graded lattice sandwich structures by multi-scale topology optimization. *Comput. Meth. Appl. Mech. Eng.* **2021**, *384*, 113949.
8. Zhang, Y.; Gao, L.; Xiao, M. Maximizing natural frequencies of inhomogeneous cellular structures by Kriging-assisted multi-scale topology optimization. *Comput. Struct.* **2020**, *230*, 106197. [CrossRef]
9. Hu, T.N.; Wang, Y.G.; Zhang, H.; Li, H.; Ding, X.H.; Izui, K.; Nishiwaki, S. Topology optimization of coated structures with layer-wise graded lattice infill for maximizing the fundamental eigenfrequency. *Comput. Struct.* **2022**, *271*, 106861. [CrossRef]
10. Ni, W.Y.; Zhang, H.; Yao, S.W. Concurrent topology optimization of composite structures for considering structural damping. *Acta Aeronaut. Et Astronaut. Sinica.* **2021**, *42*, 338–348.
11. Ali, M.A.; Shimoda, M. Toward multiphysics multi-scale concurrent topology optimization for lightweight structures with high heat conductivity and high stiffness using MATLAB. *Struct. Multidiscip. Optim.* **2022**, *65*, 207. [CrossRef]
12. Zhou, M.D.; Geng, D. Multi-scale and multi-material topology optimization of channel-cooling cellular structures for thermomechanical behaviors. *Comput. Meth Appl. Mech. Eng.* **2021**, *383*, 113896. [CrossRef]
13. Zhang, W.H.; Zhou, H.; Zhu, J.H.; Zhou, L. Material-structure integrated design for high-performance aerospace thin-walled component. *Acta Aeronaut. Et Astronaut. Sin.* **2022**, *44*, 627428.
14. Zhao, J.; Yoon, H.; Youn, B.D. An efficient concurrent topology optimization approach for frequency response problems. *Comput. Meth. Appl. Mech. Eng.* **2019**, *347*, 700–734. [CrossRef]
15. Niu, B.; Wadbro, E. Multi-scale design of coated structures with periodic uniform infill for vibration suppression. *Comput. Struct.* **2021**, *255*, 106622. [CrossRef]
16. Zhang, Y.; Zhang, L.; Ding, Z.; Gao, L.; Xiao, M.; Liao, M. A multi-scale topological design method of geometrically asymmetric porous sandwich structures for minimizing dynamic compliance. *Mater. Des.* **2022**, *214*, 110404. [CrossRef]
17. Zhang, Y.; Xiao, M.; Gao, L.; Gao, L.; Li, H. Multi-scale topology optimization for minimizing frequency responses of cellular composites with connectable graded microstructures. *Mech. Syst. Signal Process.* **2020**, *135*, 106369. [CrossRef]
18. Li, H.; Luo, Z.; Xiao, M.; Gao, L.; Gao, J. A new multi-scale topology optimization method for multiphase composite structures of frequency response with level sets. *Comput. Meth. Appl. Mech. Eng.* **2019**, *356*, 116–144. [CrossRef]
19. Zhao, L.; Xu, B.; Han, Y.S.; Rong, J.H. Concurrent design of composite macrostructure and cellular microstructure with respect to dynamic stress response under random excitations. *Compos. Struct.* **2021**, *257*, 113123. [CrossRef]
20. Gao, J.; Luo, Z.; Li, H.; Li, P.G.; Gao, L. Dynamic multi-scale topology optimization for multi-regional micro-structured cellular composites. *Compos. Struct.* **2019**, *211*, 401–417. [CrossRef]
21. Xu, B.; Huang, X.; Xie, Y. Two-scale dynamic optimal design of composite structures in the time domain using equivalent static loads. *Compos. Struct.* **2016**, *142*, 335–345. [CrossRef]
22. Zhao, J.; Yoon, B.; Youn, B.D. Concurrent topology optimization with uniform microstructure for minimizing dynamic response in the time domain. *Comput. Struct.* **2019**, *222*, 98–117. [CrossRef]
23. Le, C.; Bruns, T.E.; Tortorelli, D.A. Material microstructure optimization for linear elastodynamic energy wave management. *J. Mech. Phys. Solids.* **2012**, *60*, 351–378. [CrossRef]
24. Zhang, C.; Long, K.; Yang, A.; Zhuo, C.; Nouman, S.; Wang, X. A transient topology optimization with time-varying deformation restriction via augmented Lagrange method. *Int. J. Mech. Mater. Des.* **2022**, *18*, 683–700. [CrossRef]
25. Long, K.; Yang, X.; Saeed, N.; Tian, R.; Wen, P.; Wang, X. Topology optimization of transient problem with maximum dynamic response constraint using SOAR scheme. *Front. Mech. Eng.* **2021**, *16*, 593–606. [CrossRef]
26. Zhao, J.; Wang, C. Topology optimization for minimizing the maximum dynamic response in the time domain using aggregation functional method. *Comput. Struct.* **2017**, *190*, 41–60. [CrossRef]
27. Jensen, J.S.; Nakshatrala, P.B.; Tortorelli, D.A. On the consistency of adjoint sensitivity analysis for structural optimization of linear dynamic problems. *Struct. Multidiscip. Optim.* **2014**, *49*, 831–837. [CrossRef]
28. Zhang, L.; Zhang, Y.; Ding, L. Adjoint senility methods for transient responses of viscously damped systems and their consistency issues. *J. Theor. Appl. Mech.* **2022**, *54*, 1116–1127.
29. Ding, Z.; Zhang, L.; Gao, Q.; Liao, W.H. State-space based discretize-then-differentiate adjoint sensitivity method for transient responses of non-viscously damped systems. *Comput. Struct.* **2021**, *250*, 106540. [CrossRef]

30. Giraldo-Londono, O.; Paulino, G.H. PolyDyna: A Matlab implementation for topology optimization of structures subjected to dynamic loads. *Struct. Multidiscip. Optim.* **2021**, *64*, 957–990. [CrossRef]
31. Giraldo-Londono, O.; Aguilo, M.A.; Paulino, G.H. Local stress constraints in topology optimization of structures subjected to arbitrary dynamic loads: A stress aggregation-free approach. *Struct. Multidiscip. Optim.* **2021**, *64*, 3287–3309.
32. Yun, K.S.; Youn, S.K. Microstructural topology optimization of viscoelastic materials of damped structures subjected to dynamic loads. *Int. J. Solids Struct.* **2018**, *147*, 67–79. [CrossRef]
33. Ogawa, S.; Yamada, T. Topology optimization for transient thermomechanical coupling problems. *Appl. Math. Model.* **2022**, *109*, 536–544. [CrossRef]
34. Hansotto, K.; Niels, A. An open-source framework for large-scale transient topology optimization using PETSc. *Struct. Multidiscip. Optim.* **2022**, *65*, 295.
35. Dilgen, C.B.; Aage, N. Generalized shape optimization of transient vibroacoustic problems using cut elements. *Int. J. Numer. Meth. Eng.* **2021**, *122*, 1578–1601. [CrossRef]
36. Xu, S.; Cai, Y.; Cheng, G. Volume preserving nonlinear density filter based on heaviside functions. *Struct. Multidiscip. Optim.* **2010**, *41*, 495–505. [CrossRef]
37. Sigmund, O.; Maute, K. Topology optimization approaches. *Struct. Multidiscip. Optim.* **2013**, *48*, 1031–1055. [CrossRef]
38. Bourdin, B. Filters in topology optimization. *Int. J. Numer. Meth. Eng.* **2001**, *50*, 2143–2158. [CrossRef]
39. Wang, F.; Lazarov, B.S.; Sigmund, O. On projection methods, convergence and robust formulations in topology optimization. *Struct. Multidiscip. Optim.* **2011**, *43*, 767–784. [CrossRef]
40. Bendsøe, M.P. Optimal shape design as a material distribution problem. *Struct. Multidiscip. Optim.* **1989**, *1*, 193–202. [CrossRef]
41. Liu, L.; Yan, J.; Cheng, G. Optimum structure with homogeneous optimum truss-like material. *Comput. Struct.* **2008**, *86*, 1417–1425. [CrossRef]
42. Niu, B.; Yan, J.; Cheng, G. Optimum structure with homogeneous optimum cellular material for maximum fundamental frequency. *Struct. Multidiscip. Optim.* **2009**, *39*, 115–132. [CrossRef]
43. Xia, L.; Breitkopf, P. Design of materials using topology optimization and energy-based homogenization approach in Matlab. *Struct. Multidiscip. Optim.* **2015**, *52*, 1229–1241. [CrossRef]
44. Bransch, M.; Lehmann, L. A nonlinear HHT-α method with elastic-plastic soil-structure interaction in a coupled SBFEM/FEM approach. *Comput. Geotech.* **2011**, *38*, 80–87. [CrossRef]
45. Attili, B.S. The Hilber-Hughes-Taylor-α (HHT-α) method compared with an implicit Runge-Kutta for second-order systems. *Int. J. Comput. Math.* **2010**, *87*, 1755–1767. [CrossRef]
46. Guo, X.; Zhang, D.G.; Chen, S.J. Application of Hilber-Hughes-Taylor-α method to dynamics of flexible multibody system with contact and constraint. *Acta Phys. Sin.* **2017**, *66*, 164501.
47. Guo, H.X.; Wu, C.L. A family of unconditionally stable explicit algorithms for structural dynamics. *Shock. Vib.* **2020**, *39*, 48–56.
48. Svanberg, K. The method of moving asymptotes-a new method for structural optimization. *Int. J. Numer. Meth. Eng.* **1987**, *24*, 359–373. [CrossRef]

mathematics

Article

Construction of Supplemental Functions for Direct Serendipity and Mixed Finite Elements on Polygons

Todd Arbogast [1,2,*] and Chuning Wang [1]

1 Department of Mathematics, University of Texas at Austin, C1200, Austin, TX 78712-1202, USA; cwangaw@utexas.edu
2 Oden Institute for Computational Engineering and Sciences, University of Texas at Austin, C0200, Austin, TX 78712-1229, USA
* Correspondence: arbogast@oden.utexas.edu

Abstract: New families of direct serendipity and direct mixed finite elements on general planar, strictly convex polygons were recently defined by the authors. The finite elements of index r are H^1 and $H(\text{div})$ conforming, respectively, and approximate optimally to order $r+1$ while using the minimal number of degrees of freedom. The shape function space consists of the full set of polynomials defined directly on the element and augmented with a space of supplemental functions. The supplemental functions were constructed as rational functions, which can be difficult to integrate accurately using numerical quadrature rules when the index is high. This can result in a loss of accuracy in certain cases. In this work, we propose alternative ways to construct the supplemental functions on the element as continuous piecewise polynomials. One approach results in supplemental functions that are in H^p for any $p \geq 1$. We prove the optimal approximation property for these new finite elements. We also perform numerical tests on them, comparing results for the original supplemental functions and the various alternatives. The new piecewise polynomial supplements can be integrated accurately, and therefore show better robustness with respect to the underlying meshes used.

Keywords: serendipity finite elements; direct finite elements; optimal approximation; polygonal meshes; finite element exterior calculus

MSC: 65N30; 65N12; 65D05

1. Introduction

There has been strong interest in using polygonal and polyhedral meshes when solving certain types of problems via the finite element method. For just a few examples, we note problems in solid mechanics [1,2], elasticity [3,4], fracture mechanics [5–7], thin plates [8], shells [9], porous media [10], topology optimization [11–13], and finding eigenvalues [14]. In fact, polygonal meshes are an important motivation for the development and use of methods beyond the classic finite element method, which include, for example, the discontinuous Galerkin methods (including weak Galerkin [15] and ultra-weak methods [16–18]), mimetic methods [19–21], and virtual element methods [22–25].

Classic conforming finite element methods have also been developed for use on polygonal meshes, and especially for quadrilateral meshes. Approaches taken include the use of maps from reference finite elements [26–28], restriction to low order elements [29–32], the use of macro-elements [33], basis function enrichment [34–36], and construction using barycentric coordinates [9,37–39]. Ideally, we would have families of conforming finite elements defined for any order of accuracy. These would possess a minimal number of degrees of freedom (DoFs) subject to conformity and accuracy constraints. Finite elements based on the use of non-affine maps from reference finite elements display degraded accuracy. Accuracy is restricted if only low order elements are defined. Macro-elements, basis function enrichment, and the use of barycentric coordinates in higher order cases results in finite elements with an excess number of DoFs.

Families of conforming finite elements defined on polygons that maintain both accuracy and a minimal number of DoFs have appeared recently [40–43] (as well as some finite elements in three dimensions [44–46]). The approach taken is to begin with the space of polynomials $\mathbb{P}_r(E)$ of degree up to r defined *directly* on the physical element E to achieve accuracy of order $r+1$. To achieve conformity, one then adds in a space of supplemental functions. A basis for the supplemental functions must have certain properties on ∂E, but they must be defined over all of E by *filling in* the interior. The "supplemental function space" is sometimes called the "filling space".

In this paper, we discuss the construction of the supplemental functions, in the context of the finite elements developed by the current authors in [43], which are called *direct* finite elements. Let the element $E = E_N \subset \mathbb{R}^2$ be a closed, nondegenerate, convex polygon with $N \geq 3$ edges. The direct serendipity finite elements of index $r \geq 1$ are H^1-conforming and take the form

$$\mathcal{DS}_r(E_N) = \mathbb{P}_r(E_N) \oplus \mathbb{S}_r^{\mathcal{DS}}(E_N), \tag{1}$$

where $\mathbb{S}_r^{\mathcal{DS}}(E_N)$ is the space of supplemental functions. The direct mixed finite elements are $H(\text{div})$-conforming and take two forms,

$$\begin{aligned} \mathbf{V}_r^r(E_N) &= \mathbb{P}_r^2(E_N) \oplus \mathbf{x}\tilde{\mathbb{P}}_r(E_N) \oplus \mathbb{S}_r^{\mathbf{V}}(E_N), \\ \mathbf{V}_r^{r-1}(E_N) &= \mathbb{P}_r^2(E_N) \oplus \mathbb{S}_r^{\mathbf{V}}(E_N), \end{aligned} \tag{2}$$

for full ($r \geq 0$) and reduced ($r \geq 1$) $H(\text{div})$-approximation, respectively, where $\tilde{\mathbb{P}}_r(E_N)$ are the homogeneous polynomials of (exact) degree r. These two finite elements are related to each other by the finite element exterior calculus [47] through the de Rham complex

$$\mathbb{R} \hookrightarrow H^1 \xrightarrow{\text{curl}} H(\text{div}) \xrightarrow{\text{div}} L^2 \longrightarrow 0, \tag{3}$$

resulting in, for $s = r-1, r$ $(s \geq 0)$,

$$\mathbb{R} \hookrightarrow \mathcal{DS}_{r+1}(E_N) \xrightarrow{\text{curl}} \mathbf{V}_r^s(E_N) \xrightarrow{\text{div}} \mathbb{P}_s(E_N) \longrightarrow 0. \tag{4}$$

The consequence is that

$$\begin{aligned} \mathbf{V}_r^r(E_N) &= \operatorname{curl} \mathcal{DS}_{r+1}(E_N) \oplus \mathbf{x}\mathbb{P}_r, \\ \mathbf{V}_r^{r-1}(E_N) &= \operatorname{curl} \mathcal{DS}_{r+1}(E_N) \oplus \mathbf{x}\mathbb{P}_{r-1}, \end{aligned} \tag{5}$$

and, therefore,

$$\mathbb{S}_r^{\mathbf{V}}(E_N) = \operatorname{curl} \mathbb{S}_{r+1}^{\mathcal{DS}}(E_N). \tag{6}$$

The original construction of supplemental functions made use of rational functions (see (21)), which are difficult to numerically integrate accurately. As a consequence, when solving a partial differential equation using direct finite elements, the quadrature error may be significant, leading to poor overall approximation of the solution. This was observed in [43], although in that paper, the degradation in the approximation was attributed to poor mesh quality. While mesh quality remains an important ingredient in finite element analysis, quadrature approximation is also a critical component, especially for high order methods.

In this work, we introduce two constructions of the supplemental functions $\mathbb{S}_r^{\mathcal{DS}}(E_N)$ which involve using continuous piecewise polynomials. Such constructions are motivated by the work of Kuznetsov and Repin [33], and suggested by the work of Cockburn and Fu [41]. These new supplemental functions can then be accurately integrated by quadrature rules. (A similar, but more complex, construction in three dimensions for cuboidal hexahedra is discussed in [46]).

In the next two sections we present some basic notation and review the general definition of the original direct serendipity and direct mixed finite elements, which have supplemental functions that are C^∞-smooth. Our new families of direct finite elements based on piecewise continuous supplemental functions are given in Section 4. We give two constructions of the supplemental functions, so that one set lies in H^1 and the other in H^p for any integer $p \geq 1$. The approximation properties of these new direct finite elements are given in Section 5. The results are optimal, up to the bounding constant. The proof follows that given in [43], and we concentrate on the modifications that are required to handle the new supplements. In Section 6, we present numerical tests that compare the errors and convergence rates of the new and original direct finite elements. We conclude the paper in Section 7.

2. Notation

We choose to identify the edges and vertices of E_N adjacently in the counterclockwise direction, as depicted in Figure 1 (throughout the paper, we interpret indices modulo N). Let the edges of E_N be denoted e_i, $i = 1, 2, \ldots, N$, and the vertices be $\mathbf{x}_{v,i} = e_i \cap e_{i+1}$. Let ν_i denote the unit outer normal to edge e_i, and let τ_i denote the unit tangent vector of e_i oriented in the counterclockwise direction, for $i = 1, 2, \ldots, N$.

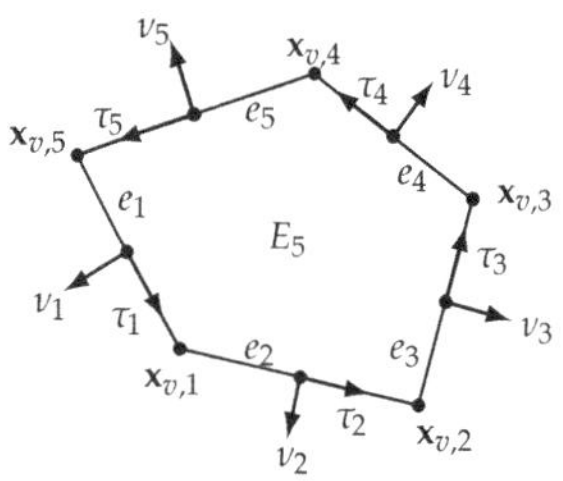

Figure 1. A pentagon E_5, with edges e_i, outer unit normals ν_i, tangents τ_i, and vertices $\mathbf{x}_{v,i}$.

For any two distinct points $\mathbf{y}_1$ and $\mathbf{y}_2$, let $\mathcal{L}[\mathbf{y}_1, \mathbf{y}_2]$ be the line passing through $\mathbf{y}_1$ and $\mathbf{y}_2$, and take $\nu[\mathbf{y}_1, \mathbf{y}_2]$ to be the unit vector normal to this line interpreted as going from $\mathbf{y}_1$ to $\mathbf{y}_2$ and then spinning 90 degrees in the clockwise direction (i.e., pointing to the right). Then we define a linear polynomial giving the signed distance of $\mathbf{x}$ to $\mathcal{L}[\mathbf{y}_1, \mathbf{y}_2]$ as

$$\lambda[\mathbf{y}_1, \mathbf{y}_2](\mathbf{x}) = -(\mathbf{x} - \mathbf{y}_2) \cdot \nu[\mathbf{y}_1, \mathbf{y}_2]. \tag{7}$$

To simplify the notation for linear functions that will be used throughout the paper, let $\mathcal{L}_i = \mathcal{L}[\mathbf{x}_{v,i-1}, \mathbf{x}_{v,i}]$ be the line containing edge e_i and let $\lambda_i(\mathbf{x})$ give the distance of $\mathbf{x} \in \mathbb{R}^2$ to edge e_i opposite the normal direction, i.e.,

$$\lambda_i(\mathbf{x}) = \lambda[\mathbf{x}_{v,i-1}, \mathbf{x}_{v,i}](\mathbf{x}) = -(\mathbf{x} - \mathbf{x}_{v,i}) \cdot \nu_i, \quad i = 1, 2, \ldots, N. \tag{8}$$

These functions are strictly positive in the interior of E_N, and λ_i vanishes on the edge e_i.

3. Direct Serendipity and Mixed Finite Elements

The general development of direct serendipity and mixed finite elements is given in [43]. The definition of the supplemental space $\mathbb{S}_r^{\mathcal{DS}}(E_N)$ in (1) is key to the construction. For completeness, we review the definitions of these direct finite elements here.

When $N = 3$ (triangles), the direct serendipity supplemental space $\mathbb{S}_r^{\mathcal{DS}}(E_3)$ is empty. When $N \geq 4$ and $1 \leq r < N - 2$, the direct serendipity spaces $\mathcal{DS}_r(E_N)$ are defined as subspaces of $\mathcal{DS}_{N-2}(E_N)$ by the rule

$$\mathcal{DS}_r(E_N) = \left\{\varphi \in \mathcal{DS}_{N-2}(E_N) : \varphi|_e \in \mathbb{P}_r(e) \text{ for all edges } e \text{ of } E_N\right\}. \tag{9}$$

Therefore, we only need to understand $\mathbb{S}_r^{\mathcal{DS}}(E_N)$ for $r \geq N - 2$ and $N \geq 4$.

To define the supplemental basis functions, two series of choices must be made for each i, j such that $1 \leq i < j \leq N$ and $2 \leq j - i \leq N - 2$ (i.e., e_i and e_j are nonadjacent edges). First, as shown in Figure 2, one must choose two distinct points $\mathbf{x}_{i,j}^1 \in \mathcal{L}_i$ and $\mathbf{x}_{i,j}^2 \in \mathcal{L}_j$ that avoid the intersection point $\mathbf{x}_{i,j} = \mathcal{L}_i \cap \mathcal{L}_j$, if it exists. Then let

$$\lambda_{i,j}(\mathbf{x}) = \lambda[\mathbf{x}_{i,j}^1, \mathbf{x}_{i,j}^2](\mathbf{x}) = -(\mathbf{x} - \mathbf{x}_{i,j}^2) \cdot \nu_{i,j}, \quad \nu_{i,j} = \nu[\mathbf{x}_{i,j}^1, \mathbf{x}_{i,j}^2], \tag{10}$$

be the linear function associated to the line $\mathcal{L}_{i,j} = \mathcal{L}[\mathbf{x}_{i,j}^1, \mathbf{x}_{i,j}^2]$. Second, $R_{i,j}$ must be chosen to satisfy

$$R_{i,j}(\mathbf{x})|_{e_i} = -1, \quad R_{i,j}(\mathbf{x})|_{e_j} = 1. \tag{11}$$

The supplemental space for $r \geq N - 2 \geq 2$ is of the form

$$\mathbb{S}_r^{\mathcal{DS}}(E_N) = \text{span}\{\phi_{s,i,j} : 1 \leq i < j \leq N,\ 2 \leq j - i \leq N - 2\}, \tag{12}$$

$$\phi_{s,i,j} = \Big(\prod_{k \neq i,j} \lambda_k\Big) \lambda_{i,j}^{r-N+2} R_{i,j}. \tag{13}$$

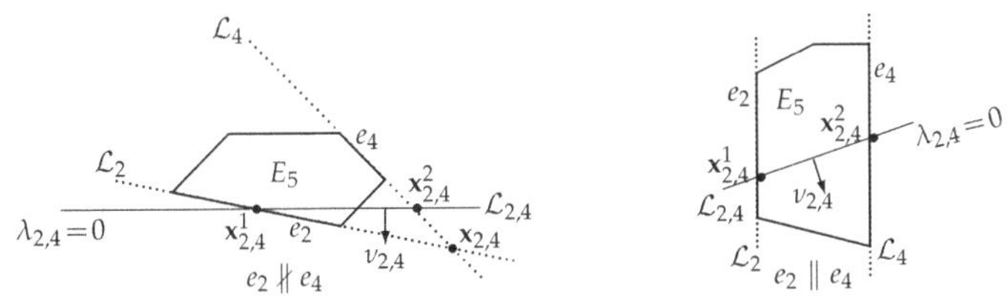

Figure 2. Illustration on E_5 of the zero line $\mathcal{L}_{2,4}$ of $\lambda_{2,4}(\mathbf{x}) = -(\mathbf{x} - \mathbf{x}_{2,4}^2) \cdot \nu_{2,4}$ and the intersection point $\mathbf{x}_{2,4} = \mathcal{L}_2 \cap \mathcal{L}_4$, if it exists.

3.1. Direct Serendipity Finite Elements

Every shape function of the direct serendipity finite element $\mathcal{DS}_r(E_N)$ is a sum of a polynomial and a linear combination of the supplemental functions, as in (1). To implement them, one must define the DoFs. For example, for $\psi \in \mathcal{DS}_r(E_N)$, one can take

$$\psi(\mathbf{x}_{v,i}), \qquad \forall i = 1, 2, \ldots, N, \tag{14}$$

$$\int_{e_i} \psi\, p\, d\sigma, \quad \forall p \in \mathbb{P}_{r-2}(e_i),\ i = 1, 2, \ldots, N, \tag{15}$$

$$\int_{E_N} \psi\, q\, dx, \quad \forall q \in \mathbb{P}_{r-N}(E_N), \tag{16}$$

where $d\sigma$ is the one dimensional surface measure. Alternatively, one can use nodal DoFs (i.e., evaluation at a node point) in place of (15) and/or (16). For the former, on each edge e_i, its corresponding edge nodes are $r - 1$ points such that they, along with the two vertices, are equally distributed on e_i. For the latter, the interior cell nodes can be set to be the Lagrange nodes of order $r - N$ of a triangle that lies strictly inside E_N.

The basis of $\mathcal{DS}_r(E_N)$ corresponding to the DoFs can be constructed. Given a computational mesh of convex polygons $\mathcal{T}_h$ over a domain Ω, the basis can be simply pieced together to form a global H^1-conforming basis of the space $\mathcal{DS}_r(\Omega) \subset H^1(\Omega)$.

3.2. Direct Mixed Finite Elements

As discussed in the introduction, full, $\mathbf{V}_r^r(E_N)$, and reduced, $\mathbf{V}_r^{r-1}(E_N)$, $H(\text{div})$-approximating mixed finite element spaces follow from a de Rham complex (3), where the direct serendipity finite elements serve as the precursor (4). The supplemental space is related to $\mathbb{S}_{r+1}^{\mathcal{DS}}(E_N)$ by the simple Formula (6).

The DoFs for these spaces (with $s = r \geq 0$ or $s = r - 1 \geq 0$) can be taken to be

$$\int_{e_i} \mathbf{v} \cdot \nu_i \, p \, d\sigma, \quad \forall p \in \mathbb{P}_r(e_i),\ i = 1, 2, \ldots, N, \tag{17}$$

$$\int_{E_N} \mathbf{v} \cdot \nabla q \, dx, \quad \forall q \in \mathbb{P}_s(E_N),\ q \text{ not constant}, \tag{18}$$

$$\int_{E_N} \mathbf{v} \cdot \boldsymbol{\psi} \, dx, \quad \forall \boldsymbol{\psi} \in \mathbb{B}_r^{\mathbf{V}}(E_N),\ \text{if } r \geq N - 1, \tag{19}$$

where the $H^1(E_N)$ and $H(\text{div}; E_N)$ bubble functions, for $r \geq N - 1$, are

$$\mathbb{B}_{r+1}(E_N) = \lambda_1 \lambda_2 \ldots \lambda_N \mathbb{P}_{r-N+1}(E_N) \quad \text{and} \quad \mathbb{B}_r^{\mathbf{V}}(E_N) = \text{curl}\, \mathbb{B}_{r+1}(E_N). \tag{20}$$

Given the mesh $\mathcal{T}_h$ over Ω, one constructs the basis and the $H(\text{div})$-conforming global space $\mathbf{V}_r^s(\Omega) \subset H(\text{div})$ (see [43] for details). As an alternative, when solving partial differential equations, one can use the hybrid form of the method [48], which does not require the construction of global basis functions.

4. Piecewise Continuous Supplements

In [43], $R_{i,j}$ satisfying (11) on E_N, for $1 \leq i < j \leq N$, $2 \leq j - i \leq N - 2$, was taken to be the simple rational function

$$R_{i,j}^{\text{rational}}(\mathbf{x}) = \frac{\lambda_i(\mathbf{x}) - \lambda_j(\mathbf{x})}{\lambda_i(\mathbf{x}) + \lambda_j(\mathbf{x})}. \tag{21}$$

These rational functions are smooth over the element. We now give new direct serendipity and mixed finite elements by providing an alternate construction of $R_{i,j}$ as a piecewise continuous polynomial defined over a sub-partition of E_N. We present two strategies, the first of which is convenient for the construction of continuous supplemental functions in $H^1(E_N)$, and the second for constructing smoother supplemental functions in $H^p(E_N)$ for integer $p \geq 1$.

4.1. Supplemental Functions in $H^1(E_N)$

Our first strategy for constructing $R_{i,j}$ requires a sub-triangulation of the element E_N, and we present two natural choices. The first sub-triangulation is depicted in Figure 3 and denoted as $\mathcal{T}^n(E_N)$. One picks a vertex $\mathbf{x}_{v,n}$ and divides E_N into $N - 2$ sub-triangles. The sub-triangles are T_m^n with vertices $\mathbf{x}_{v,n}$, $\mathbf{x}_{v,m}$, and $\mathbf{x}_{v,m+1}$, where $m = n + 1, \ldots, n + N - 2$. For the second sub-triangulation, depicted in Figure 4 and denoted as $\mathcal{T}^{\mathbf{x}_c}(E_N)$, one picks a point $\mathbf{x}_c$ in the interior of E_N and divides it into N sub-triangles. Now the sub-triangles are $T_m^{\mathbf{x}_c}$ with vertices $\mathbf{x}_c$, $\mathbf{x}_{v,m}$, and $\mathbf{x}_{v,m+1}$, where $m = 1, 2, \ldots, N$. We use the centroid of the element for $\mathbf{x}_c$.

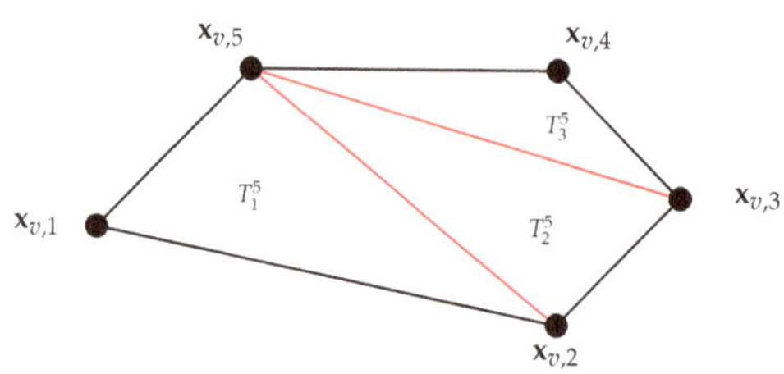

Figure 3. A sub-triangulation based on a common fixed vertex. Shown is $\mathcal{T}^5(E_5)$ using the fixed vertex $\mathbf{x}_{v,5}$.

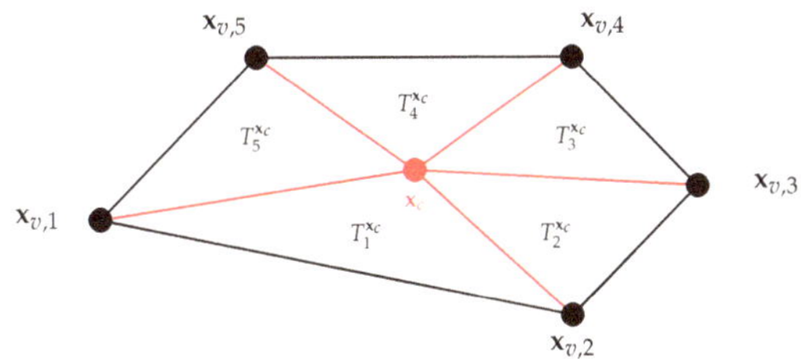

Figure 4. Sub-triangulation based on a center point. Shown is $\mathcal{T}^{\mathbf{x}_c}(E_5)$ using the centroid $\mathbf{x}_c$.

Let the piecewise polynomial function space of degree s corresponding to each sub-triangulation be

$$\mathcal{P}_s(\mathcal{T}^n(E_N)) = \{f \in C^0(E) \mid f|_{T_m^n} \in \mathbb{P}_s(T_m^n),\ m = n+1,\dots,n+N-2\}, \tag{22}$$
$$\mathcal{P}_s(\mathcal{T}^{\mathbf{x}_c}(E_N)) = \{f \in C^0(E) \mid f|_{T_m^{\mathbf{x}_c}} \in \mathbb{P}_s(T_m^{\mathbf{x}_c}),\ m = 1,2,\dots,N\}. \tag{23}$$

We construct $R_{i,j}$ in $\mathcal{P}_1(\mathcal{T}^n(E_N))$ or $\mathcal{P}_1(\mathcal{T}^{\mathbf{x}_c}(E_N))$, depending on which of the two sub-triangulations is used, such that

$$R_{i,j}|_{e_i} = -1, \quad R_{i,j}|_{e_j} = 1, \quad R_{i,j}|_{v_k} = 0, \quad \forall k \neq i-1, i, j-1, j. \tag{24}$$

by using interpolation at the vertices of the sub-triangles. If the sub-triangulation is chosen to be $\mathcal{T}^n(E_N)$, the restrictions (24) uniquely specify all the vertex values. However, if the triangulation is $\mathcal{T}^{\mathbf{x}_c}(E_N)$, the center value is not determined, so we assign $R_{i,j}(\mathbf{x}_c) = 0$.

Our construction has $R_{i,j}$ being -1 on e_i and 1 on e_j as required by (11). Moreover, $R_{i,j} \in H^1(E_N)$. After constructing the supplemental functions in (13) with this $R_{i,j}$, each $\phi_{s,i,j}$ is in $\mathcal{P}_{r+1}(\mathcal{T}^n(E_N))$ or $\mathcal{P}_{r+1}(\mathcal{T}^{\mathbf{x}_c}(E_N))$, and therefore also in $H^1(E_N)$.

4.2. Supplemental Functions in $H^p(E_N)$

We now present the second of our two strategies for constructing $R_{i,j}$ for two nonadjacent edges e_i and e_j. Recall that $\lambda_k(\mathbf{x})$ is the linear polynomial giving the (signed) distance to the line $\mathcal{L}_k$ extending edge e_k. When e_i and e_j are parallel, we simply define $R_{i,j}$ as the linear polynomial

$$R_{i,j} = \frac{\lambda_i - \lambda_j}{\lambda_i(\mathbf{x}_{v,j})}. \tag{25}$$

When e_i and e_j are not parallel, we first define a sub-partition of E_N by adding a single extra line $\ell^{i,j}$ through a point $\mathbf{x}^{i,j}$ as depicted in Figure 5. The point $\mathbf{x}^{i,j}$ is chosen so that it is closer to $\mathcal{L}_j$ than the endpoints of e_i, i.e.,

$$\lambda_j(\mathbf{x}^{i,j}) \leq \min\{\lambda_j(\mathbf{x}_{v,i-1}), \lambda_j(\mathbf{x}_{v,i})\}. \tag{26}$$

The line $\ell^{i,j}$ passes through $\mathbf{x}^{i,j}$ and is parallel to e_j. This line divides E_N into $E_N^{i,j,1}$ near e_i and $E_N^{i,j,0}$ near e_j, i.e.,

$$E_N^{i,j,1} = E_N \cap \{\mathbf{x} \mid \lambda_j(\mathbf{x}) \geq \lambda_j(\mathbf{x}^{i,j})\}, \tag{27}$$
$$E_N^{i,j,0} = E_N \cap \{\mathbf{x} \mid \lambda_j(\mathbf{x}) < \lambda_j(\mathbf{x}^{i,j})\}. \tag{28}$$

Let $\nu^{i,j} = -\nu_j$ be the unit normal vector of $\ell^{i,j}$ pointing into $E_N^{i,j,1}$, and let $\tau^{i,j} = \tau_j$ be a unit tangent vector.

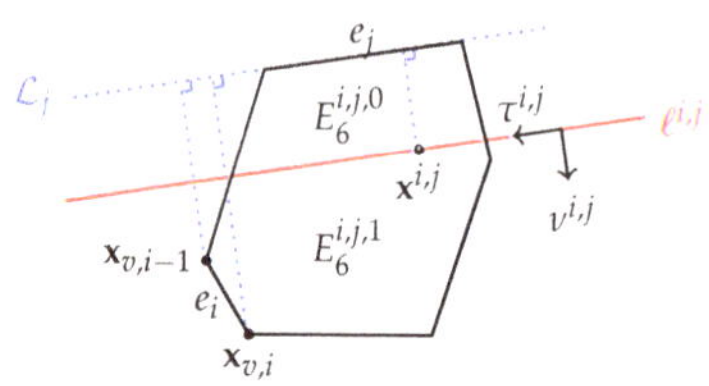

Figure 5. A sub-division of E_6 using the line $\ell^{i,j}$.

We next construct the function $\rho^{i,j}$, which is 1 on edge e_i and 0 on edge e_j. It is defined piecewise on the sub-partition of E_N as

$$\rho^{i,j}(\mathbf{x}) = \begin{cases} 1, & \mathbf{x} \in E_N^{i,j,1}, \\ 1 - \left(1 - \dfrac{\lambda_j(\mathbf{x})}{\lambda_j(\mathbf{x}^{i,j})}\right)^p, & \mathbf{x} \in E_N^{i,j,0}, \end{cases} \tag{29}$$

where $p \geq 1$ is an integer. The function is continuous, since $\lambda_j(\mathbf{x}) = \lambda_j(\mathbf{x}^{i,j})$ on $\ell^{i,j}$ implies that $\rho^{i,j}|_{\ell^{i,j}} = 1$ in either case of the definition. Moreover, in the tangential direction,

$$\frac{\partial \rho^{i,j}}{\partial \tau^{i,j}}\bigg|_{\ell^{i,j}} = 0, \tag{30}$$

and, in the normal direction,

$$\frac{\partial \rho^{i,j}}{\partial \nu^{i,j}}(\mathbf{x}) = \begin{cases} 0, & \mathbf{x} \in E_N^{i,j,1}, \\ \dfrac{p}{\lambda_j(\mathbf{x}^{i,j})}\left(1 - \dfrac{\lambda_j(\mathbf{x})}{\lambda_j(\mathbf{x}^{i,j})}\right)^{p-1}, & \mathbf{x} \in E_N^{i,j,0}, \end{cases} \tag{31}$$

which is continuous for $p > 1$, so $\rho^{i,j} \in C^1(E_N)$. By iterating the argument, we have that $\rho^{i,j} \in C^{p-1}(E_N)$ and so also in $H^p(E_N)$ for $p > 1$. If $p = 1$, $\rho^{i,j}$ is continuous, so it is in $H^1(E_N)$.

Finally, after constructing both $\rho^{i,j}$ and $\rho^{j,i}$, we define

$$R_{i,j} = \rho^{j,i} - \rho^{i,j}, \tag{32}$$

which is -1 on e_i, 1 on e_j. Moreover, $R_{i,j} \in H^p(E_N)$. The supplemental functions in (13) constructed with this $R_{i,j}$ lie in $H^p(E_N)$.

We end this section with two specific examples, using the sub-partitions shown in Figure 6, which divide E_N by N lines. The first example has a sub-partition based on the midpoints $\mathbf{x}_{e,i}^{\mathrm{M}}$ of the edges e_i, $i = 1, 2, \ldots, N$, and gives rise to the spaces denoted $\mathcal{DS}_r^{\mathrm{M}}(E_N)$ and $\mathbf{V}_r^{\mathrm{M},s}(E_N)$. We compute the minimal distance of the midpoints to the edges, i.e.,

$$h_{\mathrm{M}} = \min_{1 \leq i \leq N, k = i \pm 1} \lambda_i(\mathbf{x}_{e,k}^{\mathrm{M}}). \tag{33}$$

Then for any two non parallel and nonadjacent edges e_i and e_j, simply take the partition line $\ell^{i,j}$ to be the line parallel to e_j that is the fixed distance $h_{\mathrm{M}} > 0$ away and intersects E_N.

The second specific example uses a sub-partition based on trisecting each edge, resulting in the points, for edge e_i, being denoted counterclockwise as $\mathbf{x}_{e,i,k}$ for $k = 1, 2$, $i = 1, 2, \ldots, N$. In this case, we simply take $\mathbf{x}^{i,j}$ to be the closest of these points to $\mathcal{L}_j$, omitting $\mathbf{x}_{e,j,1}$ and $\mathbf{x}_{e,j,2}$. We denote the resulting spaces $\mathcal{DS}_r^{\mathrm{T}}(E_N)$ and $\mathbf{V}_r^{\mathrm{T},s}(E_N)$.

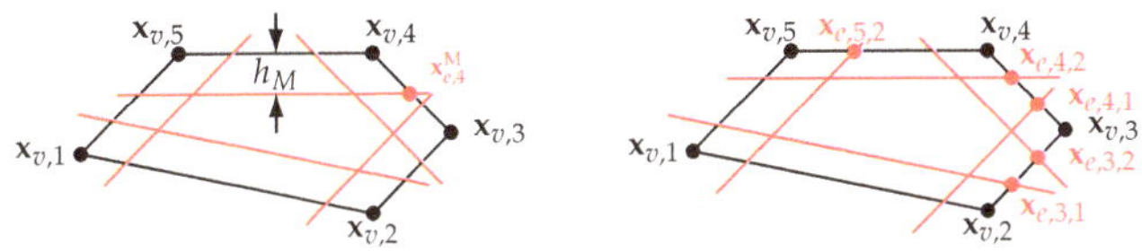

Figure 6. The two sub-partitions of E_5 used for constructing specific H^p supplemental functions. The left one is used for $\mathcal{DS}_r^{\mathrm{M}}$ and $\mathbf{V}_r^{\mathrm{M},s}$, where $h_{\mathrm{M}} = \lambda_5(\mathbf{x}_{e,4}^{\mathrm{M}})$. The right one is used for $\mathcal{DS}_r^{\mathrm{T}}$ and $\mathbf{V}_r^{\mathrm{T},s}$, where the closest trisection points are marked in red.

5. Approximation Properties

We discuss now the global approximation properties for our direct finite element spaces. The results of [43] do not directly apply here because there it was assumed that the functions $R_{i,j}$ are smooth on the element. Consider a collection of meshes $\mathcal{T}_h$ of convex polygons partitioning a domain Ω, where $h > 0$ is the maximal element diameter.

We need to make the usual assumption that our collection of meshes is uniformly shape regular [49] (pp. 104–105). For any $E_N \in \mathcal{T}_h$, let h_{E_N} be its diameter. Denote by T_i, $i = 1, 2, \ldots, N(N-1)(N-2)/6$, the sub-triangle of E_N with vertices being three of the N vertices of E_N, and define

$$\rho_{E_N} = 2 \min_{1 \le i \le N(N-1)(N-2)/6} \{\text{diameter of the largest circle inscribed in } T_i\}. \tag{34}$$

The *shape regularity parameter* of the single mesh $\mathcal{T}_h$ is

$$\sigma_{\mathcal{T}_h} = \min_{E_N \in \mathcal{T}_h} \frac{\rho_{E_N}}{h_{E_N}}. \tag{35}$$

Assumption 1. *The collection of meshes $\{\mathcal{T}_h\}_{h>0}$ is* uniformly shape regular. *That is, the shape regularity parameters are bounded below by a positive constant: there exists $\sigma_* > 0$, independent of $\mathcal{T}_h$ and $h > 0$, such that the ratio*

$$\frac{\rho_{E_N}}{h_{E_N}} \ge \sigma_* > 0 \quad \textit{for all } E_N \in \mathcal{T}_h,\ h > 0. \tag{36}$$

We also require some mild restrictions on the construction of $\mathbb{S}_r^{\mathcal{DS}}(E_N)$.

Assumption 2. *For every $E_N \in \mathcal{T}_h$, assume that the functions of $\mathbb{S}_r^{\mathcal{DS}}(E_N)$ are constructed using $\lambda_{i,j}$ such that the zero set $\mathcal{L}_{i,j}$ intersects e_i and e_j. Moreover, suppose that $R_{i,j} \in H^p(E_N)$ for some $p \ge 1$ and that the sub-partitions introduced in Section 4 for their construction depend continuously on the vertices of E_N.*

The continuous dependence requirement of the sub-partitions is met if we systematically choose the points $\mathbf{x}_c$ in Section 4.1 (say as the centroid) and $\mathbf{x}^{i,j}$ satisfying (26) in Section 4.2 (say be taking $\mathbf{x}^{i,j}$ as the closer endpoint of e_i to $\mathcal{L}_j$, or so that $\lambda_j(\mathbf{x}^{i,j}) = \frac{1}{2}\min\{\lambda_j(\mathbf{x}_{v,i-1}), \lambda_j(\mathbf{x}_{v,i})\}$).

We state first the approximation result for $\mathcal{DS}_r(\Omega)$.

Theorem 1. *Let $r \ge 1$, $1 \le p \le \infty$, and $\ell > 1/p$ (or $\ell \ge 1$ if $p = 1$). If Assumptions 1 and 2 hold (so the basis functions are in H^p on each element), then there exists a constant $C > 0$, such that for all functions $v \in W^{\ell,p}(\Omega)$,*

$$\inf_{v_h \in \mathcal{DS}_r(\Omega)} \|v - v_h\|_{W^{m,p}(\Omega)} \le C\, h^{\ell - m}\, \|v\|_{W^{\ell,p}(\Omega)}, \quad 0 \le \ell \le r+1, \quad m = 0, 1. \tag{37}$$

Proof. The methodology of the proof follows [42,43]. The key difference is that we must relax the smoothness requirement made on the supplemental functions. We highlight the differences, and leave the reader to consult [42,43] for some of the details.

Given a mesh $\mathcal{T}_h$, we construct an interpolation operator $\mathcal{I}_h^r : W_p^l(\Omega) \to \mathcal{DS}_r$ as a generalization of that defined in [50]. To do so, we use a nodal set of DoFs for the finite elements, and identify global nodal points a_i, $i = 1, 2, \dots, \dim \mathcal{DS}_r$. These nodal points must be chosen systematically with respect to the vertices of the mesh, so they depend continuously on them. The global nodal basis function for a_i is denoted φ_i.

A geometry object K_i is associated to each a_i. If a_i lies in the interior of some element, we choose the element to be K_i. Otherwise, we choose an edge containing a_i to be K_i, where we additionally ask that $K_i \subset \partial\Omega$ if $a_i \in \partial\Omega$. We use these to define the dual basis ψ_i with respect to $L^2(K_i)$, $i = 1, 2, \dots, \dim \mathcal{DS}_r$. The corresponding interpolation operator $\mathcal{I}_h^r : W_p^l(\Omega) \to \mathcal{DS}_r$ is then

$$\mathcal{I}_h^r v(\mathbf{x}) = \sum_{i=1}^{\dim \mathcal{DS}_r} \left(\int_{K_i} \psi_i(\mathbf{y})\, v(\mathbf{y})\, dy \right) \varphi_i(\mathbf{x}). \tag{38}$$

There are two essential steps towards showing the approximation property. First, the nodal basis functions are bounded,

$$\max_{1 \le i \le \dim \mathcal{DS}_r(\Omega)} \max_{E \in \mathcal{T}_h} ||\varphi_i||_{W_q^m(E)} \le C, \tag{39}$$

and, second, the dual basis functions are bounded up to a scaling factor,

$$||\psi_i||_{L^\infty(K_i)} \le C h_{K_i}^{-\dim K_i}. \tag{40}$$

We show the necessary boundedness by mapping the elements and using a continuity and compactness argument.

As depicted in Figure 7, to each element E_N, we associate a regular polygon (equilateral and equiangular) $\hat{E}_N$. We can then define a map $\mathbf{F}_{E_N} : \hat{E}_N \to E_N$ as a composition of a map that changes the geometry but not the size to $\tilde{E}_N$, and then a scaling map (see [43] for precise details).

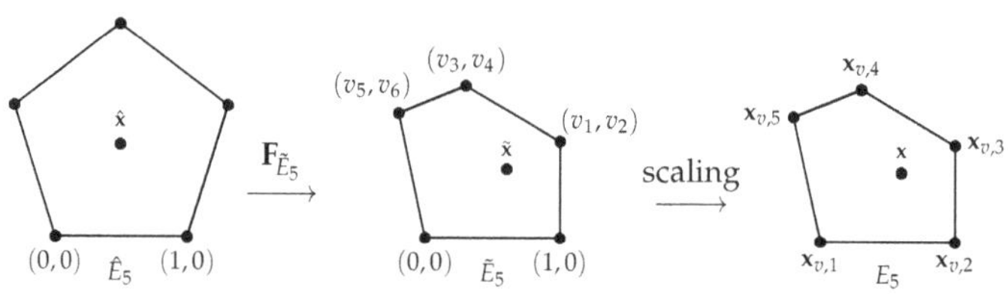

Figure 7. An element $E_5 \in \mathcal{T}_h$ is shown on the right-hand side in its translated and rotated local coordinates. It is the image of a regular reference polygon $\hat{E}_5$ on the left-hand side. The map is decomposed into one that changes the geometry but not the size $\mathbf{F}_{\tilde{E}_5} : \hat{E}_5 \to \tilde{E}_5$, and a scaling map $\tilde{\mathbf{x}} \mapsto H\tilde{\mathbf{x}}$.

Define the nodal basis functions $\varphi_i^{\tilde{E}_N}$ on $\tilde{E}_N$. It is enough to show the boundedness of their W_q^m norms. Although they are no longer smooth functions, compared to [42,43], they are continuous on $\tilde{E}_N$, and smooth on all the subregions generated by the sub-partition. Moreover, by assumption the sub-partition is required to depend continuously on the vertices of $\tilde{E}_N$. Therefore, $\varphi_i^{\tilde{E}_N}$ will still depend continuously on $\hat{\mathbf{x}} = \mathbf{F}_{\tilde{E}_N}^{-1}(\tilde{\mathbf{x}})$ and the vertices of $\tilde{E}_N$, which vary in a compact set. We conclude that the nodal basis functions are bounded in W_q^m norm. The boundedness of ψ_i in the L^∞ norm can be shown in a similar way. □

For the mixed finite elements, we have the following result, wherein we see projection operators $\pi : H(\text{div};\Omega) \cap (L^{2+\epsilon}(\Omega))^2 \to \mathbf{V}_r^s$, $s = r-1, r$, where $\epsilon > 0$, and $\mathcal{P}_{W_s}$, the L^2-orthogonal projection operator onto $W_s = \nabla \cdot \mathbf{V}_r^s$.

Theorem 2. *Let $r = s \geq 0$ or $r \geq 1$, $s = r-1$. If Assumptions 1–2 hold, then there is a constant $C > 0$, such that*

$$\|\mathbf{v} - \pi\mathbf{v}\|_{L^2(\Omega)} \leq C \|\mathbf{v}\|_{H^k(\Omega)} h^k, \qquad k = 1, \ldots, r+1, \tag{41}$$

$$\|p - \mathcal{P}_{W_s} p\|_{L^2(\Omega)} \leq C \|p\|_{H^k(\Omega)} h^k, \qquad k = 0, 1, \ldots, s+1, \tag{42}$$

$$\|\nabla \cdot (\mathbf{v} - \pi\mathbf{v})\|_{L^2(\Omega)} \leq C \|\nabla \cdot \mathbf{v}\|_{H^k(\Omega)} h^k, \quad k = 0, 1, \ldots, s+1, \tag{43}$$

where $s = r - 1 \geq 0$ and $s = r \geq 1$ for reduced and full $H(div)$-approximation, respectively. Moreover, the discrete inf-sup condition

$$\sup_{\mathbf{v}_h \in \mathbf{V}_r^s} \frac{(w_h, \nabla \cdot \mathbf{v}_h)}{\|\mathbf{v}_h\|_{H(\text{div})}} \geq \gamma \|w_h\|_{L^2(\Omega)}, \quad \forall w_h \in W_s, \tag{44}$$

holds for some $\gamma > 0$ independent of $h > 0$.

For the proof, we define the projection operator π by piecing together local operators π_E that are defined in terms of the DoFs (17)–(19). The approximation properties given in [42,43] hold with a similar proof, using now that the subregions generated by the sub-partition depend continuously on the vertices of the element.

6. Numerical Results

We present numerical experiments for our new finite elements as applied to Poisson's equation

$$-\nabla \cdot (\nabla p) = f \quad \text{in } \Omega, \tag{45}$$

$$p = 0 \quad \text{on } \partial\Omega, \tag{46}$$

where $f \in L^2(\Omega)$. The corresponding weak form finds $p \in H_0^1(\Omega)$ such that

$$(\nabla p, \nabla q) = (f, q), \quad \forall q \in H_0^1(\Omega), \tag{47}$$

where $(\cdot,\cdot)$ is the $L^2(\Omega)$ inner product. Setting

$$\mathbf{u} = -\nabla p, \tag{48}$$

we have the mixed weak form, which finds $\mathbf{u} \in H(\text{div};\Omega)$ and $p \in L^2(\Omega)$ such that

$$(\mathbf{u}, \mathbf{v}) - (p, \nabla \cdot \mathbf{v}) = 0, \qquad \forall \mathbf{v} \in H(\text{div};\Omega), \tag{49}$$

$$(\nabla \cdot \mathbf{u}, w) = (f, w), \quad \forall w \in L^2(\Omega). \tag{50}$$

These weak forms naturally give rise to finite element approximations. According to Theorems 1 and 2, the following convergence analysis holds by a standard argument [27,51].

Theorem 3. *If Assumptions 1 and 2 hold, then there exists a constant $C > 0$, independent of $\mathcal{T}_h$ and $h > 0$, such that for $r \geq 1$,*

$$\|p - p_h\|_{m,\Omega} \leq C h^{\ell+1-m} |p|_{\ell+1,\Omega}, \quad \ell = 0, 1, \ldots, r, \quad m = 0, 1, \tag{51}$$

where $p_h \in \mathcal{DS}_r(\Omega) \cap H_0^1(\Omega)$ *approximates* (47). *Moreover, with* $r = s \geq 0$ *or* $r \geq 1$, $s = r - 1$,

$$\|\mathbf{u} - \mathbf{u}_h\|_{0,\Omega} \leq C\|\mathbf{u}\|_{k,\Omega}h^k, \qquad k = 1, \ldots, r+1, \tag{52}$$

$$\|p - p_h\|_{0,\Omega} \leq C\|\mathbf{u}\|_{k,\Omega}h^k, \qquad k = 1, \ldots, s+1, \tag{53}$$

$$\|\nabla \cdot (\mathbf{u} - \mathbf{u}_h)\|_{0,\Omega} \leq C\|\nabla \cdot \mathbf{u}\|_{k,\Omega}h^k, \quad k = 0, 1, \ldots, s+1, \tag{54}$$

where $(\mathbf{u}_h, p_h) \in \mathbf{V}_r^s \times W_s$ *approximates* (49)–(50).

We perform our tests on a unit square domain $\Omega = [0,1]^2$, and take the source term $f(\mathbf{x}) = 2\pi^2 \sin(\pi x_1)\sin(\pi x_2)$, so the exact solution is $u(x_1, x_2) = \sin(\pi x_1)\sin(\pi x_2)$. We consider five types of supplemental spaces. The original direct serendipity and mixed finite element spaces will be denoted $\mathcal{DS}_r^{\mathrm{R}}$ and $\mathbf{V}_r^{\mathrm{R},s}$, respectively. These use supplements based on the rational functions (21).

For the H^1 supplemental functions introduced in Section 4.1, there are two varieties. Denote the space using supplemental functions that are constructed based on the vertex sub-triangulation as $\mathcal{DS}_r^{\mathrm{V}}$ and its corresponding mixed spaces as $\mathbf{V}_r^{\mathrm{V},s}$, and those based on the center point sub-triangulation as $\mathcal{DS}_r^{\mathrm{C}}$ and $\mathbf{V}_r^{\mathrm{C},s}$, respectively. The spaces based on the H^p supplements were described in Section 4.2 and denoted $\mathcal{DS}_r^{\mathrm{M}}, \mathbf{V}_r^{\mathrm{M},s}$ and $\mathcal{DS}_r^{\mathrm{T}}, \mathbf{V}_r^{\mathrm{T},s}$.

6.1. The Meshes Used

Approximate solutions are computed on a sequence of Voronoi meshes $\mathcal{T}_h^2$ generated by the package PolyMesher [52]. Each mesh has n^2 elements, which are generated with n^2 random initial seeds and up to 10^4 smoothing iterations to improve the shape regularity.

For comparison to the results appearing in [43], we use the same mesh sequence $\mathcal{T}_h^2$ with $n = 6$, 10, 14, 18, and 22. We show the meshes for $n = 6$ and $n = 18$ in Figure 8. The shape regularity parameters are given in Table 1. Note that the $n = 10$ and $n = 18$ meshes are the least regular.

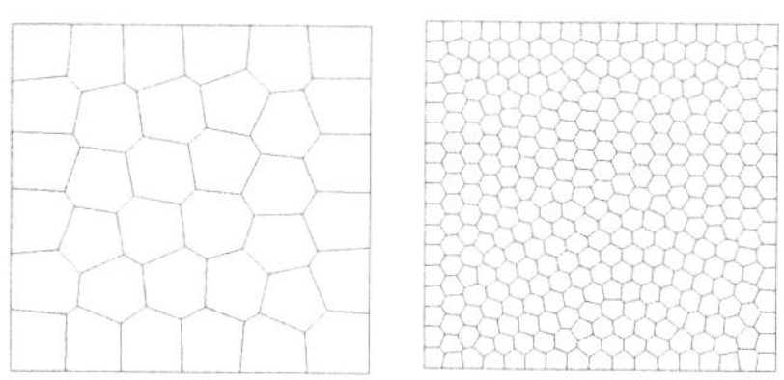

$n = 6$ $\qquad$ $n = 18$

Figure 8. Meshes with 6×6 and 18×18 elements.

Table 1. Shape regularity parameters for each mesh $\mathcal{T}_h^2$.

	$n = 6$	$n = 10$	$n = 14$	$n = 18$	$n = 22$
$\sigma_{\mathcal{T}_h}$	0.180	0.115	0.161	0.127	0.150

In [43] it was observed numerically that the $n = 18$ mesh performed well for the original direct finite elements (using rational supplemental functions) when $r = 2, 3, 4$, but had a degraded convergence rate when $r = 5$. The problem was resolved by removing short edges from the $n = 18$ mesh. However, as we will see in this section, the problem is actually due to inaccurate numerical quadrature of the rational supplemental functions, which only showed up in those tests for the more refined mesh (i.e., not $n = 10$) and higher values of r.

6.2. Results for Direct Serendipity Spaces

We present and compare the results of the numerical tests performed for $\mathcal{DS}_r^{\mathrm{R}}$, $\mathcal{DS}_r^{\mathrm{V}}$, $\mathcal{DS}_r^{\mathrm{C}}$, $\mathcal{DS}_r^{\mathrm{M}}$, and $\mathcal{DS}_r^{\mathrm{T}}$, where $r = 2,3,4,5$. We take $p = 1$ in Section 4.2 for the construction of $\mathcal{DS}_r^{\mathrm{M}}$ and $\mathcal{DS}_r^{\mathrm{T}}$, because it gives better results than a larger p in most cases. According to Theorem 3, we expect all those spaces to have the convergence rates $r+1$ for L^2 errors and r for H^1-seminorm errors. As Tables 2 and 3 suggests, the convergence rates at $n = 10,14,22$ for $\mathcal{DS}_r^{\mathrm{R}}$ are all slightly better than optimal in this test. However, we can observe a slower convergence rate at $n = 18$ for $\mathcal{DS}_r^{\mathrm{R}}$. (We interject that convergence rates are computed as improvement from the previous mesh in our sequence.)

Table 2. L^2 errors and convergence rates for $\mathcal{DS}_r^{\mathrm{R}}$ and $\mathcal{DS}_r^{\mathrm{C}}$.

	$\mathcal{DS}_2^{\mathrm{R}}$		$\mathcal{DS}_2^{\mathrm{C}}$		$\mathcal{DS}_3^{\mathrm{R}}$		$\mathcal{DS}_3^{\mathrm{C}}$	
n	error	rate	error	rate	error	rate	error	rate
10	2.160×10^{-4}	3.45	2.144×10^{-4}	3.50	8.859×10^{-6}	4.34	1.031×10^{-5}	4.35
14	7.329×10^{-5}	3.16	7.165×10^{-5}	3.21	2.175×10^{-6}	4.11	2.518×10^{-6}	4.13
18	3.452×10^{-5}	2.95	3.409×10^{-5}	2.92	7.927×10^{-7}	3.96	8.964×10^{-7}	4.05
22	1.863×10^{-5}	3.47	1.841×10^{-5}	3.46	3.555×10^{-7}	4.51	4.045×10^{-7}	4.48
	$\mathcal{DS}_4^{\mathrm{R}}$		$\mathcal{DS}_4^{\mathrm{C}}$		$\mathcal{DS}_5^{\mathrm{R}}$		$\mathcal{DS}_5^{\mathrm{C}}$	
n	error	rate	error	rate	error	rate	error	rate
10	3.467×10^{-7}	5.69	3.972×10^{-7}	6.11	1.133×10^{-8}	6.97	1.730×10^{-8}	6.61
14	5.644×10^{-8}	5.31	6.622×10^{-8}	5.24	1.202×10^{-9}	6.57	1.964×10^{-9}	6.37
18	1.530×10^{-8}	5.12	1.823×10^{-8}	5.06	4.376×10^{-10}	3.97	4.134×10^{-10}	6.12
22	5.314×10^{-9}	5.95	6.239×10^{-9}	6.03	8.905×10^{-11}	8.95	1.243×10^{-10}	6.76

Table 3. H^1-seminorm errors and convergence rates for $\mathcal{DS}_r^{\mathrm{R}}$ and $\mathcal{DS}_r^{\mathrm{C}}$.

	$\mathcal{DS}_2^{\mathrm{R}}$		$\mathcal{DS}_2^{\mathrm{C}}$		$\mathcal{DS}_3^{\mathrm{R}}$		$\mathcal{DS}_3^{\mathrm{C}}$	
n	error	rate	error	rate	error	rate	error	rate
10	3.561×10^{-3}	2.32	3.552×10^{-3}	2.36	1.933×10^{-4}	3.13	2.390×10^{-4}	3.11
14	1.683×10^{-3}	2.19	1.660×10^{-3}	2.23	6.724×10^{-5}	3.09	8.343×10^{-5}	3.08
18	1.018×10^{-3}	1.97	1.013×10^{-3}	1.94	3.144×10^{-5}	2.98	3.783×10^{-5}	3.10
22	6.712×10^{-4}	2.34	6.696×10^{-4}	2.33	1.730×10^{-5}	3.36	2.114×10^{-5}	3.27
	$\mathcal{DS}_4^{\mathrm{R}}$		$\mathcal{DS}_4^{\mathrm{C}}$		$\mathcal{DS}_5^{\mathrm{R}}$		$\mathcal{DS}_5^{\mathrm{C}}$	
n	error	rate	error	rate	error	rate	error	rate
10	8.530×10^{-6}	4.55	1.027×10^{-5}	4.91	3.103×10^{-7}	5.73	4.394×10^{-7}	5.57
14	1.973×10^{-6}	4.29	2.439×10^{-6}	4.21	4.625×10^{-8}	5.57	7.098×10^{-8}	5.34
18	6.952×10^{-7}	4.09	8.785×10^{-7}	4.01	2.646×10^{-8}	2.19	1.981×10^{-8}	5.01
22	2.969×10^{-7}	4.78	3.689×10^{-7}	4.88	5.973×10^{-9}	8.37	7.233×10^{-9}	5.66

In Table 4, we compare the results for the $n = 18$ mesh of $\mathcal{DS}_r^{\mathrm{R}}$, $\mathcal{DS}_r^{\mathrm{V}}$, $\mathcal{DS}_r^{\mathrm{C}}$, $\mathcal{DS}_r^{\mathrm{M}}$, and $\mathcal{DS}_r^{\mathrm{T}}$. On the one hand, the results suggest that the new spaces are all approximately optimal for $r = 5$, which is an obvious improvement compared to $\mathcal{DS}_5^{\mathrm{R}}$. On the other hand, the errors for $r = 2,3,4$ of the new spaces are slightly worse than those of $\mathcal{DS}_r^{\mathrm{R}}$, and among all the new spaces, $\mathcal{DS}_r^{\mathrm{C}}$ has the best performance in error. We conclude that $\mathcal{DS}_r^{\mathrm{C}}$ shows the best overall performance among all the spaces considered.

We suggest that the reason for such an observation is that the dominant errors for $r = 5$ are from the numerical quadrature applied to the integration of rational functions, especially on the elements that are less shape regular. However, for $r = 2,3,4$, the new supplements, as piecewise polynomials, cannot approximate the shape of a smooth function as well as the original rational supplements, especially those from $\mathcal{DS}_r^{\mathrm{M}}$ and $\mathcal{DS}_r^{\mathrm{T}}$, of which $R_{i,j}$ for $e_i \nparallel e_j$ are flat in the middle and oscillate near the boundary. In contrast, the supplements from $\mathcal{DS}_r^{\mathrm{V}}$ and $\mathcal{DS}_r^{\mathrm{C}}$ are more reasonably shaped, and those from $\mathcal{DS}_r^{\mathrm{C}}$ are better since its partition has sub-triangles that are more shape regular (as was shown in

Figures 3 and 4). This argument is also supported by the observation that the results are usually worse if we take larger p for $\mathcal{DS}_r^{\mathrm{M}}$ and $\mathcal{DS}_r^{\mathrm{T}}$, where the shape of the supplements are even worse.

Table 4. Errors and convergence rates at $n = 18$ computed from the previous step $n = 14$, for the direct serendipity spaces $\mathcal{DS}_r^{\mathrm{R}}$, $\mathcal{DS}_r^{\mathrm{V}}$, $\mathcal{DS}_r^{\mathrm{C}}$, $\mathcal{DS}_r^{\mathrm{M}}$, and $\mathcal{DS}_r^{\mathrm{T}}$.

	$r = 2$		$r = 3$		$r = 4$		$r = 5$	
	Error	**Rate**	**Error**	**Rate**	**Error**	**Rate**	**Error**	**Rate**
				L^2 errors and convergence rates				
$\mathcal{DS}_r^{\mathrm{R}}$	3.452×10^{-5}	2.95	7.927×10^{-7}	3.96	1.530×10^{-8}	5.12	4.376×10^{-10}	3.97
$\mathcal{DS}_r^{\mathrm{V}}$	3.554×10^{-5}	2.89	1.073×10^{-6}	3.87	2.108×10^{-8}	4.83	4.637×10^{-10}	5.92
$\mathcal{DS}_r^{\mathrm{C}}$	3.409×10^{-5}	2.92	8.964×10^{-7}	4.05	1.823×10^{-8}	5.06	4.13×10^{-10}	6.12
$\mathcal{DS}_r^{\mathrm{M}}$	6.820×10^{-5}	2.88	1.697×10^{-6}	3.85	3.095×10^{-8}	4.80	6.11×10^{-10}	6.02
$\mathcal{DS}_r^{\mathrm{T}}$	7.072×10^{-5}	2.92	1.866×10^{-6}	4.04	3.367×10^{-8}	4.91	5.83×10^{-10}	6.07
				H^1-seminorm errors and convergence rates				
$\mathcal{DS}_r^{\mathrm{R}}$	1.018×10^{-3}	1.97	3.144×10^{-5}	2.98	6.952×10^{-7}	4.09	2.646×10^{-8}	2.19
$\mathcal{DS}_r^{\mathrm{V}}$	1.059×10^{-3}	1.89	4.199×10^{-5}	2.93	9.959×10^{-7}	3.85	2.184×10^{-8}	4.80
$\mathcal{DS}_r^{\mathrm{C}}$	1.013×10^{-3}	1.94	3.783×10^{-5}	3.10	8.785×10^{-7}	4.01	1.981×10^{-8}	5.01
$\mathcal{DS}_r^{\mathrm{M}}$	1.976×10^{-3}	1.88	6.334×10^{-5}	3.01	1.590×10^{-6}	3.95	3.076×10^{-8}	4.83
$\mathcal{DS}_r^{\mathrm{T}}$	2.059×10^{-3}	1.94	6.895×10^{-5}	3.16	1.710×10^{-6}	4.04	3.008×10^{-8}	4.87

6.3. Results for Direct Mixed Spaces

We perform numerical tests for $\mathbf{V}_r^{\mathrm{R},s}$, $\mathbf{V}_r^{\mathrm{V},s}$, $\mathbf{V}_r^{\mathrm{C},s}$, $\mathbf{V}_r^{\mathrm{M},s}$, $\mathbf{V}_r^{\mathrm{T},s}$, for the full $H(\mathrm{div})$-approximation spaces where $r = s = 0, 1, 2, 3$, and the reduced $H(\mathrm{div})$-approximation spaces where $r = 1, 2, 3$, and $s = r - 1$. Since those mixed spaces are constructed from corresponding direct serendipity spaces $\mathcal{DS}_{r+1}$, it is natural that we find the comparison of the results similar to the small r cases discussed in Section 6.2. For all the spaces, we can observe the convergence rates approximately optimal in general but the errors are slightly worse for $n = 18$, especially when $r = s = 3$, as shown in Tables 5 and 6. All spaces perform similarly well, although $\mathbf{V}_r^{\mathrm{R},s}$ usually performs best in these tests. Among the new spaces, $\mathbf{V}_r^{\mathrm{C},s}$ performs a bit better, and it gives results close to those of $\mathbf{V}_r^{\mathrm{R},s}$. For reference, we provide the numerical results for $\mathbf{V}_r^{\mathrm{C},s}$ in Tables 7 and 8.

Table 5. Errors and convergence rates at $n = 18$ computed from the previous step $n = 14$, for the reduced $H(\mathrm{div})$-approximation spaces $\mathbf{V}_r^{\mathrm{R},r-1}$, $\mathbf{V}_r^{\mathrm{V},r-1}$, $\mathbf{V}_r^{\mathrm{C},r-1}$, $\mathbf{V}_r^{\mathrm{M},r-1}$, and $\mathbf{V}_r^{\mathrm{T},r-1}$.

	$\|p - p_h\|$		$\|\mathbf{u} - \mathbf{u}_h\|$		$\|\nabla \cdot (\mathbf{u} - \mathbf{u}_h)\|$	
	Error	**Rate**	**Error**	**Rate**	**Error**	**Rate**
			$r = 1$, reduced $H(\mathrm{div})$-approximation			
$\mathbf{V}_1^{\mathrm{R},0}$	7.039×10^{-2}	1.01	5.428×10^{-3}	1.98	6.988×10^{-2}	0.99
$\mathbf{V}_1^{\mathrm{V},0}$	7.039×10^{-2}	1.01	5.429×10^{-3}	1.98	6.988×10^{-2}	0.99
$\mathbf{V}_1^{\mathrm{C},0}$	7.039×10^{-2}	1.01	5.443×10^{-3}	1.98	6.988×10^{-2}	0.99
$\mathbf{V}_1^{\mathrm{M},0}$	7.039×10^{-2}	1.01	5.366×10^{-3}	1.98	6.988×10^{-2}	0.99
$\mathbf{V}_1^{\mathrm{T},0}$	7.039×10^{-2}	1.01	5.362×10^{-3}	1.98	6.988×10^{-2}	0.99

Table 5. *Cont.*

	$\|p - p_h\|$ Error	Rate	$\|\mathbf{u} - \mathbf{u}_h\|$ Error	Rate	$\|\nabla \cdot (\mathbf{u} - \mathbf{u}_h)\|$ Error	Rate
			$r = 2$, reduced $H(\text{div})$-approximation			
$\mathbf{V}_2^{R,1}$	2.614×10^{-3}	1.96	8.492×10^{-5}	2.92	2.614×10^{-3}	1.96
$\mathbf{V}_2^{V,1}$	2.614×10^{-3}	1.96	8.876×10^{-5}	2.89	2.614×10^{-3}	1.96
$\mathbf{V}_2^{C,1}$	2.614×10^{-3}	1.96	8.850×10^{-5}	2.87	2.614×10^{-3}	1.96
$\mathbf{V}_2^{M,1}$	2.614×10^{-3}	1.96	8.895×10^{-5}	2.85	2.614×10^{-3}	1.96
$\mathbf{V}_2^{T,1}$	2.614×10^{-3}	1.96	8.973×10^{-5}	2.85	2.614×10^{-3}	1.96
			$r = 3$, reduced $H(\text{div})$-approximation			
$\mathbf{V}_3^{R,2}$	6.515×10^{-5}	2.96	1.887×10^{-6}	3.90	6.515×10^{-5}	2.96
$\mathbf{V}_3^{V,2}$	6.515×10^{-5}	2.96	1.931×10^{-6}	3.89	6.515×10^{-5}	2.96
$\mathbf{V}_3^{C,2}$	6.515×10^{-5}	2.96	1.911×10^{-6}	3.89	6.515×10^{-5}	2.96
$\mathbf{V}_3^{M,2}$	6.515×10^{-5}	2.96	2.007×10^{-6}	3.81	6.515×10^{-5}	2.96
$\mathbf{V}_3^{T,2}$	6.515×10^{-5}	2.96	2.105×10^{-6}	3.83	6.515×10^{-5}	2.96

Table 6. Errors and convergence rates at $n = 18$ computed from the previous step $n = 14$, for the full $H(\text{div})$-approximation spaces $\mathbf{V}_r^{R,r}$, $\mathbf{V}_r^{V,r}$, $\mathbf{V}_r^{C,r}$, $\mathbf{V}_r^{M,r}$, and $\mathbf{V}_r^{T,r}$.

n	$\|p - p_h\|$ Error	Rate	$\|\mathbf{u} - \mathbf{u}_h\|$ Error	Rate	$\|\nabla \cdot (\mathbf{u} - \mathbf{u}_h)\|$ Error	Rate
			$r = 0$, full $H(\text{div})$-approximation			
$\mathbf{V}_0^{R,0}$	7.030×10^{-2}	1.01	2.701×10^{-2}	1.10	6.988×10^{-2}	0.99
$\mathbf{V}_0^{V,0}$	7.027×10^{-2}	1.01	3.095×10^{-2}	1.03	6.988×10^{-2}	0.99
$\mathbf{V}_0^{C,0}$	7.028×10^{-2}	1.01	2.951×10^{-2}	1.03	6.988×10^{-2}	0.99
$\mathbf{V}_0^{M,0}$	7.027×10^{-2}	1.01	3.065×10^{-2}	0.93	6.988×10^{-2}	0.99
$\mathbf{V}_0^{T,0}$	7.026×10^{-2}	1.01	3.163×10^{-2}	0.92	6.988×10^{-2}	0.99
			$r = 1$, full $H(\text{div})$-approximation			
$\mathbf{V}_1^{R,1}$	2.614×10^{-3}	1.96	4.895×10^{-4}	2.19	2.614×10^{-3}	1.96
$\mathbf{V}_1^{V,1}$	2.614×10^{-3}	1.96	5.542×10^{-4}	2.13	2.614×10^{-3}	1.96
$\mathbf{V}_1^{C,1}$	2.614×10^{-3}	1.96	5.226×10^{-4}	2.17	2.614×10^{-3}	1.96
$\mathbf{V}_1^{M,1}$	2.614×10^{-3}	1.96	7.505×10^{-4}	2.08	2.614×10^{-3}	1.96
$\mathbf{V}_1^{T,1}$	2.614×10^{-3}	1.96	7.917×10^{-4}	2.15	2.614×10^{-3}	1.96
			$r = 2$, full $H(\text{div})$-approximation			
$\mathbf{V}_2^{R,2}$	6.515×10^{-5}	2.96	8.818×10^{-6}	3.10	6.515×10^{-5}	2.96
$\mathbf{V}_2^{V,2}$	6.515×10^{-5}	2.96	1.887×10^{-5}	2.92	6.515×10^{-5}	2.96
$\mathbf{V}_2^{C,2}$	6.515×10^{-5}	2.96	1.526×10^{-5}	3.03	6.515×10^{-5}	2.96
$\mathbf{V}_2^{M,2}$	6.515×10^{-5}	2.96	2.801×10^{-5}	2.49	6.515×10^{-5}	2.96
$\mathbf{V}_2^{T,2}$	6.515×10^{-5}	2.96	3.010×10^{-5}	2.67	6.515×10^{-5}	2.96
			$r = 3$, full $H(\text{div})$-approximation			
$\mathbf{V}_3^{R,3}$	1.182×10^{-6}	3.99	2.144×10^{-7}	3.65	1.182×10^{-6}	3.99
$\mathbf{V}_3^{V,3}$	1.182×10^{-6}	3.99	3.324×10^{-7}	3.43	1.182×10^{-6}	3.99
$\mathbf{V}_3^{C,3}$	1.182×10^{-6}	3.99	2.933×10^{-7}	3.50	1.182×10^{-6}	3.99
$\mathbf{V}_3^{M,3}$	1.183×10^{-6}	3.99	1.254×10^{-6}	3.10	1.182×10^{-6}	3.99
$\mathbf{V}_3^{T,3}$	1.183×10^{-6}	3.99	1.547×10^{-6}	3.61	1.182×10^{-6}	3.99

Table 7. Errors and convergence rates in L^2 for $\mathbf{V}_r^{\mathrm{C},r-1}$.

n	$\|p - p_h\|$ Error	Rate	$\|\mathbf{u} - \mathbf{u}_h\|$ Error	Rate	$\|\nabla \cdot (\mathbf{u} - \mathbf{u}_h)\|$ Error	Rate
			$r = 1$, reduced $H(\mathrm{div})$-approximation			
10	1.290×10^{-1}	1.24	1.775×10^{-2}	2.29	1.260×10^{-1}	1.15
14	9.109×10^{-2}	1.02	9.024×10^{-3}	1.98	9.001×10^{-2}	0.98
18	7.039×10^{-2}	1.01	5.443×10^{-3}	1.98	6.988×10^{-2}	0.99
22	5.736×10^{-2}	1.15	3.630×10^{-3}	2.28	5.708×10^{-2}	1.14
			$r = 2$, reduced $H(\mathrm{div})$-approximation			
10	8.635×10^{-3}	2.23	5.210×10^{-4}	3.28	8.634×10^{-3}	2.23
14	4.308×10^{-3}	2.04	1.841×10^{-4}	3.04	4.308×10^{-3}	2.03
18	2.614×10^{-3}	1.96	8.850×10^{-5}	2.87	2.614×10^{-3}	1.96
22	1.715×10^{-3}	2.37	4.772×10^{-5}	3.47	1.715×10^{-3}	2.37
			$r = 3$, reduced $H(\mathrm{div})$-approximation			
10	3.881×10^{-4}	3.38	2.021×10^{-5}	4.39	3.881×10^{-4}	3.38
14	1.384×10^{-4}	3.02	5.151×10^{-6}	4.00	1.384×10^{-4}	3.02
18	6.515×10^{-5}	2.96	1.911×10^{-6}	3.89	6.515×10^{-5}	2.96
22	3.507×10^{-5}	3.48	8.432×10^{-7}	4.60	3.507×10^{-5}	3.48

Table 8. Errors and convergence rates in L^2 for $\mathbf{V}_r^{\mathrm{C},r}$.

n	$\|p - p_h\|$ Error	Rate	$\|\mathbf{u} - \mathbf{u}_h\|$ Error	Rate	$\|\nabla \cdot (\mathbf{u} - \mathbf{u}_h)\|$ Error	Rate
			$r = 0$, full $H(\mathrm{div})$-approximation			
10	1.281×10^{-1}	1.20	6.389×10^{-2}	1.54	1.260×10^{-1}	1.15
14	9.086×10^{-2}	1.01	3.832×10^{-2}	1.50	9.001×10^{-2}	0.98
18	7.028×10^{-2}	1.01	2.951×10^{-2}	1.03	6.988×10^{-2}	0.99
22	5.731×10^{-2}	1.15	2.145×10^{-2}	1.79	5.708×10^{-2}	1.14
			$r = 1$, full $H(\mathrm{div})$-approximation			
10	8.635×10^{-3}	2.23	2.003×10^{-3}	2.65	8.634×10^{-3}	2.23
14	4.308×10^{-3}	2.04	9.076×10^{-4}	2.32	4.308×10^{-3}	2.03
18	2.614×10^{-3}	1.96	5.226×10^{-4}	2.17	2.614×10^{-3}	1.96
22	1.715×10^{-3}	2.37	3.320×10^{-4}	2.55	1.715×10^{-3}	2.37
			$r = 2$, full $H(\mathrm{div})$-approximation			
10	3.881×10^{-4}	3.38	1.007×10^{-4}	3.47	3.881×10^{-4}	3.38
14	1.384×10^{-4}	3.02	3.303×10^{-5}	3.26	1.384×10^{-4}	3.02
18	6.515×10^{-5}	2.96	1.526×10^{-5}	3.03	6.515×10^{-5}	2.96
22	3.507×10^{-5}	3.48	7.889×10^{-6}	3.71	3.507×10^{-5}	3.48
			$r = 3$, full $H(\mathrm{div})$-approximation			
10	1.294×10^{-5}	4.60	3.537×10^{-6}	4.84	1.294×10^{-5}	4.60
14	3.270×10^{-6}	4.03	7.157×10^{-7}	4.68	3.270×10^{-6}	4.03
18	1.182×10^{-6}	3.99	2.933×10^{-7}	3.50	1.182×10^{-6}	3.99
22	5.219×10^{-7}	4.60	1.301×10^{-7}	4.57	5.219×10^{-7}	4.60

7. Conclusions

We reviewed the construction of direct serendipity and mixed finite elements on non-degenerate, planar convex polygons. The direct serendipity finite element spaces are of the form

$$\mathcal{DS}_r(E_N) = \mathbb{P}_r(E_N) \oplus \mathbb{S}_r^{\mathcal{DS}}(E_N). \tag{55}$$

The full and reduced $H(\mathrm{div})$-approximation mixed finite element spaces are obtained from a de Rham complex, where the direct serendipity finite elements serve as a precursor. The mixed spaces are of the form

$$\begin{aligned} \mathbf{V}_r^r(E_N) &= \mathbb{P}_r^2(E_N) \oplus \mathbf{x}\tilde{\mathbb{P}}_r(E_N) \oplus \mathbb{S}_r^{\mathbf{V}}(E_N), \\ \mathbf{V}_r^{r-1}(E_N) &= \mathbb{P}_r^2(E_N) \oplus \mathbb{S}_r^{\mathbf{V}}(E_N), \end{aligned} \tag{56}$$

where

$$\mathbb{S}_r^{\mathbf{V}}(E_N) = \operatorname{curl} \mathbb{S}_{r+1}^{\mathcal{DS}}(E_N). \tag{57}$$

We presented two approaches to construct the supplemental functions in $\mathbb{S}_r^{\mathcal{DS}}(E_N)$ as piecewise polynomials. The first approach divides a polygonal element E_N into sub-triangles, and constructs the supplements as continuous piecewise polynomials that lie in $H^1(E_N)$. The second approach has a more complicated subdivision of E_N that needs to be treated carefully. However, it provides a framework for constructing supplements that lie in $H^p(E_N)$ for any $p \geq 1$.

The approximation properties of the new finite elements were proved under the regularity assumption of the mesh sequences and some mild restrictions on the construction.

We performed numerical tests on a randomly generated mesh sequence and compared results for five different ways of constructing the supplemental functions, including the original construction using smooth but rational functions. The comparison suggested that it is better to use the piecewise polynomial supplements rather than the rational supplements for higher order r. Although the rational supplements are smooth and so tend to approximate better, noticeable errors could be seen due to inaccurate numerical integration, especially on meshes with short edges. Among the new spaces, it was found that the spaces with supplements based on the center point sub-triangulation (23) performed best.

Author Contributions: Conceptualization, T.A. and C.W.; Methodology, T.A. and C.W.; Software, T.A. and C.W.; Writing—original draft, T.A. and C.W.; Writing—review & editing, T.A. and C.W.; Funding acquisition, T.A. Both authors contributed about equally to the work. All authors have read and agreed to the published version of the manuscript.

Funding: This research was funded by U.S. National Science Foundation grant number DMS-2111159.

Data Availability Statement: All pertinent data generated or analyzed during this study are included in this published article. Supporting data omitted from the article are available from the corresponding author on reasonable request.

Conflicts of Interest: The authors declare no conflicts of interest.

References

1. Bishop, J.E. A displacement-based finite element formulation for general polyhedra using harmonic shape functions. *Int. J. Numer. Methods Eng.* **2014**, *97*, 1–31. [CrossRef]
2. Bishop, J.E.; Sukumar, N. Polyhedral finite elements for nonlinear solid mechanics using tetrahedral subdivisions and dual-cell aggregation. *Comput. Aided Geom. Des.* **2020**, *77*, 101812. [CrossRef]
3. Tabarraei, A.; Sukumar, N. Application of polygonal finite elements in linear elasticity. *Int. J. Comput. Methods* **2006**, *3*, 503–529. [CrossRef]
4. Paz, J.D.M. PolyDPG: A Discontinuous Petroz-Galerkin Methodology for Polytopal Meshes with Applications to Elasticity. Ph.D. Thesis, University of Texas at Austin, Austin, TX, USA, 2020.
5. Spring, D.W.; Leon, S.E.; Paulino, G.H. Unstructured polygonal meshes with adaptive refinement for the numerical simulation of dynamic cohesive fracture. *Intl. J. Fract.* **2014**, *189*, 33–57. [CrossRef]
6. Chi, H.; Talischi, C.; Lopez-Pamies, O.; Paulino, G. Polygonal finite elements for finite elasticity. *Int. J. Numer. Methods Eng.* **2015**, *101*, 305–328. [CrossRef]
7. Bishop, J.E. Applications of Polyhedral Finite Elements in Solid Mechanics. In *Generalized Barycentric Coordinates in Computer Graphics and Computational Mechanics*; CRC Press: Boca Raton, FL, USA, 2017; pp. 179–196.
8. Di Pietro, D.; Droniou, J. A fully discrete plates complex on polygonal meshes with application to the Kirchhoff–Love problem. *Math. Comput.* **2023**, *92*, 51–77. [CrossRef]
9. Ho-Nguyen-Tan, T.; Kim, H.G. Polygonal shell elements with assumed transverse shear and membrane strains. *Comput. Methods Appl. Mech. Eng.* **2019**, *349*, 595–627. [CrossRef]

10. Arbogast, T.; Tao, Z. A Direct Mixed–Enriched Galerkin Method on Quadrilaterals for Two-phase Darcy Flow. *Comput. Geosci.* **2019**, *23*, 1141–1160. [CrossRef]
11. Talischi, C.; Paulino, G.H.; Pereira, A.; Menezes, I.F. Polygonal finite elements for topology optimization: a unifying paradigm. *Int. J. Numer. Methods Eng.* **2006**, *82*, 671–698. [CrossRef]
12. Nguyen, K.C.; Tran, P.; Nguyen, H.X. Multi-material topology optimization for additive manufacturing using polytree-based adaptive polygonal finite elements. *Autom. Constr.* **2019**, *99*, 79–90. [CrossRef]
13. de Lima, C.R.; Paulino, G.H. Auxetic structure design using compliant mechanisms: A topology optimization approach with polygonal finite elements. *Adv. Eng. Softw.* **2019**, *129*, 69–80. [CrossRef]
14. Boffi, D.; Kikuchi, F.; Schöberl, J. Edge element computation of Maxwell's eigenvalues on general quadrilateral meshes. *Math. Model. Methods Appl. Sci. (M3AS)* **2006**, *16*, 265–273. [CrossRef]
15. Mu, L.; Wang, J.; Ye, X. Weak Galerkin finite element methods on polytopal meshes. *Int. J. Numer. Anal. Model.* **2015**, *12*, 31–53.
16. Demkowicz, L.; Gopalakrishnan, J. A class of discontinuous Petrov–Galerkin methods. Part I: The transport equation. *Comput. Methods Appl. Mech. Eng.* **2010**, *199*, 1558–1572. [CrossRef]
17. Vaziri, A.; Mora Paz, J.; Fuentes, F.; Demkowicz, L. High-order Polygonal Finite Elements Using Ultraweak Formulations. *Comput. Methods Appl. Mech. Eng.* **2018**, *332*, 686–711. [CrossRef]
18. Bacuta, C.; Demkowicz, L.; Mora Paz, J.; Xenophontos, C. Analysis of non-conforming DPG methods on polyhedral meshes using fractional Sobolev norms. *Comput. Math. Appl.* **2021**, *95*, 215–241. [CrossRef]
19. Brezzi, F.; Lipnikov, K.; Simoncini, V. A family of mimetic finite difference methods on polygonal and polyhedral meshes. *Math. Models Methods Appl. Sci.* **2005**, *15*, 1533–1551. [CrossRef]
20. Kuznetsov, Y.; Lipnikov, K.; Shashkov, M. The mimetic finite difference method on polygonal meshes for diffusion-type problems. *Comput. Geosci.* **2004**, *8*, 301–324. [CrossRef]
21. Manzini, G.; Russo, A.; Sukumar, N. New perspectives on polygonal and polyhedral finite element methods. *Math. Models Methods Appl. Sci.* **2014**, *24*, 1665–1699. [CrossRef]
22. Beirão da Veiga, L.; Brezzi, F.; Cangiani, A.; Manzini, G.; Marini, L.; Russo, A. Basic principles of virtual element methods. *Math. Models Meth. Appl. Sci.* **2013**, *23*, 199–214. [CrossRef]
23. Beirão da Veiga, L.; Brezzi, F.; Marini, L.; Russo, A. H(div) and H(curl)-conforming virtual element methods. *Numer. Math.* **2016**, *133*, 303–332.
24. Beirão da Veiga, L.; Brezzi, F.; Marini, L.; Russo, A. Virtual element method for general second-order elliptic problems on polygonal meshes. *Math. Models Methods Appl. Sci.* **2016**, *26*, 729–750. [CrossRef]
25. Beirão da Veiga, L.; Dassi, F.; Russo, A. High-order virtual element method on polyhedral meshes. *Comput. Math. Appl.* **2017**, *74*, 1110–1122. [CrossRef]
26. Thomas, J.M. Sur L'analyse Numerique des Methodes D'elements Finis Hybrides et Mixtes. Ph.D. Thesis, Sciences Mathematiques, à l'Universite Pierre et Marie Curie, Paris, France, 1977.
27. Brezzi, F.; Fortin, M. *Mixed and Hybrid Finite Element Methods*; Springer: New York, NY, USA, 1991.
28. Boffi, D.; Brezzi, F.; Fortin, M. *Mixed Finite Element Methods and Applications*; Number 44 in Springer Series in Computational Mathematics; Springer: Berlin/Heidelberg, Germany, 2013.
29. Shen, J. *Mixed Finite Element Methods on Distorted Rectangular Grids*; Technical Report ISC-94-13-MATH; Institute for Scientific Computation, Texas A&M University: College Station, TX, USA, 1994.
30. Bochev, P.B.; Ridzal, D. Rehabilitation of the lowest-order Raviart–Thomas element on quadrilateral grids. *SIAM J. Numer. Anal.* **2008**, *47*, 487–507. [CrossRef]
31. Kim, S.; Yim, J.; Sheen, D. Stable cheapest nonconforming finite elements for the Stokes equations. *J. Comput. Appl. Math.* **2016**, *299*, 2–14. [CrossRef]
32. Chen, W.; Wang, Y. Minimal degree H(curl) and H(div) conforming finite elements on polytopal meshes. *Math. Comp.* **2017**, *86*, 2053–2087. [CrossRef]
33. Kuznetsov, Y.; Repin, S. Mixed finite element method on polygonal and polyhedral meshes. In *Numerical Mathematics and Advanced Applications*; Springer: Berlin, Germany, 2004; pp. 615–622.
34. Arnold, D.N.; Boffi, D.; Falk, R.S. Quadrilateral H(div) Finite Elements. *SIAM. J. Numer. Anal.* **2005**, *42*, 2429–2451. [CrossRef]
35. Siqueira, D.; Devloo, P.R.B.; Gomes, S.M. A new procedure for the construction of hierarchical high order Hdiv and Hcurl finite element spaces. *J. Comput. App. Math.* **2013**, *240*, 204–214. [CrossRef]
36. Calle, J.L.D.; Devloo, P.R.B.; Gomes, S.M. Implementation of continuous hp-adaptive finite element spaces without limitations on hanging sides and distribution of approximation orders. *Comput. Math. Appl.* **2015**, *70*, 1051–1069. [CrossRef]
37. Floater, M.S.; Hormann, K.; Kós, G. A general construction of barycentric coordinates over convex polygons. *Adv. Comput. Math.* **2006**, *24*, 311–331. [CrossRef]
38. Sukumar, N. Quadratic maximum-entropy serendipity shape functions for arbitrary planar polygons. *Comput. Methods Appl. Mech. Eng.* **2013**, *263*, 27–41. [CrossRef]
39. Rand, A.; Gillette, A.; Bajaj, C. Quadratic serendipity finite elements on polygons using generalized barycentric coordinates. *Math. Comp.* **2014**, *83*, 2691–2716. [CrossRef] [PubMed]
40. Arbogast, T.; Correa, M.R. Two families of H(div) mixed finite elements on quadrilaterals of minimal dimension. *SIAM J. Numer. Anal.* **2016**, *54*, 3332–3356. [CrossRef]

41. Cockburn, B.; Fu, G. Superconvergence by M-decompositions. Part II: Construction of two-dimensional finite elements. *ESAIM Math. Model. Numer. Anal.* **2017**, *51*, 165–186. [CrossRef]
42. Arbogast, T.; Tao, Z.; Wang, C. Direct serendipity and mixed finite elements on convex quadrilaterals. *Numer. Math.* **2022**, *150*, 929–974. [CrossRef]
43. Arbogast, T.; Wang, C. Direct serendipity and mixed finite elements on convex polygons. *Numer. Algorithms* **2023**, *92*, 1451–1483. [CrossRef]
44. Cockburn, B.; Fu, G. Superconvergence by M-decompositions. Part III: Construction of three-dimensional finite elements. *ESAIM Math. Model. Numer. Anal.* **2017**, *51*, 365–398. [CrossRef]
45. Arbogast, T.; Tao, Z. Construction of H(div)-conforming mixed finite elements on cuboidal hexahedra. *Numer. Math.* **2019**, *142*, 1–32. [CrossRef]
46. Arbogast, T.; Wang, C. Direct serendipity finite elements on cuboidal hexahedra. 2023, *submitted*.
47. Arnold, D.N.; Falk, R.S.; Winther, R. Finite element exterior calculus: from Hodge theory to numerical stability. *Bull. Am. Math. Soc. (N.S.)* **2010**, *47*, 281–354. [CrossRef]
48. Arnold, D.N.; Brezzi, F. Mixed and nonconforming finite element methods: Implementation, postprocessing and error estimates. *RAIRO Model. Math. Anal. Numer.* **1985**, *19*, 7–32. [CrossRef]
49. Girault, V.; Raviart, P.A. *Finite Element Methods for Navier-Stokes Equations: Theory and Algorithms;* Springer: Berlin, Germany, 1986.
50. Scott, L.R.; Zhang, S. Finite element interpolation of nonsmooth functions satisfying boundary conditions. *Math. Comp.* **1990**, *54*, 483–493. [CrossRef]
51. Brenner, S.C.; Scott, L.R. *The Mathematical Theory of Finite Element Methods;* Springer: New York, NY, USA, 1994.
52. Talischi, C.; Paulino, G.H.; Pereira, A.; Menezes, I.F.M. PolyMesher: a general-purpose mesh generator for polygonal elements written in Matlab. *Struct. Multidisc. Optim.* **2012**, *45*, 309–328. [CrossRef]

mathematics MDPI

Article

A Bio-Chemo-Hydro-Mechanical Model for the Simulation of Biocementation in Soils: One-Dimensional Finite Element Simulations

Victor Scartezini Terra, Fernando M. F. Simões * and Rafaela Cardoso

Instituto Superior Técnico and CERIS, University of Lisbon, Av. Rovisco Pais, 1, 1049-001 Lisboa, Portugal; victor.terra@tecnico.ulisboa.pt (V.S.T.); rafaela.cardoso@tecnico.ulisboa.pt (R.C.)
* Correspondence: fernando.simoes@tecnico.ulisboa.pt

Abstract: Microbially induced calcite precipitation is a soil improvement technique in which bacteria are used to produce calcium carbonate (biocement), precipitated after the hydrolysis of urea by the urease enzyme present in the microorganisms. This technique is becoming popular, and there have been several real cases of its use; however, the dosages and reaction times used to attain a required percentage of biocement mainly stem from previous experimental tests, and calculations are not performed. Thus, it is fundamental to have more robust tools and the existence of numerical models able to compute the amount precipitated, such as the one proposed in this paper, can be an important contribution. A two-phase porous medium model is created to analyse the precipitation process. The solid phase contains soil particles, bacteria and biocement, while the fluid phase contains water, urea and other dissolved species. A coupled bio-chemo-hydro-mechanical finite element formulation is defined, embodying the biochemical reaction, water seepage, the diffusion of species and soil deformation. The main novelties of this study are as follows: (i) porosity changes are computed considering the generation of solid mass due to biocement precipitation, and, therefore, soil permeability is updated during the calculation, with these highly coupled equations being integrated in time simultaneously and not sequentially; and (ii) the model is calibrated with experimental tests conceived especially for this purpose. The model is then used to compute the biocement precipitated in a sand column simulating a real experimental test. The results of the simulations present a distribution of biocement along the column closer to that observed in the experimental tests, validating the model.

Keywords: bio-chemo-hydro-mechanical coupled model; microbially induced calcium carbonate precipitation; finite element analysis; reaction rate

MSC: 65M60

1. Introduction

Biocementation, also referred as microbially induced calcite precipitation (MICP), is a ground improvement technique that involves the use of microorganisms (particularly bacteria) to generate calcium carbonate ($CaCO_3$) predominantly in the form of calcite. The used microorganisms are usually non-pathogenic and can be found in different types of soils.

Figure 1 presents a detailed representation of the mechanism of MICP. Basically, a feeding solution with urea and calcium chloride is added to a medium of urease-producing bacteria. The urease enzymes hydrolyse urea, producing ammonium (NH_4^+) and bicarbonate (CO_3^{2-}) ions, according to the following chemical reaction (1):

$$CO(NH_2)_{(aq.)} + 2H_2O_{(l)} \rightarrow 2NH_4^+{}_{(aq.)} + CO_3^{2-}{}_{(aq.)}. \quad (1)$$

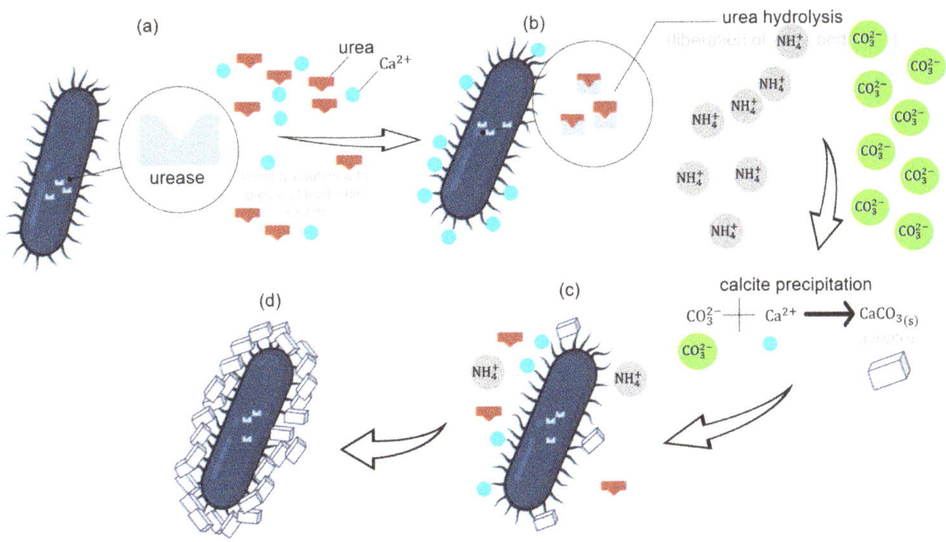

Figure 1. Schematic representation of microbially induced calcite precipitation: (**a**) urease-producing bacteria and feeding solution with urea and a calcium source; (**b**) hydrolysis of urea by urease produces ammonium (NH_4^+) and bicarbonate (CO_3^{2-}) ions; (**c**) bicarbonate ions react with calcium ions and calcite precipitates; (**d**) eventually, bacteria encapsulation occurs when the bacteria are trapped by precipitated calcite crystals.

Calcium chloride is usually supplied in the feeding solution as a calcium source, which dissolves into calcium (Ca^{2+}) and chloride ions. The bacteria cells serve as a nucleation site for calcium ions which react with the bicarbonate ions, resulting from the urea hydrolysis, precipitating solid calcium carbonate ($CaCO_3$), according to the following chemical reaction (2):

$$Ca^{2+}{}_{(aq.)} + CO_3^{2-}{}_{(aq.)} \rightarrow CaCO_{3(s)}, \tag{2}$$

This calcium carbonate, usually referred to as calcite, may lead to bacteria encapsulation when it accumulates, forming an envelope and trapping bacteria.

The precipitated $CaCO_3$ clogs the pores and bonds soil grains, thus decreasing soil permeability and increasing its stiffness and strength [1–3], sealing rock fractures [4] and increasing its resistance to erosive processes [5–8]. However, in the case of large-scale field applications, one of the main limitations of this technique is to achieve a homogenous biocement distribution in the treated volume [1,9,10].

Treatment dosages, the number of injections and the reaction time to attain a required percentage of calcium carbonate are determined through experimental tests performed in the laboratory before the field work is carried out. However, it is fundamental to have more robust tools. Numerical models able to compute the amount precipitated, such as the one proposed in this paper, would be an important contribution. The majority of the works concerning the numerical modelling of biocementation in soils are reactive transport models (e.g., [11–16]), which only focus on the fluid transport along the porous matrix by modelling water flow, chemical species transport and reactions related to MICP processes. There are also a few hydro-mechanical models (e.g., [17,18]) that consider soil as a deformable medium.

This research presents a chemo-hydro-mechanical coupled finite element model to predict precipitated calcite content in soils during biocementation and subsequent changes in the hydro-mechanical properties of this porous medium. The main purpose of this model is to be able to predict the amount of precipitated biocement for a given treatment protocol, i.e., by knowing the dosages of urea and calcium and the duration of the treatment. This new bio-chemo-hydro-mechanical model has some differences to the above-mentioned ones, listed as follows:

(i) The model considers soil grains and attached bacteria as a single species in the solid phase for the sake of simplicity. In this way, it is assumed that the attached bacteria are already homogeneously distributed in the solid matrix, and no bacterial injections are simulated;
(ii) The species present are solid grains with attached bacteria, solid calcite, water, urea, ammonium, calcium and chloride ions;
(iii) All the couplings are integrated in the formulation. Moreover, for the usual hydro-mechanical coupled behaviour in saturated soils, in which the deformation caused by mechanical actions affects the water flow (consolidation) or changes in water pore pressure affect the effective stresses, biochemical coupling is introduced. The chemical reactions result in the precipitation of solid calcium carbonate (referred to as calcite from now on) in the pores, reducing the soil porosity. At every time step, permeability changes are calculated as a function of the new porosity values (the pore-clogging effect), which may affect the flow velocity. The elastic stiffness of the medium is considered to be constant at this stage but could be updated to consider the presence of calcite forming bonds between the soil particles.

The most important novelty of the presented model is that the biochemical reaction rate parameters are calibrated experimentally with small-scale sand column tests.

Moreover, and contrary to other numerical techniques proposed in the literature, the highly coupled equations of the model, which considers porosity and permeability changes due to biocement precipitation, are simultaneously and not sequentially integrated in time.

2. Model Formulation

The formulation developed encompasses the hydro-geologic point of view (e.g., [11,12,14]), which only addresses diffusion couplings that involve water seepage and water advective diffusion/dispersion of ionic species, and the geo-mechanical point of view (e.g., [17,18]), which addresses hydro-mechanical couplings and accounts for soil deformation.

A two-phase saturated porous medium is considered, in which each phase is composed of several species, as presented by the schematic pore-scale representation in Figure 2. The solid phase (S) contains soil particles with attached bacteria, homogeneously distributed in the whole medium and jointly denoted by the symbol (s) as well as calcite, denoted by the symbol, (c). It is assumed that calcite is the only calcium carbonate morphotype that is considered as a resulting product of the ureolysis-induced calcium carbonate precipitation process. The fluid phase (W) contains water (w), urea (u), calcium (Ca), chloride (Cl) and ammonium (a) ions.

The main hypotheses of this model follow the strongly interacting model by Bataille and Kestin [19]:

i Mass balance is required for each species;
ii Momentum balance is required for the porous medium as a whole;
iii Species in the fluid phase are endowed with their own velocities; the velocity of the species in the solid phase is equal to the velocity of the phase ($\mathbf{v}_{kS} = \mathbf{v}_S$, $k \in S$);
iv The urea hydrolysis reaction, as shown in Equation (1), produces bicarbonate and ammonium ions;
v Calcium and bicarbonate ions in the fluid phase precipitate, forming calcite in the solid phase, according to Equation (2);
vi As a simplification, the reactions in iv. and v. have the same rate. Therefore, the mass of bicarbonate formed in the hydrolysis of urea immediately precipitates when the calcite is formed, and bicarbonate ions are not a part of the model.

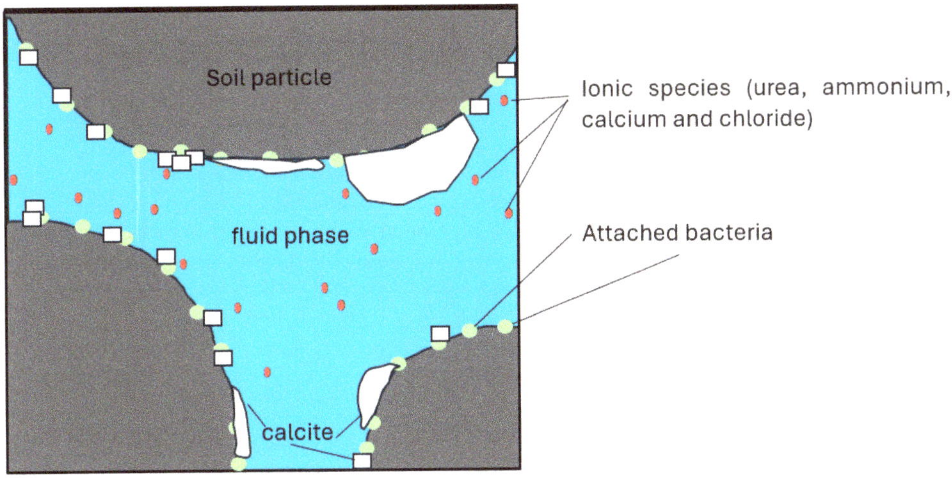

Figure 2. Pore-scale representation of main species of the model.

During the formulation, several mass and volume quantities (defined in Table 1) are used. The current volume, mass and number of moles of the species k in phase K are denoted by V_{kK}, M_{kK} and N_{kK}, respectively. The molar mass, the molar volume and the intrinsic density of the species k are denoted by $m_k^{(M)}$, $v_k^{(M)}$ and ρ_k, respectively. The initial volume of the porous medium is denoted by V_0, and the current solid, fluid and total volumes are denoted by V_S, V_W and V, respectively. Several other quantities may be defined for species k in phase K, like the volume fraction (n_{kK}), the volume content (v_{kK}), the mass content (m_{kK}), the molar concentration (c_{kW}) and the apparent density $\left(\rho^{kK}\right)$. Summing the contributions of the species, it is also possible to define the volume fraction (or porosity) of the fluid phase (n_W), the volume content of the fluid phase (v_W) and the volume content of the solid phase (v_S).

Table 1. Definition of several mass and volume quantities. The suffix kK is used in this research as a designation for the species k in phase K.

Quantity (Unit)	Definition
Current volume of solid phase—V_S (m^3)	$V_S = \sum_{k \epsilon S} V_{kS}$
Current volume of fluid phase—V_W (m^3)	$V_W = \sum_{k \epsilon W} V_{kW}$
Current total volume—V (m^3)	$V = V_S + V_W$
Volume fraction of the species—n_{kK}	$n_{kK} = V_{kK}/V$
Volume content—v_{kK}	$v_{kK} = V_{kK}/V_0$
Mass content—m_{kK} (kg m^{-3})	$m_{kK} = M_{kK}/V_0$
Molar concentration—c_{kW} (mol m^{-3})	$c_{kW} = N_{kW}/V_W$
Intrinsic density of the species k—ρ_k (kg m^{-3})	$\rho_k = m_k^{(M)}/v_k^{(M)} = M_{kK}/V_{kK}$
Apparent density of the species—ρ^{kK} (kg m^{-3})	$\rho^{kK} = M_{kK}/V = n_{kK}\rho_k$
Volume fraction (porosity) of the fluid phase—n_W	$n_W = \sum_{k \in W} n_{kW}$
Volume content of the fluid phase—v_W	$v_W = \sum_{k \in W} v_{kW}$
Volume content of the solid phase—v_S	$v_S = \sum_{k \in S} v_{kS}.$

2.1. Mass Balance of Species k in Phase K

The species mass balance can be written, in the current configuration, as presented by Loret and Simões in [20,21]:

$$\frac{\mathrm{d}^k \rho^{kK}}{\mathrm{d}t} + \rho^{kK} \mathrm{div}\, \mathbf{v}_{kK} = \hat{\rho}^{kK} \tag{3}$$

where $\mathrm{d}^k(\ )/\mathrm{d}t$ is the total time derivative as seen by an observer moving with the particles of species k, $\mathbf{v}_{kK}$ is the velocity of species k in phase K and $\hat{\rho}^{kK}$ is the rate of the mass of the species per unit of volume that is created or lost during the chemical reactions. Upon linearization, the mass balance equation in the reference configuration is as follows (see Equation (A4) in Appendix A):

$$\frac{\mathrm{d}v_{kK}}{\mathrm{d}t} + \mathrm{div}\, \mathbf{J}_{kK} = \frac{\hat{m}^{kK}}{\rho_k} \tag{4}$$

where $\mathbf{J}_{kK} = n_{kK}(\mathbf{v}_{kK} - \mathbf{v}_{\mathrm{S}})$ is the flux of the species through the solid skeleton and $\hat{m}^{kK}$ is the rate of the mass of the species per unit of volume that is created or lost during the chemical reactions, in the reference configuration.

By adding the contribution of all species $k \in \mathrm{W}$ and all species $k \in \mathrm{S}$, we obtain the following global equation of mass balance (see Equation (A10) in Appendix A):

$$\mathrm{div}\, \mathbf{v}_{\mathrm{S}} + \mathrm{div}\, \mathbf{J}_{\mathrm{W}} = \sum_{k\in \mathrm{W}} \frac{\hat{m}^{k\mathrm{W}}}{\rho_k} + \sum_{k\in \mathrm{S}} \frac{\hat{m}^{k\mathrm{S}}}{\rho_k} \tag{5}$$

where $\mathbf{J}_{\mathrm{W}} = \sum_{k\in\mathrm{W}} \mathbf{J}_{k\mathrm{W}}$ represents the flux of water.

In the case of a species $k \in \mathrm{W}$, the diffusive flux is defined as follows:

$$\mathbf{J}^{\mathrm{d}}_{k\mathrm{W}} = n_{k\mathrm{W}}(\mathbf{v}_{k\mathrm{W}} - \mathbf{v}_{\mathrm{wW}}) = \mathbf{J}_{k\mathrm{W}} - \frac{n_{k\mathrm{W}}}{n_{\mathrm{wW}}} \mathbf{J}_{\mathrm{wW}} \tag{6}$$

Therefore, the mass balance in Equation (4) for a species in the fluid phase can be rewritten as follows:

$$n_{\mathrm{w}} v_k^{(M)} \frac{\mathrm{d}c_{k\mathrm{W}}}{\mathrm{d}t} - \mathrm{div}\, \boldsymbol{\alpha}_k + v_k^{(M)} \mathbf{J}_{\mathrm{w}} \cdot \nabla c_{k\mathrm{W}} + c_{k\mathrm{W}} v_k^{(M)} \left(\sum_{l\in\mathrm{W}} \frac{\hat{m}^{l\mathrm{W}}}{\rho_k} \right) - \frac{\hat{m}^{k\mathrm{W}}}{\rho_k} = \mathbf{0}, \tag{7}$$

where $\boldsymbol{\alpha}_k = -\sum_{l\in\mathrm{W}} \left(\mathrm{I}_{kl} - c_{k\mathrm{W}} v_k^{(M)} \right) \mathbf{J}^d_{l\mathrm{W}}$, and $\mathbf{I}$ is the identity matrix.

On the other hand, for calcite, Equation (4) simply results in the following:

$$\frac{\mathrm{d}m_{c\mathrm{S}}}{\mathrm{d}t} = \hat{m}^{c\mathrm{S}}. \tag{8}$$

In the reaction of urea hydrolysis, one mole of urea is consumed when two moles of ammonium are formed at the rate r_1. Therefore, using the notation by van Wijngaarden et al. [11], the rate of the mass change of the species involved in this reaction is defined as follows:

$$\frac{\hat{m}^{u\mathrm{W}}}{\rho_u} = -v_u^{(M)} n_{\mathrm{w}} r_1 \tag{9}$$

$$\frac{\hat{m}^{a\mathrm{W}}}{\rho_a} = 2 v_a^{(M)} n_{\mathrm{w}} r_1 \tag{10}$$

In the reaction of calcite precipitation, one mole of Ca^{2+} is consumed when one mole of calcite is formed at the rate r_2. Therefore, the rate of the mass change of the species involved in this reaction is as follows:

$$\frac{\hat{m}^{cS}}{\rho_c} = v_c^{(M)} n_w r_2 \tag{11}$$

$$\frac{\hat{m}^{CaW}}{\rho_{Ca}} = -v_{Ca}^{(M)} n_w r_2 \tag{12}$$

The efficiency of the reactions of urea hydrolysis and calcium carbonate precipitation depends on several factors, such as temperature and pH [11], bacterial activity and the mineralogy of the clay particles in the soil [22]. Encapsulation by calcium carbonate crystals can also occur, creating a diffusion barrier around the bacteria. In addition, aerobic bacteria injected into an anaerobic soil may eventually die due to the lack of oxygenation [11]. All these factors can reduce the efficiency of the reaction.

Regarding the reaction of urea hydrolysis, the Michaelis–Menten kinetics mathematical model is usually used to define the reaction rate. Although some authors (e.g., [12]) defined different velocities for the reactions of urea hydrolysis and calcite precipitation, in this work, the two reactions have the same rate (as in [11]):

$$r_1 = r_2 = r = v_{max} \frac{c_{uW}}{K_m + c_{uW}} e^{\left(-\frac{t}{t_{max}}\right)} \tag{13}$$

where v_{max}, K_m and t_{max} are constants to be obtained. Since the bacteria distribution is assumed to be homogeneous, parameter v_{max} is constant, and, therefore, Equation (13) presents an exponential time decay for the reaction rate, where t_{max} is related to the lifespan or the activity of the bacteria.

Due to the simplification adopted in Equation (13), even though bicarbonate ions are involved in the reactions, their mass balance is not a part of the model since it is considered that the mass of the bicarbonate that is formed immediately precipitates when the calcite is formed.

2.2. Momentum Balance of the Species

The global equation for the conservation of linear momentum is as follows:

$$\text{div}\, \boldsymbol{\sigma} + \rho \mathbf{g} = \mathbf{0} \tag{14}$$

where $\boldsymbol{\sigma}$ is the total stress tensor, which for soils, according to Terzaghi's principle, is defined as follows:

$$\boldsymbol{\sigma} = \boldsymbol{\sigma}' - p_W \mathbf{I} \tag{15}$$

where $\boldsymbol{\sigma}'$ is the effective stress tensor, p_W is the pore–water pressure (the negative sign is introduced as it is a general convention to consider the tensile components of stress as positive [23]), $\mathbf{I}$ is the identity matrix, $\mathbf{g}$ is the gravity acceleration (9.8 m/s^2) and $\rho = \sum_{k \in W,S} \rho^{kK}$.

Assuming a linear elastic behaviour, the effective stress tensor is related to the deformation tensor $\boldsymbol{\varepsilon}$ by Hooke's law as follows:

$$\boldsymbol{\sigma}' = \mathbf{E} : \boldsymbol{\varepsilon} \tag{16}$$

where $\mathbf{E}$ is the fourth-rank elasticity tensor, and the colon denotes the double dot product. In the 1-D case, only one material constant, the Young's modulus E, is needed.

2.3. Diffusion Equation for the Ionic Species (Fick's Law)

The diffusive/dispersive flux of the ionic species is related to the concentration gradients according to Fick's law as follows:

$$\mathbf{J}^{\mathrm{d}}_{k\mathrm{W}} = -v_k^{(M)} n_{\mathrm{w}} \mathbf{D}\cdot\nabla c_{k\mathrm{W}} \tag{17}$$

where $\mathbf{D}$ is the matrix of the diffusion constants. In the 1-D case, the diffusive/dispersive flux has the following form [11]:

$$\mathbf{J}^{\mathrm{d}}_{k\mathrm{W}} = -v_k^{(M)} n_{\mathrm{w}} \alpha_L \|v_{\mathrm{wW}}\| \nabla c_{k\mathrm{W}} \tag{18}$$

where α_L is the longitudinal diffusion coefficient, which is assumed to be constant for all the ionic species.

2.4. Flow Equation for the Fluid Phase (Darcy's Law)

It is assumed that the water flow in the porous medium is governed by Darcy's law as follows:

$$\mathbf{J}_{\mathrm{w}} = -\boldsymbol{k}\cdot\left(\nabla p_{\mathrm{W}} - \frac{\rho^{\mathrm{W}}\boldsymbol{g}}{n_{\mathrm{W}}}\right), \tag{19}$$

where $\boldsymbol{k}$ is the water permeability tensor (an isotropic medium is assumed) and $\rho^{\mathrm{W}} = \sum_{k\epsilon\mathrm{W}} \rho^{k\mathrm{W}}$. Particularly for the 1-D case, the following can be written:

$$J_{\mathrm{W}} = -k_x\left(\frac{\mathrm{d}p_{\mathrm{W}}}{\mathrm{d}x} + \frac{\rho^{\mathrm{W}} g}{n_{\mathrm{W}}}\right), \tag{20}$$

where $k_x = k_h/\rho_w g$ is the longitudinal permeability obtained in $\mathrm{m^3skg^{-1}}$, and k_h is the hydraulic conductivity, related to the porosity n_{W} (see Equation (A14) in Appendix B for its update) according to the Kozeny–Carman equation as follows:

$$k_h = \bar{k}_h \frac{(n_{\mathrm{W}})^3}{(1-n_{\mathrm{W}})^2}. \tag{21}$$

3. Finite Element Formulation

3.1. The Semi-Discrete Field Equations

The 1-D finite element formulation of the problem in its weak form is obtained by multiplying the equations of the global momentum balance (14), global mass balance (5), aqueous species mass balance (7) and calcium carbonate mass balance (8) by the fields of the virtual displacement (u^*), water pressure (p^*), concentration (c^*) and mass per unit of volume (m^*), respectively. Their integration over the element volume Ω using the Gauss theorem results in the following:

$$\int_\Omega \nabla \boldsymbol{u}^* : \boldsymbol{\sigma}\mathrm{dV} - \int_\Omega \rho\boldsymbol{u}^*\cdot\mathbf{g}\mathrm{dV} = \int_{\partial\Omega} \boldsymbol{u}^*\cdot\boldsymbol{\sigma}\cdot\mathbf{n}\mathrm{dS} \tag{22}$$

$$\begin{aligned}\int_\Omega p^*\mathrm{div}\,\mathbf{v}_{\mathrm{s}}\mathrm{dV} - \int_\Omega \nabla p^*\cdot\mathbf{J}_{\mathrm{w}}\mathrm{dV} - \int_\Omega p^*\left(\textstyle\sum_{k\in\mathrm{W}} \frac{\hat{m}^{k\mathrm{W}}}{\rho_k} + \sum_{k\in\mathrm{S}} \frac{\hat{m}^{k\mathrm{S}}}{\rho_k}\right)\mathrm{dV} \\ = -\int_{\partial\Omega} p^*\mathbf{J}_{\mathrm{w}}\cdot\mathbf{n}\mathrm{dS}\end{aligned} \tag{23}$$

$$\begin{aligned}\int_\Omega c^* n_{\mathrm{W}} \tfrac{\mathrm{d}c_{k\mathrm{W}}}{\mathrm{d}t} v_k^{(M)} dV + \int_\Omega c^*\left[\left(\textstyle\sum_{l\in\mathrm{W}} \frac{\hat{m}^{l\mathrm{W}}}{\rho_l}\right) c_{k\mathrm{W}} v_k^{(M)} - \frac{\hat{m}^{k\mathrm{W}}}{\rho_k}\right]\mathrm{dV} + \int_\Omega \nabla c^*\cdot\boldsymbol{\alpha}_k\mathrm{dV} + \\ \int_\Omega c^*\mathbf{J}_{\mathrm{w}}\cdot\nabla c_{k\mathrm{W}} v_k^{(M)}\mathrm{dV} = \int_{\partial\Omega} c^*\boldsymbol{\alpha}_k\cdot\mathbf{n}\mathrm{dS},\ k = \mathrm{u, a, Ca, Cl}\end{aligned} \tag{24}$$

$$\int_\Omega m^*\left(\frac{\mathrm{d}m_{c\mathrm{S}}}{\mathrm{d}t} - \hat{m}^{c\mathrm{S}}\right)\mathrm{dV} = 0 \tag{25}$$

where $\partial\Omega$ is the element surface, and $\mathbf{n}$ is its unit normal vector.

The seven primary unknown fields (the solid displacements, water pressure, concentrations of the ionic fluid species—namely urea, ammonium, calcium and chloride—and the calcite mass per unit of volume) are approximated inside each bar finite element (e) by using a linear combination of shape functions ($\mathbf{N}_{\mathrm{U}}$, $\mathbf{N}_{\mathrm{P_W}}$, $\mathbf{N}_{\mathrm{C}}$ and $\mathbf{N}_{\mathrm{M}_c}$) and nodal values ($\mathbf{U}^{(e)}$, ${\mathbf{P}_{\mathrm{w}}}^{(e)}$, ${\mathbf{C}_{k\mathrm{W}}}^{(e)}$ and ${\mathbf{M}_c}^{(e)}$):

$$\mathbf{u}^{(e)} = \mathbf{N}_{\mathrm{U}} \cdot \mathbf{U}^{(e)} \tag{26}$$

$$p_{\mathrm{W}}{}^{(e)} = \mathbf{N}_{\mathrm{P_W}} \cdot \mathbf{P}_{\mathrm{w}}{}^{(e)} \tag{27}$$

$$c_{k\mathrm{W}}{}^{(e)} = \mathbf{N}_{\mathrm{C}} \cdot \mathbf{C}_{k\mathrm{W}}{}^{(e)},\ k = \mathrm{u}, \mathrm{a}, \mathrm{Ca}, \mathrm{Cl} \tag{28}$$

$$m_{c\mathrm{S}}{}^{(e)} = \mathbf{N}_{\mathrm{M}_c} \cdot \mathbf{M}_c{}^{(e)} \tag{29}$$

The same approximations are made for the virtual fields. Quadratic interpolation is employed for solid displacements (three nodes per element), and linear interpolation is employed for the other primary unknowns (two nodes per element).

By substituting the virtual fields' approximation into (22)–(25), we obtain the following element first-order semi-discrete equation:

$$\mathbf{F}_{\mathrm{int}}^{(\mathrm{e})} = \mathbf{F}_{\mathrm{ext}}^{(\mathrm{e})}, \tag{30}$$

where the element external forces vector is as follows:

$$\mathbf{F}_{\mathrm{ext}}^{(\mathrm{e})} = \left\{ \begin{array}{c} \int_{\partial\Omega} \mathbf{N}_{\mathrm{U}}^{\mathrm{T}} \boldsymbol{\sigma} \cdot \mathbf{n} \mathrm{dS} \\ -\int_{\partial\Omega} \mathbf{N}_{\mathrm{P_W}}^{\mathrm{T}} \mathbf{J}_{\mathrm{w}} \cdot \mathbf{n} \mathrm{dS} \\ \int_{\partial\Omega} \mathbf{N}_{\mathrm{C}}^{\mathrm{T}} \boldsymbol{\alpha}_{\mathrm{u}} \cdot \mathbf{n} \mathrm{dS} \\ \mathbf{0} \\ \int_{\partial\Omega} \mathbf{N}_{\mathrm{C}}^{\mathrm{T}} \boldsymbol{\alpha}_{\mathrm{Ca}} \cdot \mathbf{n} \mathrm{dS} \\ \int_{\partial\Omega} \mathbf{N}_{\mathrm{C}}^{\mathrm{T}} \boldsymbol{\alpha}_{\mathrm{Cl}} \cdot \mathbf{n} \mathrm{dS} \\ \mathbf{0} \end{array} \right\} \tag{31}$$

and, since $\sum_{k\in \mathrm{W}} \frac{\hat{m}^{k\mathrm{W}}}{\rho_k} = \left(-v_{\mathrm{u}}^{(M)} + 2v_{\mathrm{a}}^{(M)} - v_{\mathrm{Ca}}^{(M)}\right) \frac{1}{m_{\mathrm{c}}^{(M)}} \frac{\mathrm{d}m_{c\mathrm{S}}}{\mathrm{d}t}$ and $\sum_{k\in \mathrm{W}} \frac{\hat{m}^{k\mathrm{W}}}{\rho_k} + \sum_{k\in \mathrm{S}} \frac{\hat{m}^{k\mathrm{S}}}{\rho_k} = \left(-v_{\mathrm{u}}^{(M)} + 2v_{\mathrm{a}}^{(M)} - v_{\mathrm{Ca}}^{(M)} + v_{\mathrm{c}}^{(M)}\right) \frac{1}{m_{\mathrm{c}}^{(M)}} \frac{\mathrm{d}m_{c\mathrm{S}}}{\mathrm{d}t}$, the element internal forces vector is as follows:

$$\mathbf{F}_{\mathrm{int}}^{(\mathrm{e})} = \left\{ \begin{array}{c} \int_{\Omega} \mathbf{B}_{\mathrm{U}}^{\mathrm{T}} \sigma \mathrm{dV} - \int_{\Omega} \mathbf{N}_{\mathrm{U}}^{\mathrm{T}} \rho \mathbf{g} \mathrm{dV} \\ \hline \int_{\Omega} \mathbf{N}_{\mathrm{P_W}}^{\mathrm{T}} \mathrm{div}\, v_{\mathrm{s}} \mathrm{dV} - \int_{\Omega} \nabla \mathbf{N}_{\mathrm{P_W}}^{\mathrm{T}} \mathbf{J}_{\mathrm{w}} \mathrm{dV} \\ -\left(-v_{\mathrm{u}}^{(M)} + 2v_{\mathrm{a}}^{(M)} - v_{\mathrm{Ca}}^{(M)} + v_{\mathrm{c}}^{(M)}\right) \frac{1}{m_{\mathrm{c}}^{(M)}} \int_{\Omega} \mathbf{N}_{\mathrm{P_W}}^{\mathrm{T}} \frac{\mathrm{d}m_{c\mathrm{S}}}{\mathrm{d}t} \mathrm{dV} \\ \hline \int_{\Omega} \mathbf{N}_{\mathrm{C}}^{\mathrm{T}} n_{\mathrm{w}} \frac{\mathrm{d}c_{\mathrm{uW}}}{\mathrm{d}t} v_{\mathrm{u}}^{(M)} \mathrm{dV} + \int_{\Omega} \nabla \mathbf{N}_{\mathrm{C}}^{\mathrm{T}} \boldsymbol{\alpha}_{\mathrm{u}} \mathrm{dV} + \int_{\Omega} \mathbf{N}_{\mathrm{C}}^{\mathrm{T}} \mathbf{J}_{\mathrm{w}} \cdot \nabla c_{\mathrm{uW}} v_{\mathrm{u}}^{(M)} \mathrm{dV} \\ + \int_{\Omega} \mathbf{N}_{\mathrm{C}}^{\mathrm{T}} v_{\mathrm{u}}^{(M)} \left[c_{\mathrm{uW}} \left(-v_{\mathrm{u}}^{(M)} + 2v_{\mathrm{a}}^{(M)} - v_{\mathrm{Ca}}^{(M)}\right) + 1 \right] \frac{1}{m_{\mathrm{c}}^{(M)}} \frac{\mathrm{d}m_{c\mathrm{S}}}{\mathrm{d}t} \mathrm{dV} \\ \hline \int_{\Omega} \mathbf{N}_{\mathrm{C}}^{\mathrm{T}} n_{\mathrm{w}} \frac{\mathrm{d}c_{\mathrm{aW}}}{\mathrm{d}t} v_{\mathrm{a}}^{(M)} \mathrm{dV} + \int_{\Omega} \nabla \mathbf{N}_{\mathrm{C}}^{\mathrm{T}} \boldsymbol{\alpha}_{\mathrm{a}} \mathrm{dV} + \int_{\Omega} \mathbf{N}_{\mathrm{C}}^{\mathrm{T}} \mathbf{J}_{\mathrm{w}} \cdot \nabla c_{\mathrm{aW}} v_{\mathrm{a}}^{(M)} \mathrm{dV} \\ + \int_{\Omega} \mathbf{N}_{\mathrm{C}}^{\mathrm{T}} v_{\mathrm{a}}^{(M)} \left[c_{\mathrm{aW}} \left(-v_{\mathrm{u}}^{(M)} + 2v_{\mathrm{a}}^{(M)} - v_{\mathrm{Ca}}^{(M)}\right) - 2 \right] \frac{1}{m_{\mathrm{c}}^{(M)}} \frac{\mathrm{d}m_{c\mathrm{S}}}{\mathrm{d}t} \mathrm{dV} \\ \hline \int_{\Omega} \mathbf{N}_{\mathrm{C}}^{\mathrm{T}} n_{\mathrm{w}} \frac{\mathrm{d}c_{\mathrm{CaW}}}{\mathrm{d}t} v_{\mathrm{Ca}}^{(M)} \mathrm{dV} + \int_{\Omega} \nabla \mathbf{N}_{\mathrm{C}}^{\mathrm{T}} \boldsymbol{\alpha}_{\mathrm{Ca}} \mathrm{dV} + \int_{\Omega} \mathbf{N}_{\mathrm{C}}^{\mathrm{T}} \mathbf{J}_{\mathrm{w}} \cdot \nabla c_{\mathrm{CaW}} v_{\mathrm{Ca}}^{(M)} \mathrm{dV} \\ + \int_{\Omega} \mathbf{N}_{\mathrm{C}}^{\mathrm{T}} v_{\mathrm{Ca}}^{(M)} \left[c_{\mathrm{CaW}} \left(-v_{\mathrm{u}}^{(M)} + 2v_{\mathrm{a}}^{(M)} - v_{\mathrm{Ca}}^{(M)}\right) + 1 \right] \frac{1}{m_{\mathrm{c}}^{(M)}} \frac{\mathrm{d}m_{c\mathrm{S}}}{\mathrm{d}t} \mathrm{dV} \\ \hline \int_{\Omega} \mathbf{N}_{\mathrm{C}}^{\mathrm{T}} n_{\mathrm{w}} \frac{\mathrm{d}c_{\mathrm{ClW}}}{\mathrm{d}t} v_{\mathrm{Cl}}^{(M)} \mathrm{dV} + \int_{\Omega} \nabla \mathbf{N}_{\mathrm{C}}^{\mathrm{T}} \boldsymbol{\alpha}_{\mathrm{Cl}} \mathrm{dV} + \int_{\Omega} \mathbf{N}_{\mathrm{C}}^{\mathrm{T}} \mathbf{J}_{\mathrm{w}} \cdot \nabla c_{\mathrm{ClW}} v_{\mathrm{Cl}}^{(M)} \mathrm{dV} \\ + \int_{\Omega} \mathbf{N}_{\mathrm{C}}^{\mathrm{T}} v_{\mathrm{Cl}}^{(M)} c_{\mathrm{ClW}} \left(-v_{\mathrm{u}}^{(M)} + 2v_{\mathrm{a}}^{(M)} - v_{\mathrm{Ca}}^{(M)}\right) \frac{1}{m_{\mathrm{c}}^{(M)}} \frac{\mathrm{d}m_{c\mathrm{S}}}{\mathrm{d}t} \mathrm{dV} \\ \hline \int_{\Omega} \mathbf{N}_{\mathrm{M_C}}^{\mathrm{T}} \left(\frac{\mathrm{d}m_{c\mathrm{S}}}{\mathrm{d}t} - m_{\mathrm{c}}^{(M)} n_{\mathrm{w}} r \right) \mathrm{dV} \end{array} \right\}. \tag{32}$$

From the element internal force vector, the element tangent stiffness and tangent diffusion matrices may be retrieved as $\mathbf{K}^{(e)} = d\mathbf{F}^{(e)}_{int}/d\mathbf{X}^{(e)}$ and $\mathbf{C}^{(e)} = d\mathbf{F}^{(e)}_{int}/d\mathbf{V}^{(e)}$, where $\mathbf{X}^{(e)}$ is the unknown vector containing the nodal primary variables (displacements, water pressure, concentrations of ionic species and calcite mass content) as follows:

$$\mathbf{X}^{(e)} = \begin{bmatrix} \mathbf{U}^{(e)} & \mathbf{P_w}^{(e)} & C_{uW}{}^{(e)} & C_{aW}{}^{(e)} & C_{CaW}{}^{(e)} & C_{ClW}{}^{(e)} & \mathbf{M}_c{}^{(e)} \end{bmatrix} \tag{33}$$

and $\mathbf{V}^{(e)} = \dot{\mathbf{X}}^{(e)}$.

The Gaussian quadrature rule is applied to obtain the components of the internal forces vector (32), as well as the components of the stiffness and diffusion matrices. Due to the presence of highly nonlinear terms in this vector and in these matrices, the number of integration points per element is two, for all vectors and matrices, despite quadratic interpolation being used for the displacements and linear interpolation being used for the remaining primary variables. A list with the formulas of additional dependent variables is presented in Appendix B, while the block structure of the element diffusion and stiffness matrices can be found in Appendix C.

In this 1-D formulation, essential boundary conditions may be imposed at the top and the bottom of the soil column to specify the values of the primary variables: the displacements, water pressure or ionic concentrations. Natural boundary conditions may be imposed at the top and at the bottom of the soil column to specify forces per unit of area, the water flux or the diffusive fluxes of the urea, calcium and chloride ionic species (see (31)). On the other hand, the extension of this formulation to 2-D or 3-D biocementation problems is straightforward.

3.2. Time Integration

The formulated semi-discrete equations are integrated in time. A midpoint scheme is employed for the integration, signifying that, for each increment, the equations are evaluated at time $t_{n+\alpha} = t_n + \alpha\Delta t$, with $\alpha = 0.5$ and $\Delta t = t_{n+1} - t_n$.

Since the internal forces are a non-linear function of the nodal primary unknowns, within each step, several iterations are performed until the system's convergence is reached, that is, the residual global force $\mathbf{R}$ is zero:

$$\mathbf{R}_{n+\alpha} = \mathbf{F}^{ext}_{n+\alpha} - \mathbf{F}^{int}_{n+\alpha} \simeq \mathbf{0} \tag{34}$$

where $\mathbf{F}^{ext}$ is the global vector of external forces, dependent on the nodal "loads" $\mathbf{S}$, while the global vector of internal forces depends on $\mathbf{X}$ and $\mathbf{V}$. The quantities $\mathbf{A} = \mathbf{S}, \mathbf{X}, \mathbf{V}$, evaluated at time $t_{n+\alpha}$ are defined as $\mathbf{A}_{n+\alpha} = (1-\alpha)\mathbf{A}_n + \alpha\mathbf{A}_{n+1}$.

The Newton–Raphson method is applied, with the previous linearization of the equations around an approximation of the solution through the development of the internal forces vector in Taylor series neglecting the higher-order terms, requiring the residual vector at the next iteration to be zero:

$$\mathbf{R}^{i+1}_{n+\alpha} = \mathbf{F}^{ext}_{n+\alpha} - \mathbf{F}^{int}_{n+\alpha} \simeq \mathbf{R}^{i}_{n+\alpha} - \alpha\mathbf{C}^{*i}{}_{n+\alpha}\Delta\mathbf{V} = \mathbf{0}, \tag{35}$$

where $\mathbf{C}^{*} = \mathbf{C} + \alpha\Delta t\mathbf{K}$ is the effective tangent diffusion matrix. Equation (35) is solved in order to obtain the increment of velocity $\Delta\mathbf{V}$ that is used to update $\mathbf{V}$ and $\mathbf{X}$, according to the following:

$$\begin{cases} for\ i = 0 & \mathbf{V}^{0}_{n+1} = \mathbf{V}_n, \quad \mathbf{X}^{0}_{n+1} = \mathbf{X}_n + (1-\alpha)\Delta t\mathbf{V}_n \\ for\ i \geq 1 & \mathbf{V}^{i}_{n+1} = \mathbf{V}^{i-1}_{n+1} + \Delta\mathbf{V}, \quad \mathbf{X}^{i}_{n+1} = \mathbf{X}^{0}_{n+1} + \alpha\Delta t\mathbf{V}^{i}_{n+1}. \end{cases} \tag{36}$$

While the choice of the steps' number used in the incremental process may be variable and free, the number of iterations within each step depends on a predefined criterion of convergence. As the iteration process progresses, returning in each iteration $\Delta\mathbf{V}$ that is used to update the velocity vector, the convergence of the process is achieved when the residual, and consequently $\Delta\mathbf{V}$, vanish. Thus, the proposed convergence criterion is as follows:

$$\frac{\|\overline{\Delta\mathbf{V}}\|^{i}}{\|\overline{\Delta\mathbf{V}}\|^{0}} \leq TOL, \tag{37}$$

where $\|\overline{\Delta\mathbf{V}}\|^{i}$ is the norm of a nondimensional $\Delta\mathbf{V}$ vector at step n and iteration i, and TOL is the tolerance, which is a very small number.

The nondimensionalisation of $\Delta\mathbf{V}$ is required since both $\mathbf{X}$ and $\mathbf{V}$ encompass nodal values with different physical dimensions and orders of magnitude (e.g., displacements, water pressure, concentrations of ionic species and the mass content of calcite). Consequently, the positions related to the displacement variables in the computed $\Delta\mathbf{V}$ vectors, are divided by the corresponding maximum value occurring at the initial (0) iteration. The same is done for the positions in $\Delta\mathbf{V}$ related to the water pressure, to the concentrations of the ionic species and to the calcite mass content:

$$\left(\overline{\Delta\mathbf{V}^{i}}\right)_{\mathbf{U}} = \frac{\left(\Delta\mathbf{V}^{i}\right)_{\mathbf{U}}}{\left(\Delta\mathbf{V}^{0}\right)_{\max,\mathbf{U}}},\ \left(\overline{\Delta\mathbf{V}^{i}}\right)_{\mathbf{P}_{w}} = \frac{\left(\Delta\mathbf{V}^{i}\right)_{\mathbf{P}_{w}}}{\left(\Delta\mathbf{V}^{0}\right)_{\max,\mathbf{P}_{w}}},\ \left(\overline{\Delta\mathbf{V}^{i}}\right)_{\mathbf{C}_{kW}} = \frac{\left(\Delta\mathbf{V}^{i}\right)_{\mathbf{C}_{kW}}}{\left(\Delta\mathbf{V}^{0}\right)_{\max,\mathbf{C}_{kW}}},\ \text{and}\ \left(\overline{\Delta\mathbf{V}^{i}}\right)_{\mathbf{M}_{c}} = \frac{\left(\Delta\mathbf{V}^{i}\right)_{\mathbf{M}_{c}}}{\left(\Delta\mathbf{V}^{0}\right)_{\max,\mathbf{M}_{c}}}. \tag{38}$$

When this is performed, the same tolerance TOL may be used for all variables.

4. Experimental Procedure and Results

4.1. Soil

A uniform grading-size commercial river sand named APAS 30 was used in the experimental tests. This soil is composed of fine-sized quartz grains with a specific gravity $G_S \approx 2.6$. The samples were prepared, aiming for a bulk density around $1.50 \sim 1.52\text{g/cm}^3$, which corresponds to an initial void ratio of $e_0 \approx 0.71$ and an initial porosity (n_{W0}) of 41.5%.

4.2. Bacteria and Feeding Solution

Sporosarcina pasteurii are the bacteria selected for this study. This type of bacteria is commonly found in nature and is harmless to humans. Bacteria were supplied by the American Type Culture Collection (ATCC) entity and were lyophilized upon receipt. The growing process of *Sporosarcina pasteurii* was carried out until reaching a concentration of $\sim 10^8$ bacteria/mL. More detailed explanation on bacteria growing stages and process is presented in [3].

To produce calcium carbonate, a feeding solution had to be prepared with the nutrients that are necessary to supply to the bacteria. This solution was prepared with 0.5 M of urea and 0.5 M of calcium chloride ($CaCl_2$).

4.3. Experimental Treatment Procedure

In each experimental test, a solution with the concentration of approximately $\sim 10^8$ bacteria/mL was initially added to the sand, in order to saturate the soil (Figure 3a). The sand column tests were then carried out in small-scale specimens inside syringes with 2 cm diameter and 20 mL capacity (Figure 3b). A draining layer, composed of a geotextile and filter paper, was placed at the bottom of the syringe, followed by a layer-by-layer compaction of the sand previously saturated with bacteria. The sand column, with an assumed homogeneous distribution of bacteria, had a final height of 6 cm (Figure 3c).

The sand column tests started by irrigating 15.7 mL (the equivalent to two void volumes) of feeding solution on the top of the syringe. The upper part of the syringe was filled with feeding solution, while a downward fluid flow was established by opening the bottom of the syringe (Figure 3d). The application of feeding solution took 60 s. The exit at the bottom of the syringe was closed when the fluid on the top of the soil column achieved a constant height of 2 cm (Figure 3e), stopping fluid flow through the soil. In this manner, it was possible to investigate the precipitation of biocement with time and depth caused by diffusion of calcium and urea, assuming the bacteria would be immobile because they were attached to the soil particles. Several cases were investigated varying the time the treatment fluid was immobile at the top of the sand column, with some duplicates for estimating the experimental error, as summarized in Table 2.

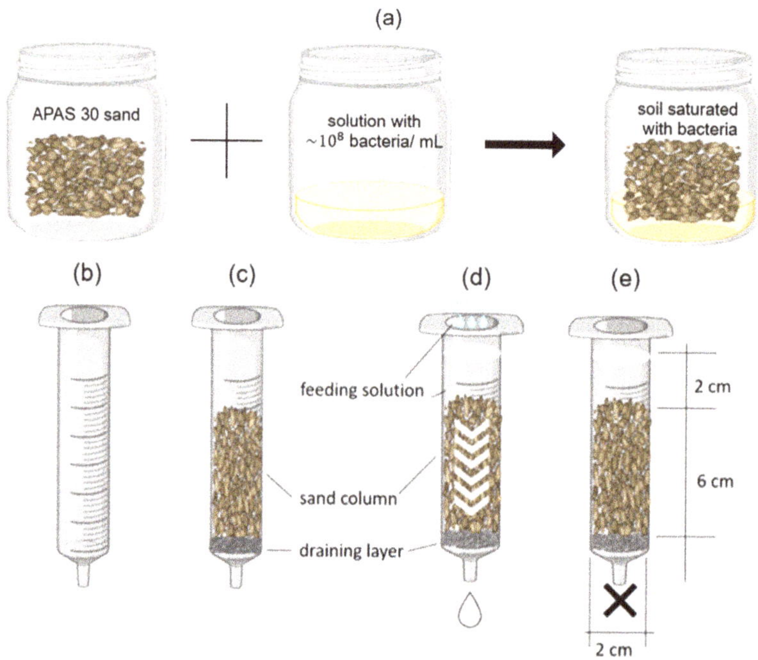

Figure 3. Representative scheme of the 1-D sand column tests: (**a**) dry soil is previously saturated with bacterial solution; (**b**) 20 mL syringe used as a mould; (**c**) soil saturated with bacterial solution is compacted inside the syringe; (**d**) feeding solution is applied from above for 60 s, generating downward flow; (**e**) the bottom exit of the syringe is closed after 60 s and a 2 cm layer of feeding solution remains on top.

Table 2. Summary of the sand column tests performed.

Duration of Treatment	Quantity of Tests Performed
1 h	4
2 h	3
3 h	4
5 h	3
12 h	3
24 h	3

For each case, at the end of the treatment, 7.85 mL (one void volume) of distilled water was applied at the top of the column to wash away the feeding solution. The soil column was then removed from the syringe and divided in three approximately equal-sized fractions (top, middle and bottom of the specimen), which were subjected to dissolution tests in hydrochloric acid to measure the calcium carbonate content and its distribution along the height of the column.

The $CaCO_3$ content was determined through acid leaching tests performed in each fraction. Prior to the leaching tests, each fraction was dried in oven for 24 h at 105 °C to determine the mass of solids (M_1). Then, the fraction was washed with hydrochloric acid (0.5 M), which dissolved the calcium carbonate. The occurrence of the reaction was verified by gas liberation and pH measurements. After that, the sample was washed with distilled water, filtered and dried again in the oven at 105 °C for 24 h to measure the final mass (M_2). The percentage of calcium carbonate content (%cc) was then calculated as follows:

$$\%\text{cc} = (M_1 - M_2)/M_1 \tag{39}$$

while the calcium carbonate mass content (referred to as calcite content, m_c) of each fraction was calculated as follows:

$$m_{cS} = \left(M_1^i - M_2^i\right)/\left(VM_1^i/\sum M_1^i\right), \tag{40}$$

where i refers to the bottom, middle and top fractions, respectively, and V is the total volume of the specimen.

4.4. Experimental Results

The percentages of calcium carbonate content, %cc, measured in all tests are presented in Table 3 (including average values for each soil column) considering the period of time that the treatment fluid was kept immobilized at the top of the columns (duration of treatment).

Table 3. Calcium carbonate content obtained from leaching tests.

Duration of Treatment (h)	Average %cc Measured in Each Column	%cc (Average)
1	0.92	0.84
	0.91	
	0.78	
	0.76	
2	0.65	0.74
	0.94	
	0.65	
3	0.62	0.68
	0.74	
	0.72	
	0.64	
5	0.79	0.69
	0.49	
	0.78	
12	0.84	0.75
	0.67	
	0.75	
24	0.95	0.83
	0.69	
	0.84	

Despite some small variations, the precipitation of calcium carbonate remained practically constant after 1 h of treatment, probably because bacterial encapsulation had occurred.

Since treatment was conducted under no-flow conditions after the first 60 s, the transport of ionic species after that time was restricted to purely diffusive flow, which occurred at very low velocities. This could also have reduced feeding fluid circulation and caused the accumulation of chemical compounds in the pores, therefore creating difficulties for the survival of bacteria [3]. On the other hand, the decrease in calcite content that sometimes was observed after 1 h of treatment could be attributed to the dissolution of irregularly shaped and less stable $CaCO_3$ minerals [24].

The first observation is in line with the findings of other authors. For example, Cuthbert et al. [25] evaluated the effects of high initial concentrations of feeding solution (0.5 M, the same concentration applied in this study) on calcite formation. They found precipitation of large calcium carbonate crystals immediately after the treatment due to higher ureolysis rate at that stage. According to the authors, these large calcium carbonate crystals that were attached to the bacteria blocked further access of the feeding solution. Xiao et al. [24] also studied the distribution of calcite in microchannels with different concentrations of the feeding solution. For larger concentrations, they observed a fast precipitation of calcium carbonate crystals without further development along the remaining treatment time. They explained this stabilization by the early encapsulation of bacteria. This type of behaviour can be mathematically described by Equation (23) for the ureolysis reaction, and therefore, experimental data could be used to calibrate the parameters in this equation. Because the amounts measured were stable after 1 h of treatment, the data found in these tests were used as reference.

Figure 4 presents the average values of the mass of calcite per unit of volume precipitated after 1 h of treatment, at the top, middle and bottom fractions. In general, more precipitated calcite was formed at the top, while less calcite mass per unit volume was formed at the bottom. This same distribution was observed in other experimental sand column studies ([26,27]) and could be explained by pore clogging of the upper fraction, occurring after the injection of the feeding solution.

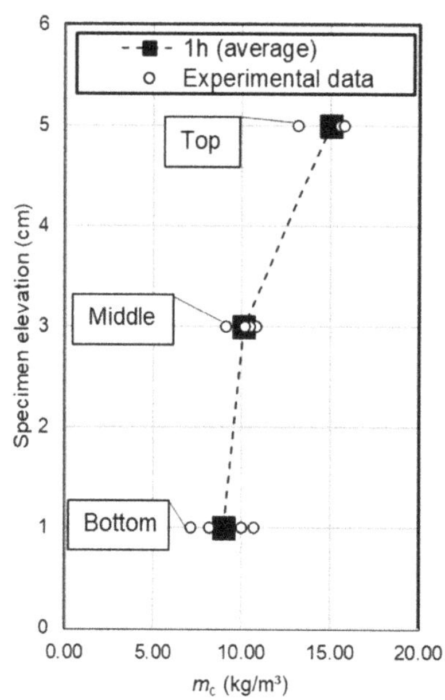

Figure 4. Calcite mass per unit volume distribution for the samples with 1 h of treatment.

5. Numerical Simulations

5.1. Model Parameters

The model was used to simulate the experiments; basically, a 1-D behaviour was observed in the soil columns. The adopted constants are presented in Table 4. The reaction rate parameters (v_{max}, K_m, t_{max}) and the diffusion constant (α_L) were calibrated to better fit the calcite mass values measured experimentally after 1 h of treatment. This calibration process will be explained later in Section 5.3.

Table 4. Values of the constants used in the simulation.

Constant	Value
Soil constants	
Specific gravity ($G_S = \rho_S/\rho_W$)	2.60
Young's modulus (E)	50×10^3 kPa
Hydraulic conductivity parameter ($\bar{k}_h$)	3.5×10^{-5} m/s
Initial porosity (n_{W0})	0.415
Chemical constants	
Calcite molar mass ($m_c^{(M)}$)	100.1×10^{-3} kg/mol
Calcite molar volume ($v_c^{(M)}$)	36.9×10^{-6} m^3/mol
Urea molar mass ($m_u^{(M)}$)	60.1×10^{-3} kg/mol
Urea molar volume ($v_u^{(M)}$)	45.4×10^{-6} m^3/mol
Ammonium molar mass ($m_a^{(M)}$)	18.0×10^{-3} kg/mol
Ammonium molar volume ($v_a^{(M)}$)	20.0×10^{-6} m^3/mol
Calcium molar mass ($m_{Ca}^{(M)}$)	40.1×10^{-3} kg/mol
Calcium molar volume ($v_{Ca}^{(M)}$)	1.75×10^{-6} m^3/mol
Chloride molar mass ($m_{Cl}^{(M)}$)	35.5×10^{-3} kg/mol
Chloride molar volume ($v_{Cl}^{(M)}$)	15.42×10^{-6} m^3/mol
Longitudinal diffusion constant (α_L)	0.02 m
Reaction rate parameters	
v_{max}	2 mol/(m^{3}s)
K_m	125 mol/m^3
t_{max}	260 s

Bar (1-D) finite elements were employed with quadratic interpolation for the solid displacements (with three nodes per element) and linear interpolation for the other primary unknowns (with two nodes per element). Several simulations were performed varying the sizes of the elements, the time steps and tolerance values, until the convergence of the results was found. In Table 5, the percentage of total calcium carbonate obtained in the numerical simulations after 1 h of treatment is shown as a function of the mesh refinement and integration time step. The chosen model had a total of 60 elements, comprising 121 nodes and 487 global degrees of freedom. A constant time step of 0.01 s and a 0.001 tolerance were used in the time integration.

Table 5. Convergence study: percentage of total calcium carbonate obtained in numerical simulations after 1 h of treatment, as a function of mesh refinement and integration time step.

Number of Elements	Time Step			
	0.05 s	**0.01 s**	**0.005 s**	**0.001 s**
30	0.75208%	0.75225%	0.75229%	0.75225%
60	0.75205%	0.75221%	0.75222%	0.75222%
90	0.75205%	0.75221%	0.75222%	0.75222%
120	0.75204%	0.75221%	0.75222%	0.75222%

5.2. Initial and Boundary Conditions

For the calculation, it was assumed that the soil column was saturated with a homogeneous bacteria distribution for the studied depth, without the presence of urea, calcium, chloride or calcite. Two time stages were considered, as described in Figure 5. The first one (for t $\leq$ 60 s) corresponded to the initial addition of the feeding solution by establishing a constant fluid flow through the column. In the second one (for t > 60 s), the fluid flow was stopped and the treatment progressed by diffusion over different periods of time. The boundary conditions corresponding to both stages are also presented in Figure 5:

- Concerning the mechanical model, the bottom boundary was restrained, and therefore, all the displacements were null during the entire calculation;
- Concerning the hydraulic model, the flow is free during the first 60 s at the bottom boundary, and the pore pressures remained constant at the top boundary after that;
- Concerning the biochemical model, at the top boundary, during the first 60 s when the feeding solution was applied, there was a sudden increase in the concentration of urea and calcium from 0 to 0.5 M and in the concentration of chloride from 0 to 1 M; these concentrations remained constant until the end of the analysis. These values were set to mimic the application of the feeding solution in the experimental tests, in which the fluid flow applied at the top of the columns was equal to 0.2 mm/s during the first 60 s of the analysis and in which a layer of feeding solution remained, with a constant height and constant concentration, at the top of the syringe until the end of the analysis.

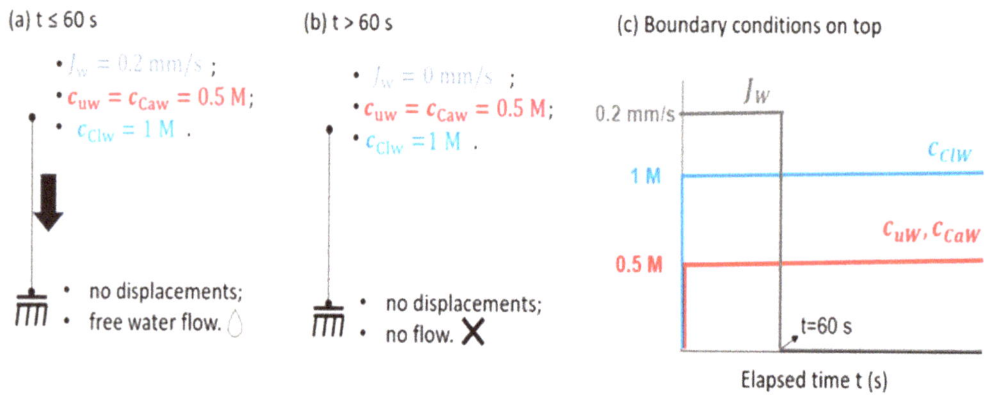

Figure 5. Boundary conditions of the bio-chemo-hydro-mechanical model: (**a**) boundary conditions for t $\leq$ 60 s; (**b**) boundary conditions for t > 60 s; (**c**) detail of the top boundary conditions.

5.3. Calibration of the Reaction Rate Parameters and of the Diffusion Constant

The calibration of the reaction rate parameters in (13) and of the diffusion constant in (18) was performed after several numerical simulations, carried out with values varying among 1~10 mol/(m^{3}s) for the maximum reaction velocity (v_{max}), 100~300 mol/m^3 for the half-saturation constant (K_m), 200~3600 s for t_{max} and 0.01~0.2 m for the diffusion constant (α_L). The values presented in Table 4 were the ones that fitted the calcite mass values measured experimentally for treatments lasting 1 h (3600 s) better.

In Figure 6a, it may be seen that the numerical profile of the mass of calcite per unit of volume obtained with the calibrated parameters presented in Table 4 fits the minimal and maximal experimental values for the top and bottom fractions, with both experimental and numerical values presenting the same distribution trend. Moreover, it may be seen in Figure 6b that, for the calibrated parameters, the reactions stopped around t = 1200 s.

5.4. Results and Discussion

Figure 7 presents the profiles along the column height of the chemical species involved in the biochemical reactions ($c_{uW}, c_{CaW}, c_{ClW}, c_{aW}$) computed at different time instants. It may be observed in Figure 7a–c that, as expected, the concentrations of urea, calcium and chloride ions remained constant at the top boundary because this was the point of application of the feeding solution. Along the sand column, it can be confirmed that the concentrations of urea (Figure 7a) and calcium (Figure 7b) decreased at the same rate with time, which is expected because urea and calcium are consumed in the reactions. The concentrations along the column of chloride ions increased only during the first 60 s, while the feeding solution was added, and then remained constant because these ions do not participate in the MICP process (Figure 7c).

The progression of the biochemical reaction was identified by the reduction in the concentrations of urea and calcium, and consequently by the increase in the ammonium concentrations (Figure 7d). Accordingly, there was an increase in the mass of calcite per unit volume with time (Figure 8a), which was always more noticeable at the top of the sand column. This calcite distribution trend is confirmed by other authors for similar boundary conditions ([11,27]). The ammonium concentrations and calcite mass remained constant after 1200 s because then the reaction rate became practically zero (see Figure 6b). The precipitation of solid calcite into the voids reduced the soil porosity, which is confirmed in Figure 8b.

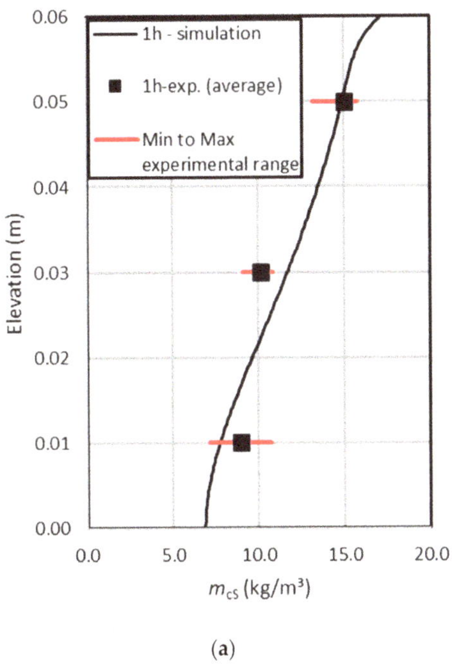

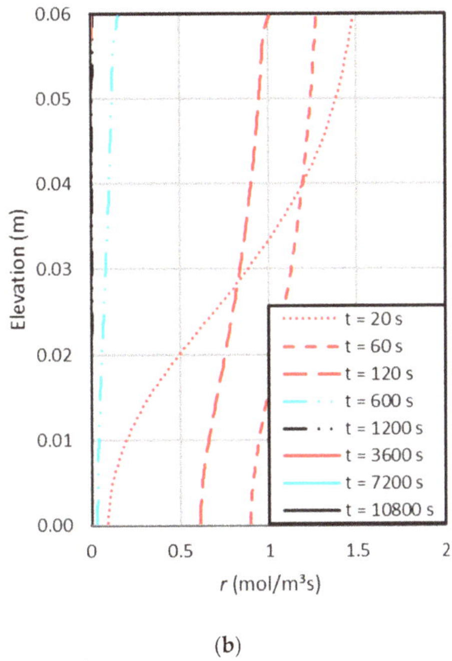

Figure 6. (**a**) Profile of mass of calcite per unit volume after 1 h of treatment, comparing experimental data and numerical simulation results; and (**b**) profile of the evolution of the reaction rate with time.

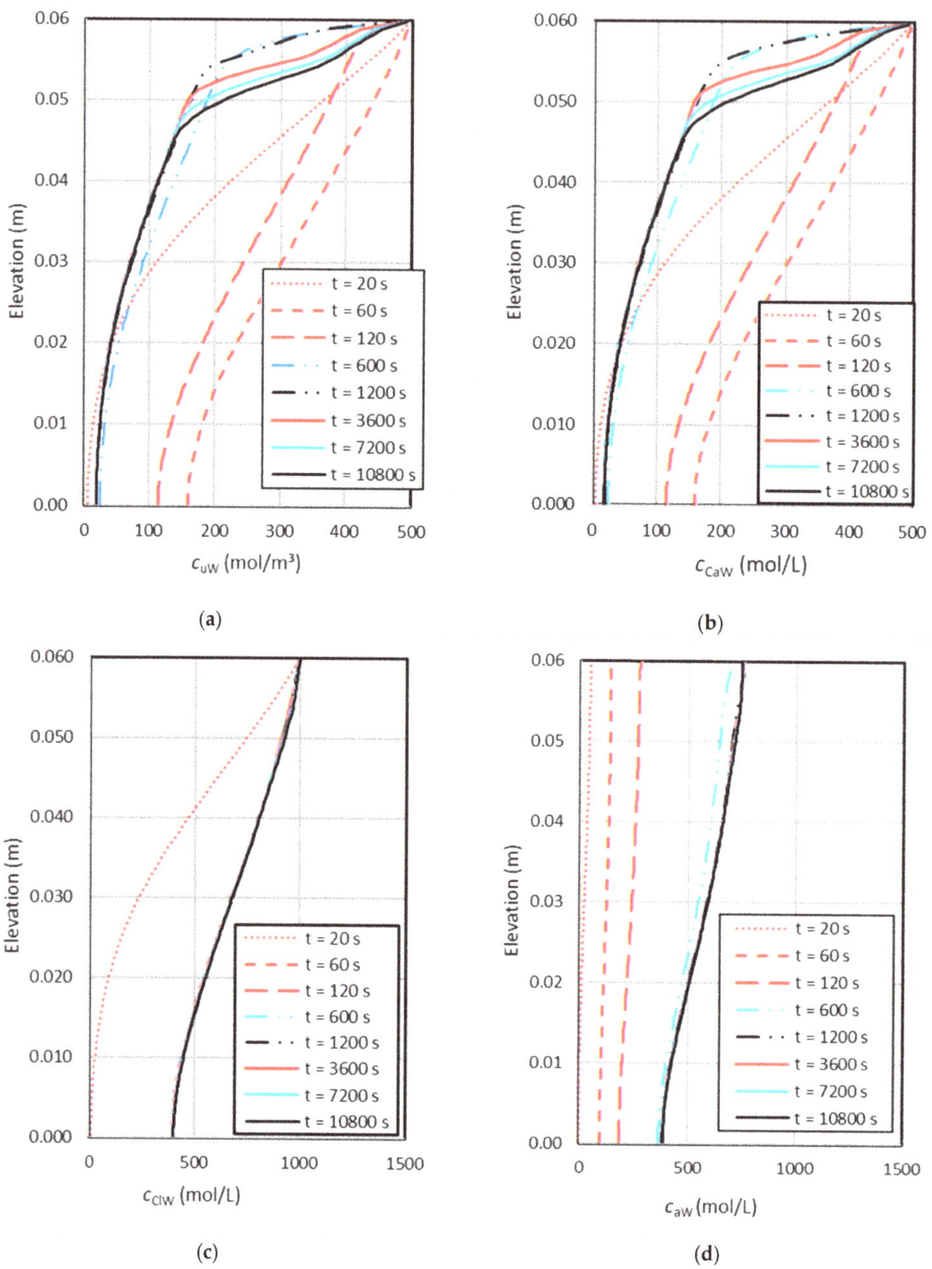

Figure 7. Time evolution of the profiles along the soil column of (**a**) urea concentration, (**b**) calcium concentration, (**c**) chloride concentration and (**d**) ammonium concentration.

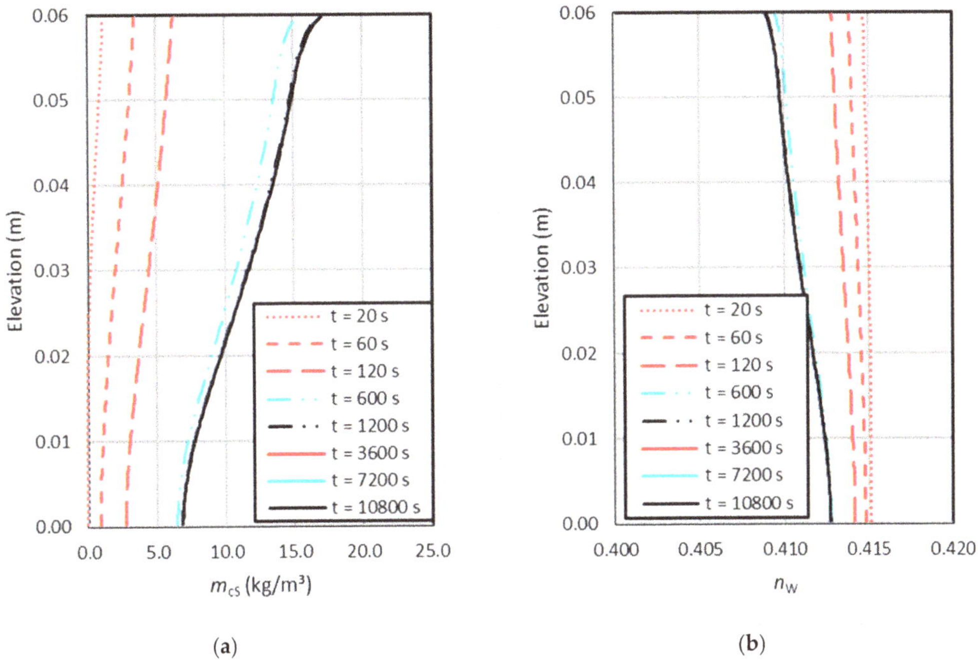

Figure 8. Time evolution of the profiles along the soil column of (**a**) mass of precipitated calcite per unit of volume, and (**b**) porosity.

The evolution with the time of fluid flow is presented in Figure 9a. During the first 60 s of the simulation, the fluid flow was practically constant along the specimen and equal to the flow applied at the top of the column; when the bottom exit was closed, the flow was reduced to zero. The evolution with time of the pore–water pressure is presented in Figure 9b. The water pressure profile started as hydrostatic before applying the boundary condition, and then it increased at the top of the column, creating a constant hydraulic gradient in the first 60 s. Then it became hydrostatic again, once the flow at the bottom was interrupted and the feeding solution accumulated above the soil column, becoming equal to the weight of the liquid column above this horizontal section. Due to the hydro-mechanical coupled behaviour, this slight pore pressure increment implies a reduction in effective stresses, and for this reason, very small swelling deformations (about 0.0067%) were computed (Figure 9c). The observed very small deformations justify the linear elastic effective stress–strain relationship that was assumed in this work.

Finally, Figure 10 presents a comparison between numerical and experimental values of the total calcium carbonate content for all tested columns and all treatment durations. The experimental average results are represented together with the minimal and maximal experimental values (see Table 3). The numerical simulation curve presents a constant value that intercepts all the experimental data range, therefore validating the model. The numerical values shown in Figure 10 are independent of the treatment duration because, according to Figure 6b, the reactions stopped around t = 1200 s. This can be explained by bacteria encapsulation, as already discussed ([24,25]). The reduction in calcite content that is sometimes observed in the experimental values in Figure 10 could possibly be attributed to the dissolution of irregular-shaped and less stable $CaCO_3$ polymorphs ([24]).

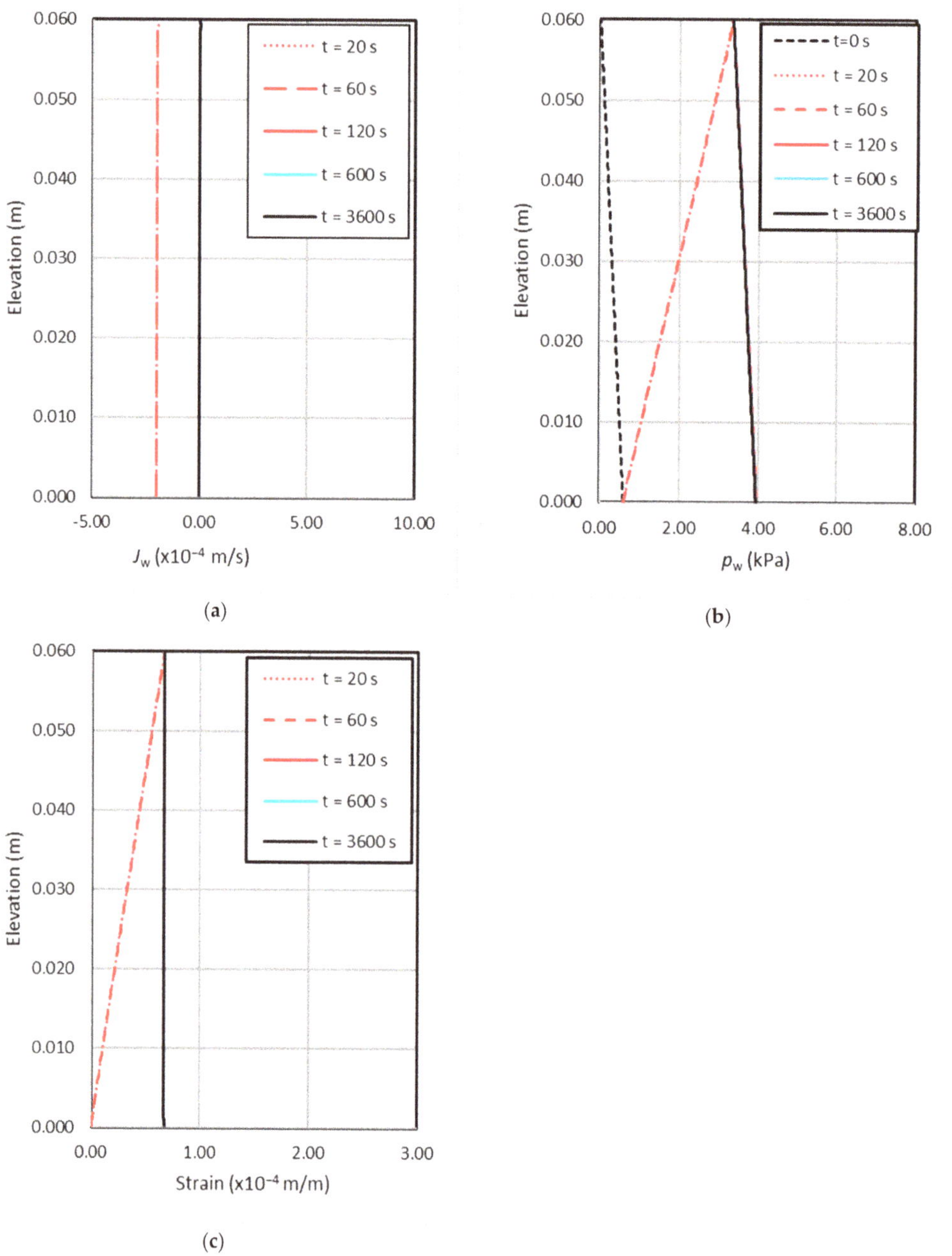

Figure 9. Time evolution of the profiles along the soil column of (**a**) water flux, (**b**) pore–water pressure and (**c**) vertical deformation.

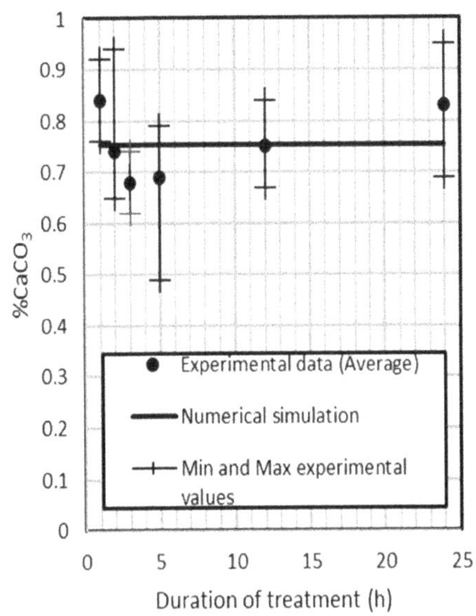

Figure 10. Validation of the numerical model showing that the results of the simulations intercept the entire experimental data range.

6. Conclusions

A finite element numerical model to perform a coupled biochemical-hydro-mechanical analysis was developed for the simulation of the biocementation process in a sand column. This was intended to be a tool to compute the amount of biocement precipitated for a given set of treatment dosages and hydraulic and mechanical boundary conditions. With the hydraulic model, it was possible to simulate the transport by conduction and diffusion of the ions, with the hydro-mechanical coupled model being related to changes in the soil's effective stresses. The precipitation of solid mass (calcite, i.e., the biocement) determined porosity changes, affecting permeability (bio-chemo-hydraulic coupling). The model is prepared to be modified to include this pore-clogging effect into stiffness and strength (bio-chemo-mechanical coupling).

The parameters of the model were calibrated with the results of experimental small-scale sand column tests, in which the biocementation treatment had a duration of 1 h. The distribution of calcite obtained in the numerical simulations, with a noticeable concentration at the column's top, was in good agreement with the experimental results for all the other tested treatment periods, therefore validating the model.

The reaction rate parameters determine the biochemical reaction and are of paramount importance in this analysis. Nevertheless, the imposed boundary conditions dictated a single application of the feeding solution and established a no-flow condition after the first 60 s of the treatment. This possibly limited the circulation of ionic specimens and lowered the bacterial activity, which explained the constancy of the calcite content value obtained for several treatment durations.

Finally, the approach adopted in this study can be used for other applications. Other bio-chemical reactions can be simulated if the chemical species and stoichiometric calculations are adapted for the specific case at hand, as well as the bacterial activity parameters. For example, it may be possible to simulate methane formation by methanogenic bacteria or corrosion by iron-oxidizing bacteria.

Author Contributions: Conceptualization, F.M.F.S. and R.C.; methodology, V.S.T., F.M.F.S. and R.C.; software, V.S.T. and F.M.F.S.; validation, V.S.T., F.M.F.S. and R.C.; formal analysis, V.S.T., F.M.F.S. and R.C.; investigation, V.S.T., F.M.F.S. and R.C.; resources, V.S.T., F.M.F.S. and R.C.; data curation, V.S.T., F.M.F.S. and R.C.; writing—original draft preparation, V.S.T. and F.M.F.S.; writing—review and editing, F.M.F.S. and R.C.; visualization, V.S.T., F.M.F.S. and R.C.; supervision, F.M.F.S. and R.C.; project administration, R.C.; funding acquisition, R.C. All authors have read and agreed to the published version of the manuscript.

Funding: This research was funded by Foundation for Science and Technology through UIDB/04625/2020 for the CERIS research unit (doi: 10.54499/UIDB/04625/2020), through the PhD scholarship 2022.10441.BD awarded to Victor Scartezini Terra and through the project CALCITE PTDC/ECI-EGC/1086/2021.

Data Availability Statement: The original contributions presented in the study are included in the article, further inquiries can be directed to the corresponding author.

Conflicts of Interest: The authors declare no conflict of interest.

Appendix A Mass Balance Equations

Since different species move with different velocities, the total derivative $\frac{\mathrm{d}^k()}{\mathrm{d}t}$ in (3) relates with the total derivative following the solid species particles $\frac{\mathrm{d}^s()}{\mathrm{d}t}$, which will be defined simply as $\frac{\mathrm{d}()}{\mathrm{d}t}$, as shown by the following:

$$\frac{\mathrm{d}^k()}{\mathrm{d}t} = \frac{\mathrm{d}()}{\mathrm{d}t} + \nabla() \cdot (\mathbf{v}_{kK} - \mathbf{v}_S), \tag{A1}$$

where $\nabla()$ is the nabla operator. Substituting (A1) in (3), we obtain the following:

$$\frac{\mathrm{d}\rho^{kK}}{\mathrm{d}t} + \rho^{kK}\mathrm{div}\ \mathbf{v}_S + \mathrm{div}\ \mathbf{M}_{kK} = \hat{\rho}^{kK} \tag{A2}$$

where $\mathbf{M}_{kK} = \rho^{kK}(\mathbf{v}_{kK} - \mathbf{v}_S)$ is the flux of mass of species k through the solid skeleton. Multiplying (A2) by $\det \mathbf{F} = V/V_0$ (where $\mathbf{F}$ is the strain gradient tensor) and using the fact that $\mathrm{d}(\det \mathbf{F})/\mathrm{d}t = \det \mathbf{F}\ \mathrm{div}\ \mathbf{v}_S$, we obtain the following mass balance equation in the reference configuration:

$$\frac{\mathrm{d}m_{kK}}{\mathrm{d}t} + \det\mathbf{F}\ \mathrm{div}\ \mathbf{M}_{kK} = \hat{m}^{kK} \tag{A3}$$

where $\hat{m}^{kK} = \hat{\rho}^{kK}\det\mathbf{F}$. Dividing (A3) by the intrinsic density of species k, we obtain the following:

$$\frac{\mathrm{d}v_{kK}}{\mathrm{d}t} + \det\mathbf{F}\ \mathrm{div}\ \mathbf{J}_{kK} = \frac{\hat{m}^{kK}}{\rho_k} \tag{A4}$$

where $\mathbf{J}_{kK} = n_{kK}(\mathbf{v}_{kK} - \mathbf{v}_S) = \mathbf{M}_{kK}/\rho_k$ is the flux of the species through the solid skeleton. For a species $k \in \mathrm{W}$, Equation (A4) may be written as follows:

$$\frac{1}{V_0}\frac{\mathrm{d}V_{k\mathrm{W}}}{\mathrm{d}t} + \det\mathbf{F}\ \mathrm{div}\ \mathbf{J}_{k\mathrm{W}} = \frac{\hat{m}^{k\mathrm{W}}}{\rho_k} \tag{A5}$$

or, upon linearization:

$$n_{k\mathrm{W}}\mathrm{div}\ \mathbf{v}_S + \frac{\mathrm{d}n_{k\mathrm{W}}}{\mathrm{d}t} + \mathrm{div}\ \mathbf{J}_{k\mathrm{W}} = \frac{\hat{m}^{k\mathrm{W}}}{\rho_k}. \tag{A6}$$

By adding the contribution of all species $k \in \mathrm{W}$, we obtain the following:

$$\frac{\mathrm{d}n_{\mathrm{W}}}{\mathrm{d}t} + n_{\mathrm{W}}\mathrm{div}\ \mathbf{v}_S + \mathrm{div}\ \mathbf{J}_{\mathrm{W}} = \sum_{k\in\mathrm{W}} \frac{\hat{m}^{k\mathrm{W}}}{\rho_k} \tag{A7}$$

where $\mathbf{J}_W = \sum_{k \in W} \mathbf{J}_{kW}$ represents the flux of water.

Summing (A4) for all species $k \in W$ and for all species $k \in S$, upon linearization, we obtain the following:

$$\frac{dv_W}{dt} + \text{div}\, \mathbf{J}_W = \sum_{k \in W} \frac{\hat{m}^{kW}}{\rho_k} \tag{A8}$$

and

$$\frac{dv_S}{dt} = \sum_{k \in S} \frac{\hat{m}^{kS}}{\rho_k} \tag{A9}$$

respectively.

Since $\frac{dv}{dt} = \frac{dv_W}{dt} + \frac{dv_S}{dt} = \text{div}\, \mathbf{v}_S$, it is possible to obtain a global equation of mass balance by summing (A8) and (A9) as follows:

$$\text{div}\, \mathbf{v}_S + \text{div}\, \mathbf{J}_W = \sum_{k \in W} \frac{\hat{m}^{kW}}{\rho_k} + \sum_{k \in S} \frac{\hat{m}^{kS}}{\rho_k} \tag{A10}$$

We may also obtain the following:

$$\frac{d\mathbf{v}_W}{dt} = \text{div}\, \mathbf{v}_S - \sum_{k \in S} \frac{\hat{m}^{kS}}{\rho_k} \tag{A11}$$

By replacing (A10) in (A.7), we obtain the following:

$$\frac{dn_W}{dt} = (1 - n_W)\text{div}\, \mathbf{v}_S - \sum_{k \in S} \frac{\hat{m}^{kS}}{\rho_k} \tag{A12}$$

which corresponds to Equation (A9) in [28].

Appendix B Dependent Variables

This section presents the equations governing the dependent variables of the developed model.

a. The total volume of the medium

The total volume of the domain is calculated as follows:

$$V = V_0 \cdot (1 + \text{tr}\, \varepsilon), \tag{A13}$$

where ε is the strain tensor.

b. The porosity

The porosity of the porous medium is obtained as follows:

$$n_W = 1 - \frac{1}{1 + \text{tr}\, \varepsilon} \left(\frac{V_{sS} + M_{cS}/\rho_c}{V_0} \right), \tag{A14}$$

c. The volume of the ionic species

The volume of the ionic species (namely urea, ammonium, calcium and chloride ions) is obtained as follows:

$$V_{kW} = c_{kW} n_W V v_k^{(M)}, \tag{A15}$$

d. The volume fraction of the ionic species

The volume fraction of the ionic species is obtained as follows:

$$n_{kW} = \frac{V_{kW}}{V}, \tag{A16}$$

e. The volume fraction of water

The volume fraction of the water is obtained as follows:

$$n_{\mathrm{wW}} = n_{\mathrm{W}}\left(1 - \sum\nolimits_{k\in \mathrm{W}} c_{k\mathrm{W}} v_k^{(\mathrm{M})}\right), \tag{A17}$$

f. The density of the water phase

The density of the water phase is obtained as follows:

$$\rho^{\mathrm{W}} = \sum\nolimits_{k\epsilon \mathrm{W}} n_{k\mathrm{W}} \rho_k, \tag{A18}$$

g. The density of the solid phase

The density of the solid phase is obtained as follows:

$$\rho^{S} = \frac{V_{\mathrm{sS}}}{V}\rho_{\mathrm{s}} + \frac{M_{\mathrm{cS}}}{V}, \tag{A19}$$

h. The water velocity

The water velocity is calculated as follows:

$$\mathbf{v}_{\mathrm{wW}} = \mathbf{v}_{\mathrm{S}} + \frac{\mathbf{J}_{\mathrm{W}} - \sum_{l\in \mathrm{W}} \mathbf{J}_{l\mathrm{W}}^{\mathrm{d}}}{n_{\mathrm{W}}}. \tag{A20}$$

Appendix C Element Diffusion and Stiffness Matrices

The element diffusion and stiffness matrices have a block structure as follows:

$$\mathbf{C}^{(e)} = \begin{bmatrix} 0 & 0 & 0 & 0 & 0 & 0 & 0 \\ \mathbf{C}^{(e)}_{\mathrm{P_w}U} & 0 & 0 & 0 & 0 & 0 & \mathbf{C}^{(e)}_{\mathrm{P_w m_{cS}}} \\ 0 & 0 & \mathbf{C}^{(e)}_{\mathrm{C_{uW}C_{uW}}} & 0 & 0 & 0 & \mathbf{C}^{(e)}_{\mathrm{C_{uW}m_{cS}}} \\ 0 & 0 & 0 & \mathbf{C}^{(e)}_{\mathrm{C_{aW}C_{aW}}} & 0 & 0 & \mathbf{C}^{(e)}_{\mathrm{C_{aW}m_{cS}}} \\ 0 & 0 & 0 & 0 & \mathbf{C}^{(e)}_{\mathrm{C_{CaW}C_{CaW}}} & 0 & \mathbf{C}^{(e)}_{\mathrm{C_{CaW}m_{cS}}} \\ 0 & 0 & 0 & 0 & 0 & \mathbf{C}^{(e)}_{\mathrm{C_{ClW}C_{ClW}}} & \mathbf{C}^{(e)}_{\mathrm{C_{ClW}m_{cS}}} \\ 0 & 0 & 0 & 0 & 0 & 0 & \mathbf{C}^{(e)}_{\mathrm{m_{cS}m_{cS}}} \end{bmatrix} \tag{A21}$$

and

$$\mathbf{K}^{(e)} = \begin{bmatrix} \mathbf{K}^{(e)}_{\mathrm{UU}} & \mathbf{K}^{(e)}_{\mathrm{UP_W}} & 0 & 0 & 0 & 0 & 0 \\ 0 & \mathbf{K}^{(e)}_{\mathrm{P_WP_W}} & 0 & 0 & 0 & 0 & 0 \\ 0 & \mathbf{K}^{(e)}_{\mathrm{C_{uW}P_W}} & \mathbf{K}^{(e)}_{\mathrm{C_{uW}C_{uW}}} & \mathbf{K}^{(e)}_{\mathrm{C_{uW}C_{aW}}} & \mathbf{K}^{(e)}_{\mathrm{C_{uW}C_{CaW}}} & \mathbf{K}^{(e)}_{\mathrm{C_{uW}C_{ClW}}} & 0 \\ 0 & \mathbf{K}^{(e)}_{\mathrm{C_{aW}P_W}} & \mathbf{K}^{(e)}_{\mathrm{C_{aW}C_{uW}}} & \mathbf{K}^{(e)}_{\mathrm{C_{aW}C_{aW}}} & \mathbf{K}^{(e)}_{\mathrm{C_{aW}C_{CaW}}} & \mathbf{K}^{(e)}_{\mathrm{C_{aW}C_{ClW}}} & 0 \\ 0 & \mathbf{K}^{(e)}_{\mathrm{C_{CaW}P_W}} & \mathbf{K}^{(e)}_{\mathrm{C_{CaW}C_{uW}}} & \mathbf{K}^{(e)}_{\mathrm{C_{CaW}C_{aW}}} & \mathbf{K}^{(e)}_{\mathrm{C_{CaW}C_{CaW}}} & \mathbf{K}^{(e)}_{\mathrm{C_{CaW}C_{ClW}}} & 0 \\ 0 & \mathbf{K}^{(e)}_{\mathrm{C_{ClW}P_W}} & \mathbf{K}^{(e)}_{\mathrm{C_{ClW}C_{uW}}} & \mathbf{K}^{(e)}_{\mathrm{C_{ClW}C_{aW}}} & \mathbf{K}^{(e)}_{\mathrm{C_{ClW}C_{CaW}}} & \mathbf{K}^{(e)}_{\mathrm{C_{ClW}C_{ClW}}} & 0 \\ 0 & 0 & \mathbf{K}^{(e)}_{\mathrm{m_{cS}C_{uW}}} & 0 & 0 & 0 & 0 \end{bmatrix} \tag{A22}$$

where

$$\mathbf{K}^{(e)}_{\mathrm{UU}} = \int_{\Omega} \mathbf{B}_u^{\mathrm{T}} \mathbf{E} \mathbf{B}_u \mathrm{dV} \tag{A23}$$

with $\mathbf{B}_u$ as the strain–displacement matrix and $\mathbf{E}$ as the elastic constant's tensor,

$$\mathbf{K}^{(e)}_{\mathrm{UP_W}} = -\int_{\Omega} \mathrm{tr}\left(\mathbf{B}_u^{\mathrm{T}}\right) \mathbf{N}_{\mathrm{P_W}} \mathrm{dV} \tag{A24}$$

$$\mathbf{K}^{(e)}_{\mathrm{P_W P_W}} = \int_\Omega (\nabla \mathbf{N}_{\mathrm{P_W}})^{\mathrm{T}} k \nabla \mathbf{N}_{\mathrm{P_W}} \mathrm{dV} \tag{A25}$$

$$\mathbf{K}^{(e)}_{\mathrm{C}_{k\mathrm{W}}\mathrm{P_W}} = \int_\Omega \mathbf{N}_{\mathrm{C}}^{\mathrm{T}} (-k_x) v_k^{(M)} \nabla C_{k\mathrm{W}} \nabla \mathbf{N}_{\mathrm{P_W}} \mathrm{dV},\ k = \mathrm{u, a, Ca, Cl.} \tag{A26}$$

$$\begin{aligned}\mathbf{K}^{(e)}_{\mathrm{C}_{k\mathrm{W}}\mathrm{C}_{l\mathrm{W}}} = & \int_\Omega \nabla \mathbf{N}_{\mathrm{C}}^{\mathrm{T}} n_{\mathrm{W}} \alpha_{\mathrm{L}} \|\mathbf{v}_{\mathrm{wW}}\| v_k^{(M)} \left(\mathrm{I}_{kl} - C_{k\mathrm{W}} v_l^{(M)}\right) \nabla \mathbf{N}_{\mathrm{C}} \mathrm{dV} \\ & + v_k^{(M)} \int_\Omega \mathbf{N}_{\mathrm{C}}^{\mathrm{T}} \mathbf{J}_{\mathrm{w}} \nabla \mathbf{N}_{\mathrm{C}} \mathrm{dV},\ k,\ l = \mathrm{u, a, Ca, Cl.}\end{aligned} \tag{A27}$$

$$\mathbf{K}^{(e)}_{\mathrm{m_{cS}C_{uW}}} = -\int_\Omega \mathbf{N}_{\mathrm{M}_c}^{\mathrm{T}} m_{\mathrm{c}}^{(M)} n_{\mathrm{W}} \frac{dr}{dc_{\mathrm{uW}}} \mathbf{N}_{\mathrm{C}} \mathrm{dV} \tag{A28}$$

$$\mathbf{C}^{(e)}_{\mathrm{P_w}U} = \int_\Omega \mathbf{N}_{\mathrm{P_W}}^{\mathrm{T}} \mathrm{tr}(\mathbf{B}_{\mathrm{U}}) \mathrm{dV} = -\mathbf{K}^{(e)}_{\mathrm{UP_W}} \tag{A29}$$

$$\mathbf{C}^{(e)}_{\mathrm{P_w m_{cS}}} = -\int_\Omega \mathbf{N}_{\mathrm{P_W}}^{\mathrm{T}} \left(-v_{\mathrm{u}}^{(M)} + 2v_{\mathrm{a}}^{(M)} - v_{\mathrm{Ca}}^{(M)} + v_c^{(M)}\right) \frac{1}{m_c^{(M)}} \mathbf{N}_{\mathrm{M}_c} \mathrm{dV} \tag{A30}$$

$$\mathbf{C}^{(e)}_{\mathrm{C}_{k\mathrm{W}}\mathrm{C}_{l\mathrm{W}}} = v_k^{(M)} \int_\Omega \mathbf{N}_{\mathrm{C}}^{\mathrm{T}} n_{\mathrm{W}} \mathbf{N}_{\mathrm{C}} \mathrm{dV} \mathrm{I}_{kl},\ k,\ l = \mathrm{u, a, Ca, Cl.} \tag{A31}$$

$$\mathbf{C}^{(e)}_{\mathrm{C}_{u\mathrm{W}}\mathrm{m_{cS}}} = \frac{v_{\mathrm{u}}^{(M)}}{m_c^{(M)}} \int_\Omega \mathbf{N}_{\mathrm{C}}^{\mathrm{T}} \left[\left(-v_{\mathrm{u}}^{(M)} + 2v_{\mathrm{a}}^{(M)} - v_{\mathrm{Ca}}^{(M)}\right) c_{\mathrm{uW}} + 1\right] \mathbf{N}_{\mathrm{M}_c} \mathrm{dV} \tag{A32}$$

$$\mathbf{C}^{(e)}_{\mathrm{C}_{a\mathrm{W}}\mathrm{m_{cS}}} = \frac{v_{\mathrm{a}}^{(M)}}{m_c^{(M)}} \int_\Omega \mathbf{N}_{\mathrm{C}}^{\mathrm{T}} \left[\left(-v_{\mathrm{u}}^{(M)} + 2v_{\mathrm{a}}^{(M)} - v_{\mathrm{Ca}}^{(M)}\right) c_{\mathrm{aW}} - 2\right] \mathbf{N}_{\mathrm{M}_c} \mathrm{dV} \tag{A33}$$

$$\mathbf{C}^{(e)}_{\mathrm{C}_{Ca\mathrm{W}}\mathrm{m_{cS}}} = \frac{v_{\mathrm{Ca}}^{(M)}}{m_c^{(M)}} \int_\Omega \mathbf{N}_{\mathrm{C}}^{\mathrm{T}} \left[\left(-v_{\mathrm{u}}^{(M)} + 2v_{\mathrm{a}}^{(M)} - v_{\mathrm{Ca}}^{(M)}\right) c_{\mathrm{CaW}} + 1\right] \mathbf{N}_{\mathrm{M}_c} \mathrm{dV} \tag{A34}$$

$$\mathbf{C}^{(e)}_{\mathrm{C_{lW}m_{cS}}} = \frac{v_{\mathrm{Cl}}^{(M)}}{m_c^{(M)}} \int_\Omega \mathbf{N}_{\mathrm{C}}^{\mathrm{T}} \left[\left(-v_{\mathrm{u}}^{(M)} + 2v_{\mathrm{a}}^{(M)} - v_{\mathrm{Ca}}^{(M)}\right) c_{\mathrm{ClW}}\right] \mathbf{N}_{\mathrm{M}_c} \mathrm{dV} \tag{A35}$$

$$\mathbf{C}^{(e)}_{\mathrm{m_{cS}m_{cS}}} = \int_\Omega \mathbf{N}_{\mathrm{M}_c}^{\mathrm{T}} \mathbf{N}_{\mathrm{M}_c} \mathrm{dV} \tag{A36}$$

Three nodes per finite element and quadratic interpolation functions were used for the bar element displacements field, while two nodes per finite element and linear interpolation functions were used for the other fields (Figure A1). This results in quadratic shape functions for $\mathbf{N}_{\mathrm{U}}$ (A37)–(A39) and linear shape functions for $\mathbf{N}_{\mathrm{P_W}}$, $\mathbf{N}_{\mathrm{C}}$ and $\mathbf{N}_{\mathrm{M}_c}$ (A40) and (A41):

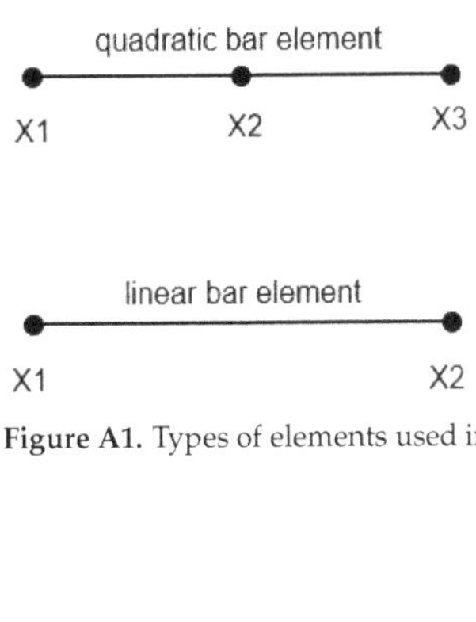

Figure A1. Types of elements used in the numerical model.

$$\mathbf{N}_{\mathrm{U1}} = -\frac{\xi}{2}(1 - \xi) \tag{A37}$$

$$\mathbf{N}_{\mathrm{U2}} = 1 - \xi^2, \tag{A38}$$

$$\mathbf{N}_{U3} = \frac{\xi}{2}(1+\xi), \tag{A39}$$

$$\mathbf{N}_{K1} = -\frac{\xi}{2} + \frac{1}{2}, \tag{A40}$$

$$\mathbf{N}_{K2} = +\frac{\xi}{2} + \frac{1}{2}, \tag{A41}$$

where $K = \mathrm{P_W},\ \mathrm{C}, \mathrm{M_c}$ and ξ is a local coordinate that varies from -1 to 1.

References

1. DeJong, J.T.; Mortensen, B.M.; Martinez, B.C.; Nelson, D.C. Bio-mediated soil improvement. *Ecol. Eng.* **2010**, *36*, 197–210. [CrossRef]
2. Al Qabany, A.; Soga, K. Effect of chemical treatment used in MICP on engineering properties of cemented soils. *Géotechnique* **2013**, *63*, 331–339. [CrossRef]
3. Cardoso, R.; Pedreira, R.; Duarte, S.O.; Monteiro, G. About calcium carbonate precipitation on sand biocementation. *Eng. Geol.* **2020**, *271*, 105612. [CrossRef]
4. Cardoso, R.; Scholler, L.; Pinto, M.M.; Flores-Colen, I.; Covas, D. Experimental analysis of biocementation technique for sealing cracks in concrete water storage tanks. *Constr. Build. Mater.* **2024**, *412*, 134854. [CrossRef]
5. Li, S.; Li, C.; Yao, D.; Wang, S. Feasibility of microbially induced carbonate precipitation and straw checkerboard barriers on desertification control and ecological restoration. *Ecol. Eng.* **2020**, *152*, 105883. [CrossRef]
6. Meng, H.; Gao, Y.; He, J.; Qi, Y.; Hang, L. Microbially induced carbonate precipitation for wind erosion control of desert soil: Field-scale tests. *Geoderma* **2021**, *383*, 114723. [CrossRef]
7. Rodríguez, R.F.; Cardoso, R. Study of biocementation treatment to prevent erosion by concentrated water flow in a small-scale sand slope. *Transp. Geotech.* **2022**, *37*, 100873. [CrossRef]
8. Wang, Y.; Sun, X.; Miao, L.; Wang, H.; Wu, L.; Shi, W.; Kawasaki, S. State-of-the-art review of soil erosion control by MICP and EICP techniques: Problems, applications, and prospects. *Sci. Total Environ.* **2024**, *912*, 169016. [CrossRef]
9. Wang, Z.; Zhang, N.; Cal, G.; Jin, Y.; Ding, N.; Shen, D. Review of ground improvement using microbial induced carbonate precipitation (MICP). *Mar. Georesources Geotechnol.* **2017**, *8*, 1135–1146. [CrossRef]
10. Fouladi, A.S.; Arulrajah, A.; Chu, J.; Horpibulsuk, S. Application of microbially induced calcite precipitation (MICP) technology in construction materials: A comprehensive review of waste stream contributions. *Constr. Build. Mater.* **2023**, *388*, 131546. [CrossRef]
11. van Wijngaarden, W.K.; Vermolen, F.J.; van Meurs, G.A.M.; Vuik, C. Modelling biogrout: A new ground improvment method based on microbial-induced carbonate precipitation. *Transp. Porous Media* **2011**, *87*, 397–420. [CrossRef]
12. Ebigbo, A.; Phillips, A.; Gerlach, R.; Helmig, R.; Cunningham, A.B.; Class, H.; Spangler, L.H. Darcy-scale modelling of microbially induced carbonate mineral precipitation in sand columns. *Water Resour. Res.* **2012**, *48*. [CrossRef]
13. Nassar, M.K.; Gurung, D.; Bastani, M.; Ginn, T.R.; Shafei, B.; Gomez, M.G.; DeJong, J.T. Large-scale experiments in microbially induced calcite precipitation (MICP): Reactive transport model development and prediction. *Water Resour. Res.* **2018**, *54*, 480–500. [CrossRef]
14. Minto, J.M.; Lunn, R.J.; El Mountassir, G. Development of a reactive transport model for field-scale simulation of microbially induced carbonate precipitation. *Water Resour. Res.* **2019**, *55*, 7229–7245. [CrossRef]
15. Wang, X.; Nackenhorst, U. A coupled bio-chemo-hydraulic model to predict porosity and permeability reduction during microbially induced calcite precipitation. *Adv. Water Resour.* **2020**, *140*, 103563. [CrossRef]
16. Faeli, Z.; Montoya, B.M.; Gabr, M.A. Elucidating factors governing MICP biogeochemical processes at macro-scale: A reactive transport model development. *Comput. Geotech.* **2023**, *160*, 105514. [CrossRef]
17. Fauriel, S.; Laloui, L. A bio-chemo-hydro-mechanical model for microbially induced calcite precipitation in soils. *Comput. Geotech.* **2012**, *46*, 104–120. [CrossRef]
18. Mehrabi, R.; Atefi-Monfared, K. A Coupled Bio-Chemo_Hydro_Mechanical Model for Bio-cementation in Porous Media. *Can. Geotech. J.* **2022**, *56*, 1266–1280. [CrossRef]
19. Bataille, J.; Kestin, J. On the structuring of thermodynamic fluxes: A direct implementation of the dissepation inequality. *Int. J. Eng. Sci.* **1977**, *17*, 563–572. [CrossRef]
20. Loret, B.; Simões, F.M.F. A framework for deformation, generalized diffusion, mass transfer and growth in multi-species multi-phase biological tissues. *Eur. J. Mech. A/Solids* **2005**, *24*, 757–781. [CrossRef]
21. Loret, B.; Simões, F.M.F. *Biomechanical Aspects of Soft Tissues*; CRC Press: Boca Raton, FL, USA; Taylor & Francis Group: Boca Raton, FL, USA, 2017.
22. Cardoso, R.; Pires, I.; Duarte, S.O.; Monteiro, G. Effects of clay's chemical interactions on biocementation. *Appl. Clay Sci.* **2018**, *156*, 96–103. [CrossRef]
23. Zienkiewicz, O.C.; Chan, A.H.C.; Pastor, M.; Schrefler, B.A.; Shiomi, T. *Computational Geomechanics*; John Wiley & Sons: Chichester, NY, USA, 1999.

24. Xiao, Y.; He, X.; Stuedlein, A.W.; Chu, J.; Evans, M.; van Paassen, L.A. Crystal growth of MICP through microfluidic chip tests. *J. Geotech. Geoenviron. Eng.* **2022**, *148*, 06022002. [CrossRef]
25. Cuthbert, M.O.; Riley, M.S.; Handley-Sidhu, S.; Renshaw, J.C.; Tobler, D.J.; Phoenix, V.R.; Mackay, R. Controls on rate of ureolysis and morphology of carbonate precipitated by *S. pausteurii* biofilms and limits due to bacterial encapsulation. *Ecol. Eng.* **2012**, *41*, 32–40. [CrossRef]
26. Whiffin, V.S.; van Paassen, L.A.; Harkes, M.P. Microbial carbonate precipitation as a soil improvement technique. *Geomicrobiol. J.* **2007**, *24*, 417–423. [CrossRef]
27. Barkouki, T.H.; Martinez, B.C.; Mortensen, B.M.; Weathers, T.S.; De Jong, J.D.; Ginn, T.R.; Spycher, N.F.; Smith, R.W.; Fujita, Y. Forward and Inverse Bio-Geochemical Modeling of Microbially Induced Calcite Precipitation in Half-Meter Column Experiments. *Transp. Porous Media* **2011**, *90*, 23–39. [CrossRef]
28. Gajo, A.; Loret, B. Finite element simulations of chemo-mechanical coupling in elastic-plastic homoionic expansive clays. *Comput. Methods Appl. Mech. Eng.* **2003**, *192*, 3489–3530. [CrossRef]

mathematics

MDPI

Article

Automatic Handling of C^0-G^0 Continuous Rational Bézier Elements Produced from T-Splines Through Bézier Extraction

Christopher Provatidis [1,*] and Ioannis Dimitriou [2]

[1] School of Mechanical Engineering, National Technical University of Athens, 15780 Zografou, Greece
[2] Department of Mechanical Design and Control Systems, National Technical University of Athens, 15780 Zografou, Greece; idimitriou@mail.ntua.gr
* Correspondence: cprovat@mail.ntua.gr; Tel.: +30-210-7721520

Abstract: This paper shows that at a certain time-point in the analysis procedure, the accuracy of T-spline based isogeometric analysis (IGA) may be substantially improved by increasing the multiplicity of the inner knots up to the polynomial degree. This task can be performed by considering the Bézier extraction operator matrix elementwise, and thus an increased number of updated control points are easily received in the geometrical and computational models. Nevertheless, after the determination of the unique control points, the Bézier elements near the T-junctions may not be well shaped, and thus minor automatic interventions are required to ensure full (i.e., C^0 and G^0) compatibility. The improved IGA-based solution may be used as a reference to determine the a posteriori error estimations in the T-spline elements of the domain, and thus may be a useful tool for IGA adaptation. The methodology is shown in BVPs dominated by Laplace–Poisson equations in rectangular and curvilinear domains, while eigenvalues and eigenvectors were extracted in a rectangular acoustic cavity.

Keywords: isogeometric analysis; T-splines; Bézier extraction operator; C^0-G^0 continuity; potential problems; Laplace equation; eigenvalue problem

MSC: 65N06; 65B99

1. Introduction

Isogeometric analysis is today's research frontier in computational methods for the solution of BVPs and eigenvalue (Sturm–Liouville) problems. According to this method, the domain is decomposed into smaller patches which are based on tensor-product NURBS approximation [1]. Later, the method was implemented in conjunction with T-spline approximation [2]. While in both of these cases the basis functions may be computed as tensor-products which are based on either global or local knot vectors, it has been proposed instead to implement the Bézier extraction (BEXT) operator [3,4].

The main advantage of this approach is that Bézier extraction, compared to the original implementation of IGA given in [1], is such that apart from the coefficients of the extraction operator, the basis functions are identical for all elements in the mesh, as is the case for classical finite elements. Therefore, there is no need to implement B-spline (basis) function evaluation routines; these are costly, from a numerical point of view. Another practical reason for using BEXT is that it reduces the communication errors in the data transfer between the geometric model and the analysis.

On the other hand, the BEXT operator is a matrix which, when multiplied by the original control points of the T-mesh, provides a greater number of new (updated) control points; these have not been exploited to date. In this paper, we propose the utilization of the new control points, which form Bézier elements of C^0-continuity, to automatically solve a parallel BVP. The latter solution is generally more accurate for the same number of elements as found in the original T-spline, and therefore may be used as a reference in an a posteriori error estimator. The next step is obviously a refined T-spline classical isogeometric analysis.

2. Conventional IGA Procedures

2.1. Tensor-Product of Local Knot Vectors (MODEL-1)

It is well known that for two given global knot vectors associated with a patch, the tensor-product B-spline (or NURBS) functions can be determined using Cox–de Boor recursion [5,6]. The same can be performed in T-spline approximation, with the only exception being that the tensor-product is based on local knot vectors associated with anchors.

For the sake of simplicity, we limit ourselves to cubic T-splines (i.e., those with polynomial degree $p = 3$). Therefore, in a usual T-spline it is sufficient to construct a matrix, let us call it U_{vec}, which for each anchor 'α' determines the knots of those other anchors to the left and the right of that under consideration, and thus forming the local knot vector $\Xi_\alpha = \{\xi_1, \xi_2, \xi_3, \xi_4, \xi_5\}$. Similarly, we need another matrix, let us call it V_{vec}, which determines the knots of those anchors at the bottom and the top of that under consideration, and thus forming the local knot vector $H_\alpha = \{\eta_1, \eta_2, \eta_3, \eta_4, \eta_5\}$. Again, for $p = 3$, the matrix U_{vec} (and similarly V_{vec}) is of the size $n_\alpha \times 5$, where n_α is the number of anchors in the T-patch. Based on these two matrices as input, for each couple (ξ, η) of the T-patch, we can determine the tensor-product of B-splines, $N_{\alpha,p}(\xi)N_{\alpha,p}(\eta)$.

The abovementioned B-spline functions, $N_{\alpha,p}(\xi)$ and $N_{\alpha,p}(\eta)$, can be easily calculated using the function `spcol` included in MATLAB® R2018, but open-source software is also available in many repositories and books (e.g., [7]).

Moreover, in the case of $p = 3$, for any set of five nondecreasing knots $\{x_1, x_2, x_3, x_4, x_5\}$, which may be a single row from the abovementioned matrix U_{vec}, there is a single piecewise cubic B-spline function $N_\alpha(x)$, which analytically is given by the following (see, e.g., [8]):

$$N_\alpha(x) = \begin{cases} \frac{(x-x_1)^3}{(x_2-x_1)(x_4-x_1)(x_3-x_1)}, & 0 < x \le x_2 \\ \frac{(x-x_1)^2(x_3-x)}{(x_3-x_2)(x_4-x_1)(x_3-x_1)} + \frac{(x_4-x)(x-x_1)(x-x_2)}{(x_3-x_2)(x_4-x_2)(x_4-x_1)} + \frac{(x_5-x)(x-x_2)^2}{(x_3-x_2)(x_5-x_2)(x_4-x_2)}, & x_2 < x \le x_3 \\ \frac{(x-x_1)(x_4-x)^2}{(x_4-x_3)(x_4-x_2)(x_4-x_1)} + \frac{(x_5-x)(x_4-x)(x-x_2)}{(x_4-x_3)(x_5-x_2)(x_4-x_2)} + \frac{(x_5-x)^2(x-x_3)}{(x_4-x_3)(x_5-x_3)(x_5-x_2)}, & x_3 < x \le x_4 \\ \frac{(x_5-x)^3}{(x_5-x_4)(x_5-x_3)(x_5-x_2)}, & x_4 < x \le x_5 \\ 0, & x \le x_1 \text{ or } x > x_5 \end{cases} \quad (1)$$

In general, the independent variable x and the knots x_1 to x_5 shown in Equation (1) may represent either of the parameters ξ or η, as well as the knots involved in the abovementioned local knot vectors $\Xi_\alpha = \{\xi_1, \xi_2, \xi_3, \xi_4, \xi_5\}$ and $H_\alpha = \{\eta_1, \eta_2, \eta_3, \eta_4, \eta_5\}$. Therefore, for each anchor 'α', Equation (1) applied to Ξ_α determines one B-spline $N_\alpha(\xi)$, and applied to H_α produces $N_\alpha(\eta)$. The range of the non-vanishing tensor-product bivariate basis function $N_{\alpha,p}(\xi)N_{\alpha,p}(\eta)$ is the rectangle $[\xi_1, \xi_5] \times [\eta_1, \eta_5]$. In general, a weight w_α is associated to the anchor $\mathbf{P}_\alpha$.

Based on the above B-spline functions $N_\alpha(\xi)$ and $N_\alpha(\eta)$, for each anchor 'α' we can calculate the bivariate blending function $B_\alpha(\xi, \eta) = N_\alpha(\xi)N_\alpha(\eta)$. When the patch is curvilinear, each anchor is also associated to a weight w_α. Following the notation in [2], if 'A' is the set of all the anchors in the patch, we define the blending functions as follows:

$$R_\alpha(\xi,\eta) = \frac{w_\alpha B_\alpha(\xi,\eta)}{\sum_{\beta\in A} w_\beta B_\beta(\xi,\eta)} \tag{2}$$

Clearly, the numerator of Equation (2) represents a weighted tensor-product of the local B-spline functions associated to the anchor 'α'. The denominator $W(\xi,\eta)$ represents the sum of the weighted tensor-products due to all the contributed anchors, and is set to ensure the partition of unity property at every point (ξ,η) of the parametric space:

$$\sum_{\alpha\in A} R_\alpha(\xi,\eta) = 1,\ \forall(\xi,\eta) \in [0,1]\times[0,1] \tag{3}$$

Based on the above blending functions $R_\alpha(\xi,\eta)$ within a curvilinear patch, and given the control points $\mathbf{P}_\alpha$, the T-spline in physical space is described by the following:

$$S(\xi,\eta) = \sum_{\alpha\in A} \mathbf{P}_a R_\alpha(\xi,\eta) \tag{4}$$

It is instructive to recall that in the special case of a NURBS tensor-product of degree $p = 3$, the abovementioned set 'A' consists of exactly $(p+1)^2$, i.e., sixteen, nonzero bivariate basis functions which fulfil Equation (3). In contrast, in a sub-patch of a T-spline, there may be more than 16 non-vanishing bivariate blending functions. Regarding an annulus, Ref. [4] shows that most T-elements are influenced by 16 (and a few of them by 17) blending functions.

As discussed above, regarding a certain T-spline patch, it is possible that a part of it (an element) is influenced by 16 non-vanishing blending functions, whereas another element might be influenced by 17. Moreover, another possibility is that the same number of 16 functions might be in evidence, but different blending functions may dominate in different elements of the same patch. In all these cases, we talk about "elements with reduced continuity", and to make these elements suitable for isogeometric analysis, it becomes necessary to subdivide them with continuity reduction lines (extended T-mesh), and thus an increased number of T-elements is produced. As a result of this process, we have an "Analysis Suitable T-spline" (AST) patch.

After the creation of analysis-suitable T-elements, the blending functions of Equation (2) may be used to estimate the mass and stiffness matrices associated with the T-patch under consideration.

2.2. The Standard Utilization of the Bézier Extraction Operator (MODEL-2)

Despite the ease in the implementation of Equation (1), and although numerical evaluations may be easily performed using open-source libraries or proprietary libraries, the tendency is to utilize the Bézier extraction (BEXT) version. The basic theory is given below.

In the theory of computer-aided geometric design (CAGD), it is well known that knot insertion does not alter the shape of a curvilinear patch, either in shape or parametrically [7]. For one-dimensional interpolation of a curve $C(\xi)$ with $p = 3$, initially we have C^2-continuity at the inner knots, and after one knot insertion it decreases to C^1-continuity. Continuing with a second knot insertion at the inner knots (thus, three equal knots in total, i.e., equal to degree p), the continuity further decreases to C^0. Therefore, when the multiplicity λ of inner knots becomes equal to the polynomial degree p, we obtain C^0-continuity at the inner knots.

Moreover, for a two-dimensional NURBS patch, the above procedure is again applicable, but then the multiplicity of the inner knot should become $\lambda = p^2$, so that C^0-continuity is obtained in both directions. As shown in [3], the column-vector including the non-zero

B-spline (basis) functions $\mathbf{N}_e$ is related to the extracted Bernstein polynomials stored in the column-vector $\mathbf{B}_e$ per element, through the following formula:

$$\mathbf{N}_e(\xi,\eta) = \mathbf{C}_e \cdot \mathbf{B}_e(\xi,\eta), \tag{5}$$

where $\mathbf{C}_e$ is the Bézier extraction operator matrix, which corresponds to the e-th B-spline tensor-product element. In general, in a NURBS patch, $\mathbf{C}_e$ is a matrix of size $(p+1)^2 \times (p+1)^2$, whereas $\mathbf{N}_e$ and $\mathbf{B}_e$ are column-vectors of size $(p+1)^2 \times 1$, due to the local-support property of B-splines.

In a similar way, for a two-dimensional T-spline patch, Scott et al. [4] presented a pseudocode and showed that multiple knot insertion leads to the "Bézier extraction operator matrix", $\mathbf{C}_e$, which may be used to estimate the C^2-continuous blending functions of the T-spline element assembly. It is clarified that $\mathbf{C}_e$ comes from the same concept as the one underlying the expression in Equation (5) for NURBS patches, but is now applied locally for the T-spline patches.

In more detail, given the initial control points $\mathbf{P}_e$ and their weights $\mathbf{w}_e$ of the C^2-continuous e-th T-spline element, the abovementioned multiple knot insertion alters the initial weights according to the following formula:

$$\mathbf{w}_e^b = \mathbf{C}_e^{\mathrm{T}} \mathbf{w}_e. \tag{6}$$

In Equation (6), $\mathbf{w}_e^b$ denotes the updated element weights after the multiple knot insertion, whereas $\mathbf{w}_e$ are the initial given element weights which are associated to the initial control points $\mathbf{P}_e$.

As we mentioned earlier, within a T-mesh there may be some sub-patches of reduced continuity, and this has been a matter of intensive research [9]. To ensure uniqueness and then perform accurate numerical integration, it becomes necessary to elongate some edges of the T-mesh and thus obtain an analysis-suitable T-mesh. Nevertheless, although this procedure leads to an increased number of analysis-suitable T-elements, a standard number of non-vanishing blending functions is not always ensured.

As we shall see later, in the benchmark test of the annulus (Example 3), which has been studied in [4], most of the elements are influenced by $(p+1)^2 = 16$ nonzero basis functions, but also there are two elements which are influenced by 17 functions. This in turn means that, for most elements, the Bézier extraction operator matrix $\mathbf{C}_e$ will be of size 16×16, but in some of them, it will be of the size 17×16.

For the sake of completeness, the computation of the blending functions is performed as follows:

From Equation (2) one may observe that the bivariate blending functions $R(\xi,\eta)$ are tensor-products of local univariate basis functions, properly normalized, as follows:

$$R_\alpha(\xi,\eta) = \frac{N_{\alpha,p}(\xi) N_{\alpha,p}(\eta) w_\alpha}{W(\xi,\eta)}, \tag{7}$$

where the denominator $W(\xi,\eta)$ is the so-called "weighting function". Each blending function $R_\alpha(\xi,\eta)$ is associated to an anchor $\mathbf{P}_\alpha$, which for the polynomial degree $p=3$ is a true control point.

At a certain point (ξ,η) of the T-patch, there are a number of 'n' nonzero bivariate basis functions, in sum approximating the value $(p+1)^2$ (e.g., $n = 16, 17, \ldots$).

Dropping out the subscript 'e' denoting the element under consideration, if $\mathbf{W}$ is the diagonal matrix which includes all the above 'n' involved weights,

$$\mathbf{W} = \begin{bmatrix} w_1 & & & \\ & w_2 & & \\ & & \ddots & \\ & & & w_n \end{bmatrix}, \tag{8}$$

and $\mathbf{N}(\xi, \eta)$ is the column-vector (of size $n \times 1$) of all the bivariate B-spline functions affecting the element under consideration, then Equation (7) is rewritten in a matrix form which provides the rational column-vector $\mathbf{R}(\xi, \eta)$ [of size $n \times 1$],

$$\mathbf{R}(\xi, \eta) = \frac{1}{W(\xi, \eta)} \mathbf{W} \mathbf{N}(\xi, \eta) \tag{9}$$

To obtain the blending functions, we still need to calculate the weighting function $W(\xi, \eta)$, which is involved in the denominator of Equation (9). The latter is written as

$$W(\xi, \eta) = \sum_{\alpha=1}^{n} N_{\alpha,p}(\xi, \eta)\, w_\alpha = \mathbf{w}^T \mathbf{N}(\xi, \eta) \tag{10}$$

Substituting the B-spline column-vector $\mathbf{N}$ from Equation (5) into Equation (10), the latter becomes

$$W(\xi, \eta) = \mathbf{w}^T \mathbf{N}(\xi, \eta) = \mathbf{w}^T \mathbf{C} \mathbf{B}(\xi, \eta) \equiv \left(\mathbf{C}^T \mathbf{w}\right)^T \mathbf{B}(\xi, \eta) \tag{11}$$

Substituting Equation (6) into Equation (11), we receive the following:

$$W(\xi, \eta) = \left(\mathbf{w}^b\right)^T \mathbf{B}(\xi, \eta) = W_b(\xi, \eta), \tag{12}$$

where $\mathbf{w}^b = \mathbf{C}^T \mathbf{w}$ is a column-vector of standard size 16×1, including the weights associated to the Bézier–Bernstein basis functions. Substituting Equations (5) and (12) into Equation (9), we eventually receive the following:

$$\mathbf{R}(\xi, \eta) = \frac{1}{W^b(\xi, \eta)} \mathbf{W} \mathbf{C} \mathbf{B}(\xi, \eta), \tag{13}$$

where $\mathbf{W}$ is the diagonal matrix including the initial weights of the control points in the C^2-continuous model (cf. Equation (8)). Equation (13) dictates that it is not necessary to directly calculate the B-spline functions, either through the recursive (Curry–Schoenberg 1966) formulas or by using the analytical ones given by Equation (1), but only the extraction matrix $\mathbf{C}$, which depends only on the knot vectors, while the expression of the tensor-product Bernstein polynomials $\mathbf{B}(\xi, \eta)$ is trivial.

Based on the blending functions given by Equation (13), the computation of the mass and stiffness matrices is straightforward.

3. The Proposed Computational Procedure (MODEL-3 and MODEL-4)

3.1. General Theory (MODEL-3)

Although Ref. [4] has focused on the estimation of the C^2-continuous blending functions according to the BEXT Equation (13), for the purposes of the present paper we focus below on the updated control points as well.

In more detail, given the initial set of control points $\mathbf{P}$ and their associated weights $\mathbf{w}$ in the C^2-continuous T-spline model, the multiple knot insertion until the multiplicity becomes equal the degree p, provides new control points $\mathbf{Q}$ according to the following formula:

$$\mathbf{Q}_e^w = \mathbf{C}_e^{\mathrm{T}} \mathbf{P}_e^w \tag{14}$$

In Equation (14), the superscript 'w' indicates projective coordinates, i.e., Cartesian coordinates multiplied by the associated updated weight, whereas the superscript 'T' indicates the transpose of the BEXT matrix $\mathbf{C}_e$. Moreover, as previously mentioned in Section 2.2, in Equation (6), $\mathbf{w}_e^b \equiv \mathbf{w}_e^Q$ denotes the updated weights of the new control points $\mathbf{Q}$ (after the multiple knot insertion), whereas $\mathbf{w}_e \equiv \mathbf{w}_e^P$ are the initially given weights associated to the initial control points $\mathbf{P}$. Note that the superscripts $\{Q\}$ and $\{P\}$ are set only to clearly indicate the status after and before knot insertion, respectively.

Regarding the size of the arrays involved, we repeat that the element Bézier extraction operator matrix $\mathbf{C}_e$ includes as many rows as the number of the non-vanishing blending functions within the T-spline element (e.g., 16, 17), whereas the number of columns is standard, and equal to 16. Therefore, in general, $\mathbf{C}_e$ is a non-square matrix. Concerning the element vector of control points $\mathbf{P}_e$ and the associated vector of element weights $\mathbf{w}_e^Q$ in the initial C^2-continuous model, each of them has exactly as many rows as the matrix $\mathbf{C}_e$ (i.e., 16, 17, etc.). Interestingly, whatever the number of rows in $\mathbf{C}_e$ is, the resulting number of updated control points $\mathbf{Q}_e$ in the C^0-continuous Bézier element equals $(p+1)^2 = 16$.

The applied algorithm of the present paper is as follows:

- Based on the initial n_P control points $\mathbf{P}$ and the given index space, create n_{ele} analysis-suitable T-spline elements.
- Apply the BEXT matrix $\mathbf{C}_e$ in each of the above n_{ele} T-spline elements, and thus determine the following:
    - The updated control points $\mathbf{Q}_e$;
    - The associated weights $\mathbf{w}_e^Q$.
- Find the unique control points $(\mathbf{Q}_e)_{\text{unique}}$ among the above $\mathbf{Q}_e$ (initially including $n_{Q'} = 16 n_{ele}$ points), and thus determine the final number of n_Q control points, which fully defines the n_{ele} rational Bézier elements. An instructive example is presented in Section 3.3. Alternatively, one could implement a variation of the Oslo algorithm [10], which is a recursive procedure designed to simultaneously handle multiple knot insertion.
- For the abovementioned n_{ele} rational Bézier elements, calculate the element stiffness matrix (and mass matrix, if necessary). Note that, since in the present paper only cubic elements have been implemented (degree $p = 3$), there are always $n_{pts} = (p+1)^2 = 16$ control points in each rational Bézier element, and thus for potential problems (one degree of freedom per node) each element matrix has a size of 16×16. Obviously, if the same concept is extended to plane elasticity problems, the stiffness (or mass) matrix of each rational Bézier element will have a size of 32×32, and so on.
- Build the total matrices of the entire T-patch, apply the boundary conditions, and solve the equations system to determine the unknown coefficients.

As we demonstrate below in the five examples of the present paper, the final number, n_Q, of control points in the proposed C^0-continuous model is larger than the initial number of n_P control points in the C^2-continuous one. By analogy to the tensor-product NURBS model, a closed-form expression will be provided below for the quantity n_Q.

3.2. Estimation of Control Points n_Q for C^0-Continuity

To establish the procedure for the estimation of the updated control points **Q** which are produced by the BEXT process, we resort to the conventional tensor-product B-spline approximation. For the sake of simplicity, we consider the piecewise cubic tensor-product B-spline patch shown in Figure 1a (of degree $p = 3$) for the following unidirectional knot vector:

$$U = [0,0,0,0,\ 1/3,2/3,\ 1,1,1,1] \tag{15}$$

Based on trivial computer-aided geometric design (CAGD)-theory [7] (p.66), the number of control points per direction is given by

$$n = m - p - 1, \tag{16}$$

where m is the number of elements in the knot vector U. Since in Equation (15) there are $m = 10$ knots and $p = 3$, we have $n = 6$ per direction, which means $n_P = n^2 = 36$ control points in the entire two-dimensional patch.

After double knot insertion at the $n_{in} = 2$ inner knots, as required by BEXT [7] (p.161), the number of control points per direction becomes

$$n' = n + n_{in}(p - 1) = 10, \tag{17}$$

and therefore, the total number of the updated control points $\{Q\}$ after BEXT will be

$$n_Q = n'^2 = 10^2 = 100. \tag{18}$$

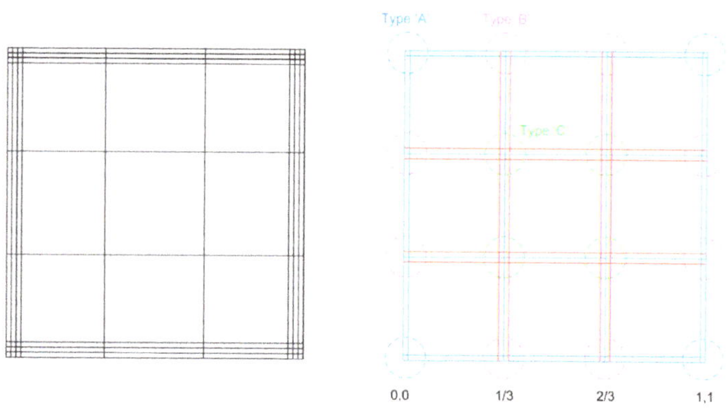

(a) (b)

Figure 1. Tensor-product (**a**) B-spline in traditional form; (**b**) T-spline form after knot insertion.

Below, the same result will be derived, considering now the tensor-product B-spline patch as a T-spline patch. The conclusions of this approach will be extended to T-spline patches as well.

Obviously, the above two-dimensional B-spline patch, as described by Equation (15), is equivalent to a T-mesh with six anchors per direction, and thus forming the following index space:

$$A_x = A_y = \{0, 0, 1/3, 2/3, 1, 1\} = \{\xi_1, \xi_2, \xi_3, \xi_4, \xi_5, \xi_6\}. \tag{19}$$

The anchors in the set described in Equation (19) are denoted by blue-colored lines in Figure 1b. The BEXT procedure requires the knot insertion at the inner knots, such as $\xi_3 = 1/3$ and $\xi_4 = 2/3$, until the multiplicity becomes $\lambda = p = 3$. This demands the introduction of the red-colored lines shown in Figure 1b, wherein one may distinguish three different types of knots, as follows:

- Type A: Knots related to the corners of the patch (four corners with four anchors per corner).
- Type B: Knots related to intermediate places along the four edges, not coinciding with the corners (six anchors per initial knot).
- Type C: Knots related to initial knots in the interior of the patch (nine anchors per initial knot).

Based on the above categorization, for the case shown in Figure 1b, in which there are four, six, and nine initial knots of categories A, B, and C, circled respectively, we have

$$\text{i.} \quad \text{Anchors at the corners:} \quad 4 \times 4 = 16 \tag{20a}$$

$$\text{ii.} \quad \text{Anchors along boundaries:} \quad 8 \times 6 = 48 \tag{20b}$$

$$\text{iii.} \quad \text{Anchors in interior:} \quad 4 \times 9 = 36 \tag{20c}$$

$$\text{SUM of anchors in the patch: } n_Q = 100, \text{ Q.E.D.} \tag{20d}$$

A procedure similar to that used to determine the number n_Q may be followed for a T-mesh, which is again divided into the above three categories, A, B, and C. The only minor exception concerns elements of reduced continuity, in which extra inner knots are added in the index space by the extension of existing connecting lines, as mentioned earlier. Depending on the location of these extra points, which may also be classified as Type C, the full number '9' or part of it may be applied to them.

3.3. On the Uniqueness of Control Points

Let us continue working with the nine tensor-product B-spline elements illustrated in Figure 1, which are based on the univariate knot vector of Equation (15).

For this configuration, the initial ($n_P = 36$) control points are shown in Figure 2a, whereas those ($n_Q = 100$) after multiple knot insertion are shown in Figure 2b. One may observe that, after the multiple knot insertion, each of the nine Bézier elements is occupied by $4 \times 4 = 16$ control points. Obviously, the number of the actual $n_Q = 100$ control points differs from the blind product $n_{Q'} = 9$ elements $\times$ 16 control points per element = 144.

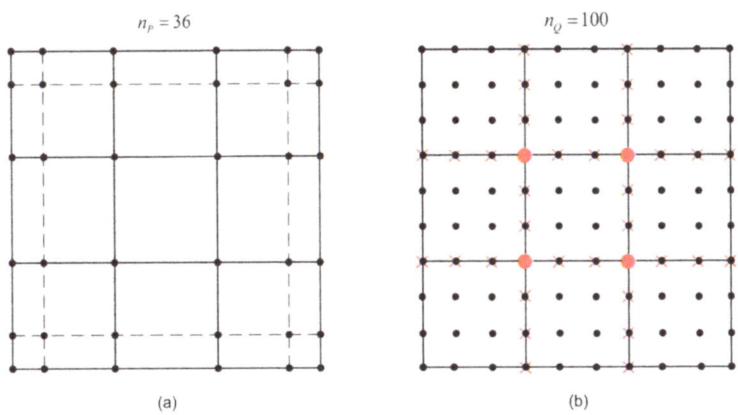

Figure 2. Control points (**a**) before and (**b**) after knot insertion (shared control points: at intersections •; along the inter-element boundaries ×).

The above discrepancy between the erroneous $n_{Q'} = 144$ and the correct $n_Q = 100$ is due to the following reasons:

- Each of the four control points at the intersections between horizontal and vertical inter-element boundaries (illustrated in Figure 2b by red circle, •) belongs to four elements, while they must be countered only once. Therefore, instead of the blind number 4 × 4 = 16, we must consider only four of them, which means that we have twelve additional fictitious points to subtract from 144.
- Each of the thirty-two control points along the inter-element boundaries (illustrated in Figure 2b by red cross, ×) belongs to two elements, and therefore a blind computation would result in 32 × 2 = 64 points. To obtain the exact number, half of them (i.e., 32) must be subtracted from 144.

Therefore, the total fictitious number of the additional control points is 12 + 32 = 44. When the latter (44) is subtracted from the blind number $n_{Q'} = 144$, we obtain the correct number, $n_Q = 100$.

3.4. Fixing C^0 and G^0-Incompatibilities (MODEL-4)

Although the procedure discussed in Section 3.1 (MODEL-3) is straightforward, sometimes there are minor shortcomings to be corrected before analysis is performed. In this context, it may happen that within a sub-patch there is a "discontinuity", and thus partitioning using an extension line is necessary for the accurate numerical integration (e.g., the dashed line GH shown in Figure 3a). For example, in the test case of [4] (p. 134), it was shown that among twenty-four T-spline elements, twenty-two of them are affected by 16 whereas the other two are affected by by 17 control points.

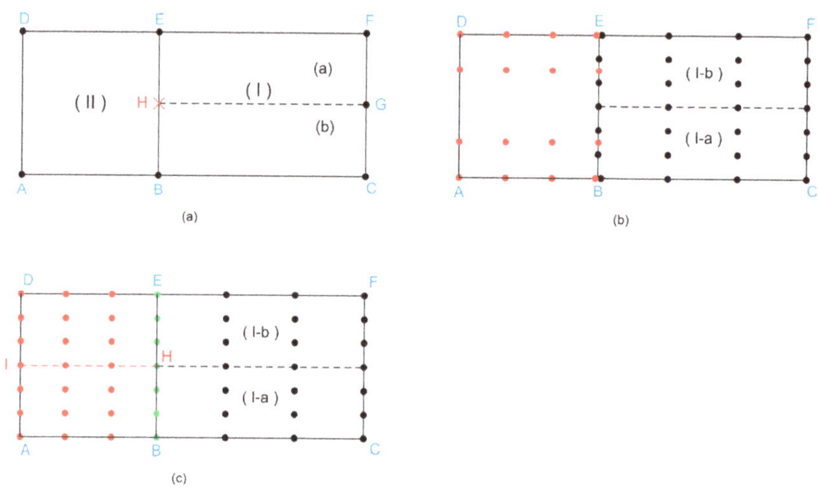

Figure 3. Formation of Bézier elements near to reduced continuity: (**a**) two sub-patches (I) and (II), (**b**) three incompatible elements, and (**c**) four compatible elements.

To be more specific, the discontinuity of the sub-patch (I) in Figure 3a demands its subdivision (using the abovementioned extension line GH) into sub-patches I(a) and I(b). After the introduction of the line GH, the model becomes "analysis-suitable" (AS). This means that each of the produced new elements I(a) = HGFE and I(b) = BCGH is continuous and thus accurate numerical integration is allowed. This task is compulsory even in the original IGA and is performed using only information provided by the index space. However, in the original IGA, the hanging node H is no problem at all, because it is not associated with an independent degree of freedom (and thus the compatibility makes no sense), but rather—as was previously mentioned—the line GH serves only for domain integration.

On the contrary, in the framework of the present paper it was found that although the abovementioned Bézier elements (I(a) and I(b)) are well formed, their neighboring Bézier element (II), which shares a common edge BE (perpendicular to the end H of the extension line GH) with the sub-patch (I) of reduced continuity, is not compatible (see also Figure 3b). Clearly, this happens although the Bézier element (II) is fully continuous. Although sometimes the accuracy of the numerical solution may be sufficient while ignoring the incompatibility, in general it becomes imperative to perform a further tessellation on the largest element (II), as shown in Figure 3c. The procedure of this tessellation is easy and is based on the common edge previously considered, from the side of the element (I) of reduced continuity. A full description of the applied numerical scheme is given in Sections A and B.

Therefore, given the index space of a T-spline, the first step in IGA is to introduce the extension lines GH, and thus the number of incompatibilities equals the number of $n_{\text{incompatible}}$ points H at the ends of them. Before the tessellation (MODEL-3), the total number of Bézier elements is n_{nele}, of which a set of $n_{\text{incompatible}}$ (like the abovementioned element (II)) is incompatible. Therefore, $(n_{\text{nele}} - n_{\text{incompatible}})$ out of the initial n_{nele} elements are compatible.

Regarding MODEL-4, we recall that the common edges at which tessellation is further conducted are perpendicular to the ends H of the extension lines GH, whereas the total number of Bézier elements becomes $(n_{\text{nele}} + n_{\text{incompatible}})$. As for the extra computation effort of MODEL-4 with respect to MODEL-3, the former includes one extra rational Bézier element per incompatibility, which means that the extra computer effort for the estimation of the element matrices is $n_{\text{incompatible}}/n_{\text{nele}}$ of the computer effort in MODEL-3. (Note that the matrices of $(n_{\text{nele}} - n_{\text{incompatible}})$ elements remain unaltered.)

4. Matrix Formulation

Numerical results refer to potential problems, particularly with reference to the Laplace equation and wave propagation equation. The latter partial differential equation is written as

$$(1/c^2)\partial^2 u/\partial t^2 - \nabla^2 u = 0. \tag{21}$$

Based on any set of control points (**P** or **Q**) associated with blending functions $\mathbf{R}_{\text{PQ}}$ (column-vector) in general, the matrix formulation of IGA is

$$\mathbf{M}\ddot{\mathbf{u}} + \mathbf{K}\mathbf{u} = \mathbf{f}(t), \tag{22}$$

where the stiffness and mass matrices as given by the following domain integrals:

$$\text{Mass matrix:} \quad \mathbf{M} = (1/c^2)\int_A \mathbf{R}_{PQ}(\mathbf{R}_{PQ})^{\mathrm{T}} dA, \tag{23}$$

and

$$\text{Stiffness matrix:} \quad \mathbf{K} = \int_A \nabla\mathbf{R}_{PQ}(\nabla\mathbf{R}_{PQ})^{\mathrm{T}} dA., \tag{24}$$

Obviously, Laplace equation ($\nabla^2 u = 0$) is a special, steady-state, case of Equation (22), and thus is described by the matrix equation

$$\mathbf{K}\mathbf{u} = \mathbf{f}, \tag{25}$$

where the force vector is given as

$$\mathbf{f} = \oint_{\Gamma} \mathbf{R}_{PQ} \frac{\partial u}{\partial n} d\Gamma. \tag{26}$$

Regarding the numerical extraction of the eigenvalues ($\lambda = \omega^2$) of an acoustic cavity, we use the following formula:

$$\det(\mathbf{K} - \lambda \mathbf{M}) = 0. \tag{27}$$

5. Results

The theory is supported by five examples. The first two examples are simple rectangles and have been devised to require edge extension in the same direction at two places to ensure analysis-suitable T-splines. The third example refers to an annulus and follows the pattern of [4], which also requires two edge extensions, but in this case, in relatively perpendicular directions. The fourth example utilizes a more complicated index space, as it refers to a fully two-dimensional problem. The fifth example has an index space similar to that of the annulus (third example) but refers to a rectangular domain.

Each example was solved using four models, as follows:

- MODEL-1: B-spline functions **N** were calculated as local tensor-product associated to control points **P**, using de Boor's spcol MATLAB® function; Equation (1) is also applicable as an alternative. Furthermore, weights and normalization were imposed to obtain the final blending functions **R**.
- MODEL-2: B-spline functions **N** were calculated using Bézier extraction operator matrices, $\mathbf{C}_e$, which were associated to initial control points **P**. Furthermore, weights and normalization were imposed to obtain the final blending functions **R**.
- MODEL-3: Basis functions **B** (Bézier–Bernstein polynomials) are known functions and were combined with the new control points **Q** on the Bézier elements of C^0-continuity.
- MODEL-4: When MODEL-3 leads to inter-element incompatibility like that demonstrated in Figure 3, the larger Bézier element is subdivided according to Sections A and B, thus eventually producing the further-updated set of control points $\mathbf{Q}'$, which is slightly larger than **Q**. Based on the further corrected weights $\mathbf{w}_{Q'}$ and the further updated set of control points $\mathbf{Q}'$, we construct the new rational Bernstein polynomials $\mathbf{B}'$ which constitute the final set of basis functions.

By the theory, MODEL-1 and MODEL-2 are identical, because they only use a different computational procedure to calculate the same B-spline functions **N**, which are associated to the same control points **P**, and at the same Gauss points. The only reason that MODEL-2 is separately mentioned here is because it crosschecks the accuracy of the computer code and thus increases confidence.

In each example, for the first three models (MODEL-1 to MODEL-3), the number of (T-spline or Bézier) elements and the number of Gauss points is the same. Nevertheless, the number of the involved DOFs of MODEL-3 differs from those of (MODEL-1 and MODEL-2), i.e., we always have $n_Q > n_P$, as was explained in Sections 3.1 and 3.2.

Furthermore, in MODEL-4 the number of elements is larger by those subdivided, whereas the number of DOFs ($n_{Q'}$) is slightly larger than n_Q.

In the steady-state problems (Laplace equation), the accuracy of the models was expressed in terms of the L_2-norm in percent (%), using the following formula:

$$L_2 = \left[\frac{\int_\Omega (u_{\text{calculated}} - u_{\text{exact}})^2 d\Omega}{\int_\Omega (u_{\text{exact}})^2 d\Omega} \right]^{\frac{1}{2}} \times 100(\%) \tag{28}$$

All computations were performed on the same PC, using MATLAB® R2018.

5.1. EXAMPLE 1: Vertical Heat Flow

In the rectangular domain of size $L \times H = 7 \times 4$, of which the index space is shown in Figure 4, the temperature is prescribed on the bottom and top edges as follows: $T_{top} = 1000$ °C (at $y = H$) and $T_{bottom} = 0$ °C (at $y = 0$); the vertical edges at $x = 0$ and $x = L$ are fully insulated ($\partial T / \partial x = 0$).

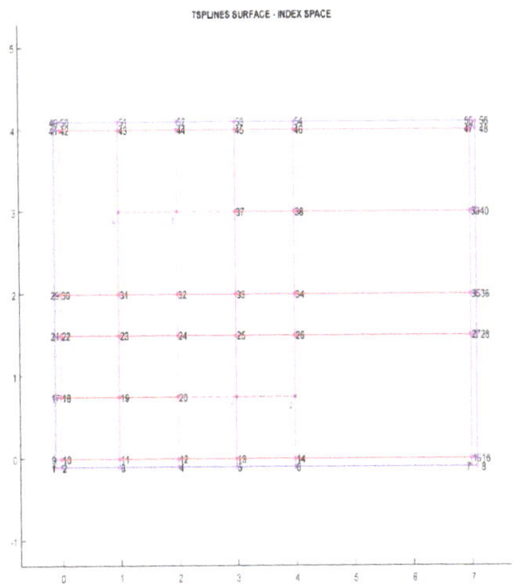

Figure 4. Index space for Example 1 and Example 2.

One may observe in Figure 4 that the index space includes $n_P = 56$ anchors and 19 initial patches. However, to ensure continuity, it becomes necessary to extend the edge 19–20 by two units to the right (thus producing the new points 1 and 2, connected by dashed line), and to extend the edge 38–37 to the left (thus producing the new points 3 and 4, connected again by dashed line). In this way, the number of degrees of freedom (DOF) remains the same at $n_{\mathrm{DOF}} = 56$, but due to the two subdivisions (each by two units), the number of T-spline elements in which Gauss integration will be performed increases, from the initial 19 to, eventually, $n_{ele} = 23$.

The numerical solution using MODEL-1 and MODEL-2, which is associated to the system of $n_{\mathrm{DOF}} = 56$ DOF shown in Figure 4, was found to coincide with the exact solution, $T_{exact}(x, y) = 250y$, with $0 \le y \le 4$.

Regarding the formation of Bézier elements produced after multiple knot insertion using BEXT (which constitutes MODEL-3), one may observe in Figure 5 two shortcomings regarding compatibility, as described in the following. The first shortcoming concerns the element at the upper left corner along the edge (31–43 in Figure 4, 108–159 in Figure 5) and the second refers to the element in the lower right corner along the edge labelled (14–26 in Figure 4, 43–64 in Figure 5). Nevertheless, the numerical solution of MODEL-3 ($n_Q = 244$ DOF) was also found to coincide with the exact solution. It is hypothesized that this happens because the heat flow is vertical, and the existing vertical edges do not interrupt the continuity of the interpolation. It is worth mentioning that the implementation of MODEL-4 (not shown but explained in Example 2) did not change the excellent result of MODEL-3 at all.

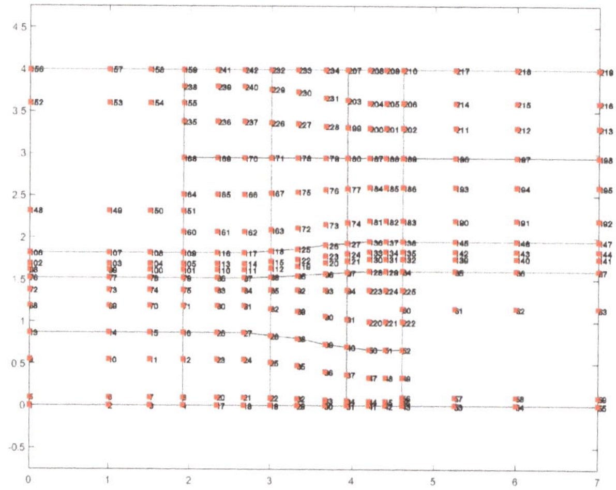

Figure 5. Bézier elements after Bézier extraction in vertical heat flow (Example 1, MODEL-3).

It is worth mentioning that the number of $n_Q = 244$ control points could be predicted by classifying the anchors into three categories according to Section 3.2. Thus, considering (A: 4 corners, B: 14 intermediate anchors on boundary, and C: 9 internal anchors including the extra ones produced after extension), the result, $n_Q = 244$, is shown in Table 1.

Table 1. Estimated number of updated control points (n_Q).

Control Points in MODEL-3			
Type A	**Type B**	**Type C**	**TOTAL (n_Q)**
4×4	14×6	16×9	244

The distribution of the temperature using MODEL-3 is shown in Figure 6, but it is the same in all four models.

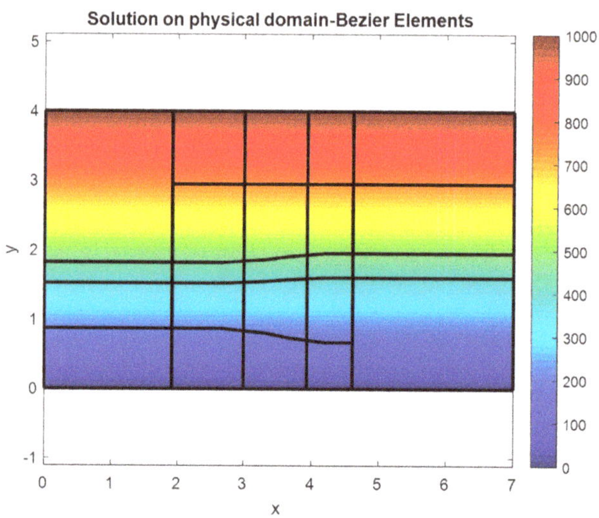

Figure 6. Temperature distribution in vertical heat flow (Example 1).

5.2. EXAMPLE 2: Horizontal Heat Flow

The same geometric model as that of Example 1 is now solved under different Dirichlet boundary conditions: $T_{left} = 0$ °C and $T_{right} = 1000$ °C on the vertical edges, whereas the bottom and top edges are now thermally insulated ($\partial T/\partial y = 0$). Obviously, the heat flow is horizontal, and the exact solution is given by $T_{exact}(x, y) = (x/7)1000$ with $0 \leq x \leq 7$.

Again, the T-mesh is the same as that shown in Figure 4, whereas the obtained set of $n_{ele} = 23$ Bézier elements after Bézier extraction is again that shown in Figure 5 (for MODEL-3).

As previously was the case, again in Example 2, MODEL-1 and MODEL-2 resulted in zero errors across the entire domain, as shown in Figure 7.

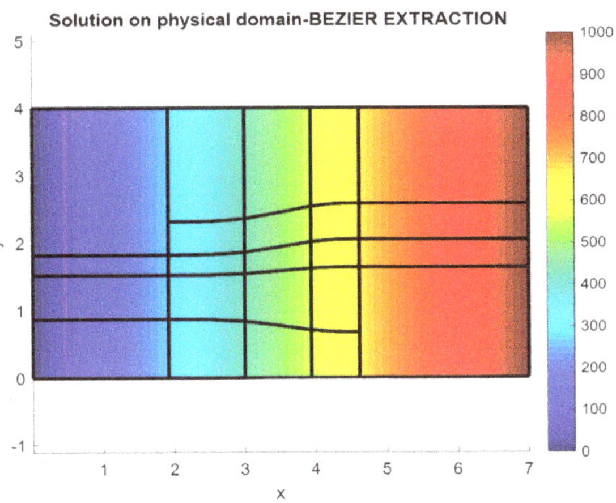

Figure 7. Temperature distribution in MODEL-1 and MODEL-2.

Nevertheless, now, the average numerical error of MODEL-3 (Figure 5, 23 Bézier elements) is substantially larger, equal to about 8.39%, as shown in Figure 8. This problematic result obviously happens because the heat flux ($\partial T/\partial x$) is discontinuous when it passes through the incompatible vertical edge 108–159 in the large Bézier element at the upper left corner, as well as from the vertical edge 43–64 in the large Bézier element at the lower right corner.

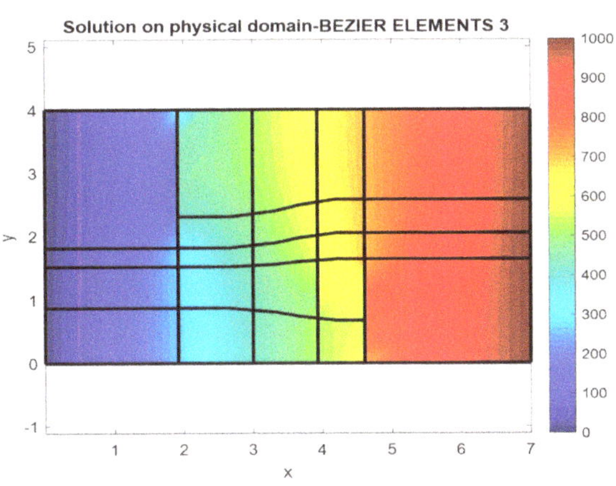

Figure 8. Temperature distribution in MODEL-3.

To fix this error, we must ensure continuity along the two abovementioned interfaces 108–159 and 43–64 by splitting the neighboring elements and thus obtaining $(n_{ele})_4 = 25$ Bézier elements (an extra 2, in addition to previously $(n_{ele})_3 = 23$ elements) associated to $n_{Q''} = 256$ nodes (previously $n_Q = 244$). This configuration defines MODEL-4, shown in Figure 9, which eventually leads to zero error (precisely, $L_2 = 4.91 \times 10^{-10}\%$). The distribution of the temperature for MODEL-4 is perfect, as shown in Figure 10.

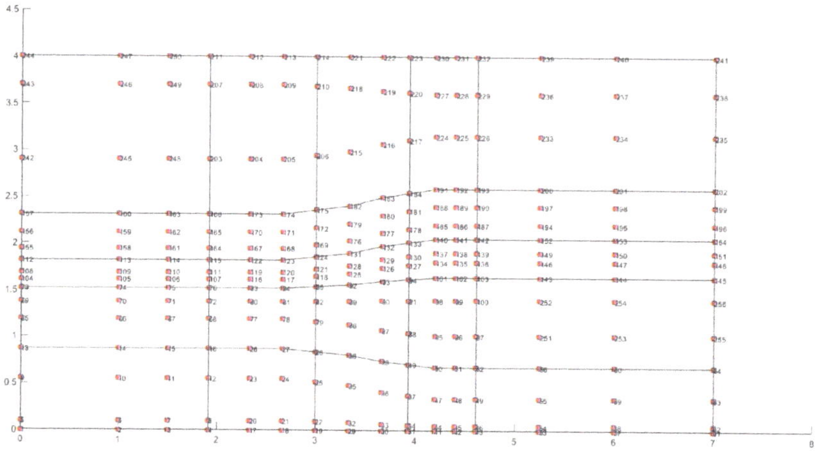

Figure 9. Final set of Bézier elements after two subdivisions (Example 2, MODEL-4).

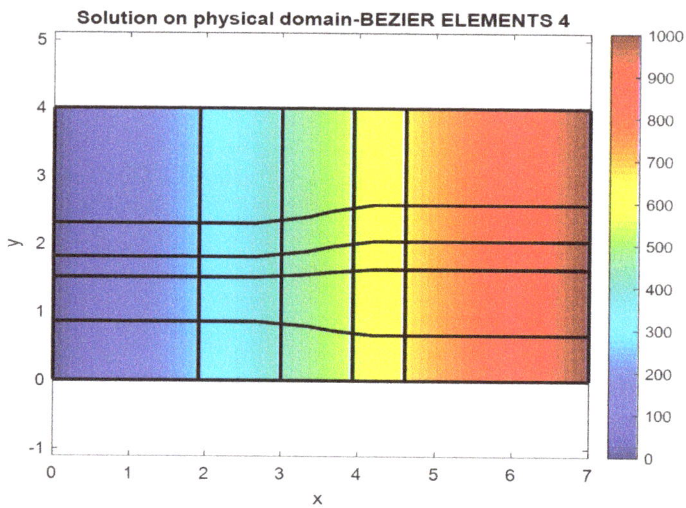

Figure 10. Example 2: Temperature distribution using MODEL-4.

5.3. EXAMPLE 3: Annulus

5.3.1. T-Spline Model

This example is a standard benchmark test [4], originally from Scott's Ph.D. thesis [11], for which all technical data (coordinates, weights) have been provided. It refers to an annulus of a central angle of 90 degrees, with internal radius $R_1 = 1.5$ and external radius $R_2 = 3$. The index space, for polynomial degree $p = 3$, is shown in Figure 11.

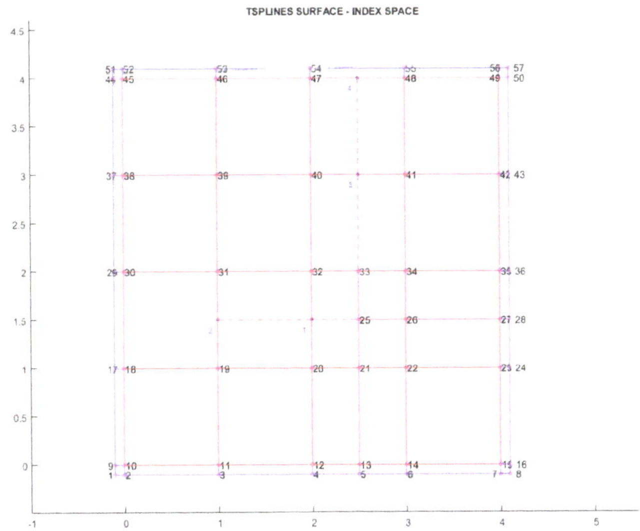

Figure 11. Example 3 and Example 4: Index space.

One may observe in Figure 11 that the index space consists of $n_P = 57$ anchors, and those numbered '25' and '33' are of valence 3. Therefore, as previously, we must extend the associated central edge ('26-25' and '25-33', respectively) to recover the reduced continuity along the pseudo-lines '25-1-2' and '33-3-4', respectively. In this way, the initial 20 sub-patches increase to $n_{ele} = 24$ T-spline elements (note that those between double boundaries are of zero area and thus ignored). In more detail, the sub-patch bounded by the anchors '19-20-32-31' splits into '19-20-1-2' and '2-1-32-31'. Similarly, the sub-patch '20-21-33-32' splits into '20-21-25-1' and '1-25-33-32'. Moreover, the sub-patch '32-33-34-41-40' splits into '32-33-3-40' and '33-34-41-3'. Finally, the sub-patch '40-41-48-47' splits into '40-3-4-47' and '3-41-48-4'. It is worth mentioning that, even after the final decomposition in $n_{ele} = 24$ C^2-continuous elements, the number of DOFs remains at the initial $n_P = 57$ anchors (the double anchors along the boundary are also included).

For the above model of $n_P = 57$ DOF (MODEL-1 and MODEL2), the result is shown in Figure 12.

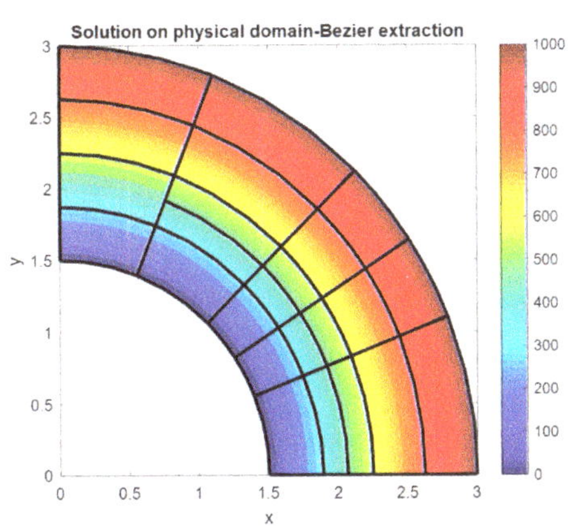

Figure 12. Example 3: Temperature distribution (MODEL-1 and MODEL-2).

Moreover, in Figure 13 we present the $n_{ele} = 24$ Bézier elements associated to $n_Q = 247$ unique nodes (MODEL-3), exactly as were produced using the Bézier extraction operator matrix. One may observe that the second element from the bottom in the first column (also shown as '18-19-31-30' in Figure 11) is not compatible with its neighboring element (the edge '19-2-31' of Figure 11).

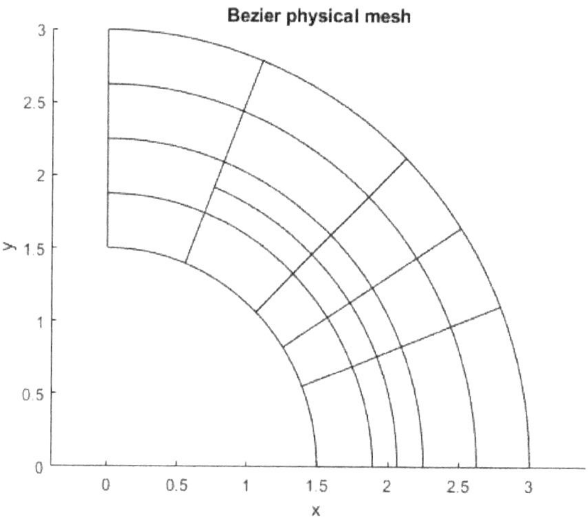

Figure 13. Example 3 and Example 4: Incompatibility near the element of reduced continuity (MODEL-3).

After the tessellation of the abovementioned element '18-19-31-30' (of Figure 11) in the vertical direction, the number of nodes in the assembly of the final $n'_{ele} = 25$ Bézier elements further increases, from $n_Q = 247$ to $n_{Q''} = 256$, as shown in Figure 14 (MODEL-4).

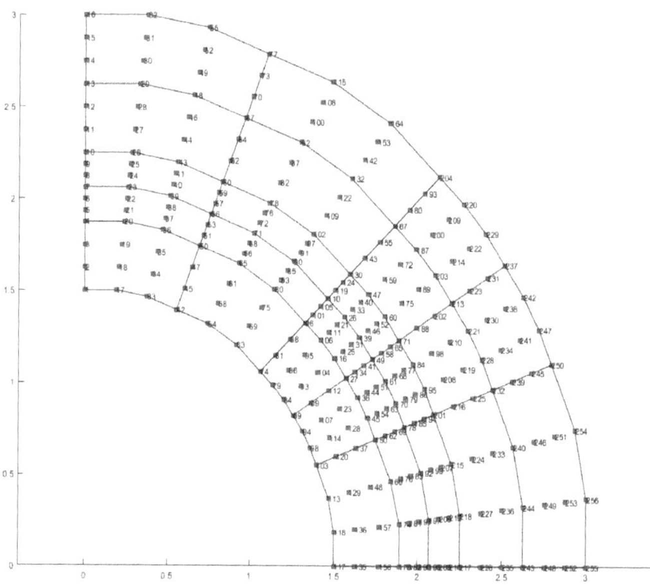

Figure 14. Final configuration of 25 compatible Bézier elements (MODEL-4).

For all of the four models, the calculated average errors, according to Equation (28), are given in Table 2. One may observe that MODEL-3 is worse than MODEL-1 and -2, the value for which was previously presented in Figure 12 (due to incompatibility), whereas MODEL-4 is the most accurate.

Table 2. Calculated errors for T-mesh (L_2-norm in percent).

L_2-Norm in Percent (%)			
MODEL-1 (57 DOF)	**MODEL-2** (57 DOF)	**MODEL-3** (247 DOF)	**MODEL-4** (256 DOF)
0.0058	0.0058	0.0098	0.0015

5.3.2. Tensor-Product Model

For the sake of completeness and to sustain the tendency of the accuracy in the four models tested, we also present results obtained using the tensor-product using uniform knot distribution. More precisely, for both directions we used the uniform knot vector:

$$U = [0,0,0,0,\ 1/4,2/4,3/4,\ 1,1,1,1]. \tag{29}$$

This means four uniform subdivisions per direction (both circumferential and radial), and thus $n_P = 7^2 = 49$ DOFs, for MODEL-1 and MODEL-2.

Regarding MODEL-3 and MODEL-4, obviously they are identical, consisting of $4 \times 4 = 16$ Bézier elements, and associated to $n_Q = 13^2 = 169$ DOFs.

For all of the four models, the results are shown in Table 3. One may observe here that, in contrast to the T-spline model (reported in Table 2), the MODEL-3 is superior to MODEL-1 and MODEL-2 (has half the error), because it also represents MODEL-4, which in all the previous cases was the best overall. However, we must consider that MODEL-4 used 3.4 times more DOFs than MODEL-1 and MODEL-2.

Table 3. Calculated errors for the tensor-product (L_2-norm, in percent).

L_2-Norm in Percent (%)			
MODEL 1 (49 DOF)	**MODEL 2** (49 DOF)	**MODEL 3** (169 DOF)	**MODEL 4** (169 DOF)
1.0785935×10^{-3}	1.0785935×10^{-3}	5.2938191×10^{-4}	5.2938191×10^{-4}

5.4. EXAMPLE 4: Thermal Analysis of Rectangular Domain

This example is a fully two-dimensional problem in which the Laplace equation dominates ($\nabla^2 u = 0$), under partial Dirichlet and Neumann boundary conditions. It refers to a rectangular domain of size $a \times b = 7 \times 4$ (Figure 15), of which the temperature along the right vertical edge is given as

$$u(x = a, y) = u_m \cos\left(\frac{\pi y}{2b}\right),\ 0 \le y \le b. \tag{30}$$

The exact solution is given as

$$u(x, y) = u_m \frac{\sinh\left(\frac{\pi x}{2b}\right)}{\sinh\left(\frac{\pi a}{2b}\right)} \cos\left(\frac{\pi y}{2b}\right),\ 0 \le x \le a, \quad 0 \le y \le b. \tag{31}$$

The index space consists of 54 anchors (Figure 16) and requires extension in all of the four directions. Therefore, using an in-house computer code we have inserted four new knots (55, 56, 57, and 58), dividing an element into three parts (i.e., 22-55-57-56, 56-57-58-31, and 55-23-32-58-57), in combination with their updated weights.

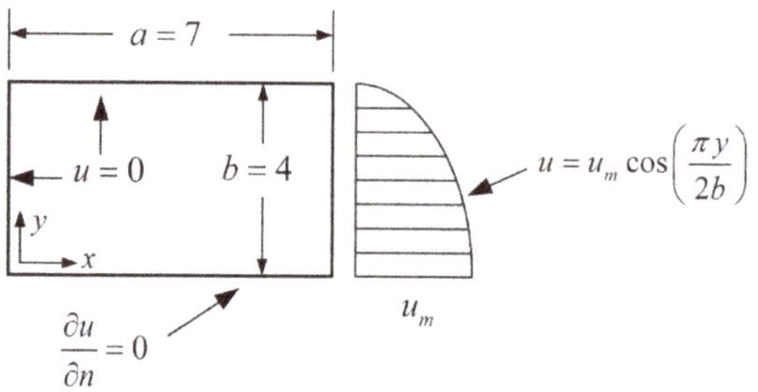

Figure 15. Dimensions and boundary conditions for the rectangular domain.

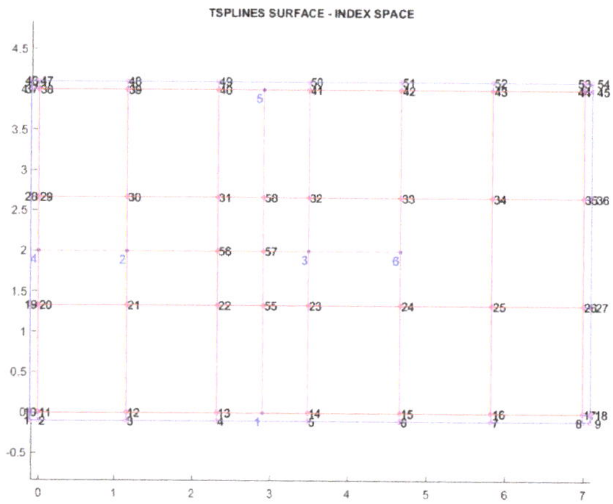

Figure 16. Index space for the rectangular domain.

The initial ANS-model consists of the 26 elements which are used in the first three computational models (MODEL-1, MODEL-2, and MODEL-3). Due to the incompatibility along the double face 24-33 shown in the index space (Figure 16), the patch (24-25-34-33) is subdivided into two parts and thus in MODEL-4 the number of Bézier elements increases (from 26) to 28, as shown in Figure 17. The deterioration of the numerical solution in MODEL-3 and its spectacular improvement in MODEL-4 is shown in Table 4. The distributions of the exact and calculated temperatures are shown in Figures 18 and 19.

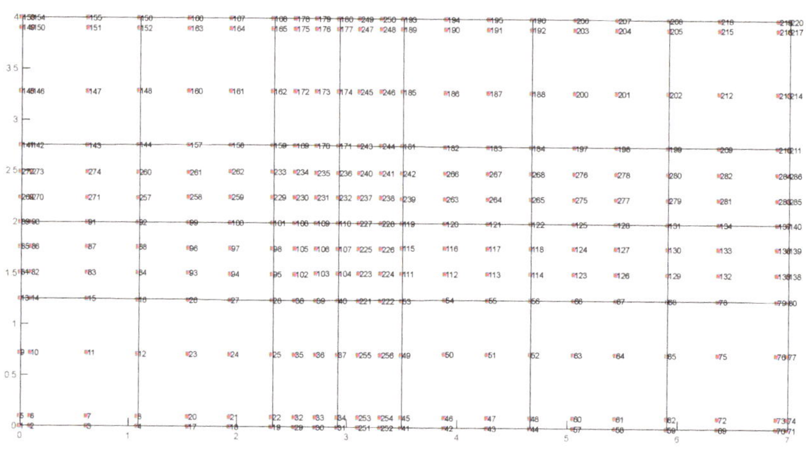

Figure 17. Final configuration of 28 Bézier elements in MODEL-4.

Table 4. Calculated errors for rectangular domain (L_2-norm, in percent).

L_2-Norm in Percent (%)			
MODEL 1 (54 DOF)	MODEL 2 (54 DOF)	MODEL 3 (270 DOF)	MODEL 4 (286 DOF)
2.6992	2.6992	4.9125	0.0051

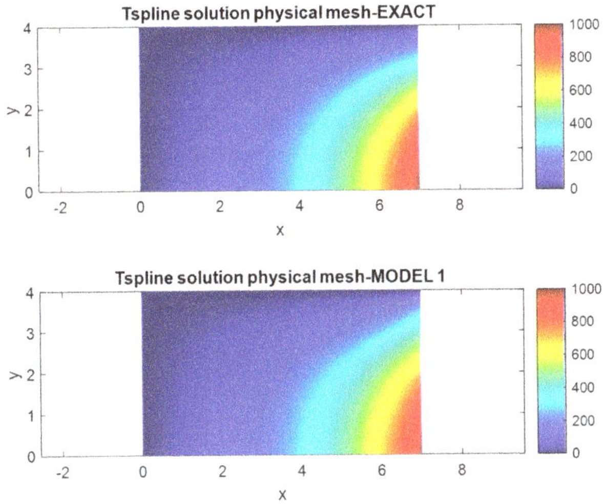

(**a**)

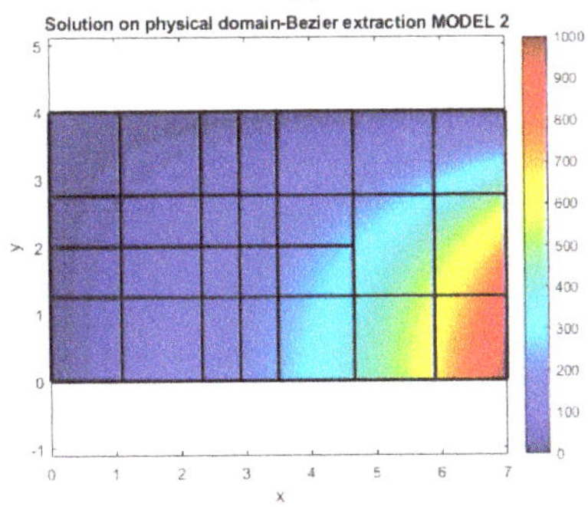

(**b**)

Figure 18. Temperature distribution (top: exact solution; bottom: (**a**) MODEL-1 and (**b**) MODEL-2).

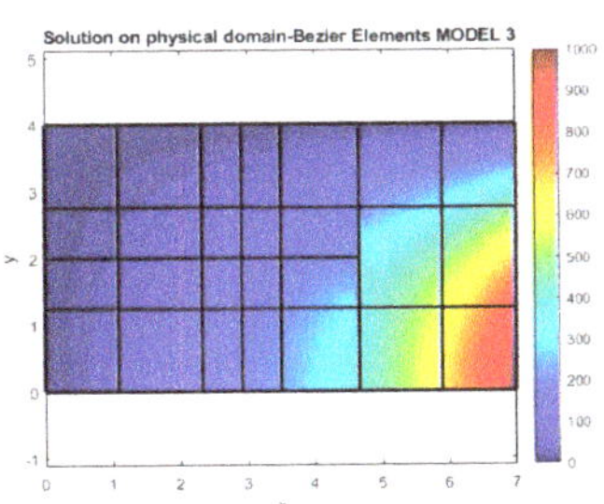

(**a**)

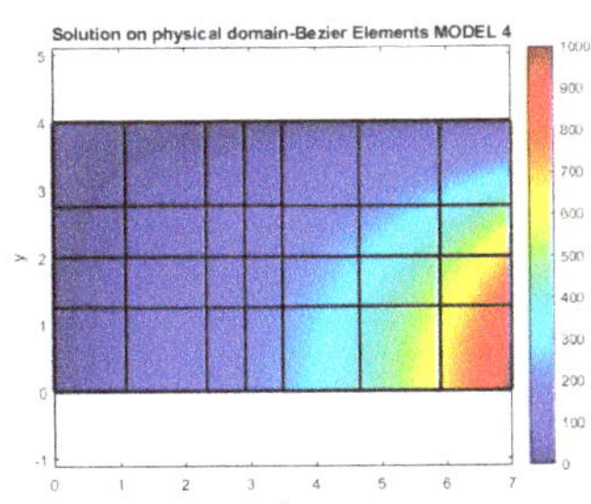

(**b**)

Figure 19. Temperature distribution ((**a**) MODEL-3 and (**b**) MODEL-4).

5.5. EXAMPLE 5: Rectangular Acoustic Cavity

We consider a rectangular cavity of size $a \times b = 3.5$ m $\times$ 1.5 m, and wave velocity $c = 1$ m/s, under Neumann boundary conditions ($\partial u/\partial n = 0$). The closed-form analytical eigenvalues may be found in [12].

The index space is shown in the previous figure, Figure 11, and thus consists of $n_P = 57$ anchors. All of the four models were taken to be the same as those in Example 3.

For each separate acoustic mode, the error (in percent) was calculated according to the following formula:

$$\text{Error(in \%)} = \frac{\omega^2_{\text{calculated}} - \omega^2_{\text{exact}}}{\omega^2_{\text{exact}}} \times 100(\%). \quad (32)$$

In Figure 20, we present the error of the first fifty calculated eigenvalues using MODEL-1 (57 DOFs, 24 elements), MODEL-3 ($n_Q = 247$ DOFs, $n_{ele} = 24$ elements), and MODEL-4 ($n'_Q = 256$ DOFs, $n'_{ele} = 25$ elements). One may observe the superiority of MODEL-4 in the entire spectrum of frequencies, mostly in the lower ones, in which MODEL-3 (although better than MODEL-1 and MODEL-2) slightly underestimates the exact eigenvalues.

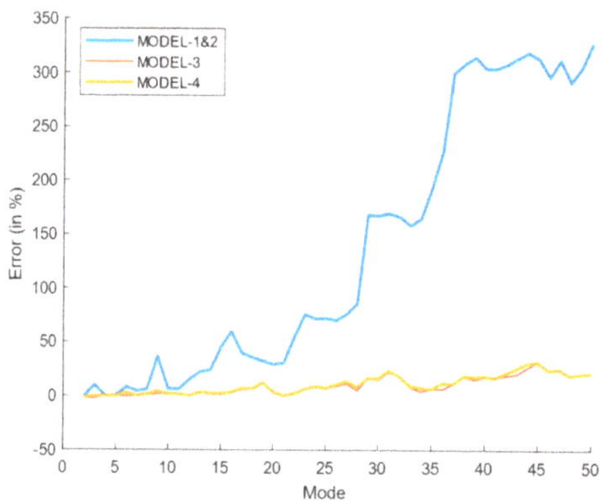

Figure 20. Calculated eigenvalues for the rectangular acoustic cavity.

Moreover, we also present the second normalized calculated eigenvector in Figure 21, as calculated in MATLAB®, which is consistent with the properly scaled exact eigenvector $u(x, y) = \cos(\pi x/a)$.

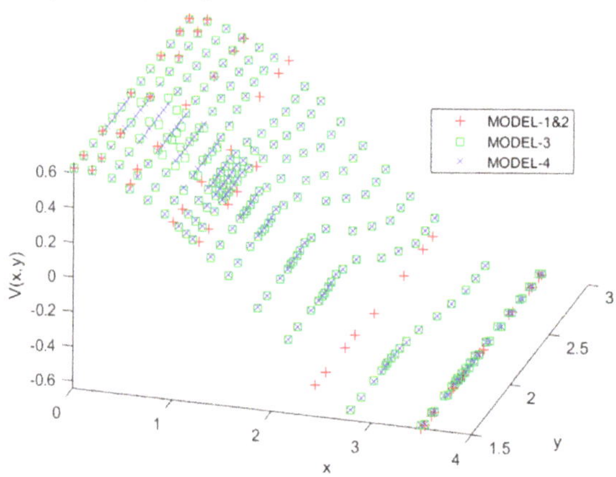

Figure 21. The second calculated eigenvector of the acoustic cavity.

Overall, one may observe that in this example, the tessellation of the one neighboring Bézier element did not seriously affect the quality of the numerical solution.

6. Computational Issues

In Section 5 we have demonstrated that once the solution of MODEL-4 is completed, we have a sufficiently accurate numerical solution across the entire domain, and one which can be used for a posteriori error estimation. Afterwards, the initial T-mesh may be properly refined following well-known (or even possible novel) procedures, and thus a second C^{p-1}-continuous IGA may follow, and so on.

In this pilot study, the approach we followed was as follows. We completed the IGA solution (MODEL-2) and then continued with the computation of the Bézier elements (MODEL-3). At the end, we performed MODEL-4. In other words, in this study each model was solved *sequentially* and separately.

However, it is possible for MODEL-2 [with element matrices $(\mathbf{K}_{P,e}, \mathbf{M}_{P,e})$ associated to n_P DOFs] and MODEL-3 [with element matrices $(\mathbf{K}_{Q,e}, \mathbf{M}_{Q,e})$ associated to n_Q DOFs] to be integrated into the same loop, at least in two alternative ways, as follows.

- The first way is to take into consideration that spline elements and Bézier elements share the *same* Gauss points and have the *same* Jacobian matrix at them (because the shape of the patch does not change after knot insertion), and thus the computer effort for the Bézier elements may be substantially reduced, if properly programmed.
- The second way is to consider Equation (5), in which the Bézier extraction operator $\mathbf{C}_e$ is the *transformation* matrix between the two sets of basis functions (spline elements denoted by the subscript 'P', and Bézier elements denoted by 'Q'). Thus, the element matrices of each Bézier element are directly calculated in terms of the associated NURBS element using the following algebraic quadratic form:

$$\mathbf{K}_{Q,e} = (\mathbf{C}_e^{-1})\mathbf{K}_{P,e}(\mathbf{C}_e^{-1})^{\mathrm{T}} \text{and } \mathbf{M}_{Q,e} = (\mathbf{C}_e^{-1})\mathbf{M}_{P,e}(\mathbf{C}_e^{-1})^{\mathrm{T}}, \tag{33}$$

without performing any numerical integration at all (see, [13]). At the end of each element loop, we will receive two sets of matrices, the former $(\mathbf{K}_{P,e}, \mathbf{M}_{P,e})$ and the latter $(\mathbf{K}_{Q,e}, \mathbf{M}_{Q,e})$, both of standard size, which will eventually occupy different positions in their corresponding total matrices $(\mathbf{K}_{\text{total}}, \mathbf{M}_{\text{total}})_P$ and $(\mathbf{K}_{\text{total}}, \mathbf{M}_{\text{total}})_Q$, according to the associated connectivity (topology) arrays, $(\text{IEN})_\text{P}$ and $(\text{IEN})_\text{Q}$, respectively.

Again, although the spline elements in a NURBS patch and the assembly of the associated Bézier elements are produced by the *same* number of *non-zero* matrix elements (k_{ij}, m_{ij}) according to Equation (33), it is their final location in the system matrices $(\mathbf{K}_{\text{total}}, \mathbf{M}_{\text{total}})_Q$ which determines a larger model for the Bézier elements ($n_Q > n_P$). In this sense, the utilization of the assembly of associated Bézier elements should not be confused with any arbitrary higher-order FEM, because this assembly is within the IGA context, having a particular quality due to the similarities of the Jacobian matrix with IGA across the entire domain.

To remove any doubt, it is instructive to discuss the NURBS model (36 control points) and its associated Bézier model (100 control points), which are shown in Figure 2a,b, respectively. Since the problem under study is potential (Laplace equation, wave equation, etc.), we have one degree of freedom per control point. The NURBS model consists of nine spline elements, each with a size of 16 × 16, and thus in principle it utilizes 9 × (16 × 16) = 2304 non-zero matrix elements, which eventually build a total stiffness matrix $(\mathbf{K}_{\text{total}})_P$ of size 36 × 36 including 900 non-zero matrix elements $(k_{ij}, m_{ij})_P$ with bandwidth 21 (Figure 22a). On the other hand, the associated assembly includes nine Bézier elements, which again utilize in principle 2304 non-zero matrix elements according to Equation (33), and eventually build a total stiffness matrix $(\mathbf{K}_{\text{total}})_Q$ of size 100 × 100 with 2116 non-zero matrix elements $(k_{ij}, m_{ij})_Q$ and bandwidth 33 (Figure 22b).

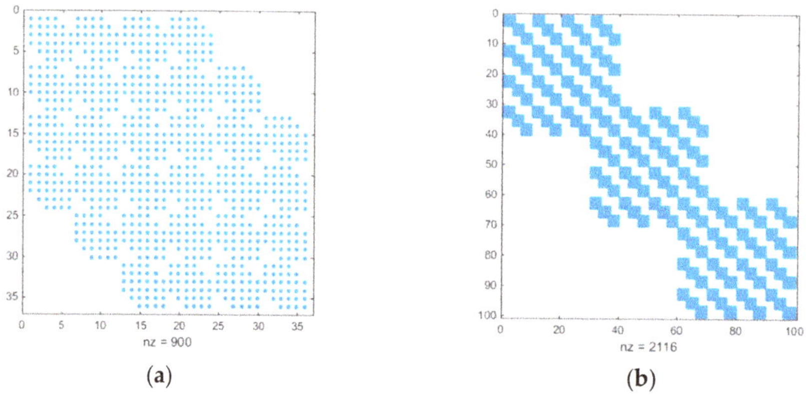

Figure 22. Sparsity patterns of total matrices: (**a**) NURBS (MODEL-2), (**b**) Bézier elements (MODEL-3).

In other words, the IGA element matrices (MODEL-2) are transformed (according to Equation (33)) and are eventually located in a matrix larger than NURBS, but less populated. This is the central point of the present paper.

Moving from the abovementioned NURBS to *T-splines*, the two alternative computational ways are again valid, but the second one may conditionally need some modifications. Therefore, since the BEXT $\mathbf{C}_e$ is *not* always a square matrix (e.g., in the present paper we noticed a few elements of size 17 × 17, whereas most of them were of the standard size 16 × 16), we cannot always construct the inverse matrix $(\mathbf{C}_e^{-1})$ as was the case in Equation (33). For these elements (larger than 16 × 16), after trivial matrix manipulation, one may easily validate that the matrices of the Bézier elements are slightly different, given by:

$$\mathbf{K}_{Q,e} = (\mathbf{C}_e^{\mathrm{T}}\mathbf{C}_e)^{-1}\mathbf{C}_e^{\mathrm{T}} \cdot \mathbf{K}_{P,e} \cdot \mathbf{C}_e(\mathbf{C}_e^{\mathrm{T}}\mathbf{C}_e)^{-1} \text{ and } \mathbf{M}_{Q,e} = (\mathbf{C}_e^{\mathrm{T}}\mathbf{C}_e)^{-1}\mathbf{C}_e^{\mathrm{T}} \cdot \mathbf{M}_{P,e} \cdot \mathbf{C}_e(\mathbf{C}_e^{\mathrm{T}}\mathbf{C}_e)^{-1}. \quad (34)$$

Equations (33) and (34) have been carefully tested, and only minor truncation errors were noticed between the several alternatives.

7. Discussion

It is well known to people working on IGA (isogeometric analysis) that knot insertion preserves the number of elements as well as the shape and the parameterization of the patch. To achieve Bézier elements of NURBS with C^0-continuity, it is adequate to insert repeated interior knots to the global knot vectors in both directions until the multiplicity equals the polynomial degree, p. This will increase the degrees of freedom, even though the element number is not changed. Since the solution space is expanded, the accuracy will be definitely improved, because the resulting solution space is a superset of the original solution space. The advantage of using the assembly of the associated Bézier elements, compared with the classical higher-order FEM, is that the shape and the parameterization of the patch, and thus the *Jacobian* matrix, are preserved, which means a mesh *quality* in the aforementioned assembly which is very consistent with IGA [13,14].

Beyond the state of the art, the present paper showed that each member in the assembly of the associated Bézier elements is merely a quadratic form (or similar, according to Equation (33) or (34)) of the same stiffness (and mass) element matrices used in continuous IGA, and thus it is the other side of the same coin. It was made quite clear that, although both formulations (MODEL-2 and MODEL-3) start with the same raw material [i.e., both with the element matrices $(\mathbf{K}_{P,e}, \mathbf{M}_{P,e})$], after the implementation of Equation (33) or Equation (34) to element matrices of sizes 16×16 or 17×17, respectively, the produced element matrices $(\mathbf{K}_{Q,e}, \mathbf{M}_{Q,e})$ of MODEL-3 (always of size 16×16) are merely stored in total (system) matrices larger than MODEL-2, according to the corresponding connectivity arrays, $(\mathrm{IEN})_\mathrm{P}$ or $(\mathrm{IEN})_\mathrm{Q}$.

At this point, it should become quite clear that the utilization of the abovementioned Bézier elements (MODEL-3 and MODEL-4) is not competitive with respect to the IGA (MODEL-2) but should be considered only as a *supplementary* step in the determination of a reasonable accurate reference value for a posteriori error estimation. Therefore, in no way do we imply the replacement of the IGA (C^{p-1}-continuity) with Bézier elements (C^0-continuity), because then we lose the CAD-based information; it is only as a step to determine the refined NURBS or T-mesh for the next continuous IGA model in an adaptive sequence. Interestingly, although the assembly of the Bézier elements (MODEL-4, with n_Q DOFs) is generally more accurate than the IGA solution (MODEL-2, with n_P DOFs), if we seek to determine the size of continuous IGA model which has the same accuracy as MODEL-4, it will be found to have more spline elements but fewer control points than MODEL-4 (i.e., $n'_P < n_Q$). In other words, ongoing research shows that it is preferrable to update the C^{p-1}-continuous spline model, rather than increase the number of Bézier elements.

The background of the present paper is as follows. In the context of T-splines IGA, basis functions are usually calculated through the Bézier extraction operator $\mathbf{C}_e$, which is derived for each T-spline element. The merits of using Bézier extraction in IGA over the standard IGA have been reported in [15] (p. 75). To derive this operator, knot insertion is implicitly applied to all the knots of the model until the multiplicity equals the polynomial degree; the outcome of this procedure was documented many years ago in the form of a pseudocode [4]. Since the usual IGA is implemented using the Bézier operator anyway, $\mathbf{C}_e$ can be further used to easily calculate the new control points that form the rational Bézier elements of C^0-continuity; a similar idea was recently implemented for the solution of topology optimization problems [16]. In other words, the control points which are implicitly involved in the already-computed Bézier extraction operator matrix can serve as a vehicle to build rational Bézier elements of C^0-continuity. This is implemented with just a multiplication of the extraction matrix $\mathbf{C}_e$ by the vector of control points of the associated e-th element, but special care is required to calculate the unique control points. Interestingly, Evans et al. [17] extended Bézier extraction to hierarchical analysis-suitable T-splines (HASTS), which are utilized as a basis for adaptive IGA.

As has been previously reported by others, "there is no one-to-one correspondence between the T-spline elements and the Bézier elements if there is T-junction" [15] (p. 78), and this issue has been handled in MODEL-4 throughout the present paper.

To make the whole procedure clear, let us describe the workflow. Designers often use commercial software such as Fusion360™ (by Autodesk), Rhinoceros 3D™ (developed by TLM, Inc., Seattle, DC, USA), and similar to develop mechanical parts. Using such programs, freely producing new geometries and finishing the procedure, we reach the point where we must perform the Analysis (IGA). Due to the design procedure, T-junctions and extraordinary points very commonly appear in the model. As a result, there is a need to check and convert (if necessary) the T-spline design from the form of "None Analysis Suitable" T-spline (N-AST) to the preferable "Analysis Suitable" T-spline (AST). For detailed explanations, the reader may refer to [18]. Clearly, AST means that there are no sub-patches of reduced continuity, and this determines a slightly higher total number of T-spline elements, compared to those existing in the initial N-AST model; this happens if either the usual IGA (MODEL-1 and MODEL-2) or the procedure relating to Bézier elements (MODEL-3 and MODEL-4) is implemented.

To overcome the above drawback, engineers use subroutines to convert any (N-AST) to (AST). Even then, geometry may include T-junctions, but then the procedure may integrate to the next phase, which is the Analysis module, without obstacles. In the proposed methodology, an AST scheme is always confirmed to present the new approach.

Although the generation of Bézier elements is a straightforward procedure in NURBS approximation [13], T-splines suffer from minor shortcomings, close to the (known in advance) borders of sub-patches with reduced continuity, i.e., those involved in the transformation from N-AST to AST. Therefore, it becomes conditionally necessary also to subdivide the closest Bézier element into the previously subdivided elements of reduced continuity. For example, one exception to this rule is when the extension reaches the boundary layer (and thus no additional Bézier element can be formed within the domain in the direction of the extension), as shown in Figure 13, in which only one element needs to be tessellated (as eventually shown in Figure 14), despite there being two elements of reduced continuity.

It was found that the abovementioned tessellation is not always necessary, but strongly depends on the boundary conditions. In Example 1, which was concerned with vertical uniaxial heat flow, no tessellation was necessary for either of the two discontinuous Bézier elements, because the line of discontinuity did not influence the flow (it was parallel to it).

In contrast, in Example 2, with the same T-mesh, but with BCs leading to horizontal flux, the lines of discontinuity were perpendicular to the flow and thus influenced it to a large degree (8.4%). It is worth mentioning that when only the Bézier element to the top-left part of the domain was tessellated, the average error decreased (from 8.4%) to only 7%, and this can be attributed to the low average temperature within it. Eventually, when both discontinuous Bézier elements were subdivided, the overall error completely vanished.

The tessellation of the neighboring Bézier elements close to them (which constitutes MODEL-4), is a standard technique which was developed in the context of the present paper. After the tessellation, the neighboring rational Bézier elements are not only C^0- but also G^0-continuous, which means that they share the same control points. Although the results are found to be very encouraging, a shortcoming of this approach is the need for tessellation in the entire row of elements until the boundary of the entire patch is reached. To resolve this drawback, instead of the tessellation of the discontinuous Bézier element and those in the same row, a single rational transient element (i.e., the one closest to the line of discontinuity) may be constructed [19,20].

In Example 3 regarding the annulus, the average error was small because, due to the small ratio of the radii, specifically, $R_1/R_2 = 1/2$, the logarithmic distribution of the temperature was almost linear in terms of the radius r. In this example, Table 2 clearly shows that MODEL-3 has an error 1.7 times larger than that in MODEL-1 and MODEL-2, whereas MODEL-4 is the most accurate among the four models (with an average error being 3.6 times smaller than that in MODEL-1 and MODEL-2). Note that all of them refer to the same number of $n_{ele} = 24$ T-spline elements; however, MODEL-3 deals with 24 Bézier elements (the same as the T-spline elements) whereas MODEL-4 deals with 25. For the avoidance of any doubt regarding the relative accuracy of the models due to round-off errors of coordinates and weights, tensor-product (NURBS) analysis was added to elucidate this example (see, Table 3), because standard coordinates and standard weights may be applied in its reproduction by any researcher.

In Example 4, concerned with the thermal analysis of a rectangular domain under fully two-dimensional boundary conditions, the quality of the results was like those of Example 3, but the value of the initial error was larger than what it was in Example 3 (in MODEL-1 and MODEL-2: about 2.7%). In more detail, MODEL-3 showed an error 1.8 times greater than that of MODEL-1 and MODEL-2, whereas MODEL-4 outperformed with an error about 500 times smaller than that of MODEL-1 and MODEL-2. Obviously, this finding is in favor of our claim that MODEL-4 can be used for a posteriori error estimation.

In Example 5, concerned with the eigenvalue–eigenvector analysis of a rectangular acoustic cavity, impressive results had been previously received for NURBS-based IGA [14] for different dimensions of the cavity (aspect ratio 2.5:1.1 ≅ 2.27 in [14], compared to 3.5:1.5 ≅ 2.33 of the present paper). Quite similarly, equally impressive results were obtained in T-spline-based IGA as well.

Overall, the superior accuracy of MODEL-4 dictates that it can take the role of a reference value for a posteriori error estimation.

In principle, the proposed methodology is applicable to the entire spectrum of computational mechanics, including elasticity, where, for the most part, the research is focused [21,22].

8. Conclusions

Bézier extraction matrices, the use of which is the golden standard in isogeometric analysis (IGA), may be used to construct updated unique control points which further determine a set of rational Bézier elements with C^0-continuity characterized by more degrees of freedom than found in the standard IGA model. This in turn leads to a second numerical solution of higher accuracy, practically without affecting the number of T-spline elements, and thus useful for a posteriori error estimation. It was found that in most cases, the blind formation of the Bézier elements using the Bézier extraction operator matrix of the patch is problematic, and thus it is necessary to further subdivide a small number of Bézier elements which share the same interface with T-spline elements of reduced continuity. Although in the present paper a standard tessellation of Bézier elements was applied, transient rational elements are also applicable. The applied methodology is generally applicable to the whole spectrum of computational mechanics as well as to three-dimensional problems.

Author Contributions: Conceptualization, C.P.; methodology, C.P. and I.D.; software, C.P. and I.D.; validation, C.P. and I.D.; writing—original draft preparation, C.P.; writing—review and editing, C.P.; visualization, I.D.; supervision, C.P.; project administration, C.P. All authors have read and agreed to the published version of the manuscript.

Funding: This research received no external funding.

Data Availability Statement: The data presented in this study are available on request from the corresponding author.

Conflicts of Interest: The authors declare no conflicts of interest.

Appendix A. Determination of Common Points in Neighboring Patches

In Appendix A we describe the procedure of the subdivision of a Bézier patch. Since the three patches shown in Figure 3c have been produced by the procedure of Bézier extraction, which preserves the shape of the patch, it is obvious that they share a unique common point H. It is apparent that the point H belongs to the position $(\xi = 0, \eta = 1)$ of the element (I-a), and to the position $(\xi = 0, \eta = 0)$ of the element (I-b); as well, as it lies along the edge AD (with $\xi_H = 1$) of the larger element ABED. Since the Cartesian coordinates (x_H, y_H) of the point H are known because it coincides with a corner control point in the two small sub-patches, the determination of the parameter η_H along the edge AD is merely to fulfil the following condition:

$$\sum_{i=1}^{n} B_{i,3}(\eta) y_i = y_H, \tag{A1}$$

where $B_{i,3}(\eta)$ are the Bernstein basis polynomials of degree $p = 3$:

$$B_{0,3}(\eta) = (1-\eta)^3,\ B_{1,3}(\eta) = 3(1-\eta)^2\eta,\ B_{2,3}(\eta) = 3(1-\eta)\eta^2,\ B_{3,3}(\eta) = \eta^3, \tag{A2}$$

while y_i is the corresponding coordinate of the i-th control point along the edge AD.

Substituting Equation (A2) into Equation (A1), we receive the following cubic equation:

$$a\eta^3 + b\eta^2 + c\eta + d = 0, \tag{A3}$$

with

$$a = (3y_1 - y_0 - 3y_2 + y_3),\ \ b = (3y_0 - 6y_1 + 3y_2),\ \ c = (3y_1 - 3y_0),\ \ d = y_0. \tag{A4}$$

The finding of the unique real root $\eta_H \in (0,1)$ of the cubic polynomial in Equation (A3) is a trivial task of numerical analysis, which may be facilitated using a mathematical package such as MATLAB®, and using the following commands: coefficients = [a, b, c, d]; root_values = roots (coefficients); in conjunction with the condition find (root_values < 1 and root_values > 0).

Appendix B. Control Points After the Subdivision

Suppressing the first subscript '3', which indicates the isoline ξ = 1, let the control points along the common edge BE (see Figure 3c) be P_0, P_1, P_2, P_3, as shown in Figure A1. Having determined the parameter η_H of the common point H, of known Cartesian coordinates (x_H, y_H) implementing Appendix A, we set it as a new control point, and continue with the subdivision of the Bézier patch ABED by the line HH'. Then, we must determine the three control points $(Q_0, Q_1, Q_2, Q_3 = H)$ on the left of H, and the other three control points $(H = Q_3, Q_4, Q_5, Q_6)$ on the right of it. Based on the same subdivision ratio η_H, it is easy to show that these seven updated projected control points, useful for the two subdivided Bézier elements, are given by the following:

$$\begin{aligned}
Q_0^w &= P_0^w, \\
Q_1^w &= (1-\eta_H)P_0^w + \eta_H P_1^w, \\
Q_2^w &= (1-\eta_H)^2 P_0^w + 2(1-\eta_H)\eta_H P_1^w + \eta_H^2 P_2^w, \\
Q_3^w &= (1-\eta_H)^3 P_0^w + 3(1-\eta_H)^2\eta_H P_1^w + 3(1-\eta_H)\eta_H^2 P_2^w + \eta_H^2 P_3^w, \\
Q_4^w &= (1-\eta_H)^2 P_1^w + 2(1-\eta_H)\eta_H P_2^w + \eta_H^2 P_3^w, \\
Q_5^w &= (1-\eta_H)P_2^w + \eta_H P_3^w, \\
Q_6^w &= P_3^w.
\end{aligned} \tag{A5}$$

The above procedure is repeated with respect to the next three polygon lines (P0, i, P1, i, and P2, i, with i = 0, 1, 2) shown in Figure A1.

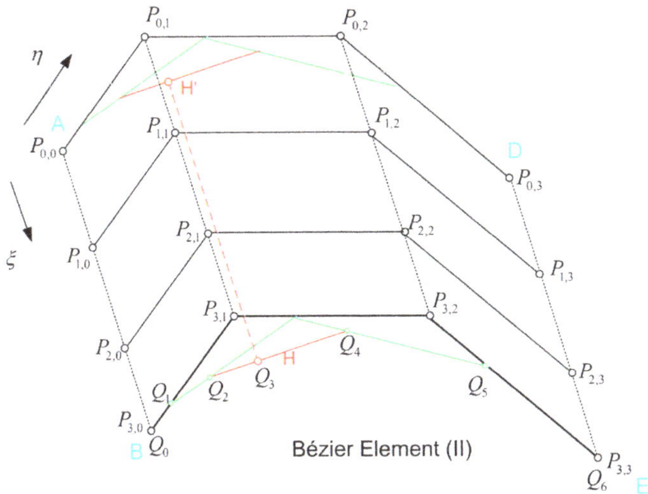

Figure A1. Element to be tessellated.

References

1. Hughes, T.J.R.; Cottrell, J.A.; Bazilevs, Y. Isogeometric analysis: CAD, finite elements, NURBS, exact geometry and mesh refinement. *Comput. Methods Appl. Mech. Eng.* **2005**, *194*, 4135–4195. [CrossRef]
2. Bazilevs, Y.; Calo, V.; Cottrell, J.; Evans, J.; Hughes, T.J.R.; Lipton, S.; Scott, M.; Sederberg, T.W. Isogeometric analysis using T-splines. *Comput. Methods Appl. Mech. Eng.* **2010**, *199*, 229–263. [CrossRef]
3. Borden, M.J.; Scott, M.A.; Evans, J.A.; Hughes, T.J.R. Isogeometric finite element data structures based on Bézier extraction of NURBS. *Int. J. Numer. Methods Eng.* **2011**, *87*, 15–47. [CrossRef]
4. Scott, M.A.; Borden, M.J.; Verhoosel, C.V.; Sederberg, T.W.; Hughes, T.J.R. Isogeometric finite element data structures based on Bézier extraction of T-splines. *Int. J. Numer. Methods Eng.* **2011**, *88*, 126–156. [CrossRef]
5. Cox, M.G. The numerical evaluation of B-splines. *J. Inst. Math. Its Appl.* **1972**, *10*, 134–149. [CrossRef]
6. De Boor, C. On calculating with B-splines. *J. Approx. Theory* **1972**, *6*, 50–62. [CrossRef]
7. Piegl, L.; Tiller, W. *The NURBS Book*; Springer: Berlin, Germany, 1997.
8. Wang, Y.; Zhang, J. *Control Point Removal Algorithm for T-Spline Surfaces*; Kim, M.-S., Shimada, K., Eds.; GMP 2006, LNCS 4077; Springer: Berlin/Heidelberg, Germany, 2006; pp. 385–396. [CrossRef]
9. Wang, A.; Li, L.; Wang, W.; Du, X.; Xiao, F.; Cai, Z.; Zhao, G. Linear Independence of T-Spline Blending Functions of Degree One for Isogeometric Analysis. *Mathematics* **2021**, *9*, 1346. [CrossRef]
10. Lyche, T.; Mørken, K. Making the Oslo Algorithm More Efficient. *SIAM J. Numer. Anal.* **1986**, *23*, 663–675. [CrossRef]
11. Scott, M.A. T-Splines as a Design-Through-Analysis Technology, Dissertation. Ph.D. Thesis, The University of Texas at Austin, Austin, TX, USA, 2011.
12. Courant, R.; Hilbert, D. *Methods of Mathematical Physics, 1st English ed.*; InterScience: New York, NY, USA, 1966; Volume I, pp. 300–304, (translated and revised from the German original).
13. Provatidis, C.G. Comparison between Bézier extraction and associated Bézier elements in eigenvalue problems. *WSEAS Trans. Syst. Control* **2022**, *17*, 605. [CrossRef]
14. Lai, W.; Yu, T.; Bui, T.Q.; Wang, Z.; Curiel-Sosa, J.L.; Das, R.; Hirose, S. 3-D elasto-plastic large deformations: IGA simulation by Bézier extraction of NURBS. *Adv. Eng. Softw.* **2017**, *108*, 68–82. [CrossRef]
15. Singh, S.K.; Singh, I.V.; Mishra, B.K.; Bhardwaj, G.; Bui, T.Q. A simple, efficient and accurate Bézier extraction based T-spline XIGA for crack simulations. *Theor. Appl. Fract. Mech.* **2017**, *88*, 74–96. [CrossRef]
16. Zhang, X.; Xiao, M.; Gao, L.; Gao, J. A T-splines-oriented isogeometric topology optimization for plate and shell structures with arbitrary geometries using Bézier extraction. *Comput. Methods Appl. Mech. Eng.* **2024**, *425*, 116929. [CrossRef]
17. Evans, E.J.; Scott, M.A.; Li, X.; Thomas, D.C. Hierarchical T-splines: Analysis suitability, Bézier extraction, and application as an adaptive basis for isogeometric analysis. *Comput. Methods Appl. Mech. Eng.* **2015**, *284*, 1–20. [CrossRef]
18. Habib, S.H.; Kezrane, C.; Hachi, B.E. Moving local mesh based on analysis-suitable T-splines and Bézier extraction for extended isogeometric finite element analysis—Application to two-dimensional crack propagation. *Finite Elem. Anal. Des.* **2023**, *213*, 103854. [CrossRef]

19. Eisenträger, S.; Eisenträger, J.; Gravenkamp, H.; Provatidis, C. High order transition elements: The xNy-element concept, Part II: Dynamics. *Comput. Methods Appl. Mech. Eng.* **2021**, *387*, 114145. [CrossRef]
20. Provatidis, C.G. Non-Rational and rational transfinite interpolation using Bernstein polynomials. *Int. J. Comput. Geom. Appl.* **2022**, *32*, 55–89. [CrossRef]
21. Guo, M.; Wang, W.; Zhao, G.; Du, X.; Zang, R.; Yang, J. T-Splines for Isogeometric Analysis of the Large Deformation of Elastoplastic Kirchhoff–Love Shells. *Appl. Sci.* **2023**, *13*, 1709. [CrossRef]
22. Fakkoussi, S.E.L.; Koubaiti, Q.; Elkhalfi, A.; Vlase, S.; Marin, M. Numerical analysis of the cylindrical shell pipe with preformed holes subjected to a compressive load using non-uniform rational B-splines and T-splines for an isogeometric analysis approach. *Axioms* **2024**, *13*, 529. [CrossRef]